Congratulations to

Fiona Maazel

Winner of the

2009 Bard Fiction Prize

Fiona Maazel, author of
Last Last Chance, joins previous
winners Nathan Englander, Emily Barton,
Monique Truong, Paul La Farge, Edie Meidav,
Peter Orner, and Salvador Plascencia.

The Bard Fiction Prize is awarded annually to a
promising emerging writer who is an American citizen
aged thirty-nine years or younger at the time
of application. In addition to a monetary award
of $30,000, the winner receives an appointment
as writer in residence at Bard College for one semester
without the expectation that he or she will teach
traditional courses. The recipient will give at least one
public lecture and meet informally with students.

For more information, please contact:

Bard Fiction Prize
Bard College
PO Box 5000
Annandale-on-Hudson, NY 12504-5000

COMING UP IN THE SPRING

Conjunctions:52
BETWIXT THE BETWEEN:
IMPOSSIBLE REALISM
Edited by Bradford Morrow and Brian Evenson

Listen: There's a hell of a good universe next door; let's go.
—e. e. cummings

Imagine an everyday world in which meat is grown in vats by men called "collies" and butchered by BattleBots creatures while adults play Frisbee with robots. Imagine a world in which secret societies meet in private to have "soft evenings" during which they travel "psychotic highways." Imagine what might follow the opening lines of a story entitled "Brain Jelly" by the brilliant novelist Stephen Wright: "Apostrophe came from a country where all the cheese was blue. The cows there ate berries the whole day long. You should see their tongues."

Postfantasy fiction that defies definition is at the center of a remarkable, groundbreaking issue edited by Bradford Morrow and Brian Evenson in the spring issue of *Conjunctions.* These and other works will be gathered in what will certainly be a muchdiscussed issue featuring stories that begin with the premise that the unfamiliar or liminal really constitutes solid though undeniably strange ground on which to walk. Contributors to *Betwixt the Between: Impossible Realism* include such veterans as China Miéville, Robert Coover, Kelly Link, Jeff VanderMeer, Peter Straub, and Ben Marcus, as well as emerging writers such as Karen Russell, Jon Enfield, Micaela Morrissette, Jedediah Berry, and Stephen Marche.

Subscriptions to *Conjunctions* are only $18 for more than eight hundred pages per year of contemporary and historical literature and art. Please send your check to *Conjunctions*, Bard College, Annandale-on-Hudson, NY 12504. Subscriptions can also be ordered by calling (845) 758-1539, or by sending an e-mail to Michael Bergstein at Conjunctions@bard.edu. For more information about current and past issues, please visit our Web site at www.Conjunctions.com.

CONJUNCTIONS

Bi-Annual Volumes of New Writing

Edited by
Bradford Morrow

Contributing Editors
Walter Abish
Chinua Achebe
John Ashbery
Martine Bellen
Mei-mei Berssenbrugge
Mary Caponegro
William H. Gass
Peter Gizzi
Robert Kelly
Ann Lauterbach
Norman Manea
Rick Moody
Howard Norman
Joan Retallack
Joanna Scott
David Shields
Peter Straub
William Weaver
John Edgar Wideman

published by Bard College

EDITOR: Bradford Morrow
MANAGING EDITOR: Michael Bergstein
SENIOR EDITORS: Robert Antoni, Peter Constantine, Brian Evenson, J. W. McCormack, Micaela Morrissette, Pat Sims, Alan Tinkler
WEBMASTER: Brian Evenson
ASSOCIATE EDITORS: Jedediah Berry, Eric Olson, Patrizia Villani
ART EDITOR: Norton Batkin
PUBLICITY: Mark R. Primoff
EDITORIAL ASSISTANTS: Lina Canney, Alice Gregory, Jessica Loudis, Elias Primoff, Kathleen Ross

CONJUNCTIONS is published in the Spring and Fall of each year by Bard College, Annandale-on-Hudson, NY 12504. This issue is made possible in part with the generous funding of the National Endowment for the Arts, and with public funds from the New York State Council on the Arts, a State Agency.

State of the Arts

NATIONAL ENDOWMENT FOR THE ARTS

A great nation deserves great art. **NYSCA**

SUBSCRIPTIONS: Send subscription orders to CONJUNCTIONS, Bard College, Annandale-on-Hudson, NY 12504. Single year (two volumes): $18.00 for individuals; $40.00 for institutions and overseas. Two years (four volumes): $32.00 for individuals; $80.00 for institutions and overseas. Patron subscription (lifetime): $500.00. Overseas subscribers please make payment by International Money Order. For information about subscriptions, back issues, and advertising, call Michael Bergstein at (845) 758-1539 or fax (845) 758-2660.

Editorial communications should be sent to Bradford Morrow, *Conjunctions*, 21 East 10th Street, New York, NY 10003. Unsolicited manuscripts cannot be returned unless accompanied by a stamped, self-addressed envelope. Electronic and simultaneous submissions will not be considered.

Conjunctions is listed and indexed in the American Humanities Index.

Visit the *Conjunctions* Web site at www.conjunctions.com.

Copyright © 2008 CONJUNCTIONS.

Cover design by Jerry Kelly, New York. Cover paintings by Peter Kettle. Front: *Gulliver*, Liquitex acrylic on gesso panel, 23 x 17 inches; rear: *The Glass Bead Game*, Liquitex acrylic on gesso panel, 28 x 22 inches. Reproduced by kind permission of the artist. Tailpiece illustration *Dream of My Late Father Walter Crane* by Lionel F. Crane, April 21, 1890.

Available through D.A.P./Distributed Art Publishers, Inc., 155 Sixth Avenue, New York, NY 10013. Telephone: (212) 627-1999. Fax: (212) 627-9484.

Printers: Edwards Brothers

Typesetter: Bill White, Typeworks

ISSN 0278-2324
ISBN 978-0-941964-67-8

Manufactured in the United States of America.

TABLE OF CONTENTS

THE DEATH ISSUE
Edited by David Shields and Bradford Morrow

Hayden Carruth
1921–2008

David Foster Wallace
1962–2008

Reginald Shepherd
1963–2008

Beloved Friends and Longtime Contributors

EDITORS' NOTE

BIRTH IS NOT INEVITABLE. Life certainly isn't. The sole inevitability of existence, the only consequence of being alive, is death. Traveling together on a train last year, the two of us, friends for nearly two decades, found ourselves talking about death. Somehow, the subject had never come up before. Outside the window, the Hudson River sparkled, and on the far shore beautiful red palisades rose up toward the sunsetting sky. The natural world—unfazed, implacable—streamed by, indifferent to our dialogue. But as we spoke, we realized there was no subject more interesting, nor one more impossible to address.

The crux of our talk was not about our own mortality, but rather about just how difficult it is to wrap words around the concept of death. Whereas once one could frame mortality within an ideology of afterlife, now the gods are either asleep or simply moribund. We can no longer speak with assurance about the immortality of art or the consolation of philosophy or the reach of heaven. Where does this leave us then?

We decided to ask forty or so fellow writers to join our conversation, each of them writing from whatever vantage they chose. We approached a wide range of novelists, poets, and essayists, and our invitation was as simple as it was demanding. How do you face death? What is death? How does death touch on your life? The responses we received are gathered here. They speak eloquently about the unspeakable, view with clarity the unseeable. Having spent many months pursuing this darkest theme, we hope that readers will find as much brilliant light in these pages as we did. While this gathering may center on death, it is ultimately about the existential fact of our ineffable selves, our mortal bodies, our very lives.

—Bradford Morrow & David Shields
October 2008
New York City & Seattle

The Sutra of Maggots and Blowflies
Sallie Tisdale

THE GREAT ENTOMOLOGIST Jean-Henri Fabre covered his desk with the carcasses of birds and snakes, opened the window, and waited. He didn't have to wait long.

From the time I was quite young, I loved cold-blooded creatures. I had to be taught not to pick things up in the woods: To me it was all good, all worth examination, from beetles to mushrooms to toads. I was stealthy, and in the thistle-ridden fields near my house, I caught many blue-belly lizards to keep as pets. My father built a cage for them, a wonderful wood-and-screen contraption that smelled of pine and grass and reptile. I kept garter snakes and frogs and chameleons too. Once, someone gave me a baby alligator. I had several praying mantises, and built them elaborate branch houses in the cage, and fed them crickets. I don't know where this came from, my appetite for the alien; it feels like an old question, long and mysterious.

My study of living things, part inquiry and part the urge to possess, became inevitably a study of predation and decay. I had to feed my pets, and most preferred live food. The mantises always died, their seasons short. The chameleons died, too delicate for my care. The alligator died. I tried to embalm it, with limited success—just good enough for an excellent presentation at show-and-tell. When one of my turtles died, my brother and I buried it in my mother's rose bed to see if we could get an empty turtle shell, which would be quite a good thing to have. When we dug it up a few weeks later, there was almost nothing left—an outcome I had not anticipated, and one that left me with a strange, disturbed feeling. The earth was more fierce than I had guessed.

In time I became specifically interested in human bodies, how they worked and how they got sick and what they looked like when they died. This did not pacify my mother, who worried aloud about my ghoulish preoccupations. I did enjoy the distress I could cause by something as simple as bringing an embalmed baby alligator to

8

school in a jar. But I was also—and for a long time I could not have explained why it was of a piece with my impassioned studies—exquisitely sensitive to the world's harsh rules. I regretted each cricket. An animal dead by the side of the road could bring me to tears, and I cried for each dead lizard, each mantis. A triad, each leg bearing weight: sensitivity, love, and logic. The weight on each leg shifts over time: now, a penetrating awareness of the cruelty seemingly built into the world's bones. Now, a colder logic, an awareness of the forces that balance systems at the cost of individuals. At times in brief pure blinks of my mind's eye, a love painful in its intensity, an unalloyed love. I love the tender, pale blossoms opening now on the cherry tree in my yard, the sudden pound of lush raindrops from the empty sky: Each thing I see is a luminous form in a sparkling world. Such love is a kind of grace; enshrined in it, all is right with the world. It is a little touch of madness, this kind of love—raw and driving.

Some years ago, I began to study the small things in the forest that I didn't understand, moving from the lovely and lethal amanita mushrooms to the stony, invincible lichens to the water skippers coasting lightly across the little creeks. I began to study insects especially and then flies in particular.

Flies are so present and innumerable that it is hard to see their presence clearly, hard to believe in their measure. There are around 120,000 species of flies, depending on who's counting, and they have many names: bee flies, cactus flies, papaya flies, warble flies, brine flies, nimble flies, biting midges, green midges, gall midges, mountain midges, dixid midges, solitary midges, net-winged midges, phantom midges—so called because the larvae are transparent and seem to disappear in water. Studying flies, my head begins to spin with suborders and divisions, tribes and clades, and the wild implications of the Latin names: Psychodidae and Sarcophagidae and *Calliphora vomitoria.*

The Order Diptera is old, as are most insects; it was well established by the Jurassic Era, 210 million years ago.[1] (Unlike all other insects, flies do not have four wings. Diptera comes from the word *di* for two and *ptera* for wings.) Fly biology is a vast and changing

---

[1] We are one kingdom with flies: Animali, and then we diverge. (You can remember the taxonomic series of kingdom, phylum, class, order, family, genera, species with an appropriate mnemonic: *Keep Pots Clean; Our Food Gets Spoiled.*) Flies are found in the Phylum Arthropoda: exoskeletons, jointed legs, and segmented bodies, a group that includes crabs, centipedes, and spiders as well. The flies are in the Subphylum

9

field. New species and subspecies of flies are always being discovered. Familiar species are found in new locations; variants between species are analyzed in new or more subtle ways, and so the taxonomic distinctions between flies are always being revised. But in the general term, flies are defined by their single set of wings, legless larvae, and mouthparts designed for biting, sucking, or lapping.

Inside these templates, there is stupefying variation. They are divided into families, genera, and species by the varied location of veins in the wings, their color, body size, type of mouthpart, the number of stages of larval development, the type and separation of eyes, antennal structure, the arrangement and number of bristles on the body, the length of the legs, and habitat—differences controversial and infinitesimally detailed.

We often know them as the most common and familiar things, as single things: individual flies rescued or swatted, struggling in webs, crawling dizzily across cold windowpanes on a milky October day. One finds flies in odd places, but so often they are not a surprise even in surprising locations—in the laundry basket or buzzing inside the medicine cabinet, or caught unaware in the wash water. Almost every fly you catch in your house will be a housefly, one of the family Muscidae, chubby and vigilant flies that can birth a dozen generations every summer. (Houseflies are found in virtually every place on earth save for Antarctica and a few isolated islets.)

Sometimes we know them as plagues: I've been battered by biting flies in forests, near mangrove and in sand, flies the size of pinheads in clouds so thick I couldn't walk twenty feet without getting a crop of angry red bites on every inch of exposed skin. These are the ones we call punkies or gnats or no-see-ums, the fly family known as Ceratopogonidae. There are more than four thousand species of them—tiny, almost invisible flies with stinging bites, inexplicable dots of pain.

The *Encyclopaedia Britannica* says simply, "It is not possible to discuss all dipteran habitats." Flies live in the air and the soil and under water and inside the stems and leaves of plants. They live high in the mountains, in sand and snow, tide pools and lakes, sulfur springs and salt lagoons. The brine fly lives in the thermal springs of Yellowstone at temperatures up to 43 degrees Celsius. There are

---

Mandibulata, which means mandibles on the second segment past the mouth opening, and just imagine that. We are not in Kansas anymore. Class Insecta means a body is divided into head, abdomen, and thorax. The insects from here on out—beetles, fleas, ants, scorpions, walking sticks, and many other types—are entirely separate orders.

flies in the volcanic hot springs of Iceland and New Zealand living at even higher temperatures. Certain flies handle extreme cold easily too, blessed with a kind of antifreeze and other strange gifts. The wingless snow fly lives underground in burrows, and wanders across the white fields during the day—wee black spots walking briskly along in the afternoon. The Himalayan glacier midge prefers temperatures around the freezing point, but has been seen active at minus 16 degrees Celsius. (When placed in a hand, it becomes agitated and then faints from heat.) One carnivorous fly lays its eggs in pools of seeping petroleum, where the larvae live until maturity. One wingless fly lives inside spiders. Certain flies can live in vinegar. There are flies munching contently on spoiled vegetables. When we eat them by accident, they just ride the peristaltic wave on through, exiting in our feces and moving along.

The single pair of wings that is crucial to the identity of flies may be very small or startlingly large or vestigial, may lie open or closed, look scaly, milky, beribboned with black veins, smoky or transparent. Instead of a second set of wings, flies have small bony structures called halteres. They are mobile gyroscopes for flight, beating in time but out of sync with the wings, twisting with every change of direction, to keep the fly from tumbling. Most are astonishing flyers, able to move in three dimensions at speeds hard to measure. Some can hover motionless and fly backward or forward or sideways like helicopters. (Flower flies, which look alarmingly like wasps but are harmless, will hover in front of your face, appearing to gaze directly into your eyes.) Midges beat their wings more than a thousand times per second; this is too fast for nerve impulses and instead involves a mysterious muscular trigger effect. A fruit fly can stay aloft for an entire afternoon, burning ten percent of its body weight every hour. There are clumsy flies: The march fly travels laboriously only a few feet off the ground, and so is continuous fodder for car radiators; march flies are often seen banging into people and bushes, and even the walls of buildings. Soldier flies can fly, but don't very often; they sit for long periods of time on leaves or flowers. Other species prefer to walk or run, sometimes on the surface of water; the louse fly, often wingless, walks sideways, like a crab.

John Clare wrote of flies that "they look like things of mind or fairies." There are flies so small they can barely be seen by human eyes; others are as wide and long as a man's hand. Their bodies may be lime green or shiny blue, glowing black, metallic or dull yellow, pearly white, leathery, variegated in browns, matted with dust. A

11

few are flecked with iridescent gold and silver. They are squat or slender or wasp waisted. Their legs may be very long and fine or stubby, delicate as a web or stout and strong. Fly genitalia, one text notes, are "extremely polymorphous." Some flies have beards or even furry coats made of bristles; others seem hairless. The hover flies mimic bees and wasps, growing yellow-brown bristly hair like the fur of a bumblebee or striped like yellow jackets. The tangle-veined fly, which is parasitic on grasshoppers, has a loud, bee-like buzz. A fly's antennae may be akin to knobs or threads or whips or feathers or pencilline brushes. Insects do not breathe exactly; they perform gas exchange in a different way from mammals, through tubes called spiracles. Their larvae breathe in many ways, through gills and snorkels, or by taking up the oxygen stored in plant roots and stems. Spiracles show up just about anywhere: beside the head, in the belly, in a maggot's anus.

What great variety they have! When Augustine argued that the fly is also made by God, he spoke of "such towering magnitude in this tininess." The family Nycteribiidae, the bat ticks, are true flies but look like spiders without heads. They live only in the fur of bats, sucking bat blood, hanging on with claws. Exposed, the stunted bugs run rapidly across the bat's fur before disappearing underneath. But the family Tipulidae, the crane flies, fill your palm. They look like giant tapered mosquitoes, with very long, slender, spiderlike legs, three eyes, and big veiny wings that may span three inches. They do not bite. These are the ballerinas of the flies, delicate and graceful. Male crane flies form mating swarms that dance above treetops at sundown, or flow over pastures in a cloud, pushed by the breeze.

So one fly seeks light and heat; another avoids both. One is a vegetarian—another a terror. They flit like tiny shadows in the night skies, crawl across the windowpane and out of the drain and into the garbage and into our eyes. Sometimes flies migrate out to sea far from anything human, flitting across the white-capped waves of the ever-moving sea for miles, for days. The fly is grotesque and frail and lovely and vigorous, quivering, shivering, lapping, flitting, jerking, sucking, panting: Theirs is an exotic genius, a design of brilliant simplicity and bewildering complexity at once.

I study flies; I am stunned by them. I love them, with a fleeting love—with the triad: love, logic, sensitivity. Did you notice how calmly I noted that there is a fly that lives inside spiders? Another that is parasitic on grasshoppers? This is a humming, buzzing world; we live in the midst of the ceaseless murmur of lives, a world of strange things whispering the poems of old Buddhas. The world's constant rustling is like the rubbing of velvet between distracted fingers; it can drive one mad. Beside the cherry tree, under that bright sky, lives the sheep bot fly. It enters a sheep's nostrils, where it gives birth to live young. The maggots crawl up the nasal passages into the sinuses, where they feed until they are grown—a process that lasts nearly a year. The sheep's nose runs with pus; it shakes its head at this odd itch, shakes and rubs its nose into the ground, grits its teeth, jumps about, growing ever weaker. The condition is sometimes called the blind staggers. One day the sheep gives a great sneeze, and out shoot mature sheep bot flies. They are ready to mate and make more babies.

It is right here with flies that I face a direct and potent challenge: What do I really believe? What do I believe about beauty and the ultimate goodness of this world?

Jean-Henri Fabre lays out his corpses by the open window. A few days later, he writes, "Let us overcome our repugnance and give a glance inside." Then he lifts the bodies, counting the flies that have come, the eggs they lay, the larvae that form ". . . a surging mass of swarming sterns and pointed heads, which emerge, wriggle, and dive in again. It suggests a seething billow." He adds, as an aside, "It turns one's stomach." He examines and measures and counts, and then gently places a few hundred eggs in a test tube with a piece of meat squeezed dry. A few days later, he pours off the liquescent remnants of the once-hard flesh, which "flows in every direction like an icicle placed before the fire." He measures it, and keeps careful notes.

"It is horrible," he adds, "most horrible."

I have been a Buddhist for more than twenty-five years, since I was a young woman. My avid urge to understand bodies didn't stop at the bodies themselves; I sought for a way to think about the fact of life, the deepest query. Buddhism in its heart is an answer to our questions about suffering and loss, a response to the inexplicable; it is a way to live with life. Its explanations, its particular vocabulary and shorthand, its gentle pressures—they have been with me throughout my adult life; they are part of my language, my thought, my view. Buddhism saved my life and controlled it; it has been liberation and censure at once.

Buddhism is blunt about suffering, its causes and its cures. The Buddha taught that nothing is permanent. He taught this in a great many ways, but most of what he said came down to this: Things change. Change hurts; change cannot be avoided. "All compounded

13

things are subject to dissolution"—this formula is basic Buddhist doctrine, it is pounded into us by the canon, by the masters, by our daily lives. It means all things are compounded and will dissolve, which means I am compounded and I will dissolve. This is not something I readily accept, and yet I am continually bombarded with the evidence. I longed to know this, this fact of life, this answer—that we are put together from other things and will be taken apart and those other things and those things we become will in turn be taken apart and built anew—that there is nothing known that escapes this fate. When one of his disciples struggled with lust or felt pride in his youth or strength, the Buddha recommended that the follower go to the charnel ground, and meditate on a corpse—on its blossoming into something new.

We feel pain because things change. We feel joy for the same reason. But suffering is not simply pain: It is our peculiar punishment that we know things change and we want this to be otherwise. We want to hang on to what is going away, keep our conditions as they are, people as they are, ourselves as we are. In Buddhist terms this is variously called thirst or desire or attachment or clinging. It means that we hold on to the hope that something will remain, even as it all slides away like sand in running water, like water from our hands. Knowing the answer does not stop the question from being asked.

Desire is not always about holding something close; it has a shadow, the urge to push things away. Buddhists usually call this aversion—the desire for the extinction of something, for separation from it. The original Pali word for aversion, *dosa*, is various and shaded, translated sometimes as anger or hatred, sometimes as denial, as projection, aggression, repulsion, and now and then as disgust or revulsion or distortion. Aversion has as much force and fascination as the positive desires we know. It may be simply a reflexive flinch, a ducking for cover; it may be much stronger. Like desire, aversion is a many-colored thing, flavored by circumstances. It is a kind of clinging—clinging to the hope of *something other than this.*

When I began to study flies, I couldn't seem to stop. Fabre wrote, "To know their habits long haunted my mind." I think of the violence with which we describe such prurient obsessions—we say we cannot tear our eyes away. My eyes are glued to flies and it is as though they are stitched open against my will. I feel revulsion, I flinch, I turn away, I duck for cover. I get squeamish, which is a rare feeling for me. But I also feel curiosity and admiration and a kind of awe. The buzz of a fly's blurred wings is one of the myriad ways the world speaks to us; it is one of the ways speech is freed from our ideas. I feel that if I could listen, if I could just listen without reacting, without judgment or preference or opinion—without reaching for a dream of how things might be otherwise—there is something I would understand that I have yet to know.

Compassion in all its flavors is woven through the enormous canon of Buddhist thought. Its root meaning is "to suffer with." We are able to feel compassion toward those beings who look like us and those who are most familiar. (These are not the same thing; dissimilar creatures can be deeply familiar, as we know from our time spent with dogs, with horses—even lizards.) At what point do we extend this circle past what is known, past what looks like us? At what point do we suffer with what is completely strange? And how far must that circle extend before it includes the sheep bot fly?

This mix of push and pull I feel when I look at insects is akin to the way the tongue longs for an acquired taste. The first time one tastes certain complex flavors they are unpleasant, even offensive. But in time it is that very flavor, its complexity—the bitterness or acidity mingling with other layers—that brings you back. Whether it is wine or chili powder or *natto*—a Japanese delicacy of soybeans bound into a sticky, cobwebbed mold—one returns in part because of the difficulty. We are sharply, pleasantly excited by the nearness of rejection, by skirting along the edge of things, the dank and sour things that instinct reads as dangerous. These shadings of flavor ever so briefly evoke poison and rot—the urine scent of beer, the lingering oily bitterness of coffee, the rank tang of certain cheeses (and I will return to cheese; it factors here). There is a brief shrinking away, perhaps very brief, minuscule, but there nonetheless.

This is a little bit of what I feel toward flies. Let us give a glance inside—a glance, a gasp, a shiver, the briefest reactivity: and then another look, a bit sideways though it may be, and then another. Then there follows the need to look: interest turning into inquiry into passion: the desire to know, to see, and something more, something crucial—the need to bear it, to be able to bear it, to be able to look as closely and thoroughly as I can.

Flies have long been considered the shells and familiars of gods, witches, and demons. They are associated with reincarnation, immortality, and sorcery. They are so unutterably strange, all swarming and speed and single-mindedness, and they cannot be avoided. I really mean that; we eat flies every day.[2] The FDA permits thirty-five fruit fly eggs in every eight ounces of golden raisins, up to twenty maggots "of any size" in a hundred grams of canned mushrooms, and a fair number of both eggs and maggots in tomato products. Last night's mushroom pizza? A womb of flies.

Flies sense the world in every way, its faintest textures: minuscule currents of shifting air, the vibration of a bird's approaching wings, the scent of decaying flowers or a mouse's corpse a half mile away. Some flies have a complex and unique ear, a flexible tympanal membrane in a complex structure behind the neck. A few parasitic flies listen for the distinct sound of their selected prey; one imagines a head carefully cocked.

They taste and smell in ways far more subtle than ours. There is no profound difference between the two senses anyway; both are a way of identifying chemicals, defining them, discriminating. They sense the sex pheromones released so hopefully by their prey, and follow; they smell the prey's feces, its breath, or the small damage done by other hunting insects. Biting flies are sensitive to stress chemicals, including the higher levels of carbon dioxide emitted when mammals exert themselves. The black flies respond directly to the scent of human sweat. Many flies have taste and smell receptors on their complex mouthparts, their antennae, the delicate legs, and fine-clawed feet. Walking, they sample the coming meal; instantly, the proboscis unwinds. Flies are sensitive to minute differences in the world's chemistry, and its surprising similarities: One of the parasitic *Lucilia* flies is attracted, according to one text, to "wild parsnips and fresh meat." One molecule attracts the male to the female; another causes the male's ritual courtship flight; a third causes the female to relax and hold still. Their world is a superdimensional

---

[2]Consider the cheese skipper, a kind of black fly found all over the world. They are so called in part because they skip, or leap, when disturbed; they curl up, grabbing the tail with the hooked mouth, tense, and then let go—springing like a coil, fast and hard. Cheese skippers are attracted to meat, cheese, and corpses, which develop a cheesy smell at a certain stage when butyric acid is present. Their family name, Piophilia, means milk loving. The larvae can be eaten accidentally, and may survive ingestion and burrow into the gut. One imagines the little thing shrugging its nonexistent shoulders and changing course. When the larvae infest a hard cheese like pecorino, they decompose the fats until the cheese turns creamy and pink, at which point the Italians call it *casu marzu*, "rotten cheese." Gourmets like it, and will blend *casu marzu* into a paste to spread on bread. Most people try to remove the maggots first. Selling this cheese is illegal in Italy, because even shredded maggot parts are dangerous—all those hooks. But not everyone does this. Some consider the maggots part of the delicacy—an aphrodisiac, or a peculiarly nutritious food.

pheromonal architecture, a mingled and vaporous mist multiplied by sight and sound and space.

Consider the compound eye, common to all insects, variously evolved in flies. A fly's eyes may be huge: the eyes of horse flies are bulging black caps filling the face. Other flies may have tiny eyes, and some flies have no eyes at all. (The pyrgotid flies have strangely shaped heads that protrude in *front* of their eyes, an evolutionary development hard to comprehend.) The eye may be flat or bulging, round or triangular in shape, shining like jewels. A deer fly's eyes are brightly colored, green or gold with patterns and zigzags. Tachinid flies have reddish eyes; dance flies have orange ones. Each facet of a compound eye is held at a unique angle, independent of all the others. They are capable of differentiating between the wavelengths of light and can distinguish the angle at which sunlight falls, allowing them to navigate off the surface of water. A fly has a thousand eyes, four thousand eyes, side by side without gap. The fly cannot focus on a single form, but sees each form from many angles at once. Each single thing is multiplied, the object broken like a mirror into shards, into shocks of light, and remade like water into a single lake, a prism, a drop of dew.

Flies eat blood and meat and feces and other insects and each other, but also pollen, nectar, algae, decaying seaweed, and fungi. Bulb fly maggots are tiny dilettantes, seeking only the inner tissue of hyacinth, tulip, narcissus, and lily bulbs. Fruit fly maggots are picky: One species eats walnut husks, another eats cherries. Pomace flies live on rotting fruit, but they don't eat the fruit; they eat the yeast that grows on rotting fruit. (This is a brief world indeed; a new generation is born every ten days or so.)

Flies bite, suck, slice, lap. Bee lice live in the mouths of bees, eating nectar. Stiletto fly larvae sometimes live in wool blankets and decaying wood. Among the black flies, which plague cattle, each species specializes in a cow part—one sucks blood from cows' bellies, one from cows' ears, and so on. The flat-footed flies, which run in a zigzag pattern across plants, include a variety called smoke flies; they are attracted to fires and eat the burned wood afterward. Eye gnats are drawn to tears, sweat flies to sweat, face flies to eyes and noses.

Flies hurt us, but only in passing; sleeping sickness, malaria, yellow fever, river blindness: mere accidents. The sheep bot fly can live in many places, including human eyes if eyes are more convenient than the sheep—but it prefers the sheep. We are simply more food,

17

more warm and meaty beings among endless beings. But what food!—palaces of muscle and blood, rich and fertile fields.

I read otherwise sober and mechanical descriptions of flies, and trip over the anthropomorphic complaint. Both Pliny and Plutarch complained that flies were impossible to train and domesticate. Among modern thinkers, one fly is "good" and the other is "bad," one is a "pest" and another a "bane" and another a "benefit." The tachinid flies are parasitic on destructive caterpillars, and snipe flies eat aphids, so they are described with kind words. Their predation does us good, but all predation does something good and not just the predator. Predation makes way. It makes room.

Even entomologists hate flies, on principle. Edwin Way Teale, who wrote of the natural world his entire life with reverence and cheer, hated the housefly. He obsessed over the number and variety of bacteria, fungi, viruses, and parasites they carried from place to place, and finally seems to have simply flung his hands into the air and given up, declaring the housefly "an insect villain with hardly a drop of redeeming virtue." Leland Howard, a USDA entomologist, wrote an encyclopedic account of insects in 1904 that is still quoted today. He called the harmless saltwater flies "sordid little flies," and the wingless bird tick "apparently too lazy to fly." Of the bluebottle, which sometimes has parasitic mites, he wrote, "It is comforting to think that the house-fly has these parasites which torment him so. Such retribution is just."

Humans are a nightmare; we tear the earth apart. We trepan mountains and pour them into rivers, take the soil apart down to its atoms, sully the sea, shred our world like giant pigs rutting after truffles. We poison our nest and each other and ourselves. We eat everything, simply everything, but we turn away from flies.

The circles of compassion can suddenly expand. Federico García Lorca wrote that he rescued flies caught at a window; they reminded him of "people / in chains." And of course I've done the same. I often do—catch flies and crickets and spiders and let them go, careful of their frailty. This brief moment of the widening circle; it is easily challenged by the maggot, by the swarm. The larvae of the fungus gnat sometimes travel in great masses, for reasons no one can guess—huge groups called worm snakes piled several deep, squirming along about an inch a minute. I know why Beelzebub is Lord of the Flies; is there any other god who would slouch so towards Bethlehem?

I long sometimes for a compound eye. It is a tenet of my religious

18

practice, an ever-present thorn, to remember that my point of view, that any point of view, is merely a point. My eyes cannot see a landscape, let alone a world. But how we judge things has everything to do with where we stand. Can I learn to see a form from many angles at once? Can I see other beings, this moment, my mistakes, my words, like this? Can I know multiplicity as a single thing?

So many flies: Mydas flies, sewage flies, robust bot flies, gout flies, scavenger flies, snipe flies. Big-headed flies, thick-headed flies, picture-winged flies, stilt-legged flies, spear-winged flies, banana-stalk flies, flower-loving flies, stalk-eyed flies, flat-footed flies, pointed-winged flies, hump-backed flies.

The literature of Zen Buddhism is thick with nature—nature images, metaphors, puzzles, and questions, but mostly the calm and serene inhuman world of clouds, seeds, spring shoots, meadow grasses, and ponds, the moon and the mountain and the wave and the plum blossom. (Kobayashi Issa, an eighteenth-century Buddhist haiku master, wrote: "Where there are humans / there are flies / and Buddhas." But he is talking, I think, rather more about humans than flies.) Such images are used as metaphors for all kinds of Buddhist concepts, but they are partly an effort to convey how Zen Buddhism describes reality itself, the world. Hongzhi, a great Zen master of China, described it as "sky and water merging in autumn"—a vast, shifting, unbounded world.

Central to Zen Buddhism is a belief in *busshō*, usually translated from the Japanese as Buddha Nature. (In English we like to capitalize words like *buddha* and *nature*, to distinguish subtly different ideas with the same sound. Today, glancing inside the seething billow of life, it seems to me an impotent fist shaking at the greatness of what we try to say with the words. But I will follow the rule.)

Busshō is shorthand for something that requires quite a few words to explain—or it is already one too many words for what can't be explained in words. Buddhism is founded on the idea that all things are impermanent, that nothing has a fixed self-nature that passes through time unchanged. Change is not an aspect of the matrix but the matrix itself. It is because no one thing is permanent that we are not separated from anything—not bounded, not contained. All beings are constantly appearing, constantly springing into existence, hurtling out of themselves, of what they were, what preceded. Buddha Nature is—what? Original nature. Perfect nature—the substrate or source of all things. But it is not God, it is not ether, it is not simply a womb that gives birth. It is all things; it is that which manifests as things—as the world—as people, rocks, stars, dewdrops, flies—all beings, all forms, all existent things. All existence.

What do I know about Buddha Nature, anyway? I can't even tell you what it is—and Buddha Nature isn't an "it" and it isn't really an "is" either; not a quality attached to anything or a state of being or a space in which things exist; Buddha Nature as I understand it—there's that "it" again—is this, this, this, here, this minuscule and gargantuan and muscular relational and organic now, the luminosity of the sparkling world, the vast inevitability of loss, and not that exactly either. I use that phrase, Buddha Nature, even as it fills my mouth with ash, to mean all those things and more—relation, aspects, moments, qualities, acts, aeons, and bodies—and I use it in a positive way, with pleasure, with outright joy, to mean that all of us—those of us who think we are something unique and those who never think about it, and all those creatures who don't do what I might call thinking but are yet alive, and all those things we bang up against and assume aren't alive at all—are in some way kin, in some way both source and effect, eternally and continually and without hesitation, spontaneously and instantaneously and infinitely giving birth to ourselves, spilling out of nothing into nothing, with great vigor—leaping, sliding, appearing, disappearing into and out of a lack of solidness, into and out of the nonexistence of permanent nature, and that because this is the law—the muscle, the hinge—of reality—it's good. It's all right. Everything is all right.

Everything is all right. The female horsefly favors large warm-blooded animals. They see quite well and will fly around their prey just out of reach, finally biting one's back or leg. (As is true with many other biting flies, including mosquitoes, only the females bite. The males live on plant pollen and juices. It so happens as well that the males live brief lives while the females live the whole long, hot summer. The story is told that the Declaration of Independence was signed on July 4 because the horseflies in Philadelphia were intolerable that year, and the delegates called for an early vote so they could get out of town.) The "phlebotomus" insects, as they are called, have anticoagulant in their saliva; after a bite, the blood continues to run, sometimes dangerously so. (To be precise, the horsefly slices rather than bites; its mouthparts are like tiny knives.) In their turn, horseflies are eaten by robber flies, who capture them on the wing and then find a convenient twig to rest on while sucking them dry.

Robber flies are sometimes called bee killers; they prize honeybees and will watch them from the shadows while the bees gather pollen, then suddenly dart out and seize one from behind, so it can't sting. They drain the bee dry and drop its empty shell; below a familiar perch, the bodies slowly pile up.

The cluster fly lays its children inside earthworms. If you crush a cluster fly, it smells like honey.

The female thick-headed fly hangs around flowers, drinking nectar, like a bully at a bar. She waits for a bee or wasp and when one comes close, she grabs it. The bee seems not to care, does not resist, while she deposits an egg before letting go. The bee flies away, the larva hatches, and burrows within. The larva eats the bee slowly until it dies, then falls to the ground within the bee's body and burrows underground to pupate. Flies are holometabolous, meaning the young undergoes a complete metamorphism into the adult form, into a completely different form. The pupa is the quiescent phase between, and may last days or weeks or even longer. The pupae of flies are not protected by cocoons like those of butterflies; they simply harden, or build a shell from soil or spit. Some flies make a puparium from their own skin. Eat the bee, crawl underground, sleep the winter through, and emerge as a fly, seeking bees. That is the cycle, the great web of its life, round and round.

Pyrgotid flies do the same thing to May beetles, except that instead of burrowing into the ground, they live in the empty beetle shell over the winter. Flesh flies live under the skin of a turtle and in the stomach of frogs. The sheep bot fly—I have described this creature already. But there is also a bot fly that infests rabbits, and a bot fly that lives in horses' throats, a bot fly that favors horses' noses, and another bot fly that prefers horses' tongues. There are bot flies specific to kangaroos, camels, warthogs, zebras, and elephants. The human bot fly, transmitted by mosquitoes, is cosmopolitan in its tastes; besides people, it infects dogs, cats, rabbits, horses, cattle, and sheep.

One of the drawbacks of a long Buddhist practice is that one sometimes has the urge to present one's self as more composed than one actually is. (Let's be clear here; I mean me.) Emotional equanimity is a Buddhist virtue, a reflection of one's ability to accept reality and a sign that one is not contributing to the heat of suffering in the world by resisting that reality. That this equanimity is a real thing to me, a true tranquillity found through steady practice, is beside the point. My tranquillity may be real but it is not immune to conditions; it is no more permanent or unchanging than my skin. At times there is a loud voice inside me, complaining indignantly: *Explain this!* Someone please explain this.

In my dreams, I could not make *Apocephalus pergandei.* It is named after Theodore Pergande, a renowned entomologist of the latter nineteenth century who was particularly interested in aphids and ants. He was observing carpenter ants one day when he saw the heads of the ants begin to fall off one at a time. When he investigated, he found what has become known colloquially as the ant-decapitating fly. The mature fly lays eggs on an ant's neck. The larvae hatch and then bore into the ant's head, eating it from the inside. Eating, the larva grows, slowly killing the ant, which apparently expires just as its head pops off. But as many of us wish we could do, it does not leave its childhood home behind. Instead, the little vermin remains inside for a while, and if you look closely that is what you will see: ants' heads, walking around, filled with the children of flies.

A Buddhist practice requires rigorous self-disclosure—mostly to one's own self—and a kind of undefended willingness to be present in one's own crappy life as it is. This means noticing how often we tell lies about ourselves. I lie about many things, to myself and others. I lie about the way that triad on which I balance tilts: sensitivity, logic, love. It limps at times, or I find myself one-legged, just plain falling down. I am not always at home in this world, not always relaxed, not always in love with this great big Buddha-Nature-ridden place.

The Tachinidae is one of the largest, most selective, and successful fly families. "Ingenious," says one entomologist, for how they have solved the problems of their peculiar niche—"respiration in particular," since it is tricky to breathe inside things. Tachinid larvae are pure parasites, infesting virtually every kind of insect. One type lays its eggs on the leaves preferred by a certain caterpillar; the caterpillar eats the eggs, and the larvae hatch inside—born, as it were, at the buffet table. Another chooses crickets and katydids. The female fly can hear the precise frequency of the cricket chirp. (She can also hear, though the calls are many times higher, the ultrasound calls of the insectivorous bats she wants to avoid.) She follows the chirp carefully through a mechanism. When she locates the host, she lays her live babies beside or on them. They burrow in and eat selectively to keep the host alive as long as possible.

Caught in a certain light, tachinid flies glow, their wings like violet veils, ovaline eyes the burnt orange of sunset. I sit in the dark summer night, pleasantly melancholy, listening to crickets and contemplating *busshō* in a pulsing world.

I can pretend to have this settled. I can pretend to not mind. Certain gall midges are parasitic on themselves: The larvae hatch inside the mother and eat her from the inside out. I am appalled, even as I recognize the marvelous efficiency. Then I turn away from my own appalled thoughts. I am practicing acceptance. I bow. I tell myself it is a kind of compassion. It is sacrifice. (As though I understand *that* in some way.)

The horsefly bites a horse, and the blood runs, and before the wound even closes the face fly creeps in and settles down to stay. The human bot fly captures a bloodsucker, such as a mosquito, and lays eggs on its body—just enough that the mosquito can still move freely. Then the mosquito finds a host and lands. The heat of the host causes the bot fly larvae to hatch; they slide off to the host's skin, down a follicle of hair, and in, another accidental gift. The larvae live just under the skin. They form a breathing hole with their hooks, keeping it open by digging constantly. This is called myiasis, flies developing in living flesh. (Many fly families indulge; the human bot fly is just one.) The maggots live under the skin until they are about an inch long. One observer of the condition wrote that myiasis causes "intense discomfort or pain," which is not a surprise. But the maggots are never still; he adds that people also complain of "the disquieting feeling of never being alone."

A person with myiasis must be patient; it is damaging to try to remove tiny larvae. One treatment is suffocation: coating the openings with paraffin or nail polish or turpentine, or lathering on chloroform dissolved in vegetable oil. One of the most effective methods for removing them is to lay strips of raw bacon across the wound; the larvae come running. Squirming, rather, in their roiling, systaltic wave.

Oh, well—parasitism is routine in the insect world. Can we call it cruel, this life governed by instinct? Consider this: Two flies glued down by their wings to a table, for convenience. A drop of paraffin is carefully poured on their backs and then scooped out into a crater. Each fly's thorax is opened into the crater with a tiny scalpel, exposing the muscle. Saline is dropped into the craters for moisture. The flies are then rotated and joined, back to back, the paraffin gently sealed with a hot needle to form a double fly. This new kind of fly can walk, sort of, each taking a turn riding the other piggyback—or it can be neatly glued to a stick. For convenience. Now the scientist has a wonderful thing, a little monster with which to study many things: metabolism, hunger, dehydration, decay.

Explain that.

The larva grows, then settles into pupation. After time, after a mountain of time, the maggot disappears, the cask opens, and a fly emerges. It is fully mature; it will grow no more. The larvae of black flies are aquatic; the matured fly secretes a bubble of air and rises in it like an astronaut to its new life in the air, bursting out of the bubble at the surface. One observer said that a sudden hatching of black flies leaves the water "in great numbers with such force and velocity" that it seemed as though they were being "shot out of a gun." In contrast, the net-winged midge makes a submarine, a stiff case that floats to the surface, where it bursts open; the adults rise from their boats as delicate as mist. At first it is a wrinkled and empty fly bag, without color or strength. The new being takes a great gulp of air and expands, incalculably vast and whole, the actualization of fly.

So many flies: tabanid flies, green bottle flies, bronze dump flies, stilt-legged flies, bush flies, stable flies, louse flies, frit flies, dung flies, rust flies, elk flies, seaweed flies, rust flies, scavenger flies, gadflies, skipper flies, soldier flies, Hessian flies, Richard flies, light flies, stone flies, sand flies, grass flies, eye gnats, wood gnats. A myriad mosquitoes.

There is something so simple and clear about the speech of flies; if I knew fly words, what would be clarified in my own? I study how flies use the world—how they make something of it that wasn't there before. They liquefy the dead, they slurp up the world, inhaling the bodies of others. They shoot out of lakes and the ground and out of bodies, joyous, filled with air. If I believe—and today, I think I do—that every being is Buddha Nature, that there is no place Buddhas cannot or will not go, then I must give a glance inside.

I don't know what a Buddha is.

One fly, its passing hum, this we know—but they mob up, don't they, into masses of flies, into rivers and mountains of life, crawling and skipping and vibrating without rest, working at disintegration and change. Phantom midges form such enormous swarms they have been mistaken for smoke plumes, humming with such force that, in the words of one observer, they sound "like a distant waterfall."

Many fly swarms are birth explosions; others are orgies. Male dance flies join in huge mating swarms, graceful ellipses that flow up and down across meadows and gardens. They make frothy structures called nuptial balloons to carry on their abdomens for attracting females. Some species put seeds or algae in their balloons; others go straight for dead bugs—the bigger, the better, as far as the female is concerned. (Female dance flies routinely eat during sex—maybe from the nuptial balloon they have accepted as part of the bargain, but often, they eat another fly.) One type of dance fly uses only saliva and air, creating a lather of emptiness; as they dance, the empty bubbles glitter like lights.

Long-legged flies do their mating dance in slow motion, their rhythms complex and mysterious; they wave black and white leg scales back and forth in front of the female like a vaudeville stripper waves her fans. Pomace flies have tufts of dark hair on their legs called sex combs, with which they hold the female still during mating. The male penetrates from behind, the female spasmodically jerking in response. Already mated females are unreceptive; they curl their abdomens under, fly away, or kick at males.

The impregnated female seeks a nest. A few flies give live birth, and a few incubate their young. The tsetse fly, keds, and bat flies all hatch within their mother and are fed with something akin to a milk gland until they are ready to pupate, at which point they are finally expelled. But most flies lay eggs—a single egg, or hundreds, or thousands. She has a telescoping ovipositor, fine and small, which emerges from her abdomen and gropes its way inside—into the soft spaces, in the dark. Flies lay their eggs in the roots and stems of plants, in fruit, in the algae of a still pond, in shit, in hair and hide, in the bodies of other insects, the stomachs of cows, the dirty hunks of wool around the anus of sheep, in the pus of an infected wound. (The preference of many carnivorous species is the corpse.) Blowflies deposit eggs in the eyes, ears, nostrils, mouth, vagina, and anus. Female flies are choosy; many have taste buds on the ovipositor to help them pick the best location—each fly to its own place. Insistent and shy, the ovipositor worms its way down: into garbage and wounds, into the rotten flecks of meat on the floor of a slaughterhouse, into stagnant water, between the membranous layers of a corpse, between fibers of living muscle, on the umbilical cord of newborn fawns—into "any convenient cavity," says the *Britannica*—and deposits tiny eggs shimmery and damp, masses of them. She is careful not to crowd them, filling first one newly made womb, and then another and another. A day later, she dies.

Sallie Tisdale

Horrible. Most horrible.

Larvae are the unfinished fly; they are like letters not yet making a word. Maggots are the simplest of larvae; they are the ur-fly, the refined essence of the fly, the marvelously simplified fly—its template, a profoundly primitive thing. Many maggots have no head, consisting only of a body and a mouth filled with hooks. They move by wavelets of muscular contraction and relaxation, grasping with the mouth hooks and other hooks along their sides. They can roll and spring and slide.

After they hatch, they eat and grow. This process may be slow or fast. The chironomid midge larva in West Africa grows in spurts, drying out and reviving through extreme temperature variations and waves of drought and rain. When it is almost completely desiccated, it enters into a condition called cryptobiosis—still alive but with no signs of metabolism. Sprinkled with water, it wakes up, takes a meal, and starts growing again until the next dry spell. Blue bottle flies require an almost totally humid atmosphere—something a corpse can easily provide in most cases—and in good conditions, hatch almost as soon as they are laid. They begin to eat, and never stop. I am being literal: They never stop. (Trashmen call maggots "disco rice" for the way they wiggle through the waste.) If undisturbed, a maggot will eat without ceasing until it is grown. There is a distinct advantage to maggots having anal spiracles; there is no need to stop eating in order to breathe.

Aristotle, like many others for most of history, believed that some flies "are not derived from living parentage, but are generated spontaneously . . . in decaying mud or dung; others in timber." They simply appear all at once from manure and corpses, with no sign of having been born. How else to explain this locomotion, this primordial fecundity?

Maggots can reduce the weight of a human body by fifty percent in a few weeks. In the decomposing of a body, there are several waves of insects, each colonizing in its turn in a strict sequence. The first wave is blowflies and houseflies of certain species; they begin to arrive within minutes of death. Their bodies are beautiful, glasslike in shimmering greens and blues, their eyes a deep, warm red. They glisten, tremble, and the larvae hatch and eat. They are ingenious little maggots. A dead body is in fact alive, a busy place full of activity—so much that the body seems to move of its own accord from their motion. The sound of all this movement, all this life, writes one entomologist, is "reminiscent of gently frying fat."

26

In time, other species of blowflies and houseflies arrive. The corpse begins to blacken, soften. (Corpses at this stage are called "wet carrion" by biologists.) The meat on which the maggots feed begins to liquefy and runs like melting butter. This is the fluid Fabre contemplated in quiet shock. "We here witness the transfusion of one animal into another," he wrote. If the maggots fail to move in time, they drown in the broth of the corpse they are eating.

By the time these larvae have fallen off into the soil to pupate, a third wave of flies arrives—fruit flies and drone flies and others, flies that prefer the liquids. Toward the end, the cheese skipper appears, drawn to the smell, and carefully cleans the bones of the remnants of tendons and connective tissue.

I contemplate my ordinary, imperfect, beloved body. I contemplate the bodies of my beloveds: individual, singular, unique, irreplaceable people, their skin and eyes and mouths and hands. I consider their skin riddled and bristling with that seething billow, I consider the digestion of their eyes and the liquefaction of those hands, my hands, my eyes—the evolution of the person into the thing, into wet carrion and eventually into a puddle, into soil, into earth, and flies. And it will come, whether I turn away or not.

We are nothing more than a collection of parts, and each part a collection of smaller parts, and smaller, the things we love and all we cherish conglomerates of tiny blocks. The blocks are built up; they will be taken apart the same way; we are nothing more. (And yet we are something more; this is one of the mysteries, I know. I cannot point to it, hold it, name it, except in the limited and awkward ways I have already tried. But there is something more, and it is the totality of this *nothing more*.)

Flies are wholehearted things, leading wholehearted lives. They understand dissolution, and by understanding I mean they live it. The parts are separated, they become something new. Pouring one's life into compoundedness without resistance, living by means of compoundedness and its subsequent falling apart—this is the wisdom of the creatures of the earth, the ones besides us, the ones who don't fight it. Because the human heart is devoted to compounded things and tries to hold them still, our hearts break. (One more thing to dissolve.) How can we know their lives? How can we understand the spongy proboscis, softly padded, with its small rasping teeth?

What better vision of the fullness of birth and the fullness of death than the maggot and the fly? A legless, headless, gill-breathing vermiform, giving way to the complete stillness of the pupa, and

27

emerging as a land-based flyer—each stage utterly unlike the others, with nothing remaining of what was before. In their turn, maggots and flies help us along in our own fullness of birth and death, until what we were is completely changed. Decomposed, recomposed, compounded, dissolved, disappearing, reappearing—a piece from here and a fleck from there, a taste of this karma, a speck of that memory, this carbon atom, that bit of water, a little protein, a pinch of pain: until a new body and a new life are made from pieces of the past. The wee bit they claim, can you begrudge it? Dissolved, our flesh is their water, and they lap us up.

"Placed in her crucibles, animals and men, beggars and kings are one and all alike," wrote Fabre. "There you have true equality, the only equality in this world of ours: equality in the presence of the maggot." What lucky flies smelled the flowery scent of the Buddha's death, and came—flowing through the air like a river in the sky, a river of flies! What lucky maggots were born in his body, in the moist heat of the afternoon while the disciples still mourned! The maggots and blowflies are the words of the old Buddhas, singing of the vast texture of things, a lullaby of birth and death. They came and turned him into juice and soil, the Buddha flowing gloriously like cream into the ground.

After a night of more routinely menacing scenes—an insecurely locked door, a strange man in a wig—I woke in the early morning from a brief, vivid dream. There had been a series of burning rooms, and finally a room completely engulfed in flames. I saw several people walking calmly through the room, untouched, smiling. I woke as one turned and looked at me, and said, "I can't tell you how safe I feel in this house."

One of the most famous parables of Buddhism is that of the burning house. The story is told by the Buddha in the Lotus Sutra. A man's children are trapped in a burning house, and won't leave when he calls them. In order to get them out, safe and free, he promises carts full of treasure, great treasure. Finally, tempted, they come out, and are saved. Fire is change, loss, the impossibility of holding on; fire is also the burning, ceaseless desire we feel to hold on to that which can't be held. The house is burning, and we stupidly stand there, refusing to leave—until we are tempted by the promise of treasure—the precious jewels of the Dharma, the practice, the Buddha himself.

28

Right here, what do I believe? I do believe in perfection, right here—and not just perfection existing in the midst of decay, but decay as a kind of perfection. I believe in beauty, especially in the moments when one least seeks it—not just the dewdrop, the grass, but beauty in the shuffling of papers on the desk in the little cubicle thick with the snuffles of the sweaty man a few inches away. Beauty in the rattle of the bus sliding halfway into the crosswalk right beside you. Beauty in the liquid aswim with maggots. In everything, in anything. I can believe this, without in any way really understanding. Even after I have my answer, the question is always being asked.

When I begin to truly accept myself as a flit, a bubble, a pile of blocks tilting over, my precious me as a passing sigh in the oceanic cosmos of change—when I accept this moment passing completely away into the next without recourse—when I begin to accept that its very fragility and perishing nature is the beauty in life, then I begin to find safety inside a burning house. I don't need to escape if I know how to live inside it. Not needing to escape, I no longer feel tempted, no longer need promises or rewards. I just walk through it, aware of fire.

The north woods in summer smell like blackberry jam, and in the pockets of sun the tiny midges dance in the heat-sweetened air. They are drunk with it, galloping round and round as their lives leak quickly away. They are points of light in the light.

Lessness
Lance Olsen

A LITTLE LESS OF US every day.

Seven words, nine syllables, twenty-three letters.

That's all that is the case, precisely what we really know about ourselves, sans irony, sans wit, sans posturing, sans philosophy, sans desperate belief: how it is impossible to reason with our own bodies.

There is hope, Franz Kafka once wrote, but not for us.

Blessed is he who expects nothing, Alexander Pope once wrote, for he shall never be disappointed.

An e-mail from a friend, her lung cancer having recently metastasized to the brain: They have me on this experimental chemo pill, long-term, which is supposed to reduce the risk of recurrence greatly. The problem is it made my face break out in this horrendous acne-like rash. So I've cut back to half a dose and begun taking antibiotics as well as using all sorts of creams. My dermatologist's assistant spent nearly an hour with me showing me how to use makeup to cover the rash. I've never used makeup in my life, and really hadn't planned on starting now, but it does seem to make a difference.

Grenz-Situationen was Karl Jaspers's term.

We seem to believe it possible to ward off death by following rules of good grooming, Don DeLillo once wrote.

How we keep writing anyway.

Grenz-Situationen: Limit situations.

How we keep writing anyway until we don't keep writing anyway.

The bioengineered replicant Roy Batty to his creator, Tyrell, in *Blade Runner*, a moment before Roy crushes Tyrell's skull, drives his thumbs into Tyrell's eyes: *I want more life, fucker.*

How I saw the writer Ronald Sukenick for the last time one humid, rainy April afternoon in his Battery Park City apartment two months before he died of inclusion body myositis, a muscle-wasting disease that eventually makes it impossible for one to swallow, then to breathe.

Jaspers's philosophy being an extended effort to explore and describe the margins of human experience, an effort to confront what he thought of, beautifully, as The Unconditioned.

Death is so terrifying, Susan Cheever once wrote, because it is so ordinary.

Ron couldn't use his fingers anymore, so he bought a voice-recognition program and wrote by means of that.

Ridley Scott reediting the scene so that in the final cut Batty says: *I want more life, Father*—thereby draining the life out of the line, making it into mere Frankensteinian, mere Oedipal cliché.

How my wife and I strolled along the banks of the Bagmati River in Kathmandu among myriad cloth-wrapped bodies burning on funeral pyres.

How Ron and I both knew this was it, how there would be no future meetings. How we both understood there were no social conventions to cover such an event. How the unsettling result was that each of our simple declarative sentences seemed anything but.

When we speak of "seriousness" in art, Thomas Pynchon once wrote, ultimately we are talking about an attitude toward death.

How, shortly before his in 1631, John Donne obtained an urn, his own burial shroud, and the services of an artist. He wrapped himself in said shroud, posed atop said urn, and had said artist render a charcoal sketch of him, which the poet kept by his bedside throughout his final illness.

The distance between the real and the ideal.

Two large framed photographs hang on the walls of my writing studio, both by Joel-Peter Witkin. They are the only ones by an established artist my wife and I have ever felt a necessity to purchase. Each is a still life, a *nature morte,* constructed from corpse parts the photographer found and posed in morgues in Mexico and France.

Families of the dead in prim circles around the pyres along the river.

Holy men spattering butter on the fires to help them burn faster.

How, to pass time on the Paris Métro once between stops, I asked my sister, with whom I was riding during a visit, how old she wanted to live to be, and, instead of answering, she began to cry.

Jaspers referred to the ultimate boundaries of being as *Das Umgreifende*—The Encompassing: the indefinite horizon in which all subjective and objective experience is possible, but which can itself never be apprehended rationally.

How, after fifty, your face becomes an accomplishment.

Eighty-three, less than a year before he died, Kurt Vonnegut: I've written books. Lots of them. Please, I've done everything I'm supposed to do. Can I go home now?

One only becoming authentically human, in other words, according to Jaspers, at the instant one allows oneself awareness of The Encompassing by confronting such unimaginables as universal contingency and the loss of the human, the loss of the body—the latter otherwise known as death.

Everything else refusal, fear, repression.

How the last words Roy Batty speaks, huddled on a dark, rainy L.A. rooftop in 2019, are some of the saddest, the most powerful, in the entire film: *All the things I have seen; these shall be lost in time.*

How it is the case, precisely, that life can be defined as a slow dying.

A terminal illness.

Birth, Beckett once wrote, was the death of him.

The goal of all life, Freud once wrote, is death.

How it is the case, precisely, that death is a protracted amnesia visited upon those who live beyond the lost one's passing.

Ernest Becker: The irony of man's condition is that the deepest need is to be free of the anxiety of death and annihilation; but it is life itself which awakens it, and so we must shrink from being fully alive.

Remembering, Milan Kundera once wrote, is a form of forgetting.

My dying friend: A lot of the brain motor difficulties that I was expecting after the first surgery seem to be appearing now. My left hand feels more or less like a stroke patient's unable to do very much except spill a glass of water on a computer keyboard or leave A. walking two blocks behind me because I had no sensation that I let go of his hand. For about two weeks there I was having some real palsy tremors, what they're calling *miniseizures.*

On a large enough time line, Chuck Palahniuk once wrote, the survival rate for everyone will drop to zero.

That's it. That's all.

How, as I was working on my novel about Friedrich Nietzsche's last mad night on earth, I couldn't shake off the abrupt uncanny realization that inside always becomes outside in the end.

The simple, brutal notion: how that which separates us from the world—our sphincterial control, our skin, our existential deep-sea suit—gradually goes away.

We are always becoming something other than we are, something other than we want to be.

Traveling.

Every once in a while Ron stopped talking, shifted in his electric wheelchair, looked out his picture window at the Hudson, then drifted back to what we were saying, and we would pick up where we had left off. I drank bourbon, Ron tea through a straw. He was having trouble swallowing. He was becoming tired very quickly. You could see it.

Every parting gives a foretaste of death, Schopenhauer once wrote.

How I could hear steam building in the skulls of the corpses as I moved along the banks of the Bagmati.

How Hemingway turned himself into a character in one of his books and shot himself in the head. How Hunter Thompson turned himself into a character in one of his books and shot himself in the head. How Yukio Mishima turned himself into a character in one of his books and committed seppuku. Publicly. In 1970.

Outside, people not cheering him on, but heckling him, jeering, as he disemboweled himself.

Gradually, or not so gradually. It depends.

I lost all my hair two weeks ago, my dying friend wrote. One of the things they talked about was the need to keep the head covered at all times and I ended up buying a large assortment of what they call chemo turbans, some of them reasonably stylish, to wear around the house. I mean, it's a perfectly good wig, and I'm sure was once a very nice beaver or groundhog or whatever it was, but I hate it. The hair of my nightmares.

The head. Not *my* head.

As if she had already begun to become something other than her own body.

My sister-in-law was in town, my dying friend wrote, and her comment was it looks OK, it just looks nothing like me. I'll use it for teaching, since it still masks hair loss, and there's no need to impose my limitations on the students. Then I decided to say screw the chemo turbans and looked at some hats. I ended up buying three outrageously exquisite retro-style felt fedoras which cover the whole head and are marvelously comfortable. You won't believe these. I've never been so stylish in my life.

Roy Batty, a replicant, virtually identical to humans in every way except for the fact that the memories he believes are his own are really someone else's, except for the fact that he has a four-year life span, is more human than the other so-called humans around him.

A ball will bounce, Richard Wilbur once wrote, but less and less.

How the sadhus, Hindi holy men who live by begging, cooked bread by burying it among shards of smoking human bones.

I want to enjoy my death, Beckett once wrote.
   Presumably with some irony.

In that race which daily hastens us toward death, Camus once wrote, the body maintains its irreparable lead.

But how Tennessee Williams accidentally swallowed the cap of his nasal spray and suffocated alone in his hotel room.

How Sherwood Anderson choked on a toothpick at a party in Panama.

How Maupassant tried killing himself by slicing his own throat, failed, was declared insane, spent the last eighteen months of his life in an asylum, dying from syphilis he contracted in his youth, as did Manet, as did Gauguin, as did Schubert, as did Nietzsche, as did Scott Joplin.

How, after a little more than an hour, I realized I should take my leave of Ron. How I don't believe I ever experienced more difficulty closing a door behind me.

How that door both shut and remained wide open.

How the only real closures come in mimetic fiction and memoir, redemption and faux wisdom hardened into commodity. Like an order of Arby's Cheesecake Poppers.

How a group of children stood knee-deep in the river, oblivious, in the black, oily water that used to be strangers, throwing a red rubber ball through gusts of coppery haze.

Charles Sanders Peirce: If man were immortal he could be perfectly sure of seeing the day when everything in which he had trusted should betray his trust, and, in short, of coming eventually to hopeless misery. He would break down, at last, as every good fortune, as every dynasty, as every civilization does. In place of this we have death.

The graveyards are full of indispensable men, Charles de Gaulle once wrote.

Death is not an event in life, Wittgenstein once wrote: We do not live to experience death.

Yes, I want to say, and no.

My mother waiting primly in her living room in suburban Dallas, also dying, also of cancer, this time breast metastasized to the spine, the liver, the brain, inventorying the clutter that took her nearly seventy-four years to quilt around herself, noting out of the blue, almost casually, to no one in particular: *All these things will forget their stories the moment I'm gone.*

A little less, and then a little less.

The first Witkin photograph on my wall: a plump old woman, the top of her head missing, her skin blotched, her body supported by wires, sitting at a chair next to a table in a sparse room. On the table is a book. Her finger holds her place, although the arm to which the finger is attached isn't itself attached to her torso. *Interrupted Reading,* the photograph is entitled.

36

Anna Karenina throws herself under a train.

His books are questions of survival of personality, Carole Maso once wrote of the narrator's former lover in *Ava*.

Yes, and no.

My cousin entered the hospital for routine hip-replacement surgery to fix his fullback years in college. The operation went off without a hitch—until an infection flowered within him, one of those virulent bacterial strains that chew through a patient's every prospect. One week my cousin was perfectly fine, minus the limp and a certain throbby stiffness. The next he was on a ventilator. The next his wife was e-mailing what amounted to acquaintances like me in an attempt to drum up something that looked like an acceptable audience for the memorial service I had absolutely no intention of attending.

Emma Bovary eats arsenic, Eva Braun cyanide, Alan Turing cyanide, Abbie Hoffman phenobarbital.

There is no boat in Hades, no ferryman Charon,
No caretaker Aiakos, no dog Cerberus.
All we who are dead below
Have become bones and ashes, but nothing else.
  Someone once carved on a Roman tombstone. Two thousand years ago.

The second Witkin photograph: a woman's untorsoed head, eyes closed, atilt on some dark surface (let's call it a table), next to which a stuffed monkey is posed.

Patrik Ouredník recounts how, during the first months Buchenwald was open for business, those in charge gave the inmates postcards that said: *Accommodation is wonderful, we are working here, we receive decent treatment and are well looked after.* The inmates were made to sign them and address them to relatives, some of whom apparently believed what they read. One Greek prisoner mailed his postcard to his father in Pyrgos. Three months later, his father arrived for a visit.

Lance Olsen

At the railroad platform, the son leaping on him and strangling him to death before the Germans could get their hands on the man.

My wife's grandmother refused to be buried, insisting on being entombed in a mausoleum instead because, she said, she didn't want to get dirty.

The distance between the real and the ideal.

Whatever opinion we may be pleased to hold on the subject of death, Proust once wrote, we may be sure that it is meaningless and valueless.

How it would be a perfect misreading of his work to suggest that Witkin's intent is to shock, disgust, exploit his subjects, his viewer's vision.

My uncle had a heart attack on a beach while feeding pigeons. A good Scandinavian, he was too embarrassed to draw attention to himself, reported his wife, who had been sitting beside him at the time, and so he expired, sotto voce, on the spot.

Diane Arbus swallows barbiturates and slashes her wrists, as does Mark Rothko.

The living being is only a species of the dead, Nietzsche once wrote, and a very rare species.

Death is the mother of—
 No, that's not it.

Another dying friend. Another e-mail. Another cancer. Another metastasis to the brain. Sorry not to have updated you sooner, but the fog is settling in so even this will have to be short. Not much news. I wish I could write something light and cheerful, at least something light and pomo-ish, but, fact is, cancer does suck. Or, rather, it's the treatment that sucks: makes me want to do nothing but sleep all day (and night). Not much pain—occasional headaches, joint aches. What's most scary is the felt deterioration of my mental abilities (such as they were)—each day, I get dumber and dumber, and know it. Memory loss, inability to follow conversations, inability to find words. B. finds it inevitably frustrating, seeing me standing in the middle of a room, clearly without a clue what I'm doing there; and never sure if I understand or will remember two minutes later something she asked me to do. Frustrating for me too—feeling like a retard who needs to have notes pinned to his shirt, reminding him what he's supposed to be doing.

Every plot being an education, ultimately, about how everything ends.

Jerzy Kosinski swallows barbiturates and puts a bag over his head, as does Michael Dorris.

While I thought that I was learning how to live, Leonardo da Vinci once wrote, I have been learning how to die.

Witkin's work performing an act of reminding.

This is how to say it.

Every narrative being, ultimately, a study in death.

Freud overdoses on morphine.

How, as one gets older, deaths begin arriving closer and closer, like mortar shells zeroing in on their target.

Death being the one idea you can't deconstruct, David Lodge once wrote.

How I was reading to my mother from Eliot's *Four Quartets* when she died. My wife was holding her hand. We were at her bedside, talking to her, trying to comfort her, even though she was already unconscious, even though she had been for more than a day. After a while, I began reading to her, to us, a little from her favorite book, *The Bhagavad-Gita*, a little from late Eliot. She suddenly flinched and stopped breathing.

She was herself and then she wasn't.

Lance Olsen

One thousand and one things change the meaning of any book on any given reading.

Witkin's goal slant-rhyming with Viktor Shklovsky's: the technique of art being to make objects *unfamiliar*, to make forms difficult, to increase the difficulty and length of perception.

Alice Bradley Sheldon, aka James Tiptree Jr., mercy-kills her terminally ill husband and then shoots herself.

Near death and incoherent, Nietzsche lay in his narrow bed in a small room on the top floor of the archives his sister Lisbeth had had built in Weimar. The people Lisbeth had brought in with the hope of establishing a lucrative cult around her brother were talking about literature. Nietzsche roused, opened his eyes briefly, said, *I too have written some good books,* then faded back into silence.

Gregor Samsa starves himself, as does the Hunger Artist, as does Kurt Gödel.

And I have come to relinquish that most modern of stances: uncertainty, Carole Maso once wrote. I am certain now of what will happen.

How my mother changed tenses before my eyes.

They said the side effects of these last two chemo sessions would be the hardest, my dying friend wrote. The latest development is that I'll suddenly pass out for a few minutes. Yesterday I was teaching and woke up as they were loading me into an ambulance. They checked my vitals, did a quick EKG, I signed a waiver stating that I didn't want to be taken to the hospital, and I went back to teach without incident.

Witkin's goal slant-rhyming with Gaston Bachelard's: Art, then, is an increase of life, a sort of competition of surprises that stimulates our consciousness and keeps it from becoming somnolent.

Edwin Armstrong, inventor of the FM radio, jumps out a window, as does Gilles Deleuze, as does F. O. Matthiessen.

In heaven all the interesting people are missing, Nietzsche once wrote.

Witkin asking his viewers to sympathize with the fragility of the human flesh, the human heart, the act of lessening that which we call ourselves.

Birth was the—

The head. Not *my* head.

Everything else refusal.

Grenz-Situationen.

Everything else fear and repression.

Yes, I want to say, and—

It happened on a Sunday when my mother was escorting my twin brother and me down the steps of the tenement where we lived, Joel-Peter Witkin once told an interviewer, recounting a pivotal moment from his childhood. We were going to church. While walking down the hallway to the entrance of the building, we heard an incredible crash mixed with screaming and cries for help. The accident involved three cars, all with families in them. Somehow, in the confusion, I was no longer holding my mother's hand. At the place where I stood at the curb, I could see something rolling from one of the overturned cars. It stopped at the curb where I stood. It was the head of a little girl. I bent down to touch the face, to speak to it, but before I could touch it someone carried me away.

Remember that we are what we are.

How the angelic four-voice vocal texture of Guillaume Dufay's masses make the day on which you hear them feel thoroughly lived. How your consciousness arranges the entire piece of theater called living into a series of remarkable paintings called recollection.

A *polyptych.*

Lance Olsen

How each morning, as you rise from your bed, the belief hums through your head that you are going to die, going to die, going to die, yes, surely, no doubt about it, but not today—an observation that will remain correct every morning of your life, except one, because—

Because—

To hope is to contradict the future, E. M. Cioran once wrote.

Leavitt's Dream
Jayne Anne Phillips

JUNE 26, 1950
CHUNGCHONG PROVINCE, SOUTH KOREA

HE CAN HEAR THE PAIN, shifting and moving, a big animal somewhere close. He knows he's hurt bad and he holds still, looking hard
into the perfect white. The pain presses at him, pushing, sliding near
and veering away, and he drifts, half conscious, waiting for it to find
him. There are banks of cloud, vast, featureless, soft. He sees a shape
below him, a curve in space, a mountainous line against a sea: the
Taebaek Range, rocky and broken, running like a north-south spine
along the Sea of Japan. They're the same barren, unforgiving mountains that rose above Taejon and overhung the lowlands he crossed
and tracked and hated during the retreat. Now they shine, banked
with clouds and spread out like some dinosaur's blasted ivory
skeleton. Beautiful country, he thinks, so hot and so cold, and knows
he's in a dream. It's winter in the mountains and the clouds are
snow, drifted and deep, horrendously white, yet he feels no cold. He
feels nothing but sees the moon set along the jagged peaks, a pale
bulge round as an orange until it settles farther down, snug against
the foothills. He hears a cry then and the land shifts, settles, and
lengthens. Like a woman, he thinks, like Lola, turning away from
him in sleep. He wants to trace the long smooth line of her body, run
his fingers from ankle to thigh to hip. The rounded globe of her belly,
seemingly within reach, glows like a moon he can touch. His legs are
senseless but he can move his arms, his empty hands. He reaches for
her but she's far away. He sees her below him, gowned as though
for a ceremony, flat on her back in a white room, the hard plane of a
steel table under her and her knees pulled up under sheets. The baby
isn't born and she's bleeding. It's her pain he hears, deepening, closing in. A burnished pewter light wavers as he tries to approach. The
pearled edges of the tableau darken, flickering every time he tries to
move.

He opens his eyes. The movement of light is tracer fire crossing against the stones above him. He's on his back in the grit of the tunnel and he feels a subtle thrum in the ground. He thinks it's the approach of tanks or heavy artillery until he remembers the stream on the other side of the tunnel wall. The tunnel exaggerates sound, displaces echo, vibration. There are indistinct voices, whispers. It's dark and the Korean girl has got them midway in, against the side of the tunnel where the dirt of the road meets the inner wall. Leavitt hears scattered artillery reports. Soldiers dug in just beyond the front and rear of the tunnel are firing sporadically. He lies still; if he doesn't move, the pain locates just beside him, and he can think. He feels the girl behind him; she's taken the boy from her back and put him on the ground between them. Now she pulls Leavitt onto his side, into the curve of the wall, and presses the boy down, behind him. Leavitt feels for the butt of his revolver against his belly, under his shirt. The gun is gone. Blindly, he feels for the revolver near him, on the ground. He has it in his hand, pulled close, when he hears the girl talking to the old woman. She's in front of them, kneeling upright. The girl is telling her to lie down, stay flat on the ground, but the old woman moves close to Leavitt and looks into his face. She's frail, smaller than the girl, her lined face almost simian. Her small eyes are black in their raisined folds. He hears her curse him under her breath, like a whisper or chant, and then she spits on him.

There's a rush of Korean words from the girl as she wipes the spittle from Leavitt's face. Crouched behind him, near the wall with the boy, she touches him with flattened palms, his eyes, the line of his jaw, his cheeks that are stubbled with a week's beard, as though to put him back together, repair the insult. Her hands are warm and dry, slim and weightless as a child's, but her touch is deliberate. Maybe she isn't a child. He remembers the shadow shape of Tompkins and his girl on the paper wall of the brothel in Seoul; the girl suspended in Tompkins's arms was probably no older than this one. It was always that girl. Tompkins let her choose which others they took upstairs with them, a means of supporting her status, winning her favor. The youngest girls called him *hyoung neem,* older brother, and formed an audience of sorts; they exclaimed like little kids as Tompkins held his girl aloft over the bed, turning her balanced on the soles of his feet as she extended her arms and legs, a performer poised in midair. Tompkins and his girl were beautiful then, siblings playing at circus games.

Leavitt hears the words, *halmoni, yogi.* The Korean girl is whispering urgently to the old woman, who sits motionless, inches away, staring at the ground. She ignores the girl and croons a kind of dirge. She might be crazy, or the war has driven her crazy; she might be a shaman, a practitioner of what the country people called Tonghak, the Heavenly Way. Superstition and magic. The elderly rural people still believe in *mudang* priestesses, *changsung* spirit posts, *chapsang* protection. Leavitt hears words, phrases. He's a murderer, she says, an evil demon, he's not alive. She spits into the dirt, then prostrates herself over her own offering as though before a temple deity. She believes he's a murderous spirit wandering among the dead.

The old woman is mistaken, Leavitt thinks ruefully. If he were a spirit he would fly from here, lifted like a mist, and take these children with him. Tompkins is looking for him, if Tompkins is alive. He's still certain he heard or sensed Tompkins's voice on the radio. *This is not enemy:* a phantom transmission. You must listen to me, Leavitt tells the girl in careful Korean. He can see, in the dark, the shapes of bodies lying where they fell, villagers wounded in the strafing who made it to the tunnel and died, or survivors killed by sporadic fire. The Koreans still alive are terrified, silent, huddled near the tunnel walls or lying flat on the ground, unmoving. The nervous American troops seem undirected, pinned down, or shooting at whim; the fire may get worse.

Leavitt wants to tell the girl to get him to the tunnel entrance at first light. He wants to keep his eyes open, focused, but he's shutting down, losing track, his consciousness manufacturing images as though to compensate for his entrapment, his injuries. The images are vivid and acute, a sensory expansion or avoidance. It doesn't feel aimless; it feels like information, direction cut adrift from space or time. He senses Tompkins's restless, impatient energy raging near him, searching. Tompkins considered himself equally menaced by North Korean troops and American command. Command kept your ass in a sling, Tompkins said, while the Communists shot at it. Leavitt knows he can't depend on Tompkins to find them. The panicked platoon may have taken casualties and scattered after the second strafing, left the wounded. Tompkins might be hurt or dying.

His attention blurs, and then sharpens: He sees Tompkins looking at him intently, peering at him as though into an enclosed space, through a window. Then they're together in open air, moving effortlessly through a densely green Korean landscape. It's a sunny day. The sound of the war roars past like a train they forgot to board, but they don't acknowledge it. They're in a country grove where it's shady and quiet. They stop under the trees, near the red wooden posts of a *hongsal-mun*, a royal grave site. Two *haet'ae* statues guard the decorative latticework of the open gates. The *haet'ae*, fierce fire-breathing creatures that resemble lions, are massive, waist-high, settled back on their haunches like big dogs. The features of their faces move and they turn their stone heads as Leavitt and Tompkins approach. Tompkins touches one of the statues and takes a round red object from its mouth; he shows it to Leavitt, a small *kusul* disc with a flame decoration. Leavitt looks past him to see Tompkins's girl and the other girls from Seoul; they're all with him, there beyond the graves, moving across the grass in a gently swirling *salpuri*, a traditional improvised dance still performed in rural hamlets. Tompkins looks at him and smiles; shakes his head as though to comment on Leavitt's illusion. Then the picture changes and they're alone, standing in the dark near a simple *myo* shrine that marks a commoner's grave. Tompkins's dark eyes are somber. His face is leaner, narrow and gaunt, his high cheekbones nearly Asiatic. He gives the *kusul* to Leavitt, closed hand to closed hand, and says it's from the mouth of the dragon: the flaring jewel of Buddhist truth. The *kusul*, compact as a small flat stone, is surprisingly heavy. Tompkins is speaking but Leavitt can't make out the words. There's something more. Something about the gun. He's saying to holster the gun.

Leavitt hears the old woman. He's in the tunnel and the old woman is mumbling in cadence, chanting or praying. The girl has pulled Leavitt onto his side with his back against her, and he can reach the empty holster strapped to his thigh. He moves his hand to the gun in the folds of his clothes and grips it, forces it securely into the holster. His arms are heavy. He knows he's passing out intermittently, but he has to keep track. He considers giving the revolver to the girl, but he reasons she'll know to take it if she needs it. The old woman, her face in the dirt, doesn't move and continues to chant. He feels the girl next to him, by the tunnel wall. He has to convince her. You must do exactly as I say, he tells her in Korean, She doesn't respond. *Ihae hashimnikka?* he asks her. Do you understand? *Ne,* she whispers, yes. Get me to the entrance of the tunnel, he says, taking care to translate correctly. If they see an American soldier alive, they'll send someone. I can tell them: no infiltrators, only villagers. The girl doesn't answer, or he can't hear her. It's hard to speak. Has he spoken? He's not sure. There's more gunfire. He hears the thug of a dropped body near them, and stifled cries. He feels the girl behind him, pulling the boy lower between them. She's a smart girl, a good girl. They need to shield the child and they need to rest, so that she

46

can pull Leavitt to the front of the tunnel. He can feel the curve of the boy against him, warm, nearly weightless. Quiet, breathing.

Gently, the girl puts something, a thickness of folded cloth, under Leavitt's head. The boy's face is against the back of Leavitt's neck. Your shy skin, his mother used to say, touching his neck at the base of his hairline. Leavitt hears her calling him. It's evening, when he was so young he didn't work in the store; he's seven or eight years old and she's calling him in from the street. If they see I'm alive, he tells her in Korean, they'll come for me. That's good, Bobby, she says. She's kneeling in front of him, combing his hair with a wet comb. He sees her young face, the face he saw as a child. This is not enemy, he says. She smoothes his hair and her hands are wet. Drink, she says in Korean. Lie still. He hears his mother talking to the old woman. It's his mother's voice, softly entreating, then it's the girl's. He sees the old woman kneeling near him in the dark. She's taken the gun from his holster and holds it in her palm as though inspecting it. Leavitt wonders calmly if she's going to shoot him. The revolver looks big in her small hand. Take the gun from her, he tells the girl in Korean, give me the gun. Before he can calibrate the old woman's intentions or try to move, she puts the gun to her head and shoots. Leavitt feels warm blood spray his face and the gun's report echoes through the arched space like thunder. The sound rolls him under like concussion, and he knows the troops dug in beyond the tunnel will think the refugees have weapons. Immediately, a volley of fire pours through the tunnel from the rear. An answering volley from troops guarding the entrance ricochets against the walls. The girl screams and pulls him against her, low and tight to the wall, out of the line of fire by inches. He loses consciousness in a roar of enveloping sound.

Questions of Death
[1892]
Eliot Weinberger

1. Is THE CAUSE of death recognized (wounds, disease, etc.), or is it assigned to some act of commission or of omission of the defunct?

2. Do the friends or relations attend upon the sick man until his death, or is it considered unlucky to be present at the supreme moment?

3. What is done with the body immediately after death? Are the limbs straightened or bent up?

4. Is ordinary clothing left upon the body, or is any special dress used?

5. Is the body left in the house or removed to any other locality before burial?

6. Is embalming practiced, and what preservatives are used? Are portions of the body treated in any way?

7. Is there any funeral procession, and who composes it?

8. Are hired mourners known?

9. Are signs of mourning worn, such as shaving the head, wearing clothes of unusual colors, etc.?

10. Is self-mutilation practiced by the mourners?

11. Are speeches (eulogies of the deceased, etc.) made at the grave? Are these pronounced by public orators, or by friends of the defunct?

12. What is the mode of burial: in trees, on platforms, in the earth?

13. Is any coffin used?

14. Are the remains left undisturbed, or are the bones removed when decay is complete?

15. What is buried with the body: any implements, weapons, food, or eating utensils, and why?

16. Are wives, servants, slaves, or favorite animals buried with the body, and what reason is assigned for this practice?

17. Are any images of wood or pottery buried with the body?

18. What is the posture of the body in the grave?

18a. Is it regarded as of importance whether the head is directed to any point of the compass? Are there any ceremonies at the digging of the grave?

19. Is a grave or coffin ever reopened for the interment of a near relation?

20. Is an interment ever made in a canoe, and is the latter provided with all necessary apparatus?

21. Are heads of friends preserved by smoking or otherwise?

22. How are these regarded, as a protection or as mere souvenirs? Will the owners readily part with them?

23. In burials by inhumation, is any mound or prominent memorial raised above the grave?

24. Are fetishes placed on the graves?

25. Are these for the good of the deceased or as a protection against him (to keep his spirit quiet)?

26. Are there any superstitious ideas about graveyards? Will the natives visit them at all times?

27. Are objects of value buried in the grave, and are they considered safe from theft?

Eliot Weinberger

28. What is the difference between the burial of a chief and of a common man or woman? Does it differ only in degree of cost?

29. Are individuals buried in their houses, and are these houses then deserted?

30. Are the persons who have handled a corpse regarded as unclean? For how long? How do they purify themselves?

30a. In what posture is the body carried to the grave?

31. Is cremation practiced as well as inhumation, tree burial, etc., and why?

32. How is the body burned, on a specially prepared pyre or in the house of the deceased?

33. Are there any ceremonies observed, or special instruments used, at the lighting of the funeral fire?

34. Are any living creatures, inanimate objects, incense, etc., burned in it?

35. Is a mound erected over the pyre, or are the bones collected and preserved or buried?

36. If buried, what is the method (form of grave and of the cinerary urn, accompanying objects, attendant ceremonies, etc.)?

37. If the calcined bones are kept aboveground, who keeps them, and how are they regarded? Is the fate of surviving relations bound up in their preservation?

38. Is desiccation of the dead body practiced?

39. Are mummies made? (Describe the process and the nature of preservatives used.)

Between the Forest and the Well: Notes on Death

Kyoko Mori

ON THE SUMMER NIGHT I realized that I too would die, my mother had left the windows open to let out the heat. Waking up to the cooler air streaming into my room, I was astonished by how puny my arm looked in the light from the street. My elbow stuck out from under the covers like a ridiculous chicken bone. My body wasn't sturdy enough to last forever. Someday, my arm—and the rest of me too— would disappear from this world. The curtains stirred in front of the windows—in, out, in, out—as though the room were struggling to catch its breath. I was eight years old. I knew my ancestors had lived and died; that's how I came to be born. Now I understood what this had meant all along: Sooner or later, it would be my turn to die. I pulled the covers over my head and hugged my knees to my chest, but there was no hiding from death. I thought I would never again be able to sleep. But before long, it was morning and my mother was shaking me awake. I had drifted off because I didn't really believe I would die, at least not any time soon.

It's amazing I didn't contemplate my death earlier and more often. All through my childhood in Japan, death was everywhere, openly feared. You did not put four cookies or apple slices on a plate at teatime because that number, pronounced *shi*, was a homonym of death. The hotels in Kobe, my hometown, did not have a fourth floor. My mother cautioned me never to pick up someone else's comb, not for reasons of hygiene but for those of luck. The word for comb, *kushi*, also meant "painful death." If I touched a stranger's *kushi* to my hair, I might die in their stead. At night, we had to be careful not to sleep with our heads pointed north, like corpses laid out for funerals. My mother got upset if my brother and I ever stuck our chopsticks in our rice bowls and left them there: that was how rice was served to our dead ancestors at the Buddhist altar—the living should always pick up their chopsticks and put them neatly on the table.

My mother's mother, Fuku, came from a line of women famous for their longevity. Fuku's grandmother, mother, aunts, and great-aunts had all lived to be over ninety. Fuku often scolded me for being a picky eater. "You won't live long eating like that," she sighed. To her, longevity was an accomplishment—something you earned by living right—and she had the backing of history. On our field trips to the temples, shrines, castles, or museums in Kyoto and Nara, my classmates and I viewed the centuries-old scrolls and tapestries depicting the lives of emperors, shoguns, and religious sages. The decorative frames around the pictures had motifs of pine trees, phoenixes, sea turtles, beetles, and other symbols of longevity. If living long was a wise man's reward and virtue, then dying young wasn't just a misfortune or disappointment. In fearing death, we feared moral failure.

But in the legends from the same feudal past made into TV movies, small bands of brave samurai warriors stormed the huge castles of their powerful enemies. Hopelessly outnumbered, our heroes—some of them only thirteen or fourteen—charged into the paths of arrows and spears with their swords raised high. Everyone died, of course. Or they won the battle but were sentenced to death afterward. Allowed to sit together one final time in their ceremonial white *kimonos*, they committed *seppuku* while their friends and families wept. The beauty of their courage was compared to that of cherry blossoms—a handful of luminous petals shedding together in the sun.

Dying gloriously, with honor, was a group activity. A virtuous death did not come to a man or a woman acting alone. When my mother chose death over her unhappy marriage, she was painfully aware of the longevity of her maternal line. At forty-one, she wasn't even halfway through her expected life span. She imagined fifty more years of crying every night, of burdening my brother and me with her unhappiness, and decided we would get over her death soon enough. My father considered her suicide so shameful that he bribed the police and the newspapers to report the cause of her death as an accidental gas leak. My brother and I were forbidden to talk about her or visit her family. My brother was eight; I was twelve. He obeyed and I didn't.

My only brush with death, so far, occurred when I was ten. My mother and I were swimming at a beach resort on the Japan Sea coast. One minute, we were riding the waves and laughing, and the next minute, I was alone in the water, struggling to stay afloat. The beach looked farther away than the longest distance—fifty meters— I'd ever swum in a pool. A blue swell, like a sand dune made of water, separated me from my mother. All the other swimmers—mothers, children, a few fathers—were clustered in the knee-deep water near the beach. When I tried to stand up to catch my breath, my legs slid sideways, a big wave went over my head, and I crashed into an under-water sandstorm. I came up just in time to get pounded down again. Then my mother was treading water beside me, telling me some-thing I couldn't hear. I propelled myself toward her and clasped my arms around her neck. As another wave crested over us, I held onto her with all my strength.

When we resurfaced, my arms and legs tangled around her neck and waist, my mother was coughing. "You have to let go," she gasped. "Otherwise, we'll both drown."

Until the day she died alone, two years later, she would praise me for loosening my grip before the next wave came and trying to float on my own. The tide was carrying us away from the beach and stir-ring up a fierce undertow. Though my mother was a strong swim-mer, even for her, it was already too late to swim back. Between us and the open sea, there was a spit of land jutting out into the water. If we stopped fighting the waves, my mother saw, we could swim to the rocks on its edge. "Look," she said, treading water and pointing behind us. "That's where we have to go." I didn't have time to worry about how we were turning our backs to the beach and swimming farther into the sea. I reached forward and pushed the water behind me. I was going to have to haul my way out of the killing waves, my legs churning their own undertow. My mother had placed herself between me and the open sea where we would surely die. She was swimming slower so I could keep pace. Before anyone on the shore realized we were in danger, we reached the rocks and climbed out of the water. From there, we were able to walk back to the beach. The year before, a man fishing at night had drowned in the same under-tow, but we didn't know till we were safely back in our hotel.

That was the last summer before my mother started crying every night. My father had been unfaithful to her throughout their mar-riage, but she was sure she had made her peace with his long absences, the late-night phone calls from his girlfriends, the lies he told and those he didn't bother to tell. She had my brother and me, her parents and brothers: All of us, she believed, needed her. Until she turned forty, my mother was a woman who feared death rather

53

than desiring it. Caught in an undertow, she did not assume that only one of us could survive.

I left Japan eight years after her suicide and spent my twenties and thirties in small Midwestern towns, first going to school and then teaching. My adult American life did not cause me to contemplate death very often. Especially in Green Bay, Wisconsin, where I eventually settled with a tenured job at a small liberal arts college, not a whole lot happened to prevent anyone from reaching their maximum life expectancy. Just once, I spun my car in a snowstorm, but the road was—typically—empty. When I hit the guardrail and stopped, the radio was still playing the same song and the car was dented but drivable. Keeping that car, with its rear-wheel drive, was perhaps the only death-defying choice I ever made.

Unlike some of my friends, I wasn't attracted to danger. In our last year of graduate school, when four of my classmates signed up for an afternoon-long skydiving orientation that culminated in jumping out of a tiny plane over a cornfield, I only went to watch. The plane circled the cornfield for nearly thirty minutes to get up to the right altitude. There was no way I could have sat through that flight, much less walked out and jumped. I did not take up rock climbing, white-water kayaking, or downhill skiing. I ran on the sidewalk, cycled on bike trails, and swam in the pool at the Y. True, no sport was completely safe. The first month I lived in Green Bay, a bowler returning from the local lanes was killed when a drunk woman rear-ended his car, causing his custom-made ball to launch itself from the backseat and hit him in the head. After that, I was careful to put anything heavy—for instance, my Smith-Corona typewriter—on the floor underneath my passenger seat, not next to me. My car was a two-seater, so no baggage could possibly clobber me from behind.

The most dangerous contact sport, of course, was marriage. My mother wouldn't have killed herself if she hadn't married my father. When Japanese couples of my parents' generation divorced, the woman lost everything. My father would have sent her home to her parents, married one of his girlfriends, and started a new life. He would have kept all his money, my brother—his son and heir—and even me. We wouldn't have been allowed to write, call, or visit our mother till we were fully grown. Dying was the only way my mother could leave her marriage and not suffer years of shame and disgrace. In the months leading up to her suicide, she had often reminded me of our near-drowning in the Japan Sea. "Remember how you let go?" she asked. "I'm so proud of you for not being afraid, for wanting to live."

To cling to someone was to be a coward or worse, to die. I only married after making sure I didn't need a husband to support me or make me happy. I had a teaching job and a writing career; I kept my own friends, my own name, my own money. If my husband hadn't been an honest and loyal person utterly unlike my father, maybe it wouldn't have taken me thirteen years to wonder why I was married at all. If I was happiest alone, why was I living with another person? I couldn't come up with a good answer. Instead, I started questioning the peace I'd made with having settled in Green Bay, my husband's hometown, where people stared at me and complimented my English and treated me like a foreigner. After our divorce, I moved one thousand miles to a big city on the East Coast. At forty-two, a year older than my mother had ever been, I was trying to be reborn without having to die.

I'm fifty-one this year, so no one would be surprised to hear that all my grandparents and both my parents are dead. My grandmother, Fuku, managed alone in her house till she was ninety-four. Though she died in a nursing home, she was only there for a week as a temporary patient. She'd hoped to recover from her pneumonia in time to attend my cousin Akira's wedding and move back home. Like all the women in her family, she ended up a widow, but my grandfather, Takeo, didn't die young either. He was in his mid-eighties when he had a heart attack, which was what killed my paternal grandfather too, at around the same age. My father and his sister both succumbed to cancer in their sixties, just like their mother before I was old enough to remember her. My father outlived his father by less than two months.

I spent a weekend with Fuku on my first return to Japan as an adult. At our parting, when she suggested we might not meet again, I laughed. "You used to say that when I was a kid," I told her. "My mother, brother, and I would be leaving your house after our summer visit and you would get all teary and predict you might not be around to welcome us the following summer. That used to upset me, until I realized you said the same thing every year. I don't believe you anymore." I don't know how long I thought she would live. She was ninety-two that summer. I didn't plan to be back in Japan again anytime soon. I had stayed away already for thirteen years. Of course she was right: That was our last visit.

My doctor in Green Bay once told me about a new patient of hers who had answered the usual screening questions about family history with, "Don't worry, Doc, people in my family all died from natural causes." When she explained that those were the causes she was particularly interested in, the man looked baffled.

The deaths in my family had seemed unreal or irrelevant to me—I had assumed—because my father, his father, Fuku, and Takeo all died after I'd left the country. I wasn't close to my father or his father anyway. Though I longed for Fuku and Takeo in my teens, their house was a long day's trip away so I only managed to see them twice, in secret, after my mother's death. Once I was in the States and had no intention of going back to Japan, everyone in my family belonged only to the past. It didn't matter whom I loved or didn't, who had died and who was still alive. Long before they died, Fuku and Takeo were as unreachable as my mother, and my father and his father might as well have been strangers. But that isn't why their dying didn't make me contemplate my own mortality. No matter how close you were to someone or how much you identified with them, other people's deaths are nothing like the possibility of your own. Losing someone and ceasing to exist are two separate problems. We experience loss often enough, many of us from an early age; however painful grief is, it's something we already know. Our own death—not the process but the result—is the one thing we can never experience, know, or understand.

I used to claim that I was afraid of dying and not of death. It was the process I dreaded, not the result. I didn't want to suffer pain, look ugly, or feel panicked and helpless. I hoped not to undergo a long, drawn-out illness like cancer because then I would have to think about my death for months, be required to read confusing medical pamphlets, and make "informed decisions," only to delay the inevitable. I wouldn't mind being dead, I insisted, if I could die suddenly, unexpectedly, painlessly, and (perhaps most important) unknowingly from a heart attack or a tree falling on my car. Or in my sleep in very old age.

One of my childhood friends had a grandmother who worshiped a Shinto god with an onomatopoetic name. If this god, Pokuri-san, decided to accept the offerings she'd been making every morning with oranges, flowers, and prayers, then one day, when she was old but still healthy, she would be doing something she enjoyed, like walking across the street to meet a friend at a tea shop, and in the midst of it, she would die instantly from a heart attack. One second, she'd be waving to her friend waiting under the tea shop's pretty awning, and the next second, *Pokuri* (or *Pow!*), she'd fall over dead—no time for panic, dread, or pain.

I still hope that I can die without suffering too, but I wouldn't waste my time praying to the god of easy death. Sometime in my forties, I came to admit the truth: The main problem with death isn't dying but being dead. Much as I'm afraid of the process, the result is unimaginably worse.

My grandmother believed that when we die, we would join the spirits of our ancestors, whom she called *hotoke-sama* (the honorable Buddha spirit) or *gosenzo-sama* (the honorable ancestors); she pictured us sitting on a pure white cloud in Buddhist heaven and watching over our descendants. Other people's grandparents prayed to various popular Shinto gods besides Pokuri-san: the kitchen god, the money god, the matchmaking god, the traffic-safety god, the education-excellence god. All of these gods were once mortal men and women; because they were especially virtuous, a more important god (just who this was, I was never sure) granted them life after death and power to hear people's prayers. Christians believed in eternal life too. At the private school I attended, which had been founded in the 1860s by an American missionary woman, I memorized Bible verses, sang Methodist hymns, and wrote essays about spirituality in two languages and won awards for my performance. In the end, none of this religious exposure or training *took*. I am afraid of death because I believe in nothing.

Or, more accurately, I am afraid of death because I cannot fully believe or disbelieve the conflicting stories. If I could just accept one—we cease to exist and become nothing, we join the ancestors, some people are turned into gods (but probably not us), or we wait for Christ to resurrect some of us and condemn others to hell—then I could make my peace with the inevitable (nothing) or proclaim my faith before it's too late to enter heaven instead of hell. Believing is the safer bet. If faith allowed me to die without fear but death proved to be an eternity of no existence, I wouldn't be around to regret my choice. That would be better than ending up in hell for having failed to believe in the right religion.

But what is the right religion, and how can I pursue any faith when my only motive is the fear of death? It wasn't always this way. As a teenager, I loved the gospel story about Peter walking on the water with Jesus until he became afraid and began to sink, or the one about the disciples meeting the resurrected Christ and recognizing him only when he sat down to break bread with them. I liked Jesus the best when he was feeding the multitude or weeping over his friend Lazarus's death, not when he refused to see his mother, brothers, and sisters who'd come to hear his sermon or when he told Martha, the busy hostess, that her sister had chosen better by sitting at his feet and listening to his stories. For a few years, between fourteen and seventeen, I believed he was real—still alive among us, as my teachers said—because no dead person, I was sure, could inspire such strong admiration and irritation at once.

By the time I went to college, though, I knew that Jesus was real in the same way as Hamlet, Jane Eyre, Jay Gatsby, Holden Caulfield, or the Makioka Sisters. I'm not saying he was fake or insubstantial. I was beginning to understand life through the lens of literature, not the other way around. Jesus and a host of other characters from books enabled me to read the people I met and analyze the complications I made with them. The characters influenced my decisions and shaped my life, but they won't change my death. When I die, I must part with all the people I loved—even those who have spent centuries inside books and attained their eternal life. They will live on, but I won't.

Those of us who don't believe in eternal life can still attain substitute or metaphorical immortality by leaving a legacy. My brother, our cousin Kazumi, and I, however, are the last of our family on my father's side with no children to carry on our name. I don't expect many people to be reading my books after my death, and I haven't worked hard enough for any cause to make a lasting difference. The closest I get to vicarious immortality is through nature. I take some comfort in thinking that even after I cease to exist, the natural world I was once a part of will cycle on with its seasons, with the flowers, grasses, and trees being reborn every spring. But I grew up in the 1960s and 1970s under the threat of worldwide nuclear annihilation, only to enter my middle age with the polar ice caps melting. The possibility of the world renewing itself forever, even if that made any difference to me after I'm dead, isn't one I can take for granted.

When I'm feeling optimistic, though, I do entertain the notion that some part of me might survive my body's demise. This undying essence would no longer be female, Japanese, five feet two inches, or any particular age, but even without a body, I imagine myself as a runner, the one consistent thing I was in life. In kindergarten and the first grade, I loved the ten-meter sprint, the air rushing past me as I hurled myself toward the white finish-line tape that touched my white gym shirt and floated around me. My first long run was in the third grade, when our physical education teacher took the sixty of us from our big combined class to the city cemetery two miles up the hill, lined us up at the gate with our backs to the garden of granite, and told us to run back to the school ground. The exhilaration of that long downhill sprint—seeing the cream-colored roof of the school building and realizing I was in the first pack of kids to be finishing—stayed with me through the thousand-meter runs I did on our high school's track team, the 10k's and half marathons I competed in during my twenties and thirties, and the five-mile run that is still the most important part of my day. If I could outlast my body and become a spirit, I would pump my air legs and air arms to sprint up and down the hill between the cemetery and my grade school and all the other hills I've ever trained on. In death, I want to be air moving through air—nothing through nothing—forever changing and unchanged.

Everything we say about death is actually about life. I like to imagine being dead as an endless run because I've always felt the most alive while running. My grandmother, who valued family above all else, longed to be reunited with her ancestors and descendants through Buddha. To her, death was a huge family gathering with plenty of food. Every morning while alive, she prayed to the family dead at the Buddhist altar by offering them tea, rice, beans, vegetables, and fruits; then she went to the kitchen to cook breakfast for her children and grandchildren. In death as in life, she wanted to be inside that same cycle of comfort and respect.

My ex-husband, Chuck, hated finishing any projects, especially those he enjoyed. In college, he declared a new major every couple of years, always thrilled with his choice until he got close to fulfilling his requirement. He took ten years to complete his BS, and when we divorced, he was enrolled in his third master's program as a no-degree candidate. It's no surprise then that he believed in reincarnation. His ideal death was an opportunity to start over indefinitely.

The hell we fear too is a metaphor for what we abhor in life. Mine would be an eternity stuck inside a small, dark coffin, unable to move, isolated from everything and everyone. The scrolls showing the Buddhist hell, where gaunt, starving souls wandered through a horrific landscape, didn't scare me quite so much even as a child. At least in that version, you were allowed to move around, you had multitudes of other sinners with whom to bemoan your fate, and the mountain of needles and the sea of blood looked spectacular, if not inviting.

Unfortunately for all these fantasies, death begins where pictures and words stop. It's the one thing we'll never be able to describe, even with our most oblique metaphors. No wonder all the heroes in Shakespeare had such long speeches as they were dying. It was their last opportunity to understand in words who they were and what they had loved and desired in life.

My last name, which means "forest" in Japanese, is death in Latin, as in *memento mori*—the medieval monks' practice of meditating on death to understand the need for salvation and enlightenment. In the name's original language too, a forest implied darkness and danger. To a Japanese rice farmer, any land covered with trees was a wilderness, a place far away from home. My ancestors would have shared Robert Frost's view of the snowy woods as lovely, dark, and deep—a place to admire from a safe distance. For my father's family, their very name reminded them of what to avoid or outwit. My mother's maiden name, by contrast, was *Nagai,* which meant "eternal wellspring." The village her ancestors came from was called *Tai,* "rice paddies and a well"—all that a farmer needed for sustenance.

To contemplate death is to balance myself between the two families that made me, to straddle the contradictions of my heritage and upbringing. While my mother rejected her legacy of longevity and died young by choice, my father died, still relatively young, from a disease he never expected to get. He had always assumed that his mother's cancer was caused by her having been in Hiroshima at the time of the atomic bomb, when he himself was safely away at college in Kyoto. People in the Mori family were not the contemplative *memento mori* types anyway. In the middle of the heart attack that would kill him before the day was over, my paternal grandfather asked my aunt to call an ambulance and then went back to his room to put on his best suit; he came out all dressed up and sat down in his formal drawing room to wait, but when the paramedics arrived, ten minutes later, he was back in his room changing into his golf shirt and sporty khaki pants—he'd decided that casual attire was more appropriate for a medical emergency. He wasn't trying to meet his death with dignity. As he did throughout his life, my grandfather was thinking first and foremost about his appearance.

Even the irreligious among us often practice a secular version of *memento mori* to evaluate the choices we've made in life. If we knew we were going to die in ten years, would we still be working the job we have today, living in the same house or city, married to the same person? What if we were going to die in five years, one year, six months, three days, or a few hours? What would we do differently? Surely my grandfather wouldn't have answered this question by saying that he would change his clothes twice. But how do we know that the choice we imagine making under the pressure of death is more true or noble? The one time I was about to die, I only wanted to avoid death and continue to live. I didn't let go of my mother in that undertow in the Japan Sea because it was the right thing to do or because I was brave. All my action proved was that I wanted to live, not how or at what cost. In this, I was more like my father's family than my mother's.

Memento mori didn't help my mother, who imagined death and chose *it* instead of finding a way to live as though she might die any day and therefore had nothing to lose. The latter would have meant leaving her marriage, going to stay with her parents, and holding on to some small hope, at least, that her parents would love and console her while she endured her disgrace or that my brother and I would come to her when we were old enough to leave our father's house. Even if we didn't, she wasn't going to lose us any more in life than she did in death, but my mother wasn't thinking of those chances. She chose the pure certainty of death over the banal compromises of life.

Because I've lived most of my life in the shadow of her suicide, I don't think of death—imagined or real—as the truth serum that would reveal our best, most honest intentions. My decision-making practice is the opposite of *memento mori*. Faced with a big career change, moral dilemma, or romantic prospect, I try to choose as though I would have to live forever with the consequences, not as though I might die tomorrow. Living to see the result of my potential mistake is just as sobering a thought as the possibility of dying with regrets, but as long as I'm alive, I can rescind, modify, or transform even the worst choices I've made. In my reverse *memento mori*, I've learned to cheat death, if only in imagination and metaphor.

Death means having no more thoughts to understand or express in words. How can I imagine not having words when that very imagining must occur in words as long as I am alive?

Memorial Church
Jay Cantor

Characters:

FIRST VOICE
SECOND VOICE
THIRD VOICE

FIRST VOICE. Today we remember the dead—

THIRD VOICE. (*Characteristically mild exasperation.*) Yes, dear, that *was* the general idea.

FIRST VOICE. (*Ignoring* THIRD.) —the people we knew from college— this one with wry wit and bold adventurousness, that one with a difficult and great vulnerability—

SECOND VOICE. —and we think someday this will happen to us, right? Not the dying, that's a cert, but I mean, if we're lucky, that someone will remember us.

FIRST VOICE. So then we must remember them today in vivid details?

THIRD VOICE. (*Sarcastic.*) Like, the way a star is remembered in *People* magazine, right? You know, like Humphrey Bogart or someone, those Camel cigarettes—

SECOND VOICE. I had this friend in Eliot House, who used to smoke unfiltered Camels. He had blue eyes—

THIRD VOICE. Or Currier. Mentholated Salems. And she'd always say as she lit one, that Muddy Waters—

SECOND VOICE. Were they blue? I'm not sure now. My God, I can't even remember the eyes of the first person I slept with!

THIRD VOICE. (*Agreeing.*) I hear you. Memory is tricky. For a while, anyway. Then it just stops altogether, and if you want to say anything you have to make it up.

FIRST VOICE. Oh, my, really, all those brands and colors, I can see now that outside of a special issue, I mean, like a thousand words, we can't come close to describing even one person.

SECOND VOICE. Maybe we should just hit the high spots then. The big achievements?

THIRD VOICE. The star's star turns, you mean?

FIRST VOICE. In ancient Greece if you were lucky—or really unlucky—you could get hung in the stars for those big moments, and anyone looking in the night sky would see you and remember you.

THIRD VOICE. The night sky a continual memorial service. The Greeks looked up, and remembered gods and people, and hoped someone would someday remember them.

SECOND VOICE. So when last week my daughter said, "Look, Mom, that's Orion"—

FIRST VOICE. Maybe, to make this more of an everyman story people could substitute the name of their wife husband lover uncle aunt self here—

SECOND VOICE. No, actually, they can't. My daughter is irreplaceable. We took the dog, though. His name is Hermes. I don't mind if you substitute a different name there. Anyway, it was in a park near our house that used to be a toxic waste dump.

FIRST VOICE. Or it used to be graveyard. A swamp. An amusement park.

SECOND VOICE. OK, it used to be a toxic waste dump, but you can make it something else, and you can change the dog's name, but remember, it was my daughter. Anyway, "See," she said, "there's Orion! He's the great hunter, Mom, the one that Artemis killed by mistake."

FIRST VOICE. Yes, the stars tell a story about the star—so we'll always remember him. Works for me.

THIRD VOICE. Not me. The stars flame out, you know, even Orion, that's something the Greeks didn't know—

FIRST VOICE. What a disenchanted age we live in!

THIRD VOICE. Orion flames out, or the constellation of Arnold, the Valedictorian, or Eloise, the Rhodes Scholar. They become black holes, I think.

SECOND VOICE. That's *cold*—

THIRD VOICE. Cold, yeah, but not chilling. It makes it so much less *why me, why her?* because, hey, it's everybody and everything, even the stars, so I can, in the absence of my self-cherishing, my blinding ego, for one glorious nanosecond, just *see*.

SECOND VOICE. That's just what my daughter said to me. "*See*," she said. "See, Mom? That's Orion's belt." I couldn't, though. My eyes aren't as good as hers. I guess my eyes are like the stars too, they wear out after a while. They're matter too—

FIRST VOICE. Which is to say energy.

THIRD VOICE. Which is to say matter. *Brute* matter. Matter becomes energy becomes matter becomes energy, until it all falls into itself, in these black holes—

SECOND VOICE. Which you keep talking about. What are they exactly when they're at home?

THIRD VOICE. (*Ever so slightly laughing at herself.*) I don't know, I read about them in the *Times* magazine once. I think a black hole's like a trash compactor, and one teaspoon of the garbage you should take out Monday night is now the weight of a thousand dinosaurs, and has so much gravitational pull that any photon that traipses by the compactor is sucked in and seen no more. And somehow, go figure, the compactor is sucked into itself too—

SECOND VOICE. That's not us yet, those black holes or that light, right?

FIRST VOICE. Not *yet*.

THIRD VOICE. No, it's us *now*, in a way. We're just so many atoms and quarks and such.

SECOND VOICE. Can we make this more cheerful? That metaphor we began with, let's all remember what's best about each other, the star turns, to thine own self be true. Nobody ever regretted not spending more time at work, etc.

65

Jay Cantor

THIRD VOICE. (*Off on her own path.*) What do we see in the stars but the billion years before us and before that, and the billion years after us? And the annihilation that awaits us and them, all of us become black holes—

SECOND VOICE. (*Still trying to make it cheerful.*) Hey, couldn't we say we look at the stars now, and someday they will look down on others looking at them, and then those people will be doing what we once did, going to Harvard, and other great stuff, and they'll remember us, the way we—

THIRD VOICE. No, we *can't* say that because then, see, they die too. And the stars die. And the sun dies. And the earth along with it.

FIRST VOICE. It's increasingly less clear to me why we invited you.

SECOND VOICE. (*Still trying. . . .*) So OK. Maybe we could say, in the stars we see a pattern that we are part of—

THIRD VOICE. No, this is the pattern of the end of patterns that I'm talking about, the words falling all over the page, just letters, and then just carbon smudges in the black sky.

SECOND VOICE. (*Desperate to make it cheerful, and so just taking over.*) So today, the dead say *memormee,* and the challenge is to hold in mind the particularity of the dead, the details of their lives, which is almost impossible, and then think of the details of your life being remembered by another mind, like yours today, and then that mind passing, but remembered by some others, perhaps, and the first time we and they looked at the stars, all maybe translated and transformed so it wasn't the night we met, because it was daytime, and the names are wrong, it wasn't Fido the dog, and besides we didn't have burgundy, we couldn't afford it. But still *something of us*—

FIRST VOICE. Who couldn't afford it? The burgundy, I mean.

THIRD VOICE. Oh, he's gone now too. He and his eyes of brown. Or blue.

SECOND VOICE. (*Trying again.*) And yet, there are our lives and this great maw of annihilation, right, and all the details more precious when seen that way, against that background?

THIRD VOICE. (*Very hipped on her own profundity.*) The maw! The maw! That's what matters. Not to thine own self be true, but the annihilation of the difference between Salems and Camels, John Grisham and James Joyce, in the Big Something that waits for everyone—

FIRST VOICE. (*Sarcastic, but a little scared.*) Our dying, if I'm not mistaken?

THIRD VOICE. Our dying, the stars dying, the universe dying. The bell tolls for thee, etc., all right, but so what, because what that really means is it tolls for everyone and everything—even for the stars.

FIRST VOICE. Lucky us, huh, the grand communion of carbon atoms everywhere—

THIRD VOICE. Right! Yes! Brilliant!

FIRST VOICE. I didn't mean to be.

THIRD VOICE. To *be*. That's our communion, yes. Classmates of 1970? Too narrow. Americans? Don't be silly. Human beings? Closer, I bet, but no. *Carbon atoms*. That's it. You get out of it what you put into it. Carbon atoms—the communion of carbon atoms. God granted us being, like the carbon atoms, wordless, mute, rapt, the ground of our sameness—

SECOND VOICE. (*Pointedly just ignoring* THIRD VOICE *now.*) "There's Orion's belt," my daughter said, exasperated. "Can't you see it?" My eyes, on their way to being carbon cinders, black holes in my face or something, don't adjust to light as well as hers. And generally I am exasperating anyway. But then I did see! "Yes," I said, "those stars together, right?" It was my daughter who showed me—

FIRST VOICE. my son—

(*Silence.* FIRST *and* SECOND *stare at* THIRD *imploringly.*)

THIRD VOICE. (*Until she joins in, as if against her will.*) my lover—

FIRST VOICE. a guy, I remember, from Hum. 5. We were out walking one night, sharing a Camel—

SECOND VOICE. A Salem. She used to walk around in her bathrobe all day and sell dope; she became a fine writer and then one night a car hit—

FIRST VOICE. my husband, I mean, before he lost his battle with—

THIRD VOICE. This friend, he ran a bank, before he put a gun to—

SECOND VOICE. this acquaintance from my dorm who, I heard—

FIRST VOICE. This classmate, this guy, this woman, said,

SECOND VOICE. "Good," my daughter said, and it was like it was a relay race, and my eyes were going, so I hand the baton to—

THIRD VOICE. The carbon atoms—

SECOND VOICE. What in God's name are you thinking of with those carbon atoms?! This is my daughter we're talking about! No grand communion of carbon atoms will comfort me for even one moment for her annihilation! She must be always remembered. This is my daughter—

FIRST VOICE. My friend, my lover, my comrade from a hundred demonstrations—

SECOND VOICE. Nothing will satisfy me but that she might live forever! (*Pausing.*) "Yes," I said, "I can see them." "See," she said, "can't you see, there's this one and this one and this one, and this, and—"

FIRST VOICE. (*Voice fading.*) And this one—

SECOND VOICE. (*And fading.*) And this one—

THIRD VOICE. (*To a whisper.*) And this—

Sick

Lucius Seneca

—Translated from Latin by John D'Agata

I AM SICK.

True, I may not be so at this moment, but I am sick nonetheless.
What are you talking about? you ask.

I am talking about this illness that has singled me out for life. That
has been with me since my birth, hangs over my head, strikes suddenly at will.

There's no reason to beat around the bush by calling it "asthma,"
like the Greeks.

I am constantly at my last breath—I am "rehearsing death," as my
doctor says—and sooner or later, without a doubt, this illness is going to permanently achieve what it's been practicing now for years.
I cannot, after all, be expected—can I?—to continue drawing on my
last breath forever.

Sure, there are other ailments in this world. And trust me, I've had
my share. But none of them, in my opinion, is more unpleasant than
this. That's not surprising—is it?—since with any other kind of illness you're only that: You're ill. Yet I am always there at death's
door, knocking.

I imagine that you're thinking now, But surely as you write this
you must be feeling better!

You're wrong. I don't. Because that's like thinking that I should
feel relieved because the latest attack is over, ignoring the fact that
soon enough another attack will come. The accused man doesn't
believe that he's won his case now does he, just because he's gotten
an extension of his trial?

Yet even as I fight for breath, day after day after day, sometimes I
find comfort by reflecting on this state.

"So," I say to Death, "you're having another go at me. Well, go
ahead! Come and get me! I had my own go at you long ago!"

You did? you ask.

I did. Back before I was born. Death, you see, is just a state of un-
being. And we have all experienced that while waiting for life to

start. Death, therefore, will be the same after our lives as it was beforehand. After all, if there's any heartache in the period that's to follow this one, surely there must have been some in the period preceding this. And yet none of us can recall any distress from that time. I ask you, then: Isn't it stupid to believe that a lamp is suffering any more after it's been put out than it was before it was lit?

We are lit and put out. We are born and die. We suffer a little in the intermission, but on either side of life I know there is deep tranquillity. I know that death doesn't follow only; I know it precedes as well. That is why it shouldn't matter to us whether we cease to be— or never even *be*—because the experience of both is simply that we are not existing.

This is how I talk to myself whenever I'm under attack. I do it quietly, of course, in spurts beneath quickened breaths. But then, little by little, the attack loosens its grip on me and my breathing returns to pants, and my thinking becomes more clear.

My latest attack still lingers, of course. I can feel its catch and release in my lungs even now. But let it do as it pleases. Just as long as my heart's still going you can be assured of this: I'm not afraid of my last hour. I'm prepared, but not planning.

It's the man who finds true joy in life, and yet who still doesn't feel remorse at having to leave what he has behind, who should be the most admired.

Yet I wouldn't know, I'm not joyful. Yet it would seem to me very hard for this man to approach death as I do. Leaving a life that one enjoys would feel like an expulsion.

I'm not being expelled, however.

I am merely departing.

A wise man cannot be evicted from a place he is not a part of.

A Solemn Pleasure
Melissa Pritchard

Helen Reilly Brown July 14, 1918–April 6, 2008
Clarence John "Jack" Brown Jr. April 17, 1918–June 13, 2003

CREMATION REQUIREMENTS

"Cremation is performed by placing the deceased in a
combustible casket or container that in turn is placed in a
cremation chamber and subjected to intense heat/flame.
Bone fragments and dust are brushed from the chamber after
cremation; however, it is impossible to remove all of the
cremated remains. Because some dust and residue always
remain in the chamber, there may be an inadvertent or
incidental commingling of residue from previous cremations.
This also may occur as a result of mechanically processing
cremated remains."

"Cremated remains may be buried, entombed, placed in a
niche, scattered over private land with permission of owner
or over public property (may require permit), or remain in
family's possession, usually in an urn (wood, marble, or metal
container)."

"Cremated remains should be collected upon notice of
availability. The crematory authority may dispose of the
remains in a legal manner 120 days after the cremation or
after agreed to pick-up date."

—Consumer Guide to Arizona Funerals Information
Arizona State Board of Funeral Directors and Embalmers

Melissa Pritchard

Funeral Services for Helen Brown

CATEGORY A—SERVICES

Professional Services

Direct Cremation (Nondeclinable)	$1,000.00
Cremation Fee	$ 300.00

Transportation

Transfer of Remains to Funeral Home—Vehicle	$ 350.00
Service/Utility Auto	$ 175.00
CATEGORY A—TOTAL	**$1,825.00**

CATEGORY B—MERCHANDISE

Minimum Cremation Container	$ 95.00
CATEGORY B—TOTAL	**$ 95.00**

CATEGORY C—CASH ADVANCES

Copies of Death Certificate	$ 150.00
Medical Examiner Permit	$ 15.00
CATEGORY C—TOTAL	**$ 165.00**

TOTAL A,B, & C	**$2,085.00**
SERVICES, MERCHANDISE AND CASH ADVANCES	
STATE AND LOCAL TAXES	$ 7.56
BALANCE DUE	**$2,092.56**

REQUIRED DISCLOSURES:

DIRECT CREMATION

A direct cremation (without ceremony) includes transfer of deceased within 50 miles; basic services of Funeral Director and Staff; refrigeration (for the first 24 hours); cleansing, handling, and care of unembalmed remains; dressing; use of facility and staff for private viewing by next of kin (up to ½ an hour); and transportation to crematory, crematory fee (for processing time greater than 48 hours from time of arrangement conference, excluding weekends and holidays). If you want to arrange a direct cremation, you can use an alternative container. Alternative containers encase the body and can be made of materials like fiberboard or composition materials (with or without an outside covering). The containers we provide are cardboard (with no pillow or bedding); basic container (totally combustible) includes pillow, bedding, and with or without fabric covering, hardwoods (either natural or stained finish) with crepe or velvet interior.

This package includes Paradise Memorial Crematory, Inc.'s cremation fee.

The deceased Helen Brown
Will be held at Messinger Indian School Mortuary
7601 East Indian School Road, Scottsdale Arizona
Until final disposition.

Melissa Pritchard
(Print Name of Responsible Party)
Date 4-06-08
Time 16:45

Melissa Pritchard

HAWTHORNDEN CASTLE
LASSWADE, MIDLOTHIAN
SCOTLAND

—*Ut honesto otio quiesceret*

SOON AFTER THE DEATH of my mother, I found myself at an international writers' retreat held in a Scottish castle named Hawthornden, an hour outside of Edinburgh. A short walk from the castle, part
of a 120-acre woodland estate running alongside the North River
Esk, is the cave that sheltered Sir William Wallace, the Scottish hero
made famous by Mel Gibson's portrayal in the film *Braveheart.*
Hawthornden Castle is part ruin, a thirteenth-century medieval castle with a warren of Pictish caves below it, hand carved of rock and
said to have hidden Robert the Bruce, Bonnie Prince Charlie, and perhaps William Wallace. The habitable half of the castle, built by Sir
James Drummond in 1638, was further improved upon by his son,
Sir William Drummond, Cavalier poet and friend of Ben Jonson,
Michael Drayton, and other literary figures of his age. Hawthornden
Castle has been an International Writers' Retreat since 1985, and
writers, selected several times a year for month-long residencies, live
in rooms, working behind doors marked Boswell, Brontë, Herrick,
Jonson, Evelyn, Shakespeare, Yeats.

In filling out my application, months before, I had whimsically
requested the use of a typewriter. Because of the noise such an anti-
quated machine would presumably make, I was separated from the
row of writers' rooms on the third floor, rooms accessed by a staircase as tightly spiraled as a nautilus shell. Instead, I was put into private quarters on the second floor reached by a short climb from the
first. The name on my door was Shakespeare.

I had come to Scotland to write, but I had also come to grieve. Our
culture is skittish of mourning, impatient and awkward with bereavement's uneven process. Friends had been exceptionally kind,
but the overall message I had gotten from society, the environment
at large, was make haste, move on, pay bills, earn your keep.

Shakespeare. My wailing room, done in dark red, dark green, and
ivory, housed a benign monster: an immense, pillared, wood-cano-
pied bed hewn of heavy timber so old and dark it appeared black. On
the headboard, formally painted in golden lettering, was the year
1651, and initials, PH and MH. Set off by hand-carved floral and

geometric patterns were human figures, two male, one at each end of the headboard, and one female, in the center, her arms crossed beneath her naked breasts, fingers encircling each erect, if slightly squared, nipple. The room had a manteled fireplace, a wardrobe, and a plain desk set before a large pair of paned windows overlooking a sea of forest, an unseen river, the North Esk, rushing along below, and above, a Gainsborough sky with shifting, scudding wreaths of silver and white cloud.

For the thirty days I lived in this room, the only sounds I heard (even better when I flung the windows wide so fresh, wind-scrubbed air could pour in) were birdsong—wrens, warblers, magpies, woodpeckers, kestrels, and others—the murmur of the Esk, and trees, an ancient woodland of oak, ash and elm, and hawthorn as well, tossed by an occasional tempest of wind, leaves flashing white and green, a sound like rough surf. Gentler sounds came from the kitchen, directly beneath my room, when the Scottish housekeeper, Mary, prepared hot porridge and coffee in the morning, and later in the day, as the French cook, Alex, slid dishes out of cupboards, chopped vegetables, conducted a muted clatter of pots and pans, her efforts sending the tantalizing savor of what we were to dine on that night drifting up the curved stairway. The spark of guilt I felt, being given such private, spacious quarters because of a typewriter I would end up never using, was quickly extinguished. Given my suppressed mourning, my blanketing sadness, this room, away from the rest, was perfect for sorrow.

The Reformation-era bed, the atmosphere, ascetic, no modernity beyond electric lights and decent plumbing—no e-mail or Internet, no phone, no television or radio, no cars—the quiet, the forest, the light—my books and my pens—my meals prepared (a basket of food left outside my door promptly at noon, a tea tray in the afternoon), laundry done, linens changed weekly—my only assignments to sleep, eat, walk, write (though no one ever inquired as to one's progress), and converse with four fellow writers during dinner and in the upstairs drawing room afterward, where we took up reading Thomas Hardy's *The Mayor of Casterbridge,* eager, each evening, for the self-induced tragedy of Michael Henchard—this cradled way of life, a childhood without chores, I called it, became a place where sorrow unveiled itself. A place thick with tales of Picts and Celts, Romans, Druids, fairies, Knights Templar, Grand Master Freemasons, Gypsies, and the pagan Green Man, with castles and ruins of castles, forests with paths wending along rivers, steep precipices, meadows pearled with sheep and lambs, lanes flanked by wild rose, foxglove, saxifrage, horsetail, bluebells. Ghosts presided too, lively and miasmic, haunting chapels and caves, appearing on forest footpaths and in Hawthornden Castle. Spirits disporting themselves as misty presences, as lights going on or off, doors opening and closing on their own, and once—we all saw it—a lamp flying across the drawing room. In my state of loss, I found such capricious afterlife cheering.

Shakespeare. My first night, I fell into a quarter sleep (the birds, still singing? the light, why so much?) tempered by a soft incredulity at my good fortune. My second and third and fourth nights passed in sporadic weeping, harsh bursts of grieving. Womb of my own dear self, source and friend, my petty quarrel and perpetual conflict, the one I had grown so intimate with in those final, terrible months. She was *gone,* a common word that had assumed grave, terrible, stony weight. *Gone.* Vanished. *Gone.* Invisible. *Gone.* No more. *Gone.* Incorporeal. *Gone.* Departed. *Gone.* Disappeared. Anglo-Saxon, *gan.* As if she had never been. There was nowhere on this earth I could ever again go to find her. She was ash in my home now, powdered and tamped into a hideous shoe-polish brown box, weighing little more than a feather, and slipcovered in a purple velvet pouch, reminiscent of Crown Royal liquor pouches, something a member of the mortuary staff had solicitously handed her to me in. My father's body, cremated by the same mortuary five years before, had not been pouched; his squared remains, as brown as his surname, *Dad-in-a-box,* had been handed to me inside a white shopping bag. Lord & Taylor. As if he were a purchase, which in some sense and by then, he was. I mentioned this to the mortuary staffer, confessing that I had stashed my boxed father behind my six published books, hidden him in my library these past five years. As a result, I was given a velvet pouch for him too. I left the mortuary, my mother tucked (my, what square, hard edges you have!) into the crook of one arm, the royal purple pouch for my father in my summer straw purse. Driving out of the parking lot while calling one of my daughters on the phone, I would have been immediately killed had not my second daughter, in the car with me, shouted for me to stop before we were slammed into by an oncoming, speeding four-wheeler. We laughed— yes, like hyenas!—at the idea of being killed exiting a mortuary, one dead mother in the car.

My parents, bagged in grape velvet, like tacky purple stuffed animals, sit side by side (*Sit?* Repose? Lounge? Tumble-bumble? Decay? What does one say of dust and knobs and shards in a box?) in an otherwise empty chest of drawers in the guest room, guests now, waiting their flight to Honolulu, where, in an outrigger canoe ceremony (as they had requested), my sister and I will sift them like ingredients, blend them into the kelpish, blue-green broth of the Pacific.

I, on the other hand, am loath to let go. Can I not keep some little of their ashes, commingled? (*"We are such stuff as dreams are made of . . ."*) But in what? Where? And why? All at once, the logic of earthly interment is apparent, a specific place to visit, to show up to on holidays and bring flowers, to erect a granite stone or marble pillar or angel. A family gathering spot, a somber picnic ground. But my parents were not religious in any conventional sense, they were affluent gypsies, and in this age of global warming and impending environmental catastrophe, burial in the ground is passé, outdated, wasteful of precious space and vanishing hardwoods (for coffins). Cremation has environmental cachet, ash is green, even if it lends itself to moments of Beckettlike absurdity and comic pathos, like "Jack," my mother's teddy bear. For the five years she flailed miserably on after my father's death, "Jack" kept her company, a teddy bear in a blue-print Hawaiian shirt, a plastic Baggie holding a few thimblefuls of my father's ashes sealed up where the bear's imaginary heart would be. He was with her at the end, snuggled beside her in a hospital bed, his little eyes gleaming loyally, if blindly, his ash heart thumping for her, his Hawaiian shirt faded, and at her demise, at her dissolution, at her burning, her auto-da-fé, Jack was there too, turning to flame in her enfolded, emaciated arms.

Father, Mother, Childe Forlorne

ROSSLYN CHAPEL

One night, in the drawing room at Hawthornden, I heard the story of Hardy, how his heart was cut out of his corpse, kept first in a biscuit tin, then interred at the cemetery he had requested his body be buried in (the rest of Mr. Hardy went to Westminster Abbey, sadly demonstrating the plight of being torn asunder, like a saint or martyr, by one's own fame). In the section of the church known as the Lady Chapel is the earliest known stone-carved "danse macabre," sixteen human figures each dancing with a skeleton. Every inch of this chapel is obsessively carved with Christian symbols as well as gargoyles, Norse dragons, angels playing bagpipes, Lucifer tied and hanging upside down, and over one hundred heads of Green Men, male faces sprouting foliage, a Celtic symbol of fertility. Rosslyn Chapel is a book in stone, written in Celtic, Masonic, Templar, Pythagorean, Gnostic, alchemical, and biblical texts. The Stone of Destiny is rumored to be buried in the chapel, as are the Holy Grail and shards of the Black Rood, or True Cross, carried from the Holy Land by William "the Seemly" Sinclair. Christ's mummified head is said by some to be hidden inside the famous Apprentice Pillar; these tales abound and inspire theories, each one wilder than the next. Stories of the Devil's Chord, of an Astral Doorway, of UFO sightings around Rosslyn, have given the tiny chapel a supernatural charisma attracting thousands of visitors. I am a visitor too, and Rosslyn Chapel, with its danse macabre, is more than a site of religious miracle and mystery. It is my second (silent) wailing room. Its graves, its symbols, speak of resurrection, of the infinite many gone into the dark.

HAWTHORNDEN CASTLE

Where better to grieve than in the same castle where a famous Scottish poet, Drummond of Hawthornden, born December 13, 1585, mourned as well? He grieved the loss of his parents, Sir John Drummond and Susannah Fowler; he mourned poor Miss Cunningham of Barnes, his betrothed, who died on the eve of their wedding. He married, much later in life, a Miss Elizabeth Logan, because she bore a tender resemblance to Miss Cunningham, and of their nine children, six perished, giving him more occasion for grief. Drummond's fine sonnets, still subjects of scholarly research, all carry the strain, the gentle rumination upon death in them, an emphasis we might find morbid today, insulated as we are by the near-promise of a medically induced old age. But Drummond lived in a time when death's gait evenly paced, if not outpaced, life's. What better spot to mourn than in the castle of a poet known for his many epitaphs and sonnets composed for departed friends, a poet who, thinking himself near death at age thirty-five, wrote for his good friend Sir William Alexander a sonnet ending with these lines:

Melissa Pritchard

To grave this short remembrance on my grave:—
Here Damon lies, whose songs did sometimes grace
The murmuring Esk: may roses shade the place!

His famous prose piece, "The Cypress Grove," a mystical meditation on death, was written in a cave inside a forest alive with
roe deer, red fox, pheasant, rabbit, squirrel, and badger, near green
meadows wandered over by horses, sheep, and cattle, in green, rain-
swept air thick with stories of battles with Romans and Norsemen,
of the Crusades, its monks and knights and ladies, of brutal warfare
with the English for freedom, of Druidic wisdom, the teachings of
the Celts still whispering if one stops to listen, in the ancient, black-
limbed oaks, the gorse and Scottish broom, the flowering hawthorn,
wild rose, and foxglove, the springing leap of white-rumped deer, or
hoarse, raucous chorus of ravens, all of which accompany me on each
daily walk, walks as healing as *Shakespeare,* with its bed, its desk,
its silence, its green view, the comforting sounds, beneath my feet,
of food being prepared, nurturance delivered to the minds and souls
of the resident writers, this writer, laboring, sorting her way to san-
ity, solitary, *danse seul,* in *Shakespeare.*

ROSSLYN CHAPEL

A poem of stone . . . powdered with stars.
—Thomas Ross
1914

I have walked fast this morning, the sky the bright, enameled blue I
remember from childhood. I left Hawthornden late, so I must walk
fast, three kilometers through woodland glen and meadow, to be at
the chapel for the Eucharist Communion at 10:30. I arrive barely in
time, hot from an hour's walking, smelling of boiled wool from my
green sweater, my hair turning to sheep's wool.

The service, preceded by organ music, is old-fashioned, sedate, as
though we have all day, and the hymns we sing, found in our faded
hymnals, are by George Herbert, Alfred Lord Tennyson, William
Blake (*For Mercy has a human heart and Pity a human face*). In the
organ loft above us, the morning's psalm is sung in plainchant by an
unseen parishioner. Even in June, the stone chapel is bleakly cold,
and the flames from white candles waver from unseen drafts. It is
easy to float backward centuries and see the chapel broken into,

78

seized as a stable for Cromwell's warhorses when he laid siege to nearby Rosslyn Castle, to smell the sweat, dung, and straw, to hear the rough shouts and curses of soldiers rather than the sweet singing of a dwindled, aging congregation of Scottish Episcopalians.

The grace of history, the dead, are those I feel most kin to now. The living seem removed, through no fault of theirs; they are meant to live and to savor all they can, and there will be that again for me as well, but for now I am more at home with the dead, with those who grieve, or with those who remember, with the reverend, and the lay reader, as I cup my hands to receive the Eucharist, kneeling at the altar, below the statue of Mary, placed there in the age of Victoria. Layers comfort me. We walk upright a while, then are divided, the lute from the player, the flesh returns to the sea or the earth or the air, the spirit becoming, perhaps, Light. A friend said of my mother, weeks before she died, she is scattering into Light. He was exactly right, and that is what we are all doing, though more slowly now than she—scattering into Light, in line to take our greater place, to be those distant stars, or a presence on the stair, unseen but felt, or that splashy, violet bloom of azalea, or that midnight call of owl or nightingale, or that uneven fringe of cerise light on the horizon, or that deer, springing silent into the glen, or that pheasant, startled, flushed from its hedgerow, or the black church cat, "William," winding himself around the legs of the reverend as he gives his Sunday announcements, his "adverts," for the church barbeque that afternoon, or for the archbishop of Brazil soon to visit, for this is the cat's home too, this chapel. We kneel above nine knights in the chapel vault, unopened for centuries. . . . The story goes that when the vault was opened and a small party went down to see, someone touched the first knight, laid out in his armor, a bell, a candle, and a book beside him, and the body, at the touch, inside its metal casing, fell to dust. The others were left undisturbed, the vault was sealed. I kneel this Sunday, June 15, Father's Day, my knees resting over the dust and bones of the St. Clair Knights Templar, five generations, my head bowed by the weight, growing lighter, of my own mortality, aging communicants on either side of me, devout, Scottish worshippers, growing lighter too, as they keep their weekly covenant of flesh and blood, as the notes of "Ave Maria" soar like sweetest birdsong above our heads, the sounds of Katherine Longville, of French Huguenot ancestry, mother of three, her boys home with their father, singing "Ave Maria" just as she had sung it the Sunday before for the wedding of a local couple, young Katherine Longville, who manages to keep up with her singing lessons every fortnight, for her boys, she says, are growing fast, and she too is only here a while. We are all engrailed.

In the woods where Drummond wrote, I write. Along mossy paths in the woodland glen where he walked, I walk. Where hearts were carved out of flesh, thus is my heart carved from my own chest, and carried by me to the chapel at Rosslyn, to be laid down, laid down too in the cemeteries I walk between, a permanent seeding of graves on either side, I, the living creature, sailing between so many dead with all the pride of uprightness, straight-upness, of breath, motion, thought, my gay distinction from poor-them, poor-dead, sorrily prone and purblind. Yet with my grandparents gone, aunts and uncles gone, parents gone, mother most recently, with all gone and but one sister living, my privilege narrows, my distinction dims, my allegiance shifting to those on either side of me, rather than with those walking all around me, strolling on a fair Saturday in June, families, visitors, the young, all of us on our way, pilgrims threading the path between two graveyards, to Rosslyn Chapel.

BETWEEN TWO GRAVES

> *Death is the sad estranger of acquaintance, the eternal divorcer of marriage, the ravisher of the children from their parents, the stealer of parents from the children, the interrer of fame, the sole cause of forgetfulness, by which the living talk of those gone away as of so many shadows, or fabulous Paladins.*

—William Drummond
"A Cypress Grove"
1620

WRITTEN IN STONE

"Lead, kindly light"

"At rest until He come"

"Sadly missed"

80

A THIMBLE OF DUST

In Loving Memory of
Helen, aged 9 and ½
And
Alexander Simmons
Aged 8
Who were tragically drowned in
The South Esk
On 26th August 1932

In memory of Jemima Arnott
Accidentally killed in an
Explosion at Roslin Gunpowder Mills
17th June 1925
Aged 20 years

Guy Justly
The dearly loved child
Of Colonel Oliver and Mary Nicholls
At Rosebank, Rosslyn
26th February, 1850
Aged 7 months
"Of such is the kingdom of heaven"

Certain names catch at one. Christina Grieve. Tibbie Porteous. Fanny Law. Euphemia Todd. Proudfoot. Or an advertisement at the bottom of one monument: Gibb Bro's. Roslin Granite Works, Aberdeen. It isn't fair. We pause, our imaginations held, by the special tragedy of young deaths, or the mixed triumph of old deaths (the oldest in both cemeteries, a woman, aged 102 years), or by the waste of the young in wars, or by parents left to grieve a child, or by the young husband left to grieve his wife, by the young killed in accidents, by disease, drowned. Less dramatic births and deaths, those whose dramas are recessed, we pass by. The sheer numbers of the dead render us frugal, we portion out sympathies.

Here Lye
Anne Watson spouse of
John Sturrock merchant
In Edinburgh, Who died
The 17the of May 1782
Aged forty years
Underneath this stone . . . Doth as . . .
Could . . . which . . .
Alive did vigor . . .
To . . . beauty as could . . .

What is it that draws us to linger over half-ruined inscriptions, puzzle out dates, to the romance of old cemeteries, stones sunk, overtipped, inscriptions blurred to unreadability, moss, scabs of lichen and rotting leaves overtaking the imperturbability of marble, the endurability of granite? One gravestone, fallen to the ground, is so covered over by an inch or more of grass and buttercup, a thick green hide, it could be mown. Near it, an angel of marble, once celestially white, soaring upward, now gray and black, tipping sideways and hidden beneath an overgrowth of hawthorn, a Cadbury biscuit wrapper obscenely prosaic by its base. All this is homily in stone, all this what we are coming to ourselves, those of us who stroll with solemn pleasure among the dead, finding poetry in the biblical or sentimental or stark inscriptions on the stones, yet glad too to end our reverie, close the iron gate and walk the graveled hill back up to the chapel or inn or tea shop, glad to turn our thoughts from a sweet melancholic ramble to our appetites, our calendars, our health, our families and friends, the petrol level in the car, the need for a drink or to take a child, or ourselves, to the bathroom. We need to pee or to kiss and hold hands, or to help Grandmother into the car, for we are, with thrilling vengeance, alive.

This passive place a summer's nimble mansion,
Where bloom and bees
Fulfilled their oriental circuit,
Then ceased like these.

—Emily Dickinson

Last Sunday, walking along the river path to Rosslyn, I came upon an injured magpie. It had tucked itself into some leaves by the side of the path, and as the sun broke over the soft green maple leaves, and with the rush of the river nearby, it seemed a not ungentle place to die. The earth is made of the dust of creatures lived before. We walk carelessly upon the dead, the world a rounded grave.

Mother, Father, Childe Forlorne

All this has laid a softness around my grieving.

In those last hours, my mother's laboring to die seemed like my own fight, as a younger woman, to give birth. The inescapability of it, the solitude, no matter who was there, the sense of magnitude. I wanted to know, to ask if it was like giving birth, this prizing apart of the flesh and the soul, but something stopped me—reserve, fear, lack of temerity, respect for my mother's profound passage. When it was time for the hospice people to help, when I mentioned the seeming labor in this dying business, they said, Oh yes, we think of ourselves as helping to birth people into the afterlife. Like midwives? Yes. Like that.

And I worried. For the eleven months she had lived after the stroke, my mother, paralyzed, smart as a whip and fully conscious, could speak but one word. *Yes.* Even when she meant no. We communicated telepathically, or through touch, or my bad jokes, which made her laugh, or with her eyes and her yes and my prattling on. Was sitting with her, watching documentaries like *Winged Migration, The Wild Parrots of Telegraph Hill,* or *Ten Questions for the Dali Lama* on my laptop, or my taking her out into the care center's garden in her wheelchair, enough? Was spooning bits of whipped cream with chocolate sauce into her mouth—the last thing she ever ate— enough? Was washing her face with a warm, then cool washcloth, combing her sparse hair, putting aloe vera chapstick on her lips, massaging her temples and earlobes, then rubbing lavender lotion on her face and hands, enough? Were these the proper rituals for death's handmaiden? Love made me clumsy, tripping after the one who led the dance.

Hours before her heart stopped, my mother bolted half up from her bed where she had been resting, struggling to breathe from the pneumonia, and grabbed hold of my sister's hand, staring at her with a look of terror my sister later refined, upon reflection, as a look that said, "Is this it then? Is this death?" It was an intense, eyes-wide-open look, and the violent grip on my sister's hand, the strength of this frail, eighty-pound woman, a baby bird nested in white, industrially washed linen, was so painful, so tight, my sister would have had to pry her fingers off if she had needed to. A death grip? I asked. We looked at one another, newly understanding the phrase.

We didn't want her to be afraid, so we asked the hospice nurse to give her a bit of morphine, a drop under her tongue, sublingua. She visibly relaxed, closed her eyes. Dozing, one might say, but for the struggle going on, the battle being lost. My sister tried to read a book she had brought; I tried to grade student essays. Who were we fooling?

When she opened her eyes twenty minutes later, we had music on, something she liked, instrumental, spiritual. I stood over her, smiling, and picked up her left hand, the paralyzed one, all bone now, and swung it gently back, forth, up, back, forth, up, as though we were waltzing. We're dancing, Mamma, I said. She smiled, then gave me a twinkling, openly flirtatious glance I remembered from childhood, the look she wore at parties, the look that had drawn so many young men to court her before I was ever born, and then, surprise upon surprise, my mother winked at me, a girl with all the world before her.

I leapt for the phone when it rang at 3 a.m. I woke my sister, who already knew. I had wanted to be there, to hold her in my arms, to murmur to her like a lover. (*I felt. I wanted. I!*) Her greatest fear, she once told me, was of dying alone. But she hadn't died alone, had she? We had all been there in the days preceding, and a nurse she'd liked, whose name I can't recall, was with her as she "passed" (the current euphemism). The hospice people say it is extremely common for people to "take their journey" (another expression) when everyone has gone home, has left the room. When we are with them, we hold on too hard, we won't let them go.

We drove the ten minutes to the care center, no traffic, the hour before dawn, took the elevator to the third floor, turned right past the dining hall, then left down the hall to her room. Helen Brown, said the sign by her door, a symbol beside it that meant: danger of falling.

(They used to find her on the floor, having rolled somehow out of her bed, so they lowered her bed each night so that it was only an inch or so from the floor, and put gym mats down to cushion her fall.) The overhead fluorescent lights were on (ugh! turn them off!); flowers bloomed on the windowsill, stargazer lilies. The artificial Christmas tree from Walgreen's that I had put up five months before and never taken down because I thought the colored lights and shiny ornaments added some cheer, and because I did not know what else to do with it, was there. The black-and-white photograph of her great-grandmother Zadrow; her grandmother, Fredericka; her mother, Rose Louise; and herself, little Helen Lorraine, five years old, hung above her bed.

She lay on her back in an overwashed gown of faded blue, her mouth gaping open. My sister said, Can't we ask them to close her mouth? We went to the nurses' station, asked, and were told they had tried, but that her jaw, loose now, as happens with death, kept falling open. We pulled the bed sheet up over the mouth that frightened us.

I asked for time alone with her. Corpse? *Mater Magnificat?* Oh, Mamma. I knelt by the bed, fell to my knees before the altar of my mother. I sensed her spirit, free, prized loose, and spoke aloud. I wept. I kissed her cheek, stroked her fine, soft hair. I went back to the nurses' station, asked for scissors, came back, and snipped a lock of her hair, tinted light brown, her weekly hair appointment a last feminine pleasure.

And death shall have no dominion.
Dead men naked they shall be one
With the man in the wind and the west moon;
When their bones are picked clean and the clean bones gone,
They shall have stars at elbow and foot . . .
                                                                —Dylan Thomas

When I was fifteen, my mother, who knew I wrote poetry and burned Chinese incense in my room but did not know how many times I rode my bicycle to the cemetery behind our house and wandered with solemn pleasure among the graves, gave me, for Christmas, a collection of poems by Dylan Thomas. I imagine her choosing this book for me, wanting to please me. She was not a literary person, she did not read poetry, yet she made the gesture within herself to understand my nature. She wrote, rather formally, in red ink, *"A Merry, Merry Christmas to our girl, with love from Mother and Dad."*

A female Anna's hummingbird appeared in my garden the morning after her death. It hovered outside my study window, looking in at me for a long, suspended time. It came back the next day and the next, hovering before that same window as I sat at my desk. And one final time, as I sat in my garden, praying to her to show me a sign that she was free now and approved of how I was handling all the earthly details of life, for I was missing her terribly and falling under my burdens, the hummingbird appeared, this time hovering, hanging in the air, inches from my face. It stayed for a very long time. The next day, I hung a feeder in the tree outside my study window, but it had disappeared. There had been no hummingbirds in my garden before and none since.

According to Tibetan Buddhist teachings, the spirit has enough energy during the first hours and days after death to give signs to the living, but after that, the spirit moves on, signs fade, then are gone. *Gan.* My mother loved birds and fed them all, especially her elusive, iridescent hummingbirds.

The day before she died, I brought her two bouquets of stargazer lilies, pink-striped, perfumed trumpets, the last blooms she would ever see. One month later, a clairvoyant came up to me and said, I see your mother has tiny little birds flying all around her—hummingbirds!—also, she says to thank you for the lilies you gave her, they have always been her favorites.

Mommy.   Mamma.   *Gan.*

Journeying through the world
To and Fro, To and Fro,
Cultivating a Small Field

—From the gravestone of
Joanna Dun, 1634
Lasswade Cemetery
Midlothian, Scotland

The Meaning of Life
Tom Robbins

THE SEARCH FOR MEANING is not a whole lot different than the yearning for certainty, which is to say, an unsuitable pursuit for any who might aspire to nimbleness of mind, amplitude of soul, or freedom of spirit.

Our human purpose, inasmuch as we have a purpose, is to consciously, deliberately evolve toward a wiser, more liberated, and luminous state of being; to return to Eden, make friends with the snake, and set up our computers among the wild apple trees. When there's meaning in this, it's because individuals created that meaning to their own specifications, rather than discovering an intrinsic, universal secret.

Deep down, all of us are probably aware that some kind of mystical evolution—a melding into the godhead, into *love*—is our true task. Yet we suppress the notion with considerable force because to admit it is to acknowledge that most of our political gyrations, religious dogmas, social ambitions, and financial ploys are not merely counterproductive but trivial.

Our mission, then, is to jettison those pointless preoccupations and take on once again the primordial cargo of inexhaustible ecstasy. Or, barring that, to turn out a good thin-crust pizza and a strong glass of beer.

Now, despite the absence of a single pixel of verifiable evidence, the pious maintain that there's an afterlife in which the tap is eternally open, the oven forever hot. However, since their tap would doubtlessly dribble only lemonade, and since those of us who've broken their rules would end up *inside* their oven, it's probably best that we eat, drink, love, and strive for higher consciousness in this one life we can actually count on, leaving the gamble on postmortem fulfillment to those who find earthly existence to be overly carbonated, too fraught with garlic and spice.

Early Dispatches
From the Land of the Dead

From the Archives of the
Shelley Jackson Vocational School
for Ghost Speakers & Hearing-Mouth Children

Shelley Jackson

THIS FILE, BELIEVED AUTHENTIC, was recovered from the archives of the SJVSGSHMC after that unfortunate incident, too well known to require mention here. It appears to document the first successful journeys to the world of the dead. Incomplete and often obscure, it does not pretend to paint a complete picture of that Land, whose Gates are barred to No One. Its merits lie in the immediacy of the impressions it records. The interleaved and waggishly titled "Tips for Travelers" were obviously added later, though their authorship is uncertain.

Indeed, most of the circumstances surrounding these dispatches are uncertain. With all due respect to those[1] who claim to have identified in them no fewer than seventeen distinctive turns of phrase frequently used by the Founder herself, we do not know who is speaking, whether it is one person or several,[2] how their impressions were transmitted and recorded, or whether they ever returned. What we do know is that in the early days of the SJVS, though the Hearing-Mouth Children were ardent in their efforts to open a passage for the voices of the dead, they did not venture down this passage themselves. They remained safely buckled into the present, even as the past rose up in their throats. But as the dead spoke about their realm, the living began to desire to see it for themselves, and to imagine ways the thing might be done.

The most successful of these seems to have employed a speech

---

[1]Blecher and Ward, "Patterns of Usage in the 'Early Dispatches': Jackson as Thanatographer?" *Death Studies*, 1977.

[2]It has often been noted that the careful pedantry that distinguishes the Second Dispatch differs markedly from the hesitance of the Third and yet again from the slovenly panache of the Fourth.

impediment[3] so extreme that the self, tied to it like a diver to a brick, was torn loose from speech-time[4] and carried down through her own mouth to that Land where words are things and language, landscape. Thoughtful readers will perceive that attempts to "phone home" or even keep a travelogue pose unique problems in regions where the scenery changes with every word. In the following dispatches, judge for yourself how well our nameless pioneer learned to navigate a terrain that she was, in the apt wording of the Sixth Dispatch, rolling out from under her own tongue.

FIRST DISPATCH

C-c-c cc ca, caaa—
    aa—
    n't. n't.
    n't.
    ca—n't. ca-n't.
    n't. n't-t-t.
    can n't.
    can n't.
    can not I
    can
    not

SECOND DISPATCH

Not.
    Not it.
    Wait . . . no.
    Not light. Not dark.
    Not sound. Not silence. Not smell nor taste of smoke.

---

[3]I employ the familiar term, but readers should note that for the SJVSGSHMC, "impediment" is a misnomer, since stuttering, stammering, etc., indicate an innate aptitude for ghost speaking.

[4]According to SJVSGSHMC philosophy, time *is* speech-time, "because speech requires the passage of time to reel out its threads from the Uninterrupted, which is silence's massy twin, a block of speech without differentiation or destination, while on the other hand time in its limpid neutrality is calibrated and furthered by the capacity of speech to ceaselessly differ from itself in a forward-looking fashion"—"72 Propositions Concerning Death," SJVS.

Not hot. Not cold. Not far, not near.

Not tasseled. Not pied. Not knit. Not knotted. Not plaited. Not patinated. Not beveled. Not bordered. Not flocked. Not cinched. Not ruched. Not fluted. Not cocked. Not felted. Not toothed. Not notched. Not ribbed. Not brindled. Not fletched. Not flensed. Not marinated. Not perforated. Not butterflied. Not bloodshot. Not beaded. Not laced. Not pursed. Not porticoed. Not hinged. Not glued. Not steel-reinforced. Not dimpled. Not pocked. Not stubbled. Not stratified. Not cileated. Not imbricated. Not gold-plated. Not enunciated. Not planned. Not done. Not undone.

Not high nor low, shallow nor deep—not. Not a thing. Not that is not even not. But that does not become something by not being not. A hole without an edge. Without anything. Without even a hole.

A hole lacking a hole.

A hole with a hole in it as big as itself. Within not, not.

Not not one now. Within not, a difference: not not. Within not not, a difference: not. Within which not not again. Stutter of not and not not forming interference patterns. Not negating not not, not not negating not, not augmenting not, not not augmenting not not. Three states of not: not, not not, and a nameless neitherness.

Name it: I.

I am not not, not not not.

I stutter, therefore I—[5]

THIRD DISPATCH

am tongue on
  I tip
  the my
  tell
  I am
  tell the time
  I
  on the tip of my tongue

---

[5]Signal lost? While the transcriptions do not mark a difference between fragmentary transmissions and those terminated by the sender, the syntax offers clues. Most commentators agree that this passage should have been followed by either "am" or "speak," though Rand, ever the maverick, proposes "ride the ass of paradox to the county fair of nonbeing."

... no time here ... no speech-time ...
... landscape time ... thing-time ...
... the the the ...
... "out order of" ...
... beginning no beginning ... end again again ... ... no next no ...

without speech-time
how can I make my report?

asking how, I do it
—tell time
—make time
—make my report

The report makes the report possible

TIPS FOR TRAVELERS

The dead do not return. Life is not interesting to the dead. Death is not interesting to the dead either. *Interest* is not interesting to the dead; it requires some distance from its object, and the dead have no distance. They are there, there, *there.* No, it is the living who haunt the dead.

There are three known routes to the land of the dead. The most popular permits only one-way traffic. We call that death. Of the two that admit return, one is through the mouth, the other through the pages of a book. Beginners may wish to consult such classics of the literature as *Charnal Days and Ways, The Last Tonsil,* or *By Foot in the Mouthlands,* but seasoned travelers will get just as far in *Let's Learn Tagalog!* or *The World of Professional Golf 1996.* Many texts offer a way; this is one.[6]

---

[6]While the Dispatches are clearly numbered, the "Tips" are not, leaving their order in question. Prudence demands, however, that we preserve the sequence in which they appeared when found, as it may be less arbitrary than it appears.

Shelley Jackson

FOURTH DISPATCH

I did not go gently. I shouldered through my lips and blew myself down my throat, tearing my larynx. I threw some grammar ahead of me as I howled past my vocal cords, and dropped into its invisible catchment.

I landed hard. It took me a while to understand myself as what might have the capacity to move against what included it.

The first thing I noticed was nothing. Normally I wouldn't have spotted it. The second was a sort of pucker. A ruck or run in nothing. Strictly speaking it was also nothing, but with a difference. I couldn't identify it, couldn't even think about it, for the moment. (I speak too freely, there are no moments here. No *about*, either, but let it pass.) What I would previously have regarded with fair certainty as thoughts—speculations, deductions, predictions, opinions, dreams, passing fancies: all that ilk—recommended themselves to my senses instead, especially the haptic. They had scratchy bits, slippery bits, bits clotting in a thin whey, bits like a stirrup or syrup, flocked bits, beveled bits, bits that bent and moved against one another with a distasteful grating, bits that swished, other bits. For the moment, excuse my language, I couldn't begin to think how to think thoughts like these.

Meanwhile those sensations I had once consigned to my body, sometimes calling them "lower," as if I personally cleared my own head by some inches, appealed now to my reason: referring and negating, proposing and refuting, and changing from moment to moment. My ankle turned a trope. My haunch was a hunch. Or would have been, had I a haunch.

In describing these impressions, in describing myself, I am, of course, describing death—nothing but. Yet something distinguished the death behind me from the death in front of me, as also the death on my left hand from the death on my right, even if, even though I cannot explain how I can speak of left hand or right, when I do not remember what it is to have hands. I know I had them once, that's all. "Hands." One of several words that may fraternize with "my," viz. also dog, God, knife, etc., though I also cannot explain "me" or "my" in any detail, saying only that it represented a difference, a very slight difference. You could call it a pucker. I called it myself, and speaking, made the mouth that made the self that said the word that made me.

92

TIPS FOR TRAVELERS

First: Stop time.

Second: Turn yourself through your mouth.

Take the path of most resistance. Feel the *o* in *no* pursing around your skull. Dive through it like a tiger through a hoop, correction, nothing so free and fiery, like a baby birthing backward, up the bone tunnel, into the meat of the problem, concentrating, concentrating, homing in on the zygote, the moment of possibility, from the wrong side. (Yes, wrong, it feels wrong, and is wrong, against the rules of time, of common sense, the rules of rules, even.) You are a word said backward, correction, nothing so airy, you are a lima bean going down the wrong hole.

Just when you think you have the hang of no, the *o* closes, leaving a little scar to mark its place. That's your road, the apostrophe in *can't, won't,* voiceless sign of omission, how can you fit through it, get beyond it, you can't, there's no through, no beyond, did you think there was, did you think death was somewhere else, it's here. It's been here all along.

You find your way by failing to get there.

FIFTH DISPATCH

I said, for it seemed to me that a tree was the first object of philosophy, "There are no trees here," and nonexistent trees stuck their roots deep into not, which cannot be imagined, and which I yet imagined, a treacly reservoir, hot, gluey, and nourishing. No trunks shot up. They were not steel gray, ropy with nonexistence, did not force out small yellow leaves, into no great gray rushing silent wind. If not has bark, these trees had that, if not does not have bark, they did not have bark, either way, this bark that they had or had not was corded, gray, black, purplish, the color of bruises, a low note on a reedy Hohner harmonica, burning film, if such qualities and objects exist or have ever existed.

I said, "There is no water," and no river drank from me and filled.

I said, "There are no objects here of any kind," and nonexistent objects bulked upon the sheer. They did not fist, they did not corner, they did not heap me with the dignity of their weight upon the shattered crust of no earth. They had no known shape, were not waxy or yellowish, taking on no flanks the gunmetal gleam of no sky. They

93

were pagan to the religion of being there, for they were not and yet persisted as such—knuckly, cuddish, aromatic, bunched.

So I said, "Additionally, there is no here here," and nowhere shot out around me in every direction as far as no horizon, where it pressed itself against no sky. The sky was cloudless, in fact it was skyless. I said, "Not a cloud," which was not a cloud, but it clouded my eyes. The sky saw the smear on my pupil, and said, "Cloud," and there was cloud. The sky came later, when I said, "Not pink," which was not pink. A word is not a color, but it flooded me with pink, and the sky saw the pink in me and blushed and, self-conscious, knew itself as sky.

I summarized, "It is not," and it, it, *it* was not, a plug of fibers, little seeds, mud, chaff, spit, what you will. Every word I said was false, brown wavy hairs did not sprout from the pale ground, did not curl into cursive against a slick rock no more there than any other turd, tooth, or other bit of alliterative ticky-tacky. Nothing was plunged to the pommel in no chafed whyever-not; no string dangled out of anywhere; the banjo jangle of a cheap radio wasn't to be heard, seeping odiously up from no next door, here where no door was opening onto no road and yet I, who was not, who was of all my lies the unlikeliest, was on my way.

SIXTH DISPATCH

I found my death legs and got moving. It was strange to feel the road peel out from under my tongue, its meridian oleanders and receding perspectives bothering themselves out of my tonsils. I blew gravel, blew my feet too, tripping along on what was being prospected out of me. There was the distance, *my* distance. Excuse me if I feel a little lump in my throat that turns out to be the moon. Its dark side, of course.

I interrupted myself with a hill or something. I mean, whatever—it was dry, speckled, vaporous, breastish, adhesive. You could call it a hill so I went up it, to see what it rose above. It was a small hill, the valleys loomed over it. Some would call it a hole with ideas above itself. Or it was nothing of the kind, it was a squat bottle with a long neck and a cork stopper, formerly containing vinegar, now white tablets, possibly aspirin. Or it was Turkey, though I've never been to Turkey. Friends, it might have been a spiny anteater, a potlatch ritual, a little wax *muchacha* with spun-sugar hair, and I'm not excluding an outdated psychology textbook. It had qualities of all these things, especially the latter, but all in all I thought it was something between a hill and a hole. In the same way that I am something between an embryo and a stiff. Namely, in a manner of speaking.

I.e., it is if I say it is.

Next minute, though, it wasn't. Things change. That's how it is in the land of the dead. That's how it is in the land of the living too, of course. But more slowly, if I remember correctly. I mean in the land of the living things rarely turn—under your eyes and so quickly you think you must have imagined it—from a vague expectation to an event, to a thing, to an idea, and from that back to an event. Do they? And then from an event sometimes to a thing, then to the idea of a thing, memory of a thing, expectation of an event, memory of an expectation unfulfilled or fulfilled only in part, then again to the event itself, which by now is past, so it's a memory again, one that already contains in itself an expectation of a future that is part past, part passing, and part to come—does it?

And that's nothing compared to the way, around here, what I would call a hill, a hole, or a butte, turns out suddenly to be an inflatable raft with a legless donkey riding on it, and then a child soldier from a small, hot country.

Someone else's death probably would have been a little different. The sky wouldn't have been so ridged and red. The ground wouldn't have lifted her up like a tongue. She wouldn't have been mispronounced, stammering through a landscape that kept reminding her of things she should have mentioned.

For her death would have been the place where all's said and done.

For me it was some kind of beginning.

I mean I am hoping so.

I mean I would like to think that death is where thinking the world and being the world are really no different. Which is why listening to my account is already traveling. I hope you packed lunch.

TIPS FOR TRAVELERS

Death is not an experience people can have; death is the cessation of experience. Nonexistence is not a property people can possess; without existence there are no people to speak of.

But still we speak of them—ourselves, dead. We imagine our unimaginable deaths. From this unreasonable behavior we derive an entire world, as real as that branch of mathematics that is based on imaginary numbers.

Death is not a place, and yet we go there.

SEVENTH DISPATCH

Death was neither here nor there. It was more like a map than most landscapes, the sky more like a description of a sky than most skies. The wind sounded like pages turning and carried a taste of ink. Hash marks sunflowered the sides of hills. Tiny letters marked the road. I told them over as I went, hoping to learn where I was: W H E R E I A M . . .

At the same time the landscape was more physical than most places. Even the farthest objects could be touched—could not *not* be touched. The faraway spire of a church was a sting in the palm of my hand. A tree in the medium distance was all over me, and while the trees I remembered were a stippled fog on a stick, here I felt every leaf. There were 629,533 of them, of which twenty-three were just at that moment letting go, and when those leaves fell I felt the absence of leaves just as keenly. Beside the tree was a blip or slur that melded a scaffold together with a cake, a hedge fund, and an unpronounceable sound emitted from a clarinet with a split reed in 1973 in Berkeley, California. The object they comprised was wedged uncomfortably between my buttocks, prying them apart, and a bit of the hedge fund was tickling my perineum. The sun squirmed into my mouth. It was softly fuzzy and surprisingly warm, with a faint taste of egg yolk.

The red sky was ribbed like a palate. Or it was a palate. In death, to resemble something is to become it. And since to look at something is to resemble it, it is foolish to look too long at anything, unless it is wise. Anyway, each looking is a likening; each likening an adhesion; each adhesion a little loss, a little wound, a place on you that used to be, that yearns to be sky, cloud, dung, donkey, another person's face. I was stuck to the sky by the back of my neck and my left wrist and it was gathering more of me to it. My toes were only just brushing the road, my clothes hiked up under my arms (I had clothes? I was clothes?). Oh, road, road, I said, and I was gravel, tarmac, pothole, rut; I unstuck myself from the sky, ripped one sole off the road and then the other, and went on grieving for the part of me that had been sky, road.

On my cloud-crossed wrist I saw other tiny, shiny scars. This is where I was a wooden frog in a wooden bow tie and wooden waistcoat from an old carousel. This is where I was a damp curl of hair. This is a drab landscape all gray sand and creosote; this, a field guide to clouds; this, an intricately crosshatched drawing of an indeterminate object. Meanwhile, somewhere there is an intricately crosshatched drawing of an indeterminate object, on which one spot freckles and sweats. Somewhere there is a wooden frog that believes it eats Grape-Nuts for breakfast and once found a gold wedding ring in a gutter on Ashby and Adeline. Somewhere an ugly stretch of desert smells like my socks after tennis.

I say somewhere, but I really mean both faraway and right here, like everything here. Like myself. I *am* that frog, drawing, etc.

I set out toward the tiny church. When I reached it, it was just as tiny as it had been when I started: smaller than a hazelnut. By now, the sting in my palm had drawn blood. It turned out that the church was inside an Ecuadoran restaurant I had not noticed, which was itself inside a laundromat, which was inside a store selling chrome-plated wheel covers. I saw the dead there: doing their laundry, eating *caldo de bola*, buying wheel covers for their vintage Pinto Bobcats. It is impossible to explain in words in what manner they were both next to and nested within one another. Each of them seemed to me to be at once its own self, an extrusion of the landscape, and an intimate part of me, so intimate I had never seen it before and knew I should not be able to see it living.

One of me who was pink and unspeakable as a pancreas came up and spoke to me. "Hello," it said. For a moment a figurehead jutted into the space between us: proud woman, green hair. "What are you doing here, who are not dead?"

"Looking around," I said, and it turned out I meant it: *around:* like when something is so familiar that you can see it from all sides no matter where you stand. When it seems to be gripped in a fist of your regard. Or mouth cunt ass. Cherished might be a better word. The whole landscape was inside me, and at the same time it was around me like an urn. Though this containing containment stretched me like clear slime on a woman's fingers I knew it was nothing compared to what I would experience when I got up the strength to die completely and I finally resembled everything.

97

EIGHTH DISPATCH

Faraway things began to hurtle past, though nearby ones barely moved. It was as if I were moving very quickly somewhere near the horizon, looking back at a distant figure in the barren landscape. The road. The plain. The beard.

Beard? Whose beard?

Just a beard.

"It is a beard made up of all beards that have ever bearded," said another, smaller beard.

"Of you too, then?" I said, for I was beginning to get the hang of it, though it tired me. I sat down (and it was the least of my difficulties that I did not know what "sitting" meant) beside a knobbly length of some yellowish substance. Rolls encircled it, interrupted by occasional dimples or divots punched deep and puckered. It had a very definite and even familiar appearance and yet I had no idea what kind of thing it was. It was stout as a log but not as stiff, and about a third of my length. It was slightly torqued. It resembled a root or, better, a grub—something that grows into something else—because it looked somehow unfinished. It had some swellings or stumps on the underside, on which its weight rested. They reminded me of the stubby legs of caterpillars, though they were not so neatly paired. On its top side a swelling distorted the folds, which swirled around it like the rings in a fingerprint. One of the deeper divots was situated here, and the folds collapsed into it as if something were tugging from the inside, and made a cleft in the side of the wen.

I ran my finger over the lip of the cleft.

"Hello," it said.

I shot off my seat.

Later I would be convinced that this had not involved moving, but some entirely different operation; in that place, distance was optional. Perhaps I did not really need legs, although the thing, which ought to know, seemed to think you did. The knobs on its underside were churning and bumping the ground as it came after me. The knobs stretched and budged until they were almost proper legs, though without knees, like a bad drawing of legs.

"I was a dog, I think," said the thing, the knobs on the underside stretching and stiffening. "Or was I a rooster?" It gathered itself back on its hindquarters and bulked out and up. Something like a comb emerged on top. "No, a dog," said the thing, acquiring what looked a bit like a tail, though it came out of the middle of its back. "Ears," it mused. The dog heard the dog in me and licked itself into shape. I wagged my tail, went on.

NINTH DISPATCH

I was passing over a great featureless plain (and when I say feature-less I mean it only in the way that an eye is featureless, when it is your own), when I was startled by a voice.

Now I must explain what sounds are like here, if they are sounds, which I believe they are, though they lack an essential component of all known sounds, namely that they are addressed to the ear. Instead they are physical objects that manifest only for an instant, seeming to travel with great speed through the air, earth, or my own "body." One does not see them come or go. One does not necessarily see them at all. Yet they have directionality, somehow. I sense that they manifest at one side first, then bulk up; by the time the other side forms the first is already gone. All this happens, of course, too fast to perceive in any detail, and perhaps the truth is much different.

I cannot tell you what the voice said. I can describe the sounds I heard, approximately, by comparing them to compounds of more familiar objects, such as "sorrowful purse with eyelashes" and "at-tent rope-cup." But no familiar object (unless one's own hand or foot or perhaps a close family member can be called an object) seems to *dwell* as they did, taking a definite shape in time as well as space, though a very brief time, or to insist on a form of attention I have to call hearing, though the way I understood them was not with my ears but with my kidneys, and if asked to paraphrase them I would have to use my fists.

TIPS FOR TRAVELERS

This is no self-help text. A self-hinder text, maybe. Death has no practical application and serves no purpose high low or middling. The barrel-chested and stoat-eyed should give it a miss and a clout with the briefcase in passing, for good measure. But you with the strained features and skinned eyeballs, haven't you always suspected that you too served no purpose? That in your cockles curls noth-ing warmer than *why not?* That you are in life like a tourist in Taiwan? Confirmed. Death is your permanent position, what kept you gainfully employed for millennia before you pitched squawking into the biological. I say "you," speaking crudely: You were not there, not as such, and later on will once again not be there, as such; this is in fact your vocation, not being there, as such. Yet being there anyway, I will insist on that. In fact never more there than when dead, whether in the long rehearsal, or the hearse. It's alive you're not quite there. Life's a leave of absence, a sabbatical from the universe. Let the other louts make themselves at home; you can't forget you're not from 'round here. You don't quite understand what's going on. You don't quite speak the language. You take some pictures, lose your wallet, get sick, and wish you were home. So go home.

TENTH DISPATCH

Today I came to a wall made of black bricks. They were quite narrow and had a greasy sheen. I knew that they were people; the bricks were dead people, piled up. They were all speaking, speaking quietly to one another. The wall, which ran through me and continued in both directions as far as I could see, was humming to itself. I walked along it until it struck me that I was no longer walking and had not been walking for some while. I was snuggling. Even the needles that had been piercing and sewing me all afternoon (in death it is always afternoon) here merely nudged me. Air was snuggling in my lungs, curling like a cat. My thoughts snuggled in my head. There was a word cozying up to my tongue. It was the word no, and it was sweeter than you could imagine. I thought, I could snuggle forever and get nowhere and not notice, this being death. I panicked, I admit, and started snuggling faster. I snuggled a blue streak, snuggled until panic snuggled into me. Finally it occurred to me to snuggle into far away. Lazily I stretched and coiled, and nudged myself right over the horizon.

Over the horizon is only a manner of speaking.

Like everything here: a manner of speaking.

ELEVENTH DISPATCH

. . . objects half-buried in the sandy turf—so I thought. Then I picked one up: It was too light: It was not a half-buried object but a half object lying on the surface. Half, but not broken or severed. A whole half. Not a broken pair of glasses but a monocle with an earpiece; not a broken china kitten, but half a kitten, intact, its cleavage plane smooth and glazed with the same stylized swirls of fur as the flanks. But what makes me call it half a kitten? It is a whole of something that has no name, and I do it a disservice by reverting to a comparison that is only half apt. Of course, that is what it is like, describing death. "Here half a thing is—" I thought, and that was a whole thought. "Thi—," I thought, and that was another.

I bent and picked up a front half of a kitten, one paw on a blue ball of string. I glanced back at the back half, which I had left tail up, as if it were tunneling into the ground.

"—kind of test?" I said.

I bent over to examine another half cat, tail up, and found I had to wrestle it from the ground. It appeared whole, but by now I knew better: It was a half of something else entirely.

"I," I thought, and knew I did not mean myself, but half of another word not spoken, a whole half, and then I thought, maybe that is what I always meant by I.

TWELFTH DISPATCH

. . . a region of very dense punctuation. Every few feet I had to force myself through what I understood to be a semicolon, a resilient jade green hedge in which myriad tiny birds—they might have been birds—shrieked their joy. Out they hustled after I passed through, rolling after me along the ground. They did not look like birds anymore.

The next stretch was a list. Initially there was a refreshing lack of connection between the parts (a forehead; a clatch of curtain rings in a pit in the sand; a slip of paper indicating that an erratum on page 204 could not be corrected in time for printing, etc.), but before long they began to frighten me; I understood that there was no reason I should ever come to the end of them. A cross-stitch Cupid; a candle stub with the wick pulled out of it; a sylvan breeze; a fotonovela; a syllogism. . . .

Shelley Jackson

THIRTEENTH DISPATCH

. . . dark flakes falling, some large and feathery and sashaying from side to side, others hurtling downward; I think you have seen snow. This snow was warm, however, although it too melted when touched. As it did it said a word. I heard *obedience*. I heard *ballpoint, tooth, countertenor*. I understood that this was a person who had recently died, and was naming the things of her or his (I thought his) life. The snowfall covered a great territory. I walked all day within that patient, thoughtful ending. The human snow blew in flurries around my feet, sometimes hurrying ahead of me. A small drift had nearly covered the—thing—what—sometimes it is hard to—sound of re-corded voice stammering—downward flame. . . .

FOURTEENTH DISPATCH

. . . blue and slotted.
. . . untoward.
. . . mouthy?
. . . pillowlets—dizzy little shrimp, or

FIFTEENTH DISPATCH

. . . a little ahead of myself.[7]

TIPS FOR TRAVELERS

Unlike life, death does not offer the consolation of an ending. Of all the things travelers must learn to get along without, this will be the most difficult to relinquish.

---

[7]This is the final document in the file. Whether it is an arbitrary cutoff point, or whether a setback at this juncture put an end to exploration for a while, is unknown. Certainly the thanatographical efforts of the SJVSGSHMC continued and even inten-sified in subsequent years, as those triumphantly detailed maps produced during the twenties and thirties testify.

Five Poems
David Guterson

PRACTICE OF THE ORDINARY

Another day so quiet it's easy to think of dying
The way I think of dying, as an organizer,
As an advertisement for financial expertise
On a remote lake reserved for people with enviable
Marriages, as matinee cinema, then walking out
Into the day, where it doesn't need to be raining
Or not raining, a sidewalk is sufficient,
The parking lot at Target,
Pie's an obvious inciter,
I'm certainly not the only patron
At Applebee's enjoying pie while
Thinking about dying, maybe for the twelfth or fifteenth
Time in an hour, those narrow fifty-mile-an-hour lanes
Between the mall and the interstate
Full of crazed teenagers also thinking about dying,
But not in the same way I'm thinking about it
Because they're so eroticized, though it should be noted
Here that they're suicidal too, still
Capable of the romantic view, and fierce.

Outside my window, fruit trees are blooming.
I should thin their buds but,
Putting things in order,
There are two fallen trees in the field
That might get mixed up with the long grass
If I don't go now in the name of the brush hog.
Still, what I would really like to do today
Is clean the shop, which I think with patience
Could be done from a wheelchair. The sole purpose
Of a minute's death. What's easy now
Will be hard later. Everything I do could be practice.

David Guterson

COYOTES CALLING

Tonight the frogs are loud enough,
Less rhythmical than crickets,
Calling the raccoon.

I didn't look for the moon this evening,
But my daughter's right about the willow
In the dark. It shouldn't be seen by me alone.

In the greenhouse a swollen bee
Worked the glass today. I watched it
While looking for a handful of string.

It's spring. A mallard hen and drake,
In the rain this morning,
Flew down the center of the road toward the stream.

Soon the garden voles will take the field.
Each year, the same—
They seem fled, then they return.

Today I lifted my shovel carelessly.
My mind went to the spider
In the corner of the cart.

I shoveled in a dream instead of
Shoveling, but now and then a worm woke me up
With the opportunity not to end its life.

And maybe, dying, I'll hear coyotes calling.
Will it be enough then to say that I lived on this earth
And pursued my salvation haphazardly?

David Guterson

TIME

All morning I've threatened
To do something nameless
And, desiring to desire,
Ignored good advice:
To read the sutras like everything depended on it.
I've let languor in,
As if I had time to name names,
Or seconds to dismiss looking forward.
Watching the toaster's an option,
But so is putting it back in the cupboard.
If I'm choosing between myself
And the world, is that a vain consideration?
The prospect of travel next week
Shouldn't overwhelm my morning,
Since I might be dead before New Jersey:
No itinerary for that.
And now I remember—last night I dreamed
Of an earthquake that, with an effort,
I took seriously.
There are mouths to feed, I'm sure of this.
I see my daughter drink tea
While wrapped in a blanket and think,
Keeping to the middle on clear mornings isn't easy.
What else should I do while being human?

David Guterson

PAVERS

At first light
I'm laying pavers
With stinging fingers.
I'm finding my grade.
The petals on the Frederick Minstrel fall—
Spring snow in high country.

This work is overcast with silence.
Hours pass.
Evening—I sit on pavers watching
The bubble in the level
As if air is absolute.
The straight line pleases.

Still, the fact is,
I'm wrong again,
And what else is there?
I will have to go back
To the skewed line and maul it in,
Or pull the pavers out and lay them true.

JUSTIFICATION FOR IDLENESS

Because tomorrow illuminates itself,
This autumn day is disposable.

One thing and then another,
And then one day, not another.

Like a thousand leaves in a storm,
My thoughts rake leaves.

My mind rakes all the leaves it can find
While others fall.

Leaves, please demonstrate how to waste time carefully.
Let me go as you do, down, naked to the wind and rain.

Wages of Love
David Huddle

SOMETHING EVER SO LIGHTLY brushes a tender place in her mind. His eyes finding her and not looking away. She blinks but doesn't stop feasting on the sight of him.

At a party. At the country club. Eve's sixteen.

*

HORACE IS A PRICK! Clara prints out the words slowly. A medium receiving dictation.

Horace has been dead for about three hours.

Clara's lips feel twisted tight across her teeth. *Not myself,* she tells herself. In her whole life, she's never written or said aloud the word *prick.* In her fifty-two years of marriage to him, she never entertained calling Horace any name other than *dear* or *sweetheart* or— as a joke that offended him the one time she said it aloud in the car after a party at which she'd had a third glass of wine—*Horace Porridge.* Now her hand won't stop. Her fingers press the pen across the magazine page. Her tight lips shape the words as they appear before her eyes. PIG FUCKER. DEVIL'S RECTUM.

*

Eve moves toward him. It feels like sleepwalking. She wonders if she'll be able to keep from touching him. When she's close enough to him to do that, he disables her with a smile. It makes her catch her breath. But she sees it's only incidentally for her. Like he's caught sight of himself in a mirror over her shoulder. She's not too gaga to receive a little burst of understanding. Nothing measures up to the sight of himself. Maybe he can't really see anything else. Her face, her body, her new dress and shoes that she's adored until this moment, even her newly shaved and still slightly stinging armpits are merely a mirror for this boy. He looks at her and sees a plain girl panting and thinks, *Oh yeah, I don't blame her, I'd pant for me too.*

107

David Huddle

What she understands doesn't trouble her. And anyway, to walk away now is out of the question. She does what her grandfather has taught her to do with strangers of note. Extends her hand and speaks in a clear voice. "Hello, I'm Eve Collins, I don't think we've met."

*

CLARA IS A WHORE, Clara writes. She feels her eyes widen at the sight of the words. She wants to cry out but the last thing she wants at this moment is for Hannah to come running upstairs to see what's the matter with her. Clara would have to tell her. *I'm a whore. Don't you see what I've written here? All these years I didn't quite know what I was. Now I know.*

The thought of saying such nonsense to her daughter amuses her enough to make her mouth relax into what she thinks might pass for a smile. Maybe this thing that's taken hold of her will pass quickly. It could be just a little step up into proper grieving.

Still. *Whore.* It's something to consider. Never made any money. Seventy-five years old. Had sex with only one man. Even so, maybe *whore* is the name of what I am. What I was all that time.

*

A tongue of flame sweeps across her shoulders and the top of her chest. Because that's where his eyes go when she extends her hand toward him. Down. Away from her face to her chest. "I'm Sylvester," he says. He barely places his fingers into her hand. It's the handshake her grandfather calls the please-don't-hurt-me. Eve can see he doesn't like her making him touch her. He didn't like what he saw of her chest. He doesn't want to be near her.

She laughs at him. Not in a mean way. "Here," she says. "You don't know how to do this." With her left hand, she grasps his wrist to hold it steady, then pushes her right hand forward, firmly grips his right hand, removes her left hand, and gives his right hand three firm shakes. "That's how," she says. Because he's cast his eyes down at their hands, she drills his face with her own eyes. "And look straight at the person you're meeting when you do it," she says.

He still won't look at her. "You're a teacher," he murmurs off to the side. His eyes lift but stop at the level of her mouth. Study her mouth. "So am I," he says. Removes his right hand from Eve's. With

108

the top of his index finger touches the center of her collarbone. Turns and walks toward the punchbowl.

Joan of Arc, she's tied to the stake. Flames blaze up from beneath her feet. Agony and slow death. At the edge of the dance floor in the Burlington Country Club. Fifty adolescent boys and girls moiling around.

His hair is long as a girl's. And he uses conditioner. So it wafts in the slight breeze of his walking away from her.

*

Clara hadn't asked to be left alone with Horace. But they seemed to think she should be. "Take your time," someone whispered. They left the room. Softly closed the door behind them.

Her first impulse was to open it and step right out behind them. *Wait for me*, she could call. But she stood where she was.

Dead, he's anybody, was her next thought. *What difference does it make what I say? Or do?*

Another thought came too. *Most alone I've been in my life.* Horace had been her companion. Before him, her mother and father, her sister. All of them gone now. The ones outside, in the hallway—Hannah and Eve and Bill, they were . . . She couldn't finish that thought, but they weren't, couldn't be, what Horace had been. As if what she thought, he thought too. Or something like that.

Here he was. What was left. Which wasn't really him.

She stepped to the bed. They'd—what could she call it?—cleaned him up. Combed his hair. She looked closely. They must have shaved him with his electric razor just before she arrived. Arranged his head on the pillow, the covers across his chest and shoulders, the sheets fresh to the bed.

Here he was. She snorted. Here he wasn't.

This was the moment when her hands seemed to receive signals that didn't come from her mind.

Her hand raked the covers down to his waist.

She couldn't say what rose in her at that moment. Or she'd say meanness, except that so far as she knew, she'd felt no meanness since grade school. She'd had no reason to feel it. Then or now.

The hair on his chest had gone wispy, gray, and sparse. His ribs were visible beneath the skin. His chest was boxy. His chin—which people didn't hesitate to tell him was strong—now jutted up from his neck as if he were about to speak with some kind of heartfelt conviction. The vague little path of hair that began at his belly button was covered by the sheet she'd disrupted.

She heard herself breathing. She still had her coat on. Ridiculous that she hadn't thought to take it off. She did so.

Whatever it was—meanness, rage, or some mutated version of sadness—stayed steady in her.

She wasn't about to throw herself on top of Horace's body and begin to wail. It occurred to her that that's exactly what they wanted her to do, the ones out there or in the reception area down at the end of the hallway. Hearing the first sounds of her grieving, they would nod their heads and take comfort from her noise.

She ripped the covers all the way down. Even off his feet at the bottom of the bed.

Not a stitch.

*

He's all the way across the room, but Eve thinks he knows her eyes are following him. He gives her a look that is no smile at all, jerks his head so slightly she's certain she's the only one who's seen it. She's certain, too, he's intended it for her. Then he steps through the curtained doors out onto the balcony, where she knows the boys go to smoke.

I'm not going out there, she tells herself.

All the while moving that way.

*

A little puff of gray-brown pubic hair, like an exotic forest plant. Penis atop scrotum, the latter tightened, the former relaxed. *No more duties for you, old fellow.*

Horace is thin, and his body looks stretched here on the sheet, as if someone had held his shoulders and another had pulled on his feet. His belly is concave between his rib cage and the upthrust of his hipbones. His thighs seem to have lost all their hair—they're the shade of white that Clara associates with breasts that haven't seen sunlight. He looks so utterly vulnerable that she can't help imagining awful things being done to him.

You'd like a look at 'im, wouldn't you?—somebody's voice whispering in her mind, she doesn't know whose. It's true, though, she did want to see him. Like this. As, while he had the life in him,

110

she never would have been allowed to see him.

But that's not exactly true. It wasn't a matter of his allowing her to look. Horace would have obliged her if she'd ever asked. He was vain. A dear man, but one who knew exactly how handsome he was and didn't mind anyone looking at him. He'd have said, *Of course you can, my dear.* And lain down naked and stretched out exactly as he is here. Probably closed his eyes so as not to embarrass her.

*

He's about to light a cigarette. It's in his mouth. He flicks the lighter just as she steps out. She suspects it's a little show he's putting on.

She walks to him, plucks the thing from his lips, and tosses it from the balcony.

I wasn't going to light it, he says. Behind him the stars are out, the black sky milky with light, thin clouds, a sliver of moon. It's cold out here.

Eve Collins, he says. Doesn't say so much as murmur. A little sound only she can hear.

You shouldn't be out here with me, he says. Softer if anything.

She won't speak to him. Won't give him that. Or anything more, she swears.

In one step he's close enough that she can smell his breath. He wasn't lying—he doesn't smell like cigarettes. The cold out here stings her face, makes her feel brave for staring straight at him, refusing to look away.

His own eyes are invisible to her, black sockets of a skull. He has his back to the light, and she knows it makes her face visible for him. It doesn't matter, she won't look away.

Then she feels the lightest touch. So soft a brushing she thinks she must be imagining it. Each nipple through her dress and bra. He wouldn't.

She won't look away or step back.

He is. With the backs of his fingers. Brushing.

He leans toward her ear, murmurs something, the syllables more a silent transmission than sound. It takes her a moment to receive and process it.

You're very beautiful.

She hits him hard, where her grandfather told her to strike if she ever had to hit a boy. In the solar plexus. *Because that will paralyze*

111

him, at least for long enough that you can get away, he'd said and she'd remembered.

The boy goes down. Sylvester. Puppet whose strings got snipped.

She steps back inside. Softly closes the door behind her. Hot in here. Feels her blood rocketing through her veins. Walks among the others who take no notice of her.

I'm not beautiful. Her lips move. *Not even close.*

*

Clara taught him. Taught him manners, taste, books, music, painting. Even tennis. On their honeymoon, they played every day. When he hit a ball badly, he threw his racket, cursed. Stomped off the court. She doesn't know where she found the patience to put up with him, overlook his roughness, ignorance, self-absorption, errors in grammar, tone deafness, wrong choices of color and clothes. He was heavy footed, the least elegant tennis player she'd ever seen.

But he listened to her. He learned. He was good at that.

When they were first married, they discovered that neither of them knew how to cook anything more than soup from a can or hamburgers in a frying pan. So they learned together. About matters of preparing food, they rarely argued, because their knowledge was equally thin.

She read aloud to him—Tolstoy, Flaubert, Faulkner, Katherine Mansfield, Jane Austen, T. S. Eliot, Robert Frost, Edwin Arlington Robinson. He was the best listener she'd ever known. He'd ask for the book and read back to her the poem or passage she'd just read.

Music too. He knew the popular stuff, the big bands from years back. Tone deaf though he was, he was nevertheless crazy about Elvis and Little Richard and Bill Haley, the Coasters. *Yakety yak,* one would say to the other when that one was talking too much. The other would say, *Don't talk back,* and that would make them both smile. But she helped him hear what Bach and Vivaldi could tell him. In the third year of their marriage, they spent evening after evening listening to the Beethoven symphonies, then the string quartets. He had an appetite for it. When he heard *Così fan tutte,* it was as if he'd been waiting for years for music such as that. For months, he insisted on nothing but Mozart.

The truth of it, though—the miracle, the secret, the explanation— was desire. Not so much hers for him, which was adequate, at least most of the time, but his for her. He wanted her. She knew that about him almost from the first sight she had of him. It was like a sea breeze, always there, always pleasing to her. Something steady and bracing that had entered her life. At first she thought it would surely diminish, maybe go away altogether. At some point—nine or ten years in—she understood that maybe it wouldn't.

In his sexual attention to her, he was ardent, he was alert, he was (so far as she could tell, which wasn't very far because he was the complete story of her sexual experience) the most attentive lover a woman could ever have. But what would she know about that? It occurred to her that she never considered anyone else. It was in his shocking understanding of her body that he became elegant to her. She didn't know how he could have learned what he knew about her. Even if he'd asked her, she couldn't have told him.

Also, his desire for her was so constant and at the ready that it amused her. Hers never rose to the level of his. They had this little joke that his prick belonged to them both and that it was a "darned dependable piece of equipment."

In that regard, Horace had been her teacher. Or maybe he was just the one who had the aptitude for learning it as they went along.

There were plenty of times when she wanted to, but she took some pride in never having refused him.

But there it was. *Whore.*

Goddamn him!

*

In that year—her junior, his senior—Sylvester takes on a role in their high-school life. He's arrogant and feminine and fearless. He's rail thin, and someone has tailored his clothes to fit him perfectly, his jeans tight as a girl's and shirts fit to the waist but big—almost flow-ing—in the sleeves. Maybe he orders them that way from a catalog. When he walks through the halls, he gives off the sense of a man-nishly dressed female model striding into a slight wind. His Asian-dark hair shifts and ripples and flows as he walks. His face seems to say that he can't be touched, that he has no need for friends, that he has little pity for most of his schoolmates, that he leads a life of far greater importance than anyone in those hallways, that he knows sources of pleasure that are unreachable by ordinary teenagers, that his future is probably unimaginable to anyone who sees him at this very temporary phase of his life.

Eve can't help watching him. But she thinks her view of him isn't the same as everyone else's.

It's ridiculous what she thinks, but it makes sense to her—he's touched her, he's tried to touch her intimately, and she's dropped him to his knees. Therefore there has been this exchange between them in which she's proven herself superior to him. Thus, arrogant and self-contained as he is, she's seen him otherwise. And he knows she's seen him that way.

Every now and then, maybe once a week or every ten days, he passes by her, sometimes at her locker, sometimes coming up on each other face to face, and she'll hear—or feel—his murmured greeting. *Hey, Eve Collins.* She can never be certain he's actually said it. His lips don't seem to move. His eyes don't fall on her. She starts thinking of it as his no-look hello.

Older boys, jocks, punks of one kind or another call him names— faggot, girl-boy, Miss Pissy, and of course worse than that, much worse. The names seem not to affect him. Once or twice he gives the name caller a pitying look. He has a way of walking around and away from name callers that makes them look powerless and idiotic.

But they laugh about his name. Sylvester.

In the hallway traffic, Robert Alley, the very big boy who's their school's all-state defensive tackle, likes to bump him with his shoulder or give him a hockey hip, then point at him and say, "Get out of my way, Sylvia!"

She doesn't see it when it happens, but the account comes to her, of Robert Alley's aiming to bump Sylvester but missing because Sylvester sidesteps him—*like a ninja!* is the phrase every teller of this account uses for Sylvester's footwork—and Robert lurches against an open locker door, gashing a nostril half off his face.

She, and everyone else, expects quick and harsh retribution to come to Sylvester. They keep waiting. Finally one morning Sylvester arrives at school with a heavy bruise around his eye. Two or three boys and even one of the senior girls ask him what happened. To the boys he merely shakes his head. To the girl, he says, "What makes you think anything happened?" and walks around and away from her.

This is his talent. Walking away.

And photography. There's a class in it, where evidently Sylvester is the star pupil. His pictures are put up in the teachers' lounge, the principal's office, even downtown in the lobby of the Merchants Bank. Black-and-white portraits. A boy with his head down in a pout.

A girl running to catch a bus with her skirt flapping at her knees. A girl and a boy walking down an empty hallway, very close together, shoulders touching.

Only occasionally does she ever see Sylvester with a camera. She tries to decide if she wants him to take a picture of her. Some days she does want it. Others not.

A picture of Robert Alley standing by his car in the parking lot, sharing a joint with two of his friends, results in the three of them being suspended from school and Robert getting kicked off the football team for the last two games of the season.

A myth arises out of the school gossip—there's been a confrontation downtown between Sylvester and Robert Alley and his friends. The myth is that Sylvester stands his ground and says, "I have some other pictures, Robert. Some pictures that explain how you get your spending money."

They stop calling him names. They leave him alone. He makes no effort to be friends with anyone. Boy or girl. To maybe half a dozen of the members of his photography class, he nods. And that's it. He's the most alone person Eve has ever observed.

Which makes his occasionally passing near her and saying—or transmitting—*Hey, Eve Collins,* the moments of her nearly unbearable sophomore year of high school that she treasures like Aztec coins.

*

Clara was horrified at her grieving self. She could barely stand the company of anyone. Thus she became a master evader of social occasions, or a shortener of those occasions she couldn't evade. Solitude was what she wanted. She wanted to be alone all the time.

She assigned herself to go through Horace's papers. A good excuse for evading or minimizing visits. "I'm sorting through his files. I hope you don't mind, I'm right in the middle of something."

People intruded in spite of her tactics. They thought she needed company. Thought she needed to talk about him. About the old days with him. *Would you like to hear about the first time I ever saw his penis?* she thought of asking. *Would you like to know what we found out that we both liked? Would you like to know our nicknames for our sexual parts?*

So she was almost always in a state of guilt. *Whore* and *slut,* she called herself—and sometimes printed out on scrap paper, a compulsion that seemed utterly crazy to her when she gave into it. It was as if she were a prosecutor trying to pin a crime on an innocent person—herself. Nothing of her life would testify to her having been promiscuous or a sexual manipulator or even a flirt. But something in her wanted to insist that these names fit her. She went on with it. The name calling. Which must have been a form of inquiry. She couldn't see an end to it. But of course that's what she longed for. Not company.

She'd have been willing to be locked up if she could have stopped feeling what she felt.

She could tell no one what was wrong.

No one could have guessed.

*

In the spring of that year Sylvester starts to sit where Eve sits in the cafeteria. Catty-corner from her. Empty chairs usually around them both. Doesn't speak to or look at her. It's not that they have a table to themselves but that they both take places at a table understood to be for outcasts, losers, geeks, etc. There's little conversation. Kids who sit here are ashamed of sitting here.

Except Sylvester, who, though he says nothing, somehow conveys the idea that he sits here to get away from the trash and riffraff of the rest of the lunchroom crowd, the popular kids, the jocks, the kiss-ass honor students. It's not so much a smirk he wears as that serene, can't-touch-me, ironic-in-a-way-you-couldn't-possibly-understand, tight-lipped smile.

She makes herself look away from him. Mostly she's successful.

This one time, though, when she does look, he catches her eye.

Doesn't wink. The universe would dissolve into a river of monkey snot if that boy ever winked at anybody.

OK, so she can't break the stare between them as quickly as she should have.

Next day at lunch he takes the seat directly across from her. Still has nothing to say. And manages not to look at her. So far as she can tell, though, he might be doing it when she's successful in her will not to look at him. Good thing nobody's making movies here because these scenes would be funny in a way that would not amuse either of them. Girl and boy determined not to look at each other.

That's where he sits from then on.

One day when he's set his tray down and he's settled into his chair, he looks directly at her and says, "Hey, Eve." Like an ordinary boy.

"Hey," she squeaks. Little dormouse. Little blind mole. Little bat baby.

She shakes it off. "Hello, Sylvester," she says in the firm voice her grandfather made her practice with him when she was ten years old. He'd be proud of her for remembering how to speak up in a social situation. Though of course he'd be horrified at the boy on whom she's wasted the valuable training he gave her.

*

It wasn't the end—Clara knew that much—but there was a kind of release that came to her in April, when she could go outdoors. The awful words and thoughts didn't come to her when she was bending to pull up the ravenous weeds that had invaded her perennial bed. *It'll get better when I can get down on my knees,* she thought. It was too cold and wet for her to do that now, though ten or fifteen years ago she would have been right down there on the soggy ground. *An old lady has to have a decent day before she gets down in the dirt,* she told herself. A grieving widow.

When she came indoors—couldn't stop herself!—she went straight to the phone pad and printed out CUNT SNIFFER.

She stood there shaking, wondering if she should call Hannah to come get her and take her to the hospital. Commit her.

Stood a long while. Took a deep breath. Let her hand with the pen in it go back to the paper.

BEGONIA, she wrote.

*

Why the kids let them alone she can't understand. Why Hannah and Bill allow it to happen she understands but thinks they should know better. The first boy who's shown an interest in her? Of course they're not going to interfere, no matter how freakish he might seem to them. It's the kids who ought to be mocking them, telling her mean gossip about him or giving him accounts of all the humiliating episodes of her grade-school life that most of them know perfectly well.

Everybody stays out of their way. Lets it evolve. Sure, they're interested; Eve can feel the ten thousand eyes on her as she's never felt them in the past. Boys to whom she's been invisible at least

117

now seem to grant her a physical presence. Girls who've treated her with contempt now give her a level stare as if they're trying to fathom some secret she might have, something they haven't previously recognized.

But all it is between them is a little talking. There's no touching. If anything, she can feel him avoiding any contact between his skin and hers. Which—given how he touched her out on that balcony two years ago—seems all the weirder.

Eve knows it isn't a real courtship. Or whatever you call it when a couple becomes a couple. They're a couple, and Eve has a term she's invented for how it makes her feel. She's "tragically excited" all the time. She just wishes she had someone she could say those words to who wouldn't laugh in her face. Or she wishes Sylvester would reach for her hand. If he'd just touch her, she wouldn't mind it so much that she can't discuss him with anyone.

*

A long time ago she'd gradually taken the gardening away from Horace. He'd had no gift for it, but when they first moved into the house on Prospect Street, she'd had her hands full with Hannah as a preschooler, and so Horace had dutifully tended to the flower beds. *Tended* wasn't the right word, because she's pretty certain he did more harm than good. *Presided over,* maybe. He pulled up trillium that she knew the previous owners of the house must have treasured. When he wondered aloud why the bulbs he'd ordered hadn't come up, she'd asked him whether he'd planted them with the pointed end turned up or down. And watched his face turn red. Even so, crocuses appeared their first spring. A few grape hyacinths. Old bulbs planted by the previous owner. Later on, the rose bush by the chimney bloomed as if to show them what might be possible if anyone in the house could show some aptitude for horticulture.

"You've got a black thumb," she told him on the day he ran the lawn mower over the little hydrangea bush for which she'd had such high hopes. She'd said it in mild anger, but when she saw him smile, she realized it was funny. From then on, his black thumb was their joke.

The fall Hannah started first grade, Clara ordered the bulbs and put them in. A hundred and twelve of them. Tulips and daffodils. That first year, she let him dig the holes, but from then on, she even did that work, which was the least pleasant labor she'd ever carried out.

"It's a fair price to pay for what they bring us when they come up," she told him.

Horace hadn't ever argued with her. On the second day of May, while she was out in the side yard counting tulip buds, it occurred to her that once or twice he'd fallen into some silent pouting—kept quiet and kept out of her way. But he just didn't have it in him to argue with her. Even when she herself knew she was being unreasonable. The morning sun was warming her shoulders, and she was standing in a trance, realizing something completely obvious about her husband that she should have known all that time.

If she had him back, she'd force him to argue with her. The nerve of him!

Yes, she was crying, and she had to go inside to blow her nose and get her face cleaned up. But he'd had no business treating her that way. Wasn't it a sign of respect if you argued with somebody?

It'd been three weeks since she'd written one of those words.

*

It's Ansel Adams, Edward Weston, and Alfred Stieglitz he wants to tell her about. Brings art books to school and shows her pictures. Sometimes postcards. At lunchtime, they find a place out on the school grounds where the other kids can't see what he's showing her. Photographs of Georgia O'Keeffe nude when she must have been in her twenties. Of Georgia O'Keeffe's hands. Of Georgia O'Keeffe the old lady with the good witch's smile on her face. Adams's pictures of mountains, trees, snow. Weston's picture of a nude floating faceup in a swimming pool. Weston's picture of a nude in an upstairs window, the woman looking down on the photographer with an expression of peculiar seriousness.

"That's how you look!" Eve tells him. "When you're walking through the hallways. Just like that. Like *Who are all these midgets out here getting in my way?*"

He has this way of laughing that's soundless. You have to see his face to know that's what he's doing. "I read this thing Henry Miller wrote," he says. "'I piss on it all from considerable height.' You see me with that look on my face? That's what I'm saying. Words to get me through the valley of the shadow."

She thinks she's been accidentally trained by her father and grandfather to understand the way Sylvester talks to her. Bill seems to talk mostly to himself, and Horace talks like he's practicing a speech.

119

Sylvester doesn't talk a lot, but when he does, he speaks directly and only to her. What he has to say has *drama* to it, like he's confiding in her something he hasn't told anybody else.

The pictures of Georgia O'Keeffe—hands, breasts, stomach, old lady face—make her feel strange and secret.

Sylvester keeps quiet when they look at the nude pictures. But she thinks he steals little glances at her face.

*

She liked working through late afternoon into twilight. *Dusk* was a word that came to her when she was out there kneeling and leaning back on her heels to rest her back after a long time weeding. The air turned cool, but she was hot from the work. All around her was the smell of plants, roots, raw earth. *Dusk,* she thought. *Dusk.*

PANSIES, BEGONIAS, IMPATIENS. She was back to keeping her gardening diary. She thought it was as close as she ever came to writing in a real diary. It amused her now to see that this was where she'd taken up printing. Years ago, when she took over the flower gardens from Horace. A way to write out words so crudely no one could mistake them for anything else. DUSK, she printed. OLD WOMAN SWEAT, she set down. STINK, she wrote. And tried to sketch herself on her knees drawing her wrist across her forehead. Amused at how no one looking at her picture would have the slightest idea what it represented. No talent for making pictures. GOOD STINK, she set down, the letters almost as perfect as a typewriter's. She sketched two silly flowers beside the knees of the figure of her unrecognizable self.

*

Toulouse-Lautrec isn't anyone Eve knows about, but now Sylvester's absorbed in reading about him. Little French dwarf who painted posters for dance halls. Sylvester has a single page ripped from a book. He shows it to her, a picture called *The Kiss.* It makes her skip a breath. The two of them stare at it. They say nothing. "Where did you get this?" she finally asks. He shakes his head. After a moment, he picks it up off the grass where he's set it for her to see, puts it back in its envelope, back in his notebook.

She's pretty sure she's blushing. "It's sex with him, isn't it?" She says it the way Bill would—a question not really asked, just something wondered aloud.

"They're pretty sure he couldn't do it himself," Sylvester says—and this too sort of randomly uttered, as if it's OK if she hears him but it's also OK if she doesn't. "Something wrong with him."

Eve isn't about to ask for details.

Sylvester leans back on his elbows. They have only a couple more minutes before they have to go in for their fourth-period classes. "But the guy spent a lot of time in brothels," he says.

All afternoon she can't get that word out of her mind. Silently she sounds it. It makes her lips open, then requires her tongue to touch the roof of her mouth just behind her teeth. She looks it up. *Brothel. Wretch, scoundrel, scapegrace, good-for-nothing. An abandoned woman.*

*

Once and once only, she and Horace went outdoors. Their second anniversary. They'd gone to Café Shelburne for dinner, then come home. She knew he was in a state, and that excited her. They'd finished their bottle of wine. In the car, in the driveway, he held her and whispered what he wanted them to do. They went into the house without turning on the lights. Took off their clothes in the living room, streetlights shining through the windows. Anyone stopping to look might have made them out in the shadows. He was fast getting out of his clothes. She didn't look directly at him, but she was pretty sure he gazed at her the whole time she was taking off her slip, underwear, and stockings.

Then they went out into the backyard. No blanket. No shoes. Nothing but themselves. She believed him when he said they were hidden from sight—a fence, a hedge, the garage, their house, trees overhead. But there was moonlight sifting down through the leaves, plenty of it. They stood half sideways and kissed such a long time, touched each other with their hands. She didn't want to lie down on the cold grass. He quickly got down there, then turned on his back—a blue-white slab against black nothingness—and raised his arms to her. So she lay on top of him, while they kissed some more. Then she knelt over him, raised her hips, and let him go up into her. She wasn't quite ready for him, but ready enough. Over him that way, moonlight turning them into a pewter man and woman, she could see his face clearly enough to understand he had focused on the sight of her, the feeling of her. The planet stretched out around them, the star-speckled sky and the moon soared overhead, galaxies zoomed out away even farther, and a billion people moved through their lives on islands and continents far away. He was blind, deaf, mindless to it all. Intent on her alone and only her.

She didn't come or even bother to pretend that she had. It was too cold, and the ground hurt her knees, and she couldn't make herself concentrate the way he did without even trying. It didn't matter; this was for him anyway. When he started to shout the way she knew he would, she put her hand over his mouth.

But all these years later, she hadn't forgotten what it felt like to look down on him that way, to know that in that moment she'd made him forget the world and everything in it. No future, no past, nothing. Only her. The feeling wasn't what she understood sex to be, but maybe it was something she liked better. A step beyond sex. Or off to the side.

It was just that once. She wouldn't go outside with him again. She didn't know exactly why. Maybe that feeling seemed wrong to her— realizing she was his entire consciousness. Taking her pleasure from that. It was wrong. And indoors it wasn't possible.

*

He's teaching her about the camera. Eve can tell it makes him anxious. Like she can't even hold it right. She'd stop him and say she doesn't care about learning how it works if her handling the camera is going to make him speak to her this way. But she can tell he's already really trying to be patient with her. Even though it's awkward, this is the most intimate he's allowed himself to be with her since that time on the balcony. His hands touch hers as he moves her fingers to the buttons and switches on the camera. Their faces are close. His straight black hair and her slightly curly brown hair hover over the stupid little apparatus. Define a little space around them.

*

Clara was sitting in his study when she opened a file that contained that old picture of them at Cape May. Her sister had taken it with Horace's Brownie Hawkeye, and Horace had shown it to her before he'd taken the negative to Photo Garden to have the picture enlarged. He'd said that her sister was a genius photographer. The two of them, Clara and Horace, out in the surf. Now Clara stared so hard she could feel the ocean water rising and falling around her legs, splashing halfway up and shocking her thighs. Her mouth was slightly open; she was saying something to him—teasing him maybe. They were both so slender they looked like teenagers. His shoulders seemed broader than she'd remembered them being. But that was something she liked about him, those shoulders he held so straight. She shook her head at the sight of them. What was she saying? She couldn't bring it back. She turned the picture over. In his fine hand, he'd written, *Horace Houseman and Clara Woodford, Cape May Point, June 5, 1953.* That was a year before they were married. She was twenty years old, he was twenty-four. Later that summer he'd ask her to marry him.

Something did come back to her. The night before, they'd walked along the beach until they'd come to a lifeguard stand. They'd climbed up and sat for a long while, not really necking, because she wasn't sure yet about him. People walked by them, murmuring greetings the way people will do when they're at the beach. Horace noticed how many couples there were. Old and young. Even one boy and girl who couldn't have been more than ten or eleven, and Clara had refused to count them as a couple, though Horace insisted they were—you could be in love at that age even if it didn't amount to anything. Maybe more intensely in love than when you got old enough for it to amount to something. And she'd asked him, "What does that mean, 'amount to something?'" He'd laughed and said, "I guess we'll find out."

Which was when she knew that he'd made up his mind about her. Even if she hadn't yet made hers up about him.

*

"An Odalisque," Sylvester explained to her, "was a slave." He shows her picture after picture. Paintings and photographs, some modern, some old, of nudes on daybeds or sofas, with their backs turned or lying faceup with their hands covering themselves discreetly. Eve's cheeks go warm as she looks at the pictures. A black-and-white photograph of a woman with large breasts and a hat on. A painting of a pleasant-faced woman with a very large derriere that makes her look like she should quickly put her clothes back on. Sylvester talks quickly. He's nervous. She knows he likes saying these names— *Boucher, Ingres, Horst, Degas, Lefebvre, Picasso, Delacroix.* He wants to do a project. "Digital Odalisque." He wants her to help. There's something naked about his face. Or maybe she's just seeing

123

it that way because the pictures have embarrassed her. But she's seventeen. Nearly old enough to vote.

She is, however, a virgin. Very much so.

It comes to her that he is too. That's maybe what she's seeing in his face, hearing in his voice.

She likes the idea of both of them being innocent.

She's not absolutely certain she's got it right, but she says OK to helping him.

*

Still in his study, with the Cape May photograph on the desk in front of her, Clara came around to thinking again of Horace's dirty movies. The bag of them she found in his Rise and Shine crate. She leaned forward, put her elbows on the desk, steepled her fingers as she'd seen Horace do a hundred times. Here and elsewhere. She'd never tried imitating his pose. Maybe she should go up to his closet and deck herself out in his clothes, come back and sit here this way. See what it would tell her about him. Her husband. A man who'd have a secret like that.

Since his death she hadn't revisited the day she found the movies and made herself sick looking at the pictures on their cases. She counted that day among the worst of her life. She'd called Hannah, which was a stupid thing to do. But she'd thought that since Hannah and Horace were so close, Hannah would be able to explain it to her in a way that would help. She wasn't crying or hysterical when she talked with Hannah. And Hannah was shocked too that her father would have those things hidden away. Though she couldn't say much because Eve was in the room when she took the call, Hannah had had sensible advice: *Talk to him,* she'd said. And Clara probably would not have talked to him about it if Hannah hadn't advised it.

So she did.

On a Saturday afternoon, she'd knocked at the door to the study. He'd invited her in, very pleasant and sort of mock formal about her visit. He gestured to the chair in front of the desk. She sat down, and she told Horace what she'd found. "Right down there," she'd pointed toward the crate, which was within kicking distance of Horace's left foot. "I know what kind of filth you have down there," she said.

She was proud of herself for her composure. Her voice had had an edge of anger to it—just the right amount—but what it hadn't revealed was how afraid she was of where the conversation might take them. Dirty movies weren't another woman. But they did, if you were the wife who found them, tell you that your husband wasn't the man you'd thought he was. The man about whom you'd thought you knew just about everything—and now this! It wasn't a huge leap from that piece of knowledge to a mutual acknowledging that maybe they shouldn't be married at all.

She didn't want that. And whatever he said after she'd accused him could take them right there in an instant. *Maybe we shouldn't be married.*

He'd sat as she was sitting right that moment. Elbows on the desk, fingers steepled against his lips.

As she'd spoken, he'd looked straight at her.

In his face, she'd seen fear too. The same as hers. Or maybe because she felt it so powerfully in the silence that followed her little speech to him, she projected it into how she saw him. She couldn't know. But she had to trust what she thought she saw.

He never looked away from her. Never turned in the chair. He did, however—when he was sure she wasn't going to say anything more and it was his turn to speak—take his hands down from in front of his mouth.

"They're Sonny's," he said. "I tried to look at them, but I couldn't." His voice was level. His eyes didn't move away from her face.

She let the silence stretch. Because she thought that would be a proper test. Let his words hover in the air.

Finally she said, "I don't believe you." Because it was a preposterous answer. Anyone would think so.

He let some silence pass too. But then he said, "I think you do, Clara. I think you do believe me."

That too was preposterous. And she wasn't about to tell him that he was right.

After a moment, she got up and left the room and closed the door behind her.

They didn't discuss it again.

Their lives went on.

*

Sylvester lives with his grandparents, the Dusablons. It's a new house, a big one in the development just across Dorset Street from Vermont Country Club. Eve and Sylvester have driven here in Bill's old truck, which he's given to Eve for her last two years of high school. It's Friday afternoon. From school, Sylvester has directed her to the house, Dusablon Manor, he calls it. She's wondered where he lived, and now she knows. Also she knows his parents are in Montreal, and they've sent him to live with his grandparents. He doesn't say why. She doesn't ask.

He instructs her to park diagonally across from the front of the house. "That door," he tells her, pointing. Tells her she's to enter without knocking, to walk straight through the kitchen and the dining room. "You'll come to a hallway. On the other side is the living room. There'll be double doors that will be pulled to but not all the way closed. Open them, pull them to behind you. You'll see the camera on the table in front of you. I'll tell you what to do."

She sits still, heart crazy in her chest. She studies him. He won't look at her. Instead keeps his eyes fixed on the house. She wills herself not to blurt out that this scares her. That she's afraid to trust him. That it worries her, how she's made him up in her head, but the person she's made up might not be him at all. She hopes he'll look at her.

He doesn't. She knows he's deliberately avoiding it.

"Your name is Dusablon too," she says softly. "Like your grandparents."

He nods. "In Montreal," he says, "you say you know Sylvester Dusablon, people will know who you mean. They will give you respect. Except they will think you mean my father." He laughs softly.

This little bit of new information and his laugh make her feel no better. *I might not show up,* she thinks of telling him but doesn't. But it's how she thinks of it when he gets out of the truck. "Tomorrow," he says, giving her just the flash of a look through the passenger window before he turns to the house. Then she's driving back into town, wanting to speed but forcing herself to obey the speed limit. "I might not show up," she says aloud. She has time to decide. The thought of being a no-show and him waiting for her is a comfort. Something to help her stay calm from now until then. When she's supposed to be back at Dusablon Manor.

*

Clara knew a lot of time had passed since she first sat down here at his desk. *I'm about to dissolve,* she thought. The Cape May photo remained facedown on the desk. *Horace Houseman and Clara*

126

Woodford, Cape May Point, June 5, 1953, the back of it told her whenever her eyes flicked down to it. As if it were some kind of message.

Clara Woodford is as dead as Horace Houseman, she thought. Deader. *What we have here is Clara Houseman*, she thought. *And who might that be?* came the question.

Something she'd seen very recently touched a switch in her mind. Made her stand up and turn to the open drawer of the file cabinet, where she found the folder with the Cape May picture in it.

The ever orderly Horace. That folder was marked merely *Personal*—which is what made her want to see what was in it in the first place, to see what he'd designate as personal. But of course there were other folders there, but they were named. *William Collins. Eve Collins. Hannah Houseman. Hannah Collins. Clara Houseman. Clara Woodford.*

That was the one she took out now. She sat down again and set it on the desk in front of her. *Clara Woodford.*

Hesitated to open it.

But did.

Pictures of all sorts. Newspaper clippings. Snapshots. Clara's senior picture taken for the Northfield yearbook. A family portrait that must have been taken when Clara was confirmed—twelve and in a white dress with a huge collar. Clara looking proud and happy with her Northfield tennis team, each girl cradling her racket by its head, as no tennis player would ever hold it. Clara with her toes pointed and her hands raised above her head on a diving board. Clara receiving an honor at summer camp when she was nine. Clara in her prom dress. Clara at a restaurant raising a champagne glass on her twenty-first birthday. Some of these pictures were very old, but she remembered them all. As if they were portraits of a friend she hadn't seen for years.

Then this one. Which she had never seen. A black-and-white taken fairly close to the subject. Clara asleep. On her side. A summer nightgown, lopsided and slipped off her shoulder. The beginning of her breast. A sweet look on her face. Lips very slightly parted. It was a compelling picture. Clara of the study couldn't stop studying the sleeping Clara's bare shoulder. Her breast wasn't exposed, but the slipped-down nightgown at the center of the picture insisted that the eyes take note. There was the shape underneath the flimsy cotton. Maybe even the shadow of her nipple.

But you had to look for that to see it at all. The girl looked sweet. It was a nice picture.

She knew it was at Cape May that same summer. He was there with her family in the big house they rented. Otherwise well behaved, he'd been a little obnoxious with that camera, taking pictures of them all when they just wanted to enjoy themselves. He said they didn't have to smile, just to go about their business and not to mind him.

She thought she'd seen all those pictures.

This one meant he'd slipped into the bedroom she shared with her sister. Or now that she thought of it, there were two nights when her sister had gone to Philadelphia to stay with a girlfriend. This was late enough in the morning that he didn't need a flash to take it.

It was an unusual picture. Something about her own sweetness caught like that—in a way she never could have seen in her waking life—made her smile at the girl she was then. Though that girl was certainly old enough to be considered a woman.

Again, she sank into such a trance that she lost track of where she was. A memory surfaced. Waking to Horace in her room. *I was just coming to tell you breakfast is ready,* he had explained, with such a smile on his face. She never thought to doubt him. Even though he had that camera in his hand. So he must have taken this picture just before she opened her eyes. Maybe it was the camera's snap that had wakened her. But he'd never mentioned taking it, never shown it to her.

She picked it up with her fingers—it was like something he'd stolen from her. What did it mean that he'd kept it like that? A little secret.

She can't ask him, of course, and nothing she knows about him tells her the answer. But she can't help smiling. To think she'd printed out such names for him. And for herself. From the dead he's whispered to her, *Just look at this pretty girl!*

*

It's dreamlike, following his directions for parking, entering the house, moving through these rooms. Until this moment she hasn't questioned that this is his grandparents' house. But it could belong to anyone. Kidnappers. One of those men who captures girls and chains them up in a basement torture chamber. Maybe Sylvester—

The double doors are ajar just as he said they would be. The house is so silent she thinks he must not be here as he said he would be. But those doors standing ever so slightly open reassure her. If he's here, then he must know she's out in the hallway. She stands still just a moment before opening them and stepping into—

He's there on the sofa, turned away from her, the pale skin of his back lighted extraordinarily within the shadowy living room. The curtains are pulled against the sunny spring day outside. But she can see how he's arranged the lights to make a bright oasis in the middle of the shadows. *He must have borrowed them from school,* she thinks.

"Pick up the camera," he tells her, his voice as conversational in tone as if they were chatting out on the school grounds. "It's on automatic but without the flash, and so you don't have to do anything except focus, and then snap it."

She picks it up and steps forward.

"Stand right there and take the first one," he tells her.

Through the viewfinder, he's a figure at the center of a picture. Shining length of a boy's back in the light of paradise. She focuses and snaps.

I understand this, she tells herself. It's at least half true—she does understand it, and she's so greatly relieved that he hasn't pulled some awful trick on her. Even so, that he's completely nude—this is the word that comes to her instead of the crude one, *naked*—has her in a state of mild outrage. But then she thinks, *If I had thought about it, I would have known this was what he had in mind. This was what he was telling me he wanted to do.*

"Now down there," he tells her, pointing toward the table at the foot of the sofa. "Take at least two shots each time," he says. "Take enough shots; one or two of them are bound to be good."

She knows he's talking to her to help her move through the shock he must know she's feeling. But then she thinks, *I can do this. He knows I'm perfectly capable.*

And she is, though it jacks her blood pressure up a couple of notches when he turns over and presents the whole front of himself to the bright lights. Eve's only seen pictures of male genitalia.

"Are you OK?" he asks. "Because if you aren't, I don't mind covering up. But I'd prefer this to be straightforward."

"I'm fine," she says. Saying it helps. She even steps forward and focuses. The viewfinder helps too. *A penis is just a penis,* she tells herself. And Sylvester's could hardly be less threatening. Pale thumb of flesh in a nest of ink black hair. Pinkish scrotum. *There it is,* she thinks. *Nothing to it.*

Two snaps. A third for good measure.

*

On the last day of his life, Clara visited Horace at the hospice house and met her granddaughter just as she was leaving. "How is he?" Clara asked, but Eve shook her head and wasn't able to say anything to her. When Clara opened her arms, Eve moved against her and hugged her so hard Clara thought she might have to ask her to let go.

So she knew this would be the day. Eve had divorced her husband before there were children, and she'd come back to Burlington to be close to her family. Clara knew it was Horace she mostly meant by family. That child had loved her grandfather, and she thought it would probably go harder on Eve than it would on herself when Horace was gone.

Before she went in, the nurse told her she'd just helped him back into bed.

His eyes were on her when she entered the room. She took her time closing the door behind her back, holding Horace's gaze all the while. He nodded very slightly and watched her take off her coat. Didn't try to smile. Watched her while she pulled the chair up beside him and sat down.

Still, neither of them spoke. That whole week Horace hadn't been strong enough to say more than a sentence or two at a time. Less each day.

"A nice visit with Eve?" she finally asked.

He nodded. Even that was an effort.

She was quiet. It was all right to sit like this, just saying a word or two every now and then. They'd both gotten used to it.

"Do you think," he began. And swallowed.

Clara waited.

". . . she'll be all right?"

She had no choice but to tell him yes. But then she said—and the thought came to her in the saying of it—"She's been through the worst of it. She'll be fine. She's lucky she's had you to talk to all these years."

He nodded, and she thought she saw a little smile come to his lips. His eyes were half closed. But then they opened and turned directly to her. "You?" There wasn't any sound, but there was no mistaking what he'd asked.

She bit her lip and felt herself shaking her head. "I can't answer that," she said.

And stood up and leaned down to hug him. Gently enough to tell him how much she cared for him but hard enough that he'd know how much she'd miss him.

*

Eve hasn't counted the shots, but when he asks her to hand him the camera so that he can switch it to black and white, she thinks maybe she's already taken thirty-five or forty. And then she takes almost that many again in the new round. She has no idea how much time has passed. By the time he says he thinks they should stop, she feels as if she's driven to some distant place, a journey that started yesterday afternoon and has taken most of the night.

"Do you mind waiting for me in the hall while I put on my clothes?" he asks. He's kept his place on the sofa, but he's picked up a pillow and covered himself with it.

She grins at him because she's amused that after hours of lying there nude in her presence, he doesn't want her to watch him get dressed. But she takes it that he's being thoughtful of her. "Not a problem," she says.

Such intense sunlight washes the hallway that it makes her blink. She feels dizzy. And stands in front of the big mirror by the front door. Considers the thoroughly unremarkable person staring back at her. Brown-haired girl in a sweatshirt and blue jeans. So-so complexion, eyes neither brown nor green. "Strong chin," her father once said of her at a holiday dinner. "And her grandmother's lovely high forehead," chimed in her grandfather. Eve's still studying her otherwise nondescript self when Sylvester steps out, blinks, even raises a hand in front of his eyes.

"I left a robe for you. Just on the chair in there. You'll see when you go in. In case you want it."

She turns to face him. A boy in jeans like tights and a fitted black shirt. Long hair black as midnight and eyes so blue they could cut you like razors. Anybody looking at him would wonder what's up with this kid. She knows her eyebrows are raised.

"Your turn," he explains.

She says nothing. Just stares at him. Knows her mouth is slightly open.

"You knew, didn't you?" he asks. He's not quite looking at her. "I thought you'd figure it out," he murmurs.

She still doesn't say anything. But now that he's said it, she realizes that she did know. At some level, like in some hidden room deep down in herself, she had already figured it out. She did know. *But I don't have to do this,* she tells herself. *Nothing can make me.*

Then he meets her eyes.

And after a moment, she nods. Takes a breath. Steps through the double doors.

*

She knows they won't bother her as long as that door is shut. Or they'll knock before they come in.

She places her index finger against the cool skin over his rib. The short, last rib at the bottom of the cage.

She takes away her finger and stands like that until a drop of water falls onto his forearm right beside her stomach. *Where is that coming from?* she thinks. Then she knows.

Dear Husband,
Joyce Carol Oates

DEAR HUSBAND,

Let no man cast asunder what God hath brought together is my belief. And so I have faith that you will not abandon me in my hour of need. Dear husband, you will forgive me and you will pray for me as you alone will know the truth of what has happened in this house, in the early hours 6:10 a.m. to 6:50 a.m. as you alone have the right to condemn me. For it was my failure as a wife and the mother of your children that is my true crime. I am confessing this crime only to you, dear husband, for it is you I have wronged. Our children were to be beautiful souls in the eyes of God. You led our prayers: Heavenly Father, we will be perfect in your eyes. And in the eyes of Jesus Christ. "With men it is impossible but not with God: for with God all things are possible." Our firstborn son named for you, dear husband, was most beloved of you, I think. Though you were careful not to say so. For a father must love all his children equally, as a mother must. Loell Jr. was meant to be perfect. And Loell Jr. was a very happy baby. That he would not be a "fast learner" like some in your family was hurtful to him, for children can be cruel, but he did not cry overmuch in his crib. It is true your mother fretted over him for her grandson did not "thrive" as Mother McKeon would say. Loell Jr. had such warm brown eyes!—a sparkle in his eyes though he came late to speech and could not seem to hear words spoken to him unless loudly, and you were facing him. It was God's wish to cause our firstborn to be as he was. And then God sent us twin daughters: Rosalyn and Rosanna. Bright, lively girls with white-blonde hair so much prettier than their mother's hair, which has grown darker— "dirty blonde"—with each year. The twins were closest to Mommy's heart, when they were not misbehaving. And little Paul, with his daddy's sharp eyes and wavy hair, and little Dolores Ann: Dolly-Ann, our "sudden gift" from God, born within a year of your second son. All of my life here in Meridian City has been our family, dear husband. You said, I will make a home for us. Like a city on a hill our family will be, shining in the sun for all to behold. You are praised as a draftsman and the plans you work with, blueprints out of a computer, I can't comprehend. It is like a foreign language to me, which you can so easily speak. Though in high school I took algebra, geometry, trigonometry, one of the few girls in Meridian High in Mr. Ryce's class, I did not do badly. Each semester my name was on the honor roll and I was president of Hi-Y in senior year and a guard on the girls' basketball team and at the Christian Youth Conference in Atlanta, I was a delegate in my senior year. You would not remember, for you were three years older than "Lauri Lynn Mueller" and a popular boy on the football team, yearbook staff, studying mechanical engineering, and one of those to receive scholarships at Georgia Poly Tech. It was unbelievable to me that Loell McKeon would wish to date me, still less to marry me, I must pinch myself to believe it! Dear husband, this letter I will be leaving for you on the kitchen table, where I have cleared a space. My handwriting is poor, I know. My hand is shaky, I must steady it as I write. I will dial 911 when it is time. Within the hour, I think. On the counter, there are three knives. Who has placed them there so shiny sharp, I am not certain. The longest is the carving knife, which has been so clumsy in my hand, you would take it from me to carve our roasts. I have swallowed five OxyContin tablets you did not know that I had saved out of my prescription, and there are twelve more I am to swallow when God so instructs me, it is time. I am so grateful, each step has been urged on me, by God. NO STEP OF OUR LIVES IS WITHOUT GOD. Upstairs, the children are peaceful at last. They have been placed on our bed in the exact order of their age for it is this order in which God sent them to us. There is Loell Jr., and there is Rosalyn, and there is Rosanna, and there is Paul and there is Dolly-Ann, and you would believe those children are beautiful children, so peaceful! Dear husband, when the "bad feelings" first began, even before I went to that doctor you believed to be Pakistani, or Indian, from the health plan, I would have a dream while awake and my eyes staring open driving out on the highway and my hands would turn the wheel of the car to the right—quick!—quick as a lightning flash!—before any of the children could perceive it, we would crash into the concrete wall at the overpass and all would be over in an explosion of flame. This dream was so searing, dear husband, my eyes have burned with it. It is the purest of all flame, all is cleansed within it both the wickedness and the goodness of humankind in that flame annihilated for as Reverend Hewett has preached to us out of the pulpit, *Unto every one that hath shall be given, and he shall have abundance: but from him that hath not shall be taken away even that which he hath.* This was long ago it seems when Rosalyn and Rosanna were still in car seats in the back, and Loell Jr. was buckled in beside me, fretting and kicking. A later time, when Paulie was in back with the twins, it was the station wagon I was driving, on Route 19 South, and the children were fretting as usual, for a kind of devil would come into them, when Mommy was behind the wheel and anxious in traffic, little Paulie would shriek to torment me, his cries were sharp like an ice pick in my brain! Mother McKeon said—she did not mean to be harsh but was kindly in her speech—Can't you control these children, Lauri Lynn? It should not be that hard, you are their mother. Your mother looks at me with such disappointment, I do not blame her, of course. Your mother has a right to expect so much better of Loell McKeon's wife, all of the family has a right to expect this for you are their shining son. Now in her face there is disappointment like a creased glove someone has crushed in his hand. Mother McKeon had no difficulty raising her three children. You, and Benjamin, and Emily May. You are perfect, God has blessed you. To some, it is given. From others, it is taken away. Why this is, Reverend Hewett has said, is a mystery we must not question. At Thanksgiving, I was very anxious. You said, why on earth are you hiding away in the kitchen washing dishes before the meal is concluded, why do you behave so rudely, what is wrong with you?—you were on the honor roll at school, you won the *Meridian Times* essay prize, $300 and publication in the paper—"Why Good Citizenship Is Our Responsibility in a Democracy." Little Dolly-Ann had diarrhea and the twins could not be seated together for their giggling and squabbling and Loell Jr. ate so fast, with his head lowered, and was so messy, and Paulie sulked, wanting to play his videos, and shoved at me saying, Go away, Mommy, I don't love you, Mommy. The children eat so fast, and are so messy, Mother McKeon crinkled her nose saying, You'd think these children are starving, and nobody taught them table manners, look at the messes they make. It is sweet things that make them so excitable, out of control. Always at family meals there are many sweet things. Even squash, and cranberry sauce, your mother laces with sugar. Dear husband, I have tried to keep them bathed. It is hard to fight them sometimes, for they kick and splash in the bath knowing how fearful I am, the floor will get wet, and the tile will warp, and water will drip down through the dining-room ceiling. I have tried to keep this house clean. You would laugh at me, your angry laugh like silk tearing, dear husband, but it is so, that I have tried. When the police come into this house this morning, I am ashamed to think what they will see. Of the houses on Fox Run Lane, you would not believe that 37 is the house of shame for from the street, it looks like all the others. Of all the "colonials" in New Meridian Estates, you would not believe that this is the house of shame. The bathrooms are not clean. The toilets cannot be kept clean. Beneath the cellar steps, there is something so shameful, I could not bring myself to reveal it to you. You have been so disgusted, dear husband, and I know that you are right. I know that it is not what you expected of this marriage, and what was promised to you. And you are working such long hours, and you are away more often at Atlanta. I know that I am the mother, and I am the wife. I do not need anyone to help me. Mother McKeon is right, it is a dangerous idea to bring strangers into our homes, to carry away stories of us. Such wrong stories as are told of Loell Jr. at his school, that he bites his own fingers and arms, it is in frustration with the other children teasing him. Yet, as a baby, his eyes were so happy and unclouded, your mother said what a blessed baby, look at those eyes. For in Loell Jr.'s eyes, your mother perceived your eyes, dear husband. None of this is your fault, dear husband. At Christmastime you bought me an excellent vacuum cleaner to replace the old. It is a fine machine. I have seen it advertised on TV. It is a heavier machine than the other, which is needed in this house. It is difficult to drag up the stairs, I am ashamed of what the police officers will discover. The boys' rooms are not clean. The boys' bedclothes are stained. There is a harsh smell of the baby's diapers and of bleach. The twins' hair cannot be kept free of snarls. They push at my hands, they whimper and kick, when I try to comb their hair. And so many dirtied clothes, socks and sneakers, and towels. Worse yet are certain things that have been hidden. I am so ashamed of what will be revealed to you, after I am gone. It was my fault, to provoke you to say such things. I know that such terrible words would never erupt from your mouth, dear husband, except for me. And never would you strike a woman. My jaw still hurts but it is a good hurt. A waking-up hurt. You said, Lauri Lynn, what the hell do you do all day long, look at this house. You have nothing to do but take care of the children and this house and look at this house, Lauri Lynn. You are a failure as a mother as you are a failure as a wife, Lauri Lynn. Tricked me into marrying you, pretending to be someone you are not. You were right to say such things, dear husband. Many times I have said them to myself. In a weak moment, when little Paulie was just born, I

136

asked you could the Morse girl drop by after school to help me some-times, I would pay her out of my household money. I was not beg-ging from the neighbors, dear husband! I was not telling "sob stories" as you have accused. I did take counsel with Reverend Hewett, as you know. Reverend Hewett was kindly and patient saying God will not send us any burdens greater than we can bear, that is God's promise to mankind. I began to cry, I said I am a failed mother. I am a failed wife. My children are not good children, Reverend. My chil-dren are flawed and broken like dolls, like the dolls and toys they break, the stuffed animals they have torn. I am so tired, Reverend Hewett. It was held against me that at Sunday services, I slept. I could not keep my eyes open, and I slept. Our church is the most beautiful of all churches in New Meridian, we are very proud of our church. It is a vision of heaven in our Church of the Risen Christ, which is only three years old, like an ark it is built with its prow rising. Two thou-sand worshippers can gather in our church and sing praises to the Lord, it is like a single voice so strong you can believe it would rise to heaven to be heard. In such joyous sound, Lauri Lynn was but a tiny bubble and what sorrow there is in a tiny bubble is of no conse-quence. I am the Way, the Truth, and the Life so Jesus has promised but Jesus was disgusted with Lauri Lynn, you could not blame him. If I could sleep, I would be happy again. I do not deserve to be happy ever again, I know. It is for this reason, I think, that this morning at last I acted, as God has instructed. For now what is done is done. For now it cannot be undone. Mommy! Rosanna cried but I did not heed her, for the strength of God flowed through my limbs. When we were first married, dear husband, I weighed 126 pounds but after the babies, these past few years my weight has been 160, I am so heavy, my thighs are so heavy, the veins are blue and broken in my flesh like lard and my breasts are loose sagging sacs, you would not believe that I am twenty-eight years old, which is not old. I stand in front of the mirror gripping my breasts in my hands and I am so ashamed, yet there is a fascination in it, what I have become. For I am not now Lauri Lynn who was a plain girl but known for her smiles, to make others feel welcome. And in some snapshots, I am almost pretty. Where that girl has gone, I do not know. Truly she was not a "trick" to beguile you, dear husband! You will say, Lauri Lynn will abide in hell. But Lauri Lynn is not here, the children scarcely knew her. In the 7-Eleven if there are teenaged boys outside, I am ashamed to walk past. These boys jeering and mocking as boys had done with my friend Nola, who weighed 150 pounds when we were girls. Look at the cow, look at the fat cow, look at the udders on that cow, moo-cow, moo-cow, moooo-cow like hyenas the boys laughed, for nothing is so funny to them as a female who is not attractive. We must not pay attention to such crude remarks, and yet. And yet in your eyes, dear husband, I see that scorn. It is the scorn of the male, it cannot be contested. In the mirror, in my own eyes, I see it. In Jesus's eyes, I see it. I am a bad mother, and now all the world will know. It is time, all the world should know. It was very hard to force them, dear husband. Like you they are not patient with me any longer, they have smelled the weakness in me. In animals, weakness must be hidden. For a weak animal will be destroyed by its own kind. There is a logic to this. I began with Loell Jr. for he was the oldest, and the biggest. Loell Jr. I had to chase for he seemed to know what Mommy wished to do, to make things right again. Loell Jr. is named for you, he is your firstborn son though he has been a disappointment to you, I know. For Loell Jr. cannot comprehend arithmetic, the numerals "fly" in his head he says. He fought me, I was surprised. When I chased him in the upstairs hallway he ran screaming and squealing like one of our games except when I caught him he didn't giggle—I didn't tickle him—the "spider tickle" he used to love—he fought me, and bit my fingers, but I was too strong for him, and carried him back to the bathroom and to the tub where the water was just warm the way the children like it, and now there is so much water on the floor, it is leaking through the floor and through the dining-room ceiling, you will be so disgusted. Some parts of what happened, I don't remember. I remember laying Loell Jr. on our bed, his pajamas so wet, the bedspread became wet. Next was Rosanna, for she had wakened, and Rosalyn was still sleeping. (This was very early, dear husband. At the Days Inn in Atlanta, you would still be asleep.) Jesus said to me, It is true that you are a bad mother but there is a way: "If thine eye offend thee, pluck it out." There is a way to be forgiven, and cleansed. Dear husband, I wish that the toilet was not so stained but the stain is in the porcelain and cannot be scrubbed out. And the tub, I have scoured with cleanser so many times tearful and in a fury but the stains will not come out. Even steel wool would not clean it, please forgive me. After Loell Jr. the others were wakening and God instructed me, Lauri Lynn! You must act now. A feeling of flames ran through the upstairs hall, I could see this flame like heat waves in the summer and from these flames, which were the flames of God, I drew strength. From these flames, I understood what was ordained. For he who hath not, from him shall be taken away even that which he hath, I had not understood until now is God's mercy, and God's pity. It is not God's punishment for God is a spirit, who does not punish. So swiftly this truth ran through me, I cried aloud in joy. The little ones believed it was their bath time. And the promise of bath time in the morning is breakfast, and if they do not misbehave, they can have their favorite cereal, which is Count Chocula, which is covered in chocolate. It was so very early—not yet dawn! The house is quiet before the start of the long day. The children must be scrubbed if they have soiled themselves in the night and they must be readied for school except for Paulie and the baby and then there is the return from school, noise and excitement, it is a very long day like a corridor in a great motel where you cannot see the end of it, for the lighting is poor, and the rooms are strangely numbered. Mommy is so tired! Which of those doors in the corridor is Mommy's door is not certain. For the day has no end. My sister said, chiding, You look so tired, Lauri Lynn, you should see a doctor. I was furious with her poking her nose in our business, I said, I am not tired! I will not break down and cry. I will not be ridiculed, or pitied. I will not be laughed at. I am not a TV woman, to spill her guts to strangers, to reveal such shameful secrets, to receive applause. I have done a good job, I think, to hide from them. From the McKeons especially. But it is too hard, I am so tired, one by one I drowned them in the tub, it was not so very different from bathing them, for always they kicked, and splashed, and whimpered, and whined, and made such ugly faces. Some parts of what God instructed me, I can recall, but others are faded already now, like a dream this is so powerful when you are asleep, you would wish to keep it, but when your eyes open, already it begins to fade. It was a hard task but needed to be accomplished for the children had not turned out right, that is the simple fact. As at birth, some babies are not right, malformed, or their hearts are too small, or their brains, or the baby itself is too small, and God does not mean for such babies to survive, in his infinite wisdom. These children, who did not show their deformities to the eye, except sometimes Loell Jr., when he twisted his mouth as he did, and made that bellowing sound. I am a bad mother, I confess this. For a long time I did not wish to acknowledge this fact, in my pride. But the flames cleanse us of all pride. Even Reverend Hewett would not know, for in his heart he is a proud man, that pride is but a burden, and when it is taken from you, what joy enters your heart! In your eyes, dear husband, I hope that this is restitution. I hope that this is a good way of beginning again for you. The baby did not suffer, I promise. Like the others Dolly-Ann thrashed and kicked with surprising strength for a five-month infant but could not fight her mother as the others tried to do, and beneath the water little Dolly-Ann could not scream. How many times you have pressed your hands over your ears, dear husband: Why does that baby scream so? Why is it our baby that screams? It is a cleansing now. God has instructed me, and Jesus Christ has guided my hand. As I am a bad mother I will be punished by the laws of man, I will be strapped into the chair of infamy, and flames will leap from my head, but I will not be punished by God for God has forgiven me. Dear husband, you will be called at work, in Atlanta. You will be asked to return home. In heaven, the children will be at peace. They will no longer be dirty, and squabbling, but they will be perfect as they were meant to be. Always you will know from this day forward, your beloved children are with God, and are perfect in his bosom. There will be strangers in this house, which has been a house of pride too long. To the police officers who are men like yourself you will say with your angry laugh, there is not a clean glass in this house, if one of the police officers requests a glass of water. And the broken toys on the floor. Ugly Robo-Boy that Mommy could not fix, for the battery did not fit right, that provoked Paulie to scream, It won't walk! It won't walk! Mommy, I hate you! The twins, I have wrapped in their new plaid coats, to lay on the bed. I brushed out their snarled hair like halos around their heads. The others are in their pajamas, which are wet, and I have hidden their faces with a sheet. These are not beautiful children, I am afraid. For their mother was not a beautiful woman. My big girl, you called me. My breasts filled to bursting with milk, you held in your two hands in wonder. My big-busty girl, you moaned making love to me, lying on top of me and a sob in your throat, your weight was heavy upon me, often I could not breathe, and your breath was sour in my face sometimes, a smell as of something coppery, I hid such thoughts from you of course. No you are released from our wedding vows, dear husband. In the place where I am going, I will not have children. If I had been strong enough, the fire would consume me. But the fire has burnt down now, I am very tired, it is all that I can do to swallow these pills, and take up the carving knife, at the kitchen sink. You will find another woman to honor and to cherish and to bear your children and they will be beautiful as you deserve, and they will be perfect. Lastly, dear husband, I beg you to forgive me for the heavy casserole dish hidden beneath the cellar stairs, that is badly scorched and disgusting for not even steel wool could scrape away the burnt macaroni and cheese, now in cold water it has been soaking since Thanksgiving. I could not hide it in the trash to dispose of for it is a gift from your mother, it is Corning-Ware and expensive and might yet be scoured clean and made usable again, by another's hand.

Your loving wife,
Lauri Lynn

What Will Survive of Us
Geoff Dyer

THE FIRST ONE I SAW was on the corner of West Thirty-sixth Street and Sixth Avenue: a racing bicycle, painted completely white (tires, saddle, spokes—everything) and chained to a street sign ("Left Lane Must Turn Left"). Plastic flowers had been threaded through the wheels and around the crossbar. New York, that week, was hosting a clutch of art events so I assumed that the white bike was a spin-off from the Pulse or Armory art fairs; either that or a harmless bit of street art. Or maybe it was a prop belonging to one of those irritating mimes, like the ones you get in Covent Garden, presumably painted in matching white and performing nearby. But no, there was no human accompaniment, just this white bike with—I could see as I drew close—cards attached to the sign and to the crossbar:

DAVID SMITH
63 Years Old
Killed by Car
December 5, 2007

A memorial, then, but unlike any I had ever seen before.

The habit of placing flowers or other tributes at the scene of a murder or fatal accident is well established in Britain and America. Two new novels offer vivid essays in contrast between the default style of commemoration in London and New York respectively. For the East End–based narrator of Emily Perkins's *Novel about My Wife* these "tawdry plastic sheaths of flowers in memory of a loving color-photocopied mum or restless young chav who's got in the way of somebody's else's crack-fueled Stanley knife" are "a new form of urban decoration, mawkish post-Diana grief." The Lower East Side equivalent, as seen in Richard Price's *Lush Life*, is altogether more extravagant: "There were dozens of lit botanica candles, a scattering of coins on a velvet cloth, a reed cross laid flat on a large round stone, a CD player running Jeff Buckley's "Hallelujah" on an endless loop, a videocassette of Mel Gibson's *The Passion* still sealed in its box, a

143

paperback of *Black Elk Speaks,* some kind of unidentifiable white pelt, a few petrified-looking joints, bags of assorted herbs, coils of still-smoldering incense that gave off competing scents, and a jar of olive oil." Just four nights later, this wild, neo-Kienholzian shrine is on its way to becoming visual compost. Already it seems "all wrong, sodden and charred, sardonic and vaguely threatening; as if to say, this is what time does, what becomes of us mere hours after the tears and flowers."

This bike, though, had advanced the practice to a far higher level of commemoration and artistic expression. With its poignantly flat tires the white bike was unmissable and yet, even in the crowded streets of midtown Manhattan, it didn't get in anyone's way. Robert Musil writes somewhere that nothing is as invisible as a monument; this unmonumental memorial was distinctly visible and yet so modest as to be *almost not there.* As they waited to cross the street, several people touched the bike: a casual version of the gesture made by Catholics of crossing themselves when they pass over a threshold. By virtue of the white bike a completely innocuous corner of Manhattan—one of thousands—had been imbued with a uniquely gentle aura. Perhaps I am being sentimental but it felt as if this was the safest intersection in the whole of the city.

I had no idea how the white bike came to be there or how it was regarded by the authorities. After a few more months would the chain be cut and the bicycle discreetly removed? Or would it be allowed to remain perpetually in the sun and rain, like the cars and bikes that have been left to fade, rust, and rot at Oradour-sur-Glane in France since the massacre that took place there on June 10, 1944? I assumed it was a one-off guerrilla action but, in the course of a week in the city, I noticed two more of these white bikes: at Houston and Lafayette, and on the Hudson bike path (in memory of Eric Ng, aged 22), right by the Pulse Art Fair:

ERIC NG
22 Years Old
Killed By
Drunk Driver
December 1, 2006
Love & Rage

So these bikes *were* part of an organized if unofficial campaign of remembrance. As far as I can work out, the first so-called Ghost Bike appeared in St Louis, Missouri, in 2003. The ongoing initiative is now part of a loose alliance of Web sites and organizations such as Visual Resistance and the NYC Street Memorial Project (another strand of which commemorates pedestrian fatalities). According to ghostbike.org there are now similar memorials in more than thirty cities across the world. I've never seen one in London but there are, apparently, ghost bikes in Manchester, Oxford, and Brighton. On the ghostbike Web site, Ryan, a volunteer, had written about the creation of the bike I had seen outside the Pulse Art Fair:

"I started making ghost bikes for strangers in June 2005. A year and a half later, my friend was killed by a drunk driver while riding on the West Side bike path. Eric was 22 and had just started teaching math in a Brooklyn high school. He was the kind of person that made you want to live a little more. A year later I still expect to see him when I show up somewhere. His death ripped a hole in my heart. When we make ghost bikes we tap into the hurt of the world. Each person is part of the soul of their city. These stories can make headlines one day and are forgotten the next—we try to make the city remember. We choose to honor that stranger we know could just as easily be our friend, our sister, our own self. That choice makes us whole."

As well as being part of a web of activist organizations, the ghost bikes can be seen in the context of the ad hoc accumulation of street art generally, from loutish graffiti litter to Banksy's ironic—now ironically iconic and commodified—stencils, to community-based murals. In civic ambition the ghost bikes are like a quiet and respectful aspect of the old Reclaim the Streets initiatives—except they proceed from the premise that the streets do not need to be reclaimed by confrontation, that they are *already* ours. But the bikes also throw into relief something about the inadequacy of much public art generally and "official" memorial art in particular.

At its worst, public art in Britain typically defaults to the level of the Norman Wisdom sculpture outside Edgware Road tube station or the justly derided couple kissing goodbye at St. Pancras. The fact that the latest round of proposals for the fourth plinth at Trafalgar Square included Tracey Emin's idea for a little group of sculpted meerkats as "a symbol of unity and safety" reconfirms what everyone already knows: that it is possible to gain a reputation as a serious and important artist on the basis of work devoid of seriousness or importance. With the odd honorable exception—Antony Gormley's *Angel of the North*, for example—most contemporary public sculpture prompts the viewer to echo the question posed fifty years ago by Randall Jarrell in *Pictures from an Institution:* Well, it's ugly, but is it Art?

Rituals of remembrance now come freighted with worries about whether they will be properly observed. As the singing stops and the players find their spot "around the ten-yard circle that until / tonight seemed redundant" (Paul Farley, "A Minute's Silence"), the possibility that homage will turn to insult hangs over football stadiums like a threat of terror. State-sponsored memorials like the Diana fountain near the Serpentine are distinguished by their failure to give voice to the sum of individual feelings they are designed to articulate. In Britain one has to go back to the numbed aftermath of the First World War, to Charles Sargeant Jagger's statue of a soldier reading a letter at Paddington Station (by platform 1) or to the Cenotaph (designed by Sir Edwin Lutyens) on Whitehall to find memorials of high aesthetic quality that are also in step with the needs of a grieving populace.

Most deaths, of course, cannot be expected to be recorded and memorialized on the official monuments of a large city. Nor should artists be required to devote themselves to creating anything other than exactly what they feel like making at any given time. But the hope that the larger needs of society might coincide with the deepest, uncoerced urges of the best artists can never be entirely extinguished. Perhaps it is a sign not only of the solipsism of the contemporary art world but of a wider social failing that it is on the margins—and beyond—of the competitive, hedge fund–powered art market that one finds evidence that art rather than being an amusing diversion or a profitable investment might be integrated with a broader goal of social progress. The flip side of the art boom of recent years has been that one notion of value—cash—has become so engorged as to have caused other, ultimately more valuable, ones to wilt. This is not to hark back to the earnest early 1960s when John Berger, then art critic of the *New Statesman,* was content to ask a single simple question of any piece of art: "Does this work help or encourage men to know and claim their social rights?" Nor does it date back to the heady days of the Bolshevik Revolution when artists eagerly put their shoulders to the Soviet wheel that would eventually break them. No, this takes us much further back, to the prehistoric dawn of art and of human consciousness, to the realization that, as Lewis Mumford famously expressed it in *The City in History,* "The performance of art itself added something just as essential to primitive man's life as the carnal rewards of the hunt."

The *Temple of Tears* and the *Temple of Joy* were created by David Best at Burning Man in the Black Rock Desert of Nevada in 2001 and 2002 respectively. Made out of the wooden offcuts from a toy factory, these huge, Balinese-style structures were constructed by changing teams of volunteers in the course of the week-long festival. As the temples were being built, people left photographs and keepsakes, or wrote prayers and messages on the wood to loved ones who had died. With the understanding that suicide places the greatest burden on the ones who are left behind to mourn, the altar of the *Temple of Tears* was dedicated to those who had died by their own hand. Needless to say, there were no notices or guards stipulating appropriate behavior. (Solemnity, it is worth remembering, is usually a form of decorum, a way of behaving that is entirely compatible with a *lack* of feeling.) The boom of sound systems could be heard in the distance; people wandered through in their wild, sex-crazed costumes, but the atmosphere of compassion and kindness was palpable—overwhelming, in fact. In scale and intensity of effect, these temples were comparable to Lutyens's memorial to the Missing of the Somme at Thiepval. The difference, of course, is that whereas Lutyens's monument was built to last, the temples were built in order to be ceremoniously burned within days of their completion. In a postreligious culture that lacks appropriate rituals of grieving and mourning—and the solace that such rites provided—there was something perfectly appropriate about this: a memorial predicated on transience, a work of art that was absolutely inseparable from the temporary city and the community it was designed to help and to please.

In their less spectacular, more modest—and, already, more lasting—way, the ghost bikes do the same thing: honor the dead, delight the living, make the world a safer, nicer place. If that is too humble a definition of art, then one wonders why it is so rarely achieved elsewhere.

Postscript: A friend who was in New York about a month after I was sent me a picture of the first ghost bike I'd seen, the one on Thirty-sixth and Sixth. It had been completely vandalized: wheels buckled, signs and tires torn off. This was sad, but in a way the mangled bike looks even more poignant than in its original pristine condition.

Two Poems
Mary Jo Bang

DEATH AND DISAPPEARANCE

A plague. The population shaped by the spread.
The meeting with mammals whose bones are not found
Upright anymore. The slow pandemic and its subsequent
Effect. The unusually high rate of devastation.
Winter and spring. Take any year and it's possible to infer
The purple spots on abdomen or limbs.
The overwhelming priority. The impoverishment with
Every outbreak. The corpses in recurrent waves.
A pyre burning the molecular biology
Of the virulent strain and taking with it the haunting evocation
Of a face. A cluster of cases provides whatever
With no knowledge of exactly how. With no possible
Undermining flowering of certainty. The outsider status
Of the mechanical animal. Gear churn. Lung bellow.
A foot thumping in the rib cage. Back and forth.
The limited skills for finding what can no longer be seen.
Only a surround where one feels seriously cheated.
As if beat handily. As if exploited. As if a wide variety of poses
That resemble manikins. The fascinating nature of
The stratagems of staggering forward with exhaustion
Into the final further line of inquiry.
The body becoming meat and bone and the iconographic
Culture saturated with reaction. The subject itself now manifested
In any number of ways as a formless arc. Swaddled
In the basic fact of layers of purpose that simply become
Profoundly brutal. The aura escaping description
Except as an empire of trouble. A dreadful definite pattern.

N AS IN NEVERMORE

The raven is stuffed now,
Into the shape of a principal
Taxidermic moment. The snapshot shows it

As it was when it was alive and staring
Down from the door frame
And onto what we are when all but defeated.

To define is to make material, so says the raven—
Below it is the eerie highway
Known as an ever-death.

Ravaged by war and wars' enigmatic attacks
By a rocket constructed of parts
And blended into an incendiary whole.

One way to see the bird is to look at it
As a fragment of violence mixing its message
With the cold roar of constant utterance.

Quoth the raven, Give me more—.
Mis- means mistake as in shell game catastrophe.
The arm is a line that points to the start.

A bar or six at the window and dying
Again. And on the small screen
The bird turns back into the whining operatic.

Into the story of key elements:
Accident and design with an ending
That ties up the plot rather nicely.

Although outside the box there is mockery spilling over
Onto the unwitting wish: to be and to be and to be
Better. And over that, love's layer of happy shellac.

Mary Jo Bang

"Only when I'm posing do I feel real,"
This from the invisible crowd, this
From the death's-head. This from the bird

Looking down on a square where
A woman is brushing back her hair.
Her name is Lenore Nevermore.

Mere Oblivion
Nicholas Delbanco

EUBIE BLAKE, THE RAGTIME pianist, was one hundred years old when he died. Blake stayed quick witted, nimble tongued—and nimble fingered in his music making—till the very end. At his centenary celebration, the pioneer of boogie-woogie said, "If I'd known I was gonna live this long, I'd have taken better care of myself."

Grandma Moses did take care, dying at 101. Her family still runs a vegetable stand in the village of Eagle Bridge, New York, and the landscape she reported on looks much the same. Photographs and video clips of the spry white-haired old lady suggest she loved the role she played: America's bespectacled witness, painstakingly outlining hay fields and snowfields and horses and barns and fruit trees and, from household chimneys, smoke. Self-taught and wholly familiar with the upstate world she memorialized, "Grandma" took late fame in stride, one senses; journalists would seek her out, not the other way around.

Many great artists live long. We know that Titian—Tiziano Vecellio—died in the city of Venice on August 27, 1576, having been for sixty years the undisputed master of the Venetian School. Although a large proportion of his thousand canvases were worked on by assistants, he remains among the most prolific and accomplished painters of all time. His color sense was sumptuous, his compositions unerring, and his fleshy nudes and "Titian-haired" beauties still appear to breathe. The portrait of Pietro Aretino hanging in New York's Frick Museum is a masterpiece of psychological acuteness; shave the man and change his clothes and he could be paying a visit to that collection today. Titian claimed to have been born in 1477, which would make him ninety-nine at death; birth records of the period are inexact, however, and he may have been a stripling who died at ninety-five.

Nonagenarians are frequent in the history of art. An incomplete if not quite random sampling would include the Italian painter Giorgio de Chirico and the Greek dramatist Sophocles, who wrote *Oedipus at Colonus* near the end of his very long life. According to tradition,

Sophocles demonstrated competence—disproving his son's accusation that he had grown feebleminded—by reciting entire speeches from *Colonus* while a rapt audience wept.

Elliott Carter, born in 1908, continues to compose. At ninety-one Somerset Maugham expired, as did Jean Sibelius and Pablo Picasso; Knut Hamsun died at ninety-two, P. G. Wodehouse at ninety-three. Oskar Kokoschka and George Bernard Shaw both kept working till the age of ninety-four; Louise Bourgeois has a retrospective exhibition now at ninety-six. Octogenarians include the painter Francesco Guardi, poet William Wordsworth, and the sculptor Donatello; those who lived till eighty-one include the artists Lucas Cranach the Elder, Constantin Brancusi, Georges Braque, Walter Sickert, Edgar Varèse, and George Stubbs. Johann Wolfgang von Goethe, Leo Tolstoy, and Francisco Goya had their lives end at eighty-two, while Victor Hugo and Edgar Degas died at eighty-three. Henri Matisse and Max Ernst died when eighty-four; so too did Seán O'Casey and Grace Paley; Herman Hesse, Harriet Beecher Stowe, Richard Strauss, and Ralph Vaughan Williams all died one year older, at the age of eighty-five. Giovanni Bellini, Michelangelo Buonarroti, Frans Hals, Thomas Hardy, Jean Auguste Dominique Ingres, Arthur Miller, Claude Monet, Ezra Pound, Georges Rouault, and Igor Stravinsky all lived to their late eighties, and Hokusai—the self-described "old man mad about painting"—died at eighty-nine in 1849.

As Henry Wadsworth Longfellow points out in his *Morituri Salutamus:* "Cato learned Greek at eighty; Sophocles / Wrote his grand O*edipus,* and Simonides / Bore off the prize for verse from his compeers, / When each had numbered more than fourscore years." This is a writer writing about writers, but there are other professions particularly congenial seeming to the elderly. The architects Christopher Wren and Frank Lloyd Wright died at ninety and ninety-one respectively, and Alvar Aalto, Walter Gropius, and Ludwig Mies van der Rohe all lived past eighty. Architects require time to rise through the ranks of an office, or to establish their own; they rarely receive important commissions till fifty or sixty years old. Marcel Breuer, Le Corbusier, and Louis Kahn—to name only a few practitioners—were at work in their late last years. Most present stars of the architectural firmament—Norman Foster, Frank Gehry, Rafael Moneo, I. M. Pei, Renzo Piano, and Richard Rogers among them—have reached "a certain age."

Another such profession is that of conductor. The aerobic exercise of conducting from a podium is self-evidently healthful, and elderly orchestra leaders seem not the exception but the rule. Men such as

Thomas Beecham, Adrian Boult, Arthur Fiedler, Otto Klemperer, Pierre Monteux, and Arturo Toscanini worked into their seventies and eighties; Leopold Stokowski died at ninety-five. There are, of course, precocious conductors and visionary architects who compel admiration when young, but the generality would seem to hold; it helps here to be "mature."

Artists in their seventies are legion. The briefest of lists might include—grouped not alphabetically but by their age at death—Hans Christian Andersen, Canaletto, Benvenuto Cellini, Honoré Daumier (seventy); Daniel Defoe, Piet Mondrian, Nicolas Poussin, Maurice Utrillo, Tennessee Williams (seventy-one); Barbara Hepworth, Henry James, Algernon Charles Swinburne, Walt Whitman (seventy-two); Noel Coward, Antonio Gaudí, El Greco, William Butler Yeats (seventy-three); Jean Honoré Fragonard, George Frederick Handel, Fernand Léger, Tiepolo, Mark Twain, Euripides (seventy-four); Raul Dufy, Samuel Johnson, Jacopo Tintoretto (seventy-five); Edward Elgar, T. S. Eliot, Joseph Turner (seventy-six); Edith Sitwell, Jules Verne (seventy-seven); Alexander Calder, Jean-Baptiste-Camille Corot, Vladimir Nabokov, Paolo Uccello (seventy-eight); and Pierre Bonnard, who lived until seventy-nine. What the French have called the *troisième age*—that third category beyond childhood and maturity—now extends indefinitely; a fourth or *quatrième age* may prove necessary soon.

All this raises the question of actuarial tables and life expectancy as such. During the Roman Empire and in the "Pax Romana," the average life span of the citizen is thought to have been twenty-eight; today in the "Pax Americana," the average citizen expects fifty additional years. As recently as 1900, the average life expectancy was a mere forty-seven. And, as those who deal with Medicare and Medicaid and the Social Security Administration more and more urgently remind us, the fastest-growing segment of the American population is the elderly. Our aging populace constitutes a major shift of emphasis within the "body politic," and the effects thereof are just beginning to come clear.

One need be neither a sociologist nor politician to understand that changes must be made in our treatment of "senior citizens"; medical, fiscal, housing, retirement, and transportation policies all need to be adjusted as the nation's men and women grow older month by year. Teleologically speaking, and if we count back from the end

153

point, it's almost as though we no longer need die; we gain in life expectancy for every year we live. It's a form of Zeno's paradox: We halve the distance to our "goal" yet never quite attain it—or only when the complex system of the body at last stops functioning. Too, a disproportionate amount of our medical costs and expenditures are incurred in the final six months.

These are not merely American issues. Countries as diverse as Finland and San Marino face the same questions acutely—and the longer lived their populace, the more urgent the problems become. The population of the planet is growing exponentially in part because of longer life: Pandemics are averted, child-bearing years extend, and we do not die as rapidly once ill. When William Butler Yeats observed, "That is no country for old men" and set sail for Byzantium, he was referring to an Ireland that now is newly prosperous and where the old live well.

Instead it's the youthful population that's, worldwide, at risk. The infant mortality rate remains a major factor in any statistical survey of how long we live. Malnutrition and starvation and the failure to inoculate against disease all take their lethal toll. Many of the countries with the lowest life expectancies (such as Botswana, Lesotho, Zimbabwe, Zambia, Mozambique, Malawi, South Africa, the Central African Republic, Namibia, and Guinea-Bissau) suffer from very high rates of HIV/AIDS infection, with adult prevalence rates ranging from ten to thirty-eight percent. Those who inhabit Swaziland will live an average of 32.23 years. Almost without exception, the men and women who contract HIV/AIDS in these impoverished nations will rapidly succumb.

For them, the Hobbesian description of life as "nasty, brutish, and short" holds all too true. (Hobbes wrote *Leviathan* while in his sixties and lived till ninety-one.) Sex traffic, gang warfare, and child slavery: Each constitutes a human scourge that also impacts age. The danger of conscription or forced manual labor—life in the army or the mines—further reduces the life span of those whom Frantz Fanon called "the Wretched of the Earth." And it would seem to be the case that those who live past fifty are less exposed to mortal shocks than their youthful counterparts; the chance, at fifty-nine, of making it to sixty is better than the chance of turning twenty if you are nineteen.

Still, by whatever measure and plotted on whichever graph, it's clear we're getting older, and one crucial aspect of mortality is how well we function near life's end. According to the *World Factbook* for 2007, worldwide average life expectancy is now 65.82 years—

men can expect to live 63.89 and women on an average 67.84 years. The longest-lived nationals inhabit Andorra, with a life span of 83.52 years; they are followed by the citizens of Macau at 82.27 and Japan at 82.02. The United States—for all its vaunted prosperity and medical expertise—ranks forty-fifth worldwide, with an average life expectancy of 78 years. Its impoverished neighbor, Cuba, after decades of embargo, has a population that can expect nearly the same.

"Retirement communities" may be a boon to real estate developers, and the well-heeled use motorized wheelchairs, but the poor in urban and rural America die young. (Infant mortality here would seem to be the variable that keeps us comparatively low on life expectancy charts.) And youth itself means something new; we're far more precocious as well as later starting than would have been the case two hundred years ago. We're both more independent and dependent than was the rule in previous times, both more connected to the world and protected from it. A cell phone permits us to travel yet stay in touch with home. A credit card enables both purchasing power and debt. The paradox attaching to our nation's young is everywhere made manifest; childbearing gets deferred by those who marry late or embark on careers—and when these no longer quite-so-fertile couples require fertility treatments, quadruplets may result. . . .

My focus here, however, is on what happens in old age. We keep our teeth longer, our backs are less bent. X-rays and antibiotics have had an effect on the species as important as that of gunpowder and the opposable thumb. Central heat, indoor plumbing, and air-conditioning have changed the expectations attaching to productivity as well as to hygiene. Viagra and Cialis and an arsenal of face creams promise perpetual youth. And, as TV ads for pharmaceuticals constantly remind us, "You're only as old as you feel."

Yet if you study photographs of soldiers in the Civil War or look at those who stood on bread lines in the Great Depression, you'll see a different national profile than describes our nation now. Our waistlines have enlarged. We drive and fly great distances but rarely walk more than a mile. Jackie Gleason's sitcom character in the 1950s—the foul-mouthed, big-bellied Ralph Kramden—would seem svelte by comparison with reality show contestants today. The epidemic of obesity that threatens to make our generation the first to live fewer years than its parents is a new phenomenon, engendered by junk food and insufficient exercise. "Assisted Living" compounds and "Home Health-Care Givers" are new phenomena also, and will almost surely increase.

155

Nicholas Delbanco

All this belabors the obvious, but life expectancy itself is coming into question as a useful measure; "health years" and "life years" are being proposed as substitutes for "health span" and "life span." Some gerontologists suggest we consider such terms as "disability-free years" and the idea—at the end—of "compressed morbidity"; it's possible to live for decades in a near-vegetal state.

As Lisa Picard writes in *Elizabeth's London*, "We do not have reliable contemporary figures from which to calculate the expectation of life at birth, in London, in the Elizabethan era. For men it has been estimated at twenty to twenty-five years in the poorer parishes, and thirty to thirty-five in the wealthier parts of London, with many prosperous men surviving into their fifties. . . . A diarist born in 1528 recorded sadly that he was 'growing towards the age of forty, at which year begins the first part of the old man's age.'"[1]

Is thirty thirty, forty forty? I mean by this that the meaning of such numbers may itself have changed. Anthropologists and archaeologists and paleontologists and forensic experts have accumulated evidence of bone and body mass in the young and elderly of previous times; we have some understanding of what it entailed to enter into combat in Thermopylae or Carthage or in the Third Crusade. We know about lead poisoning and calcification in hips. But it's impossible to truly know—to inhabit, as it were—the bodies of the ancient dead and feel what they were feeling when they made their morning oblation or drank their cup of wine. It's natural enough for us to imagine that Julius Caesar and a contemporary actor or Cleopatra and a modern movie star are similar of stature—that the hair and legs and breasts and waistlines of our famous ancestors look more or less equivalent in those who portray them today. But a visit to the catacombs or a hall of armor dispels that illusion in terms of *size;* we're larger as a species and will no doubt continue to grow. If our breadth and bones have altered, if matters of shelter and nutrition transform the way we sleep and defecate, why would it not be also true that our ways of feeling young and old have changed?

Is it possible that Keats and Mozart and the rest had used up their allotted span and did not in fact die young? When Shakespeare retired to Stratford-upon-Avon—having been born in that village in April 1564 and fated to die there in April 1616—was he a very old man?

---

[1] *Elizabeth's London: Everyday Life in Elizabethan London,* Lisa Picard (Weidenfeld & Nicolson, London), 2003, p. 89.

William Shakespeare can't provide a true case study of the creative artist in old age, since his is a case apart. The dimensions of his genius make him nonrepresentative; he is one of a kind. Perhaps no one in history—and certainly not in the English language—has reported on a greater range of characters and social class; from gardener to bishop, from fool to king, from "rude mechanical" to courtier he moved with almost insouciant ease and a dramatist's all-seeing eye. Lawyers believe him a lawyer, scholars construe him a scholar; those whose expertise is philosophy or religion or soldiering believe he must have been trained as philosopher, cleric, or soldier. His "I" is multitudes.

What this means in theatrical terms is that he could shape-shift at "will." As Keats observed, the dramatist was supremely possessed of the faculty of "negative capability"—the ability to enter a consciousness other than his own. The writer can argue both sides of a single question, inhabit warring adversaries and phrase opposing views. This is a sine qua non of the theater, where men and women up on stage aren't stand-ins for their author but motivated characters with conflicting needs. And it's therefore doubly hard to say, *This* Shakespeare endorses, *that* he rejects, *these* are his opinions, and they do not change.

Take three of his great plays about love: *Romeo and Juliet, Antony and Cleopatra,* and *The Winter's Tale.* They represent a progression from adolescent to middle-aged erotics and then to enduring devotion (as in Hermione's sixteen years of faithfulness to the husband who had banished her). *Othello* and *Twelfth Night* and *Troilus and Cressida* and *A Midsummer Night's Dream* also are importantly concerned with romance and its entanglements. But do they mirror the mind of their creator, his own passionate infatuations, or are they simply charts of love's terrain? Are any of the antics so brilliantly portrayed on stage in some way self-reflexive? It's clear when he wrote them and clear in which order, but not so simple to interpret them in terms of autobiography. Did he consider suicide as does Romeo or find himself spellbound as was Antony or jealous as Leontes? Did he lust for ass-eared Bottom as does Queen Titania; was he seduced by someone's look-alike or enamored of cross-dressing twins? Does he endorse or disagree with his creature's famed pronouncement as to romantic behavior (in *A Midsummer Night's Dream*): "Lord, what fools these mortals be!"[2]

---

[2] This and all other quotations from Shakespeare come from *The Riverside Shakespeare, Second Edition, The Complete Works,* eds. Evans, Tobin, et al. (Houghton Mifflin Co., Boston), 1997.

We cannot know. We have too little evidence of Shakespeare's personal history to speculate with profit on his transition from youth to age and how or what he learned. To try—in the modern manner—to establish a connection between personal experience and articulated art is to be baffled throughout. We think he played the part of "old Adam" in *As You Like It* and possibly Sir Oliver Martext. But did his son Hamnet's death importantly inflect his portrait of Prince Hamlet, and did he suffer depression while writing *Measure for Measure* or *King Lear*? Is *Troilus* the record of nervous collapse and does *Titus Andronicus* suggest he took pleasure in pain? Do *The Merry Wives of Windsor* and *All's Well That Ends Well* mean his sunny disposition was slated to prevail?

The answers are uncertain, and the only certainty is that we cannot tell. We have documentary evidence of birth and weddings, death and lawsuits, and within the welter of the plays reside a few fixed notions. There's the probably unhappy marriage to a woman some years his senior, the probably authentic devotion to a man some years his junior, the probably sincere conviction that daughters should obey their fathers, and the dislike of dogs. All else is open to interpretation or, as Matthew Arnold put it, "Others abide our question. Thou art free."

Still, it's possible by reading him to come to a kind of consensus opinion on his thoughts about mortality and what death entails. When proud King Lear declares himself "an old, fond, foolish man" and repeats his despairing "Never, never, never, never . . ." because his child will "come no more," we hear the voice of bitter wisdom and see a searing portrait of man at the end of his days. Near the very end, in fact, in *The Two Noble Kinsmen* (which he most likely cowrote with the playwright John Fletcher in 1613–14), Shakespeare describes an ancient grotesque in terms that one can only hope do not include self-portraiture:

> The aged cramp
> Had screwed his square foot round,
> That gout had knit his fingers into knots,
> Torturing convulsions from his globy eyes
> Had almost drawn their spheres, that what was life
> In him seemed torture.
>
> (V, ii, 42–47)

From Macbeth's "sere and yellow leaf" to Prospero's announce-
ment that "Every third thought shall be my grave," the Swan of
Avon seems to have been haunted by the prospect and then actuality
of death. And long before "Tomorrow and tomorrow and tomorrow"
engaged the bard's attention, he understood the stages of incremental age. Some of this is formulaic, a matter of convention, but the
elderly were with him from the start. His assertion that "Old men
forget" (*Henry V*), his characterization of John of Gaunt in *Richard
II*, and his description of "second childishness" as the final act of
seven (*As You Like It*) all have the ring of witnessed truth and not
mere rhetoric.

By and large, however, life is a "brief candle" and soon to gutter
out. When young Harry Percy dies (having been bested in single
combat by Prince Hal) in *Henry IV, I*, he says gaspingly—there's only
one word of these twenty-three that's more than monosyllabic—

> But thoughts, the slaves of life, and life, time's fool,
> And time, that takes survey of all the world,
> Must have a stop . . .
>
> (V, iv, 81–83)

"The fools of time" are everywhere in Shakespeare, and "the whirli-
gig of time" will "bring in its revenges." He possessed the stoic's
conviction that "death, a necessary end, will come when it will
come"—or phrases this conviction through characters such as the
soon-to-be-assassinated Julius Caesar. When her husband tells
Calpurnia, "Of all the wonders that I yet have heard, it seems to me
most strange that men should fear . . ." he reproves those who pro-
long their lives by caution. When Prince Hamlet tells Horatio "we
defy augury" and urges acceptance —"Let be"—he's saying, in effect,
there's no gainsaying death. The "divinity that shapes our ends /
rough-hew them how we will" suggests both a willed acquiescence
in fate, and the farmer's skilled ability to "finish off" a hedge.

Think of that hedge as the form of a play, with its shaped duration.
The hours and acts of theatrical time encompass decades often—particularly so in the romances, where the logic of chronology gives way
to a synoptic rendering of years. If in the comedies and history plays
and tragedies Shakespeare busied himself with coherence—striving
to make sense of things, stressing causal connections and linked
tales—the late plays are less sequence bound or yoked to plausibility.
It's as if the peerless artificer has had enough of artifice and now

159

simply wants to tell stories (moving closer to the strategies of fiction than of verse). The masques and dumb shows honor *entertainment,* and if a character gets pursued by a bear, why that's just part of the spectacle; the playwright had spent years competing with the bear-baiting rink next door. . . .

Still, there's a growing impatience. The romances echo the rhyming assertion in *Cymbeline* that—soon or late, no matter how we attempt to deny it— "golden lads and girls all must / as chimney sweepers, come to dust." One has the sense, in *The Tempest,* of incremental weariness—an old magician's readiness to "drown my book." That "our revels now are ended" comes almost as relief. When Caliban reminds his master that "You taught me language, and my profit on't / is I know how to curse" there's more than mere humor involved; such language is a burdensome gift, and one that its possessor seems willing to renounce.

Before this, of course, comes sweet music. If in *Cymbeline* we're told to "Fear no more the heat of the sun," during Ariel's song in *The Tempest* we're invited to imagine an almost-alchemical shift:

> Full fathom five thy father lies.
> Of his bones are coral made;
> Those are pearls that were his eyes;
> Nothing of him that doth fade
> But doth suffer a sea-change
> Into something rich and strange.
>
> (I, ii, 400–405)

That "something rich and strange," as many critics have observed, has to do with necromancy, and takes as its near antecedent the transformation of Hermione from stone to flesh in the final sequence of *The Winter's Tale.* Both acts are quasimagical, with the playwright as the mage, the "sea-change" from living to lasting has to do with what endures when flesh "doth fade." And in such a reading, possibly, the fools of time are jesters at least as much as dupes; it's Feste and Lear's creature who most completely understand the way the cold wind blowing may turn to perfumed air—as well as the reverse. So when Prospero describes his own "most potent art" and announces himself ready to abjure it, he nonetheless has mustered "cloud-capp'd towers" and "the great globe itself"—all conjured into language while the pageant fades. The playwright, ready to retire, must have known (in the very act of declaring he'd leave "not a rack behind") that the play would last.

In the sonnets in particular, Shakespeare considers what endures—even with an adleaven of boastfulness in such couplets as: "So long as men can breathe, and eyes can see / So long lives this, and this gives life to thee." Or, "If this be error, and upon me proved / I never writ, nor no man ever loved." The dramas have few such referents to the act of composition; they were intended for performance and not written down. When Malvolio pens a letter or Hamlet forges the king's orders, the business of writing is stage business, and often as not those who rely on pen and paper are made fun of or made to seem inept.

Indeed, since his "scripts" antedate copyright protection, there was a kind of premium on *not* being published. The text was a closely held secret. John Heminge and Henry Condell, fellow members of his acting troupe, made a profit out of Shakespeare's writing only when he no longer produced it, and the first folio appeared seven years after the playwright's death. The company of the King's Men did not want their language copied by rivals in the provinces; the quarto of a play existed more as prompter's script than speeches intended for strangers to read. The practical man of the theater from Stratford would no doubt be amazed to know how widely his dramas are published and how often studied in silence today.

But this is not the case with poetry, which by the sixteenth century had a long-standing tradition as written artifact. When Shakespeare penned his sonnets, he did so in the expectation that they would be preserved. The *page* is much referenced here. As suggested above (and in contradistinction to the plays), the poems are full of allusions to their own written existence, and they stake claims on the future. The theme of "immortality" in verse was a conventional one, much practiced by his predecessors; the ravages of time and mutability and their effects on youthful beauty were established as a subject before the sonnet form.

Holding "the mirror up to nature," his poetry describes what will not last. Shakespeare was always precocious; he had a quicker ratio to the passage of time than ordinary men. And when he wrote the following, he would have been barely thirty. No recognition of old age, no description of youth's fleetingness is more achingly incisive than his

Nicholas Delbanco

SONNET 73

That time of year thou mayst in me behold
When yellow leaves, or none, or few do hang
Upon those boughs which shake against the cold,
Bare ruin'd choirs where late the sweet birds sang.
In me thou seest the twilight of such day
As after sunset fadeth in the west,
Which by and by black night doth take away,
Death's second self, that seals up all in rest.
In me thou seest the glowing of such fire
That on the ashes of his youth doth lie,
As the death-bed whereon it must expire,
Consum'd with that which it was nourish'd by.
This thou perceivs't, which makes thy love more strong
To love that well, which thou must leave ere long.

We do know he moved to the country, with only a few trips to London in the final years. He bought New Place, one of the principal dwellings in Stratford-upon-Avon, as early as 1597. Shakespeare's father had been prosperous there before his fortunes altered, and Anne Hathaway's family came from solid local stock. But the playwright earned real money in his chosen trade, and he seems to have known he would spend it at home; for years he made long-distance purchases, both large and small, of land. "In May 1602 and again in July 1605 Shakespeare made very substantial investments in 'yardlands' and leases of tithes in the Stratford area. He was now, in addition to a successful playwright and actor, a significant local rentier and one of Stratford's leading citizens."[3] While in London he had lived modestly, in rented rooms; once back in the place of his birth he planned to make a show.

The Tempest, with its great renunciation scene, has long been read as a kind of retirement party the playwright threw for himself. Prospero, who can do almost anything, does next to nothing in punishment of the rivals by whom he has been wronged. Instead, he mounts a fete: "The rarer action is in virtue than in vengeance," he proclaims. Then, having done well by his daughter Miranda (as would Shakespeare by his beloved daughter Susanna), the duke withdraws

---

[3]*Will in the World*, by Stephen Greenblatt (W. W. Norton & Co., New York), 2004, p. 330.

to meditation and "every third thought" of the grave. So when he begs the audience, in the play's final moment, to "let your indulgence set me free," he's asking for more than applause; like Caliban and Ariel he hopes to be released. Though we have little evidence of his physical condition, it's likely the writer expected a longer life of retirement than the one he lived; he was buried, according to the Stratford register, on April 25, 1616, at the age of fifty-two.

It was a quiet passing: sudden, unremarked, and in one account occasioned by a drinking bout with his old cronies Michael Drayton and Ben Jonson. But there's no real record of excess, and not many die of a night in a bar—as did young Christopher Marlowe in a tavern brawl. We don't really know what killed Shakespeare, whether he suffered a wasting disease or caught a sudden chill. What's clear is he had *wanted* to leave the theater and was not forced to do so, and also that his planned withdrawal was not absolute. Stratford was to be his principal but not sole residence; by analogy he now might be a retired chief executive of the company of the King's Men who remains on a retainer or serves as a consultant. From time to time he lent a hand to his hand-picked successor, John Fletcher (witness his work on *The Two Noble Kinsmen*), and he did purchase a place in Blackfriar's as, plausibly, a pied-à-terre as well as a London investment. The best guess is he'd had enough of the hurly-burly of daily production and wanted, as it were, to leave "the cloud-capped towers, the gorgeous palaces, the solemn temples, the great globe itself . . . behind." He was tired; he'd worked long and hard.

Yet the charms of domesticity were never compelling to Shakespeare, and he famously left his wife only his "second-best bed." His daughter Judith married a man of whom he disapproved, and to whom he left nothing by name. There were several small bequests— Shakespeare's sword to Thomas Combe, money to buy "rings" for his old colleagues Heminge, Condell, and Richard Burbage, five pounds to Thomas Russell—and the bulk of the estate to Susanna (whose husband, John Arden, was a man he trusted). His last will and testament was conceived of in January 1616 and signed by him in a shaky hand on March 25. That he died at New Place some twenty days later suggests he knew he wasn't well and wanted to put things in order.

The poetry and plays were of unequalled quality; he no doubt knew that too. To play at word games as did he, they were Will's true testament, and had been built to last. But death was everywhere, life brief, and the whole notion of permanence would have looked a little different in Jacobean England. The great lost works of Greece and

Rome had only recently been found again, the great words of the Bible were being newly minted in the King James version. We've come, as a civilization, to value that which went before and to preserve it zealously; in the expansive Renaissance of which Shakespeare was principal spokesman, what mattered was forward-facing discovery and not pious retrospect.

This is arguable, of course. Yet no one who wrote in English ever invented more of it, and neologism is in its very essence a strategy of innovation; it pays the past scant heed. "What's past is prologue," as he wrote, and even the history plays would have provided his audience with newfound information; the Plantagenet and Tudor kings whom Shakespeare brought to life onstage are familiar to us now *because* he imagined them then.

Further, one can argue that the playwright's use of source material is in its nature piratical; the past was there for plundering, the histories and chronicles available for alteration like the New Place he newly tricked out. He was "disrespectful" of Plutarch and Holinshed and others, and it seems fair to say he would have expected equivalent treatment from those who might adapt him in their turn. Now we are scrupulous to a fault, particular and scholarly to the best of our cautious discernment—but Thomas Bowdler, who censored him, or those who let Cordelia and Lear enjoy a happy ending are in some sense faithful to the playwright's revisionist spirit. Contemporary productions that offer the Civil War as a backdrop for *Macbeth* or turn the Capulets and Montagues into motorcycle gangs are not necessarily misguided; his work thrived upon analogy and used what came to hand. . . .

In *Becoming Shakespeare: The Unlikely Afterlife That Turned a Provincial Playwright into the Bard,*[4] Jack Lynch convincingly argues that our response to Shakespeare was scarcely foreordained. A series of events took place, a series of sponsors emerged, and the collective efforts of later generations were necessary before the provincial playwright and theater manager became the "Immortal Bard." This takes nothing away from his greatness but may put it in perspective; while alive he did not have the currency his work enjoys today.

So it would seem unlikely he spent his last years worrying about the future fate of *Coriolanus* or *Two Gentlemen of Verona*—a self-appointed archivist of the self-engendered canon. More likely that he supervised his gardens than his texts. And as suggested at this essay's

---

[4]*Becoming Shakespeare: The Unlikely Afterlife That Turned a Provincial Playwright into the Bard,* Jack Lynch (Walker and Co., NY), 2007.

start, what a seventeenth-century man in his early fifties might have been feeling in physical terms is open to conjecture. He may well have been old and weak by the time he wrote *The Tempest,* and Prospero's brave spectacle making proved a last hurrah. But when—as in Jacques's soliloquy—the "last stage of all" would end "this strange eventful history," it would not arrive as "mere oblivion." For here is our preeminent example both of lastingness and its description; Shakespeare's gallery of characters includes both those who die on stage and those who live to render them immortal. Continually he tries—as Hamlet urges Horatio—to "tell my story right."

Last year, at ninety-eight, my father died. A painter, art collector, and dealer, he liked to assert, "A painting a day keeps the doctor away." And, for a long time, it did. When his decline began, nearly two years before, I flew to New York City to see him in the hospital; he'd had a fall. As I approached his hospital bed, he opened his eyes and recognized and smiled at me and said, "I am not dying yet." Then he said something I'll never forget: "But I am more ready for death than for life."

This was, I think, a truth told. He did recover and return to his apartment and was not dying yet. But, as Prince Hamlet says in his rumination on the fall of a sparrow, "If it be now, 'tis not to come; if it be not to come, it will be now; if it be not now, yet it will come—the readiness is all." I flew to see my father one final time last November 14, two days before he did in fact die, and we had an excellent visit: played chess, argued over the comparative artistic and financial value of late Goya prints. He complimented my tie, as usual, and as usual insulted my shirt. These years I saw him often, as often as I could, and lately had the sense of a willed, wise shutting down. When I'd ask how he was feeling, he had a new refrain: "I'm getting old," he'd announce, with a mixture of pride and surprise.

Now that I too am getting old I start to take the measure of the astonishing span of his life. My father called three countries home; he prospered for nearly a century, lived in two, and saw the millennium in. He learned to drive automobiles, to fly in airplanes, to shift languages and professions and use television and Xerox machines and predict—sometimes accurately—the future while celebrating the past. Our family has a long history, and often he would dwell on it and, during the final months, *in* it, but "mere oblivion" was something he avoided, and for that I am grateful and have composed these lines.

Floating Away
John Ashbery

As virtuous men float mildly away
so do our minutes hasten toward the rain,
some speckled, some merely numinous,
and so it goes. The Traveler and his Shadow
find much to concur on. The wreckage of the sky
serves to confirm us in delicious error.
Congratulations on your life
anyway.
Not even doing it
makes up for the loss it guaranteed.
Only a 28-year water supply
shields us from the desert.

Sticker shock awaits plaid gutter boys
pissing out over a stream. Surely if you were
going to count that against him the others would befall too.
That's not what he was saying, Uncle.
We're going to have a friendly chat with him
in the belief that someone will vote for you.

Pleated regret that is easier
by the end of the war inhibits only cats.

Some other holy man was here before
and the eunuchs made much over him.
In the small garden a harmonica was heard braying.

Morto

Susan Daitch

A BLINDFOLDED MAN, SMILING and disheveled, breaks through the stone wall of his turret prison. *We wrap your chains around me. . . . And you hold on very tight.* He's carrying an old man, a fellow prisoner, and tangles of iron links fly behind them as they jump from a great height; they bounce from wall to wall like *par cour* athletes, finally landing in a courtyard hundreds of feet below. Hooded guards wielding swords and shields quickly surround the two escaped prisoners. There can be no flight now. Maybe. This is Matthew Murdock, blinded by radiation, but notorious for his hypersharp senses. Though he appears vulnerable, he levitates and smashes opponents with aerial kicks and punches, thereby avoiding death and injury.

One of the most important features of superheroes is that, for the most part, they don't die permanently. If, in the course of a comic, it appears they've been killed, often as not, it's a ruse. They don't stay dead for long. Superman died but always came back. Even nonsuperheroes Tom and Jerry suffered horrible deaths, injury, mutilation, throwing sticks of dynamite at each other, burning to cinders starting with their tails, flattened against walls, peeling off surfaces, always bouncing back for more injury and other deaths. There are hundreds of Green Lanterns who all have the same powers, just in different amounts. If one Green Lantern dies he passes his ring, the source of his power, something akin to King Solomon's ring, to the next Green Lantern, so death is tricked.

Marvel's X-Men, renegade mutants with their broad range of powers and beleaguered status, are among the most death defying of the Marvel and DC universes. They come close, once in a while one succumbs, but just as they twist and turn in the breeze, they're yanked back from the precipice. Unlike other superheroes, the X-Men aren't entirely separate from us walking-around human drudges, fallible and temporary. We're genetically linked to Jack Kirby and Stan Lee's X-Men (*homo superior*), the next step in human evolution. Viewed

167

with suspicion and dread by lesser mortals, their superpowers help them evade hot water in an infinite variety of forms, but, for all their skills and dazzling appearances, the X-Men and others are no less accepted by the majority. They're stand-ins for all misfits, subject to attempted genocides, purges, and ordinary one-on-one bullying.

Neil Gaiman first met the X-Men when he was as a child in 1967 as the American series was exported to the UK in the form of black-and-white reprints. He went on to write comic series like *Sandman, Miracleman,* and many others, but Gaiman hadn't written an X-Men story until he was approached by Marvel shortly after September 11, 2001. In writing about those who could defy death he wanted to jettison images of planes, burning buildings, people leaping who couldn't fly upward before hitting the sidewalk. Gaiman took the superheroes back to Elizabethan England and created a hybrid story of historical record, science fiction, a futuristic lunar landscape, and a faltering utopian community in the New World. Even without the falling towers, plumes of smoke, office workers running from fire and ash, *Marvel 1602* bears many footprints of the present moment.

At the opening of the story Queen Elizabeth meets with her spy-master, Sir Nicholas Fury, and Dr. Stephen Strange, her personal physician trained in Ankara and points east. Strange, angular features, black and gray goatee, goes into trances before double mirrors and practices an amalgam of magic and medicine in rooms full of creatures in tanks and glass globes including a blowfish that, *when dried and ground, causes a man to feel no pain.* Nicholas Fury, nose scarred, patch over his left eye, is loyal and physically imposing; he towers over the hunched queen, who can barely stand. Elizabeth sinks into a plain wooden chair, not a throne, coughs up blood. At the end of her life she often fainted and had difficulty moving under the weight of her robes. When ill she refused to take to her bed, and in the comic her face is clown white, sagging, contorted, yet no one around seems to grasp the perilousness of the situation with the quickness of the aged queen. Dr. Strange reports that he's been entrusted with the safe passage of something powerful and dangerous being transported from Jerusalem by the Knights Templar. Whatever the thing is, were it to fall into the wrong hands, the result would be catastrophic for the West. Fury, the voice of pragmatic skepticism, shrugs the rumor off, but the queen is stern with both him and Strange.

"*. . . let us hope that the world does not* end, *eh, Sir Nicholas? Eh, good Doctor? At least let it not end before I do.*"

168

James VI of Scotland covets Queen Elizabeth's throne and plots to assassinate her. Though cunning, James is drawn differently from the others. He has small eyes, speaks like a dolt, the sort of character whose speeches you imagine are punctuated by a high, nervous laugh. The king of Scotland has an uneasy alliance with the Spanish Inquisition. When assailants are caught in the palace, Fury suspects agents of King James. He wants to torture them to learn exactly who sent them but Queen Elizabeth tells him, *We do* not *torture. We are not* barbarians.

The panels are dark, the queen's face illuminated by a single candle. In the last frame the camera is high above her and Fury. She's crumpled in her ordinary chair; shadows are long, and Sir Nicholas stands before her, arms crossed, cape over one shoulder in a drawing style reminiscent of Hal Foster's *Prince Valiant*. Having no superpowers, Queen Elizabeth finally is assassinated, throwing the world of *Marvel 1602* into chaos and panic. (Queen Elizabeth actually died in March 1603, either from lead poisoning absorbed from her white makeup, or as a result of a chill caught while out walking. It's believed she might have fought the illness and recovered, but Elizabeth was tired, she'd outlived her friends, felt isolated in her own court. Far from suffering assassination, she gave up, willed her own death, an anti-heroine who rather than trick death over and over, was ready to go.) The Marvel Queen is vulnerable to mortality, and her departure from the planet coincides with a rash of aberrant weather: floods, fantastic lightning storms. Mortals and mutants alike believe these are signs that the world is about to end.

King James I succeeds Elizabeth and charges Sir Nicholas Fury with the elimination of Carlos Javier and his school full of mutants, hidden away somewhere in England. The mutants, future X-Men, are outsiders, persecuted in England and Europe where, if caught by the grand inquisitor, they'll be burned at the stake. In the seventeenth century they're not yet called X-Men but members of the "witchbreed." They take refuge in Professor Javier's school for mutants just as they will in later centuries. Fury lays siege to the school, though he has no intention of an ethnic cleansing. The X-Men fear death just as ordinary humans do, and the hunt for them is real, but their special powers—extreme strength, mind control, power of flight, invisibility, rays that project through walls or ice or fire—make them difficult quarry. None are strangers to the role of outlaw. At the behest of the Vatican, in an uneasy alliance with the inquisitor, a genocidal mission has been in place before the opening of the story. The death of Queen Elizabeth only makes their situation more desperate.

There are many plots and subplots in *Marvel 1602*, several sets of villains and potential villains. Constructed with rapid jump cuts between threads, all stories are interconnected. Potential evildoers and sympathetic fellow travelers, often at the side of the heroes, aren't entirely what they appear to be. Some who advertise themselves as loyal to the X-Men will turn out to double-cross the mutants. Sometimes they look similar. Even in their clothing, sometimes a hybrid of Elizabethan starched collars, farthingales, and tights, both the X-Men and their adversaries look as if they've spent a lot of time in some kind of Tudor gym working out like there really is no tomorrow. Many, from the evil Otto Van Doom to Fury, have high cheekbones and distinctively pronounced corners of the eyes, unlike the round eyes of animated Disney characters, manga or anime figures. The fact that there can be a resemblance between the good and the bad indicates some things aren't as different as they claim, and appearances shouldn't ever be entirely trusted.

In the middle of *Marvel 1602* the whole story turns on a dime. Dr. Stephen Strange is called to the moon by one of the Watchers, a bald creature with sweeping drapery, big eyes, and a high forehead who is concerned that someone called the Forerunner is in Elizabethan England who shouldn't be and is gumming up the works. If the universe implodes and discontinues itself, there will be nothing left to watch. Bereft of subjects, voyeurs will be out of business. He issues a caution to the doctor that he, Strange, can say nothing about their meeting or the pending apocalypse, then sends him back to earth to lie barely conscious on a stone floor outside dark parapets. Coming out of his trip to the moon and parley with one of the Watchers, Strange is arrested, sent to the Tower, and ultimately beheaded as witnessed by the young Peter Parquagh (future Peter Parker/Spiderman of Queens). Could the death of Strange be a trick of some kind? Is it really curtains for the magician, despite his ability to see the future and other talents? It appears this is a real death. King James puts the head on a pike outside the tower, though it won't stay there long.

Rifts split King James and the inquisitor, and divide the inquisitor, himself a masked superhero, from the pope, all of them strange bedfellows to begin with. The grand inquisitor is revealed to be a Jew from the Venetian ghetto and sentenced to burn at the stake. At the last possible moment, while flames lick his feet, he bursts his chains and takes to the air. The inquisitor, Enrique, is really Magneto, who, hundreds of years later, will lose his parents in Auschwitz. To prevent the end of the world, Carlos Javier and Enrique form an alliance. What are the Jewish inquisitor's choices? Count Otto Von Doom of Latveria, lurking in other chapters, makes his presence known as the evil behind other evils. The count is a worse alternative, and Enrique, despite his past as a torturer of the hero mutants, is, for the moment, redeemed.

The Marvel universe may be full of betrayals, but Von Doom is one of the most unreconstructed villains. It will turn out that he was responsible for the queen's murder and the torture and imprisonment of the brilliant and mutable Mr. Fantastic, among other Supernaturals. In a *Kiss Me Deadly* moment, his curiosity gets the better of him, and he tangles with the fake, but still powerful, Templar weapon. The frame explodes into multibranched lightning, leaving Von Doom a heap of mangled parts. He seems to have finally expired but will reappear as intent on world domination as ever. Only one aspect of Von Doom has changed. The formerly handsome count has suffered terrible disfigurement. Complicating matters, there are circumstances beyond anyone's control: more freakish weather with violent rainstorms and hurricane winds, phenomena that seem to foreshadow global warming and climate change as yet unheralded by carbon emissions.

The X-Men escape on a ship, the *Fantastick,* whose name echoes a particular band of superheroes present on board as it sails for the New World. The Fantastic Four (The Thing, a rocky monster; Invisible Woman, who can project force fields; Mr. Fantastic; the Human Torch, who can turn himself into a fireball, fly, and shoot fire simultaneously) are captured by Von Doom but escape, then join forces with the X-Men. Europe has become a death trap for the mutants. Peter Parquagh, who has already begun his four hundred years of worry about his aunt and uncle, will later join them. Though dead, Strange will make his presence known below deck. His head was preserved in brandy (a sailor carelessly drank from the keg and went mad). Clea, Strange's wife, brought the head to the New World, so it can communicate with Sir Nicholas Fury, Javier, and others who have taken refuge there. When lifted from its preservative bath, Dr. Strange's head has opaque white eyes, drips fluid, his face appears frozen in a scream.

Also on the *Fantastick* is Rojhaz, a blond native American sent from Virginia on a mission to the queen; his light hair is seen as evidence that Welsh sailors had landed in the New World long before the colony of Roanoke was founded. When the opportunity presents itself, Rojhaz sounds like Boris Karloff's Frankenstein, whose speech is truncated into bulletlike assertions: *Friend. Good.* Later he'll be catapulted back to the twentieth century, where, as Captain America, his speech will metamorphose from brittle aggressive phrases into complete sentences conveying longing and disappointment. Spoken language is a marker of his transformation and time travel through a Marvel tesseract. His story is the only one that flashes forward to his future in the New World and his fight against the "President for Life," who looks a great deal like the what-me-worry *Mad Magazine* image of the forty-third chief executive. He's traveled back to the earliest days of colonies with the intention of correcting America's problems from the very beginning and thereby preventing the ills of subsequent centuries. It's Captain America's displaced time travel that is gumming up the seventeenth-century works. He's the Forerunner the watcher warned about and must be launched forward into his own time. His project to save twenty-first-century America by traveling back four hundred years is a heroic idea, but impossible to carry out.

Even in the refuge of America the end of the world is constantly imminent, constantly to be worried about, and prevented, even if the means of preventing the apocalypse can only be temporary. Death is evaded, but each character comes very close, so close the reader is almost always tricked, at the edge of his or her seat, sure that even the Hulk, Thor, Ice Man, the Human Torch, and their confreres are severely tested despite their powers. Someone is always one trick ahead. There is always another muscle behind the one thought to be most powerful. Behind each backstage full of puppet masters there's another backstage. Doom, the Inquisitor, Javier, and so on are dust motes dancing in the light for the critical amusement of the watchers on the moon, and then there's a King Watcher overseeing Watcher Junior.

Death is imminent and possible; one is fooled over and over again. Even the powers of flight, invisibility, speed, and superhuman strength can't stop it all the time, you would think. Fatality is tremendously possible, always at the door, storming the gates, around the corner. There are moments when the reader knows more than the characters, knows how rare death is, and so is all the more surprised, has more pleasure in their survival, their squeaking by once again.

—Thanks to Nissim Ram for his advice, suggestions, and expertise on all things comic.

II. PAINTBALL

FAKE DEATH

When we entered the paintball arena in Long Island City, a father of one of the boys, who had once been employed as a projectionist, said, "I haven't walked on a floor this sticky since I worked in Times Square." The entrance was decorated with paintings of figures holding weaponry; a painting of a woman in an Afro and thong, holding a gun, reminded me of the painting in Scatman Crothers's apartment in *The Shining*. Four guys in their twenties, shaved heads, cans of Coke in hand, sat on a bench along one wall. The former projectionist asked what was fun about paintball. None of them answered, so he asked again. Finally one said, "You get to shoot people."

Paintball is a self-contained universe with its own laws, food, clothing, weapons, and language. Located in an industrial stretch of Queens, but close enough to the city itself so someone driving from midtown can be there within minutes, Long Island City Paintball occupies an area about the size of a small airplane hangar. You walk through the corridor to a large space segmented by green netting separating barrackslike areas. There are two large battlefields dotted with big chopped-off pyramid inflatables called Aztecs. Kids and adults alike put on camouflage suits, bulletproof vests, helmets, and visors, and the air is misty from the netting and the haze of exploded paint shells. The guns look real, not like Super Soakers or cap guns, not like a plastic prop or toy. Adult paintballers, mostly men, look like real soldiers, and the children like miniature versions of the same. Are they servicemen about to go to Iraq, or just back from Afghanistan, or the kind of guys who hang out at the watercooler talking about wanting to take out, as in kill, Jack the prick from human resources? The tables behind the netting seem to be self-segregated by race: African-American, Hispanic, Asian, white guys. All squadrons look very serious. That the green netting is probably more reminiscent of the bases of the Mekong Delta than of Mosul doesn't dissipate the echoes of the current war, however removed from the Tigris Basin you may be.

A referee barks out the rules to the table of twelve-year-olds. It's difficult to hear above the sound of gunfire, and he shouts, "Do you understand me?" over and over like a drill sergeant. Ammo is distributed in bags; orange and olive pellets filled with fish oil, they squish underfoot. A lot of them are spilled as guns are loaded, and parts of the floor look like a pool of eggs spawned by a giant sturgeon. There are rumors it hurts when you're hit, and some of the kids are apprehensive. The ref says you can't be closer than ten feet, because then it will really hurt when you're hit, but how will they know what the exact limits of ten feet are? Their estimates aren't accurate.

Paintball was invented in 1976 by writer Charles Gaines, who wanted to reproduce the experience he'd had hunting in Africa. Along with two of his friends, he eventually came up with the scheme of teams engaging one another with paintball guns that were originally bought from an agricultural catalog. The guns were used by the forestry service to mark trees and by ranchers to identify cattle without branding. As the equipment evolved, Nelson Paint Company and National Survival Game developed a monopoly on the products and were extremely profitable in a very short period of time. Now guns with names like the Kingman Spyder Xtra and the Kingman Pilot with Anti-Chop System are more efficient. They boast front-mounted pumps to make recocking easier and gravity-fed hoppers. Web sites for paintball facilities utilize a variety of martial imagery: guns, barbed wire, targets. However, if you go to New York Paintball and click on Reservations, an image of Che Guevara appears, though whether this is intended as a random image of battle or symbol of leftist guerrilla movements or both is up for interpretation.

The bursts of gunfire are deafening, the referee screams that if participants bring their weapons to the table they'll be retired for the night. He shouts again, *"Do you understand me?"* He does sound desperate and convincing—the enemy is vicious and is at the gate. What if this were real? What if some apocalypse had hit the city and the survival of the human race depended on only the band of twelve-year-olds celebrating a birthday and crews of grown-ups out for a Saturday night shooting spree? What if shelter in Long Island City Paintball in the middle of this industrial no-man's-land was all that was left? There is a survivalist aspect to paintball, and so maybe these are the people who would figure out how to get by, how to build snare traps, construct stoves out of rocks, and jimmy open all those locked doors.

This artificial battlefield, a hidden New York, is itself probably doomed. Just as factories and warehouses are displaced, the Long Island City establishment could easily be looking the wrecking ball straight in the eye as phalanxes of luxury condos eat away at the edges of the urban landscape. The city has a passion for rewriting and reinventing itself. Certain kinds of amusements from Coney Island to midtown Laser Park are in their death throes or have already disappeared. LIC Paintball will be converted into a tower advertising city views, underground parking, and concierge service. Someone high in their glass-and-steel tower may, just as the sun sets over the East River, smell the chemical fumes of paintball and wonder what on earth the source of the noxious vapors could possibly be. Perhaps, like native American ghosts that are said to haunt the houses built over their gravesites, an unidentifiable haze and the sound of paint guns in the hands of imaginary soldiers will haunt the condominiums. Residents will find themselves walking with an inexplicable swagger and in the middle of the night hear someone say, over and over, *Do you understand me? Do you understand me?* Whispers in the dead language of the imaginary battlefield, its military gamer talk, echo the hot speech of the long-gone soldiers who speak of *Aztecs, Blind Fire, Condom, Dorito, Ghost, Hoser, Hell Hole, Noob, Ramping,* and *Sweet Spotters.* Or will the ghosts only be what they call *Dead Men Walking*, only pretending to be eliminated until the next round?

III. OJ IN CONEY ISLAND

Coney Island has its share of ghosts; bits of many past Coney Islands cling to the shore. Futurism and anachronism vie for the skyline with the projects to the west and Brighton Beach to the east. Only the parachute jump is left of George C. Tilyou's Steeplechase Park, where mechanical horses once raced around a metal track. Nothing remains of the Blowhole Theater, where air was blasted up women's skirts and dwarves poked male visitors with electric cattle prods. Fire eaters, human cannonballs, the freakishly contorted, tiny, or obese, the sword swallowers, and snake seducers are mostly in retirement or only work weekends. The boardwalk is close to deserted, and the former Steeplechase is now a baseball stadium, KeySpan Park, home of the Brooklyn Cyclones. Leaning against the ticket booth at the entrance to KeySpan Park a man is telling OJ jokes, and he attaches himself to us. Someone made eye contact, and now he sticks to us. No one asks him why he's telling OJ jokes. No one acknowledges he's started to follow us.

Knock. Knock.

Susan Daitch

Who's there? One of the kids takes the bait.
OJ.
OJ who?
You can be on a jury.

The children don't get the joke. They don't know who OJ is, and they don't care. To them the joke isn't funny. Not many people visit Coney Island in the middle of the week, so it's slim pickings for those looking for easy marks or a captive audience who might have some patience with vocalized ramblings, conspiracy theories, or the funny stories of some professional lollygagger you've never seen before. The man, hood covering the top half of his face, follows us down Surf Avenue, past Pete's Clam House, sprouting fake rooftop palms; a restaurant advertising surf and turf; past Nathan's Famous; and the crumbling, boarded-up Coney Island Museum; past Shoot 'Em Win shooting gallery and the boarded-up Shore Hotel. Pinned to his gray padded jacket is a NIXON NOW button.

What's the motto of OJ's limo service? We get you to the airport with time to kill.

The man scratches his butt and laughs. George C. Tilyou recognized that people laughed easily at the embarrassments and humiliations of others. In Coney Island he made a lot of money from this knowledge. Now shuffling as if the demands of narration are too much, the man attaches himself to another small crowd walking down Surf Avenue, telling more jokes, but he's not so far away we can't hear him. At West Tenth Street, when he reaches the Cyclone, one of the last of the gravity-propelled wooden roller coasters, a white snake looping toward the beach, someone tires of his banter and tells him to get lost, but he doesn't. One ride that has shut down keeps attack dogs who circle, barking, snarling, jumping up the chain-link fence only to fall back. The man waves at the dogs; they're old friends. This might have been the site of Luna Park with its riot of crescent moons, giant spinning candy apple red rosettes, squatting gargoyles, plaster Venetian palazzos with their turrets and cupolas, and famous ride: A Trip to the Moon. Was Little Nemo's Slumberland modeled after this confection of architectural delights or was it the other way around? A fire in 1944 destroyed Luna Park, and it was never rebuilt. Projects called the Luna Park Houses rise on the other side of the elevated subway tracks to the west, and Luna Park

176

Furniture, boasting of low, low prices in English and Russian, sits facing the Atlantic.

OJ's lawyer says I have some good news and some bad news. The bad news is your blood is everywhere. The good news is you have low cholesterol.

Freud, who visited Coney Island in 1909, wrote in *Jokes and Their Relation to the Unconscious*, "A favorite definition of joking has long been the ability to find similarity between dissimilar things— that is, hidden similarities." The man who follows us around Coney Island ties together murder, cholesterol, and a limo service. He's a fountain of dissimilarities, as are the landscapes he traverses. Did Freud visit Dreamland? Sailing into New York Harbor, the lights of its 375-foot-high tower were visible before the lights of the Statue of Liberty until Dreamland too was destroyed by fire.

OJ's driver knocks on his door. There's no answer, so he knocks again. Finally OJ opens the door, and his driver asks him if he wants to go to the airport. Just a minute, he says, I have to go axe my wife.

The man resumes trailing us until we get to the New York Aquarium, built on the site of Dreamland in 1955. Inside its sand-colored cinderblock walls a traveling exhibit of jellyfish glows in the dark. He stops here for a moment because he has no intention of shelling out admission to watch the performing sea lions or the two o'clock feeding of the hammerheads, then he disappears, taking his OJ jokes with him. I imagine him out on the boardwalk, Wonderwheel directly behind him like a giant green-and-orange halo as he looks for another audience, until the object of his humor becomes as obscure and as archaic as a promised trip to the moon in a wooden boat, or a Coney Island Red Hot that only costs a nickel. All of Coney is due to fall under the wrecking ball, destined to be rebuilt as a Vegas-style family entertainment complex. Plans were submitted by Thor Equities. Thor's demolition of Coney Island began, though it was suspected it was carried out illegally, before permits had been issued or plans thoroughly approved. Thor's vision of Coney Island portrays a neat walkway framed by glass towers and fountainlike structures echoing the iconographic shape of the parachute jump. Presentations of the future Coney Island are Disneylike, clean and shiny, no visible freaks or shysters, no hot dog–eating contests, no tattooed women in dreads and high heels eating grubs and insects. This isn't a playground where you can hear people shouting in macaronics, shilling for gyros, empanadas, or substances best consumed under the boardwalk.

In *Marvel 1602* the secret weapon husbanded away by the Knights Templar turned out to be the staff of Thor, a stick capable of atomsplitting power. All the superheroes, those subject to mortality and those who appear resistant to it, fear the staff falling into the wrong hands, risking the ultimate apocalypse. As a symbol of power Thor transmogrifies, as the name changes hands. Thor becomes associated with a megadeveloper, a great leveler capable of flattening an urban landscape with all its quirks, obsolete and dangerous (to some) amusements, itinerant nutjobs, all ultimately overtaken by the canary yellow bulldozer with a Megadeth decal on its door. Daredevils, propaintballers, weekend revelers, weirdo jokesters off their meds flirt with death, poke a stick in its eye only to be swallowed by the quicksand of the landscape itself. The amusement park falls victim to its own success as waterfront property values skyrocket, and just as the gears and motors wear out on the rides Thor finds another way to split atoms. Death comes in the back door, sneaks up, and taps you on the shoulder pretending to look like you and be your friend. A developer's visualized digital model fiddles with and reconstructs a processed echo of the park's former self, and finally some kind of mortality wins through the final destruction of the place. For the moment nothing has yet been built, some of the rides remain, and the OJ guy still taps along the herringbone planks of the boardwalk. Alone in the rain a few stragglers walk along the water, though signs are posted warning of dangerous currents and steep drop-offs, and there are no lifeguards in sight. "We have met the enemy and he is us," said Walt Kelly's Pogo. The solitary moments on the shore are among the most threatened. Perhaps, in part, he had this endangered city in mind.

From The Woman Who Lost Her Soul
Bob Shacochis

We are about to speak of very ugly matters.

—Stendhal
The Charterhouse of Parma

DURING THE FINAL DAYS of the German occupation of Croatia, there was an eight-year-old boy in Dubrovnik, Stjepan Kovacevic, who would be introduced in the most indelible fashion to his destiny, the spiritual map that guides each person finally to the door of the cage that contains his soul, and in his hand a key that will turn the lock, or the wrong key, or no key at all.

In Stjepan's case, the map was drawn by an act of retribution: the brutal death of his father, beheaded before his eyes by Tito's Partisans, Serbs and Bosnians, Communists and Muslims, men who shit on God and men he would spend the rest of his life calling, as all Slavic Christians, Roman and Orthodox, called such men who bowed to Mecca, the Turks—their origin hardly mattered—and much of his future would be devoted to their ultimate defeat. One apostate held the boy with a forearm clamped across his throat, the canvas sleeve of his uniform reeking of paraffin; two men escorted his mother upstairs for "interrogation"; three more forced his father to prostrate himself before the hearth in the kitchen, then side-kicked his head into the fire like a soccer ball, the boy crying as much from shame as terror because for months now, as the war turned against his people, he had been ravaged by hunger, and the smell of his father's sizzling flesh made his mouth water and his stomach foam.

The Serb who held him said, And this one?

The Bosnian Partisan who had wielded the crude saber stepped away from the headless corpse, muttering introspectively. Who is the beast? Is it me? I am a slayer of beasts. Who kills children? I do not kill children, even Fascist brats with fathers who kill children, he said and came and stooped before the boy, taking his measure, the son of Europe in the hands of the barbarians. Stjepan, who would not look at him, remembered little more than the stink of black tobacco steaming from his mustache, the splatter of paternal blood on his

179

greasy trousers, the winter mud streaked on his boots. My name is Kresimir mrtvac, he told the son of the former Ustashe vice commander who had orchestrated the pogroms in central Bosnia. Kresimir mrtvac, Kresimir the corpse. When you are a man, come find me, OK, he said, and I will kill you then. He lifted the boy's quivering chin with blood-slick fingers—Yes? Promise?—but Stjepan kept his eyes downcast and finally the Bosnian chuckled drily and patted him on the cheek as if he were his own. Good, he said. Don't forget.

The Partisans left to continue their orgiastic purge of Dubrovnik and Stjepan stood in place, exactly where he had been released from the grip of the man who held him, the satin pool of his father's blood inching toward his shoes. Over the crack and stutter of gunfire in the nearby rialto he strained to hear any sound from the floor above to tell him his mother was alive, not knowing then that she listened too, lying in catatonic stillness where the men had left her in her child's urine-smelling bed, commending to the Almighty the souls of her husband and the boy, convinced they were both lost to her on this earth but absorbed by eternity as martyrs of God and saints of the fatherland, their names already on the lips of unborn avengers, a future generation of patriots. To have such a prayer to pray was an honor, and lifelong.

Outside the house, the old city shrieked and whistled and banged, but inside endless minutes passed in catastrophic silence until she heard the boy retching and bolted down the stairs into the kitchen in time to see him drop his father's charred skull, which he had managed to recover from the flames with cast-iron tongs, into a pail of dishwater. She wiped the vomit from his slack mouth with a rag, pulled his soiled sweater over his head and replaced it with two clean ones, made him put on his overcoat and gloves, scarf, and felt hat as she ran back upstairs for their documents and cache of banknotes— what was there to buy anymore with all this money?—toothbrushes and hairbrush, a bar of homemade soap and hand towels, extra underwear and sewing kit, jewelry with sentimental value, saints' reliquaries and an ivory-beaded rosary blessed by the pope, a confirmation gift from her parents, and the few family photographs she cherished, rushed to the toilet to cleanse herself and empty her mind of the rape, buttoned a sweater on over her housedress and a stylish wool jacket over the sweater and hurried back downstairs to where the boy stood in the ruins of his world, a speck of a world exploding outward with a pulverizing flash, his face ashen and immobile, a tiny manikin fattened by winter clothes staring eyeless into space. She

made the sign of the cross over her dead husband and fished his bill-
fold from his pocket and his gold crucifix and its chain from a pud-
ding of blood. We're leaving now, she said, and pushed her son out
the door, away once again from the city of her birth into the peril of
a future known only by its past.

With other panicked refugees they fled the walled city to its outermost quays and were packed aboard the fishing boats that would
take them that night and the next day north to Split, Ustashe controlled and two weeks in front of the Partisans' advance, where Dido
Kvaternik's men secured passage for them on a convoy to Zagreb, the
city rising from the plain in a dome of sulfurous fog, arriving two
days before Christmas 1944. In Zagreb, they shared a bedroom in his
aunt Mara's lugubrious apartment, like a private chapel infused with
grief, on the northwestern corner of Jelacic Square—his mother's
sister, widowed herself by Chetniks earlier in the war. For months
it seemed they did little more than huddle together in its sunless
freezing rooms, insensate, bewitched by the fizzing radio and its dia-
bolic spew of contradictory reports, waiting for the end, leaving the
apartment's sanctuary only to plod uphill to Dolac and its barren
stalls, scavenging for bread and turnips and coal, or attend mass at
the cathedral, over which his father's cousin reigned as archbishop,
spiritual leader of the land described in 1519 by Pope Leo X as Ante-
murale Christianitatis, the outermost ramparts of Christendom, a
belated and feeble acknowledgment of a reality superior to geogra-
phy—Asia meets Europe not where the seas divide the continents
but here, deep in the savage wilderness of the Balkans, where empires
and religions grate against each other to produce a limitless supply of
bloody slush flowing east and west into the gutters of civilization.

In February Mostar fell to the Bolsheviks, the same month his
mother fell ill drinking an herbal remedy and afterward lay curled
into herself like a sick cat, mewling in bed throughout Lent, and
it would be years before he knew this medicine was a traditional
midwife's abortifacient meant to trigger miscarriage. In April, Srijem,
Vukovar, and Valpovo followed Mostar into Stalinist hell. As May
approached and the Partisans moved inexorably westward toward
Zagreb, Stjepan and the two wraithlike widows joined the city's
exodus—hundreds of thousands of soldiers and civilians—on a Bosch-
ian trek toward the Austrian frontier, the army and home guard—
naïveté being as much of a result of an excess of moral purity as
excess itself—choosing to surrender to the Allies and not the Reds.

But at the River Drava the national troops of the Independent State of Croatia were disarmed by the unsympathetic and ideologically ambivalent British, shuttled aboard overcrowded trains, and transported straight back to Yugoslavia into the hands of the Communists, massacred as they filed out from the boxcars like the eighty thousand Jews they had dutifully shipped to Poland throughout the war. By the time this Biblical-seeming justice occurred, however, the boy and his exhausted mother and increasingly demented aunt had already turned back from the border, deterred by Partisan raids on the tail of the column where they trudged like stock animals in a desperate herd of hollow-eyed, disheveled women and bawling children, reaching the deserted streets of the city only hours before Zagreb fell to Tito on the eighth of May, the same day Germany surrendered.

They stayed indoors, the heavy brocade curtains drawn across the apartment's bay windows, fearing every sound as they dreaded every silence, phantom shapes in flickering candlelight, saying the rosary together in hushed voices or lying like invalids numb in their beds, the boy occasionally taking a book from the shelves of his uncle's library to stare with zero reaction at pictures of farm machinery or let his mind fall into a sentence and wander aimlessly through the shadowy canyon of its words. On Sunday mornings they ventured out for mass, scurrying along the damp pavement uphill toward the beckoning spires of the cathedral like frightened mice. It had been in this same cathedral, two years earlier on the feast day of Christ the King, that the boy and his parents had heard the archbishop's sermon condemning religious and racial intolerance—*all men and all races are the children of God . . . one cannot exterminate Gypsies or Jews because one considers them of an inferior race*—although the boy had forgotten everything about the service but the heroic presence of his father sitting next to him, a rare occasion because his duties generally kept them separated. His harried, preoccupied father, his beautiful uniform smelling of saddle soap and rain and peppery gunpowder, had been ordered back to the capital from the Bosnian front for consultations, his wife and son joining him from Dubrovnik for a holiday in the Esplanade, the grand hotel across from the train station. *What's a Jew?* he remembered asking, too loudly, and he remembered his father lightly pinching the side of his bony thigh and whispering, *Someone preferable to a Turk, now shh,* the expression in his father's friendly gray eyes fixed on something far away, and not friendly, not forgiving.

After church they walked hand in hand in hand to a café, the parents sometimes swinging the child between them like a bell of joy;

Stjepan ate ice cream with berry preserves, his parents laughed and drank beer with the Waffen-SS, and even the obliging waiters seemed like emissaries of happiness, that lost Sunday afternoon in the middle of war.

The archbishop, released from Partisan custody the first week in June, distributed flour and the comfort of absolution to his burgeoning congregation of refugees, and Stjepan, who had only known compassion from women and never from men, fell in love with the priest, the dark crescents of mercy like bruises beneath the archbishop's eyes, the pure hand of tenderness rested on the boy's shoulder, kneading the back of his rigid neck or warming the top of his shaven head, the compressed grace of his beatific smile in a city where smiles were as unlikely as roasted chickens and laughter had been consigned for safekeeping to the insane. The Sunday when Stjepan announced to the archbishop that at the moment he received the Eucharist and felt the buttery melt of the consecrated host on his tongue, he had heard God's voice instructing him to join the priesthood, the archbishop, deeply touched by the child's faith, studied Stjepan with sad resignation. My son, he told the boy, I am reluctant to encourage you, it is a difficult time to want to be a priest in Croatia—Partisans were hunting down and executing Catholic clergy throughout the parishes, intent on decapitating the church with as forceful a blow as they had lopped off the heads of the Ustashe puppets; the archbishop himself accused of inspiring, if not advocating, war crimes—but he nevertheless admitted Stjepan to the ranks of altar boys serving the cathedral. In this role, and in the starched, incense-fragrant security of its ritual, Stjepan began to reawaken from his family's coma of defeat, his excitement uncontainable when in July, the new regime, for the first and last time, granted permission to the archbishop to hold the city's annual procession to the shrine of Marija Bistrica, north of Zagreb, the boy selected to lead the file of priests in scarlet cassocks and white lace mantles, swinging a brass censer, dizzied by the puffs of frankincense he created. Behind, in the flock of forty thousand pilgrims, walked the two sisters, his mother and aunt. Tito's soldiers, many still dressed like forest Partisans but others wearing the new uniforms of the Yugoslav army, lined the route, inflamed by the audacity of so large a crowd, the impertinent bereavement of the families of the Ustashe collaborators, the husbands and sons and fathers who had been annihilated while trying to surrender at the frontier. No shots were fired but the verbal abuse escalated, sporadic, convulsive, to acts of violence, as sudden and

183

unpredictable as lightning bolts. Somewhere along the route of the procession, a bull-faced Partisan thrust himself into the flow of pilgrims to block the path of the widows.

Do you recognize me? he demanded of the boy's aunt Mara. I am from Siroki Brijeg—her husband's village.

Yes, she said, get out of my way.

I am from Siroki Brijeg, he repeated like an imbecile, bellowing.

Yes, his aunt Mara said, I often saw the drunken slut they called your mother fucking Turks in the alley.

For her insolence she received a rifle butt to the head, the stock turned sideways, striking cheekbone to cheekbone, her aquiline nose crushed backward into her sinus cavities. After the benediction at the shrine, the boy, yearning for praise, looked for the women and was disappointed but not overly surprised when he failed to locate them among the vast expanse of the devout, who had pressed onward in their pilgrimage despite the harassment. Meanwhile, his aunt and mother had been taken back to the city by a white-haired peasant with his horse-drawn wagon, first to a clinic where his once glamourous aunt was hastily diagnosed as "unfixable," the weary doctor injecting her with a syringe of precious morphine after settling on the amount of his bribe, then to the apartment, where his mother stood on the street pleading with passersby to help carry the delirious, half-conscious woman up the steps, her pale blonde hair gelled with black blood, eyes like tomatoes, swollen closed, purple face bloated beyond recognition. When the boy returned at sundown, he found the women in the musty parlor, his tall scarecrow aunt laid out on the sofa, his mother kneeling by her head with a washbasin of cold water and a mound of bloody tea towels, the sound of his mother's prayers entwined with the gurgle of agony coming from his slowly suffocating aunt.

Go to bed, Stjepan, his mother said when she realized he had returned home. Get some rest. If she dies, we are leaving tomorrow.

His mother's side of their bed remained an empty blue glow that night, her absence a bottomless pool daring him to come close and swim away, and in the morning he found the two sisters together still but irreconcilably, his aunt in a royal shroud of velvet curtains patterned with silvery fleurs-de-lis, his mother asleep on her suffering knees, her head cradled atop her sister's unused womb, her right hand cupping the dead woman's left hand, its cold whiteness stuck out from the folds of the shroud as if to catch at life's shreds, the parlor bathed in what the boy experienced as an angelic aura of radiance from the columns of banished sunshine entering the apartment. He knelt beside his mother, praying mindlessly, until she cracked open her eyes.

She was just like your father, his mother murmured. If you want a Dalmatian to shut his trap, what can you do but kill him. She opened her reddened eyes fully, looking at Stjepan without expression or feeling. Get dressed and pack your valise, she said.

Where are we going? he asked, and an edge of rebelliousness in his tone made her raise her head from the corpse of her older sister and straighten her back to look down gravely on the boy.

We are going away, she said.

Where?

God willing, we are going to the coast to find a boat.

To go where?

Be careful how you speak to me, she warned.

I won't leave, he said, uncustomarily stubborn.

Stjepan, we cannot live with the Communists, she explained impatiently. And we cannot live without God. You are old enough to understand these things.

His anger reared up and he told her he had decided to live with the others—the fugitives—at the archbishop's palace.

Soon Tito will come for the archbishop too, she said. He will die alone a martyr in Lepoglava. Get dressed now. Not another word.

No, he said, his face bright red, shrieking. I must stay.

She prodded him to explain why until he confessed he had made a deal that prevented him from leaving and she thought he meant the bargain he had struck with God to join the clergy and tried to hug him, perhaps to mitigate his piety with the touch of her flesh, but he flapped away from her arms like a bird. Stjepan, she said, they don't want priests here anymore. You can study to be a priest in Italy.

No, he screamed, eyes spurting a fury of tears. I promised.

Stop this, she said. You promised what? To whom? To God?

A heart-piercing wail—Yes, God.

Quiet. Calm down. Promised what, darling?

To kill the men who killed my father, he said.

Ah, I see, she said. You and I will talk about this.

To protest openly would reveal the sin of his thoughts—worse, expose the sin's appeal—and so he kept quiet and watched with sullen resentment, later that morning in the sacristy of the national cathedral, as his mother negotiated with one of the priests, trading a bundle of currency wrapped in newspaper and tied with butcher's string for the promise that the church would attend to the remains of his aunt Mara, Stjepan thinking bitterly, Why are we bothering with her? What makes her so special? And then, unwittingly, he found himself back across the bridge in his mind to where he had abandoned his father in the fog on the other side. Who buried Father? Maybe they buried him without his head. Was his head soaking still in the kitchen bucket? But if they buried him, did they place the head with the body? Wasn't that more evil than even killing, to put his head over here and his body over there? Shouldn't he and his mother return immediately to Dubrovnik to make sure these unspeakably important matters were properly addressed? Why didn't she care? She didn't care.

They called at the archbishop's private residence at the massive neo-Gothic palace behind the cathedral, his mother desperate for any assistance her husband's cousin might find in his heart to offer for the difficult journey ahead into exile—their second exile together, although the boy had no knowledge of the first. She was determined to make contact with the Americans but remained terrified of the allied forces, foremost the treacherous British, the venomous sting of their centuries-old contempt for the Croats, who controlled the border crossings along the northern frontier and continued their unconscionable wartime alliance with Moscow and the Partisans. Italy, which she had spent much of her life admonishing—in fluent Italian, no less—seemed for the second time in her life the only reasonable destination, and to her relief, the archbishop, inviting the woman and the boy into his sitting room for the forgotten luxury of coffee and biscuits, counseled her to go to the Italians and pray for the best. There is a ship, he told her, that would arrive soon in Zadar to pick up refugees and take them across the Adriatic to Ancona. On this ship, he said, he hoped to place an envoy, who would report to the Vatican on the relentless persecution of the church. She and her son should consider accompanying the envoy to the coast, where passage might also be arranged for them on the ship.

Should, she repeated to herself. *Might.*

Marija, before you say yes, the archbishop said solemnly, there is one complication you must know about—the boat has been leased by Zionists; the refugees they will collect are Jews. Are you guilty of anti-Semitism? the archbishop asked his mother.

No, she said, let the Jews live in peace, but they will throw us overboard and who could blame them, Father. In Bosnia, my husband had orders to send them all to the camps.

And did he obey? asked the archbishop.

Father, who could not obey? she said, adding with a sigh—He was a soldier.

Yes, everyone obeyed, some more than others, said the archbishop, reciting the platitudes that could be thrown like a golden cape over the shoulders of atrocity. Your husband never drew a breath nor, I am certain, extinguished another's that he did not commend to the glory of God and nation, and all Christians who are patriots must live and die this way with the moral force of their beliefs or their lives are worth nothing. To be honest, I don't think he cared much about the Jews one way or another. The Jews were never a genuine problem in this country—not like the Masons, for instance—only scapegoats for other problems. Why bother with these poor souls when the devil himself is at the door? In any case, trust in God these Jews on the boat will not put you in the water.

Surreptitiously, the boy ate the last biscuit; the archbishop stood to extend his hand. Mother and son lowered themselves side by side to their knees to press their lips to the papal ring and receive his blessings. Without warning, Stjepan became inconsolable and the archbishop finally had to pry the sobbing child's fingers away from his own.

They spent the night with other refugees housed in the overcrowded, fetid recesses of the archbishop's palace, the boy forbidden by his mother to speak to anyone of their plans; spies were the reason she gave him but secretly she feared the jealousy of the others should they learn of their privilege, beneficiaries of the archbishop's personal intervention. In the morning they walked with their belongings to the cathedral to attend a mass for the dead, his aunt Mara occupying one of the seven pine-board coffins arrayed between the nave and the left side of the altar, the pews filled with anonymous mourners, the air weighted by the humidity of their bereavement and the gloom-heavy fumes of beeswax, but the grave diggers were days behind in their labor and to remain in the city for her burial was out of the question. After mass, his mother led him down the aisle to the forbidding row of coffins. Which one is Aunt Mara's? he asked. I don't know, she said, kiss them all.

They returned to the pews, where the boy stretched out and fell asleep to the anguished susurration of his mother's rosary, and she did not have the heart to wake him when the archbishop's driver

arrived but scooped him into her arms and carried him to the car.
(On the ship, to make him laugh, she invented a ribald game when
the boy, lost in serious thought, suddenly announced that the driver
must have carried him asleep from the cathedral, not his mother. I'm
too heavy, he insisted. No, she said, you weigh less than a fart in a
bottle. And another time—No, it wasn't so difficult to carry you.
You weigh no more than a feather on a duck's ass. Or later on—It's
true, the tits of a chicken are heavier than you—and he would begin
to giggle, monkeylike, and clap a hand over his mouth, deliciously
scandalized.)

She folded the boy onto the front seat while the driver, a large but
elderly man with white cropped hair and the piercing amber eyes of
a raptor, tied their bags to the roof and then she sat in back, sharing
the seat with a pugnacious-looking man dressed in a brown worsted
suit, unsuitable for summer weather; red, meaty hands resting on his
knees; his brush-cut black hair and steel eyeglasses amplifying the
severe virility of his face. The driver too, despite his age, seemed
intimidating. He had the rolling, flat-footed gait of a brawler, one of
those men who would rather fight than explain themselves, his
bulky face sculpted by pugilism, she thought, and engraved with a
vestigial sharpness she vaguely associated with criminals—perhaps
the war had done this, branded him with its harshness, or perhaps
he was a redeemed thug come home to serve the church. Both men,
she realized, made her uneasy. The driver slid behind the wheel, bringing with him a lemony trace of hair tonic, and as they drove west
through the maze of Zagreb's colorless streets she waited in vain for
her fellow passenger to present himself, say something, say anything,
the small courtesy of a greeting, an acknowledgment of their common humanity, a gesture of fellowship based on the danger they now
faced together, but the man offered nothing beyond the arrogant profile of a glare directed out the windscreen.

Where is the archbishop's envoy? she finally found the courage to
ask.

I am the envoy, he said without turning to look at her.

Yes? she said. I thought you would be a priest.

I am a priest, he replied with a trill of strange glee. He crossed his
arms over his chest and tilted his head her way, as if to share a confidence, but with no interest still to look at her. Today, however, he
said, lowering his voice, and tomorrow, and until we are on the boat,
I am your husband—and now he looked at her with icy blue eyes and
a patronizing smile. With your permission, he said. In name only, of

course—and shifted his body to glare again at the streets.

What is your name? she said dully, resigning herself to this unexpected ruse.

Our name is Bauer, he said. I am Slavko.

I see, she said. And what is our business in Zadar?

Your business, madam, is to be my wife.

At first she was concerned but then overwhelmingly gratified that her son, as if he'd been drugged senseless, would not wake up, his surrender so deep that he slept through two checkpoints, the first on the outskirts of the city and the second a few kilometers beyond. The driver proved himself to be well versed in the protocols of danger, exceedingly calm, cautiously gregarious, his deflections a humble art she had not imagined he possessed, exiting the car in his dark suit and yellowing dress shirt unbuttoned at the collar and his eyes shining with camaraderie to smoke with the Partisans, packs of contraband cigarettes handed around, opening the trunk for a bottle of plum brandy, telling barnyard jokes and mumbling lies, the passengers overlooked and soon forgotten. Those interminable minutes at the checkpoints she thought she would faint from terror, anticipating the boy surfacing back to reality, confused and innocent, unable to recognize the peril they were in and not understanding truth was a poison they would not survive. The privilege of the archbishop's assistance, she now realized, came at a price she had not been clever enough to foresee.

The road was in poor condition, cratered and rutted, trafficked by oxcarts and an occasional jeep, its soggy ditches littered with curious wreckage and the torn remains of animals, women distant in the fields scything barley hay, chimneys rising above the ruins of the countryside, infrequent reminders that nothing was settled—a crossroads where she saw a gouged and severed head mounted on a stake, a turn in the road that slowly revealed a tidy row of executed men, naked, facedown in wildflowers, their bound hands crossed palms up atop the pumpkinlike swelling of their buttocks. There were no more checkpoints that afternoon until twilight, at the entrance to Karlovac, and at the same moment she noticed the barrier across the road the boy began to rouse and sit up. Listen to me, she screamed, diving halfway into the front seat, shaking the boy by the shoulders while he stared at her, dumbstruck with horror by his mother's assault. Talk to nobody, she said frantically, if you talk they will kill us. But she had frightened him needlessly, her heart thundering as the soldiers inexplicably raised the wooden bar across the road and waved them onward into the city.

In an alley behind the central square, the envoy disappeared into the rectory of Holy Trinity Church and they did not see him again until the morning, when she and the boy and the driver emerged from the housekeeper's apartment where they had passed the night, their stomachs rumbling from bowls of ratatouille, left over from dinner and laden with paprika, reheated and served for breakfast. There was the car in the alley just as they had left it, and there was the envoy in the backseat, unchanged in every respect from the day before, though he carried on his breath the slightly decrepit scent of vinegar, she noticed as she eased in beside him, as if he'd been eating pickles or rotten apples or drinking bad wine. Good morning, she said, and because he offered no other response than an aloof nod she did not ask him if he had slept well or poorly or not at all, to hell with him. As they had prepared themselves for bed, she had tried to explain to the boy how important it was, should they be stopped by the rebels, to keep his mouth zipped, but he seemed increasingly withdrawn and restless, and she sensed her control over him slipping away. I don't know who this priest is, she said, who cannot travel as a priest under the flag of the archbishop. Maybe he is just afraid, like the rest of us, she told her unresponsive son, yet he wants us to pretend we are his family. So OK, if I say he is my husband, you say yes, if I say he is your father, you say yes, but if I don't say these things, you will not say these things. Do you understand? You must understand, Stjepan. You must agree.

She had slept fitfully, dreading the likelihood that the boy would be tested, his childhood again trapped like a fly between the hands of life and death, and that morning she did not have to wait for her fear to manifest itself because it sprang, iron jawed, upon them instantly, the car turning a corner out of the alley into the central square suddenly occupied by soldiers jumping down from the flatbeds of two battered trucks, an officer sprinting forward, signaling to the archbishop's driver. Halt! his voice punctured the air. Out! To the driver— Step away! To the woman and boy—Stand by him!—the officer gesturing toward the envoy. She clasped the boy protectively to her legs and stared into the air at pigeons taking flight until her vision spiraled with black confetti, jittery particles that were not pigeons but a dissipation of reality. The soldiers formed a horseshoe and they waited, for what she didn't know, no one speaking, the sun too bright in her eyes and life vertiginous but without motion and the world itself blurred to an abstraction.

Then in the unnatural stillness the painful vividness of everything ebbed back into her consciousness with the rhythmic purr of engines somewhere nearby in the otherwise silent city, faint at first and louder as they approached the square, the mushy rip of tires on the cobblestones preceding the dreamlike appearance of a pair of familiar black sedans, German made and previously favored—Who wouldn't know?—by the Gestapo. The envoy tried to grasp her elbow and without a thought she shrugged away his hand. Two men in ordinary streetclothes but with holstered pistols strapped on military belts got out of the second sedan and spoke briefly with the officer and then they were standing in front of her and the boy was pulled from her arms, the man turning Stjepan around so that she could observe his reaction, but the man could not see what she could see on her son's face, only how it shocked her, how his expression broke her spell-like drift away from what was happening and cast her into a clear-headed state of alertness, she would say many times in the future, seeing for the first time in the eyes of the boy his intractable disregard for authority, the impudent but desolate fearlessness he now assumed in the face of danger, some unbreakable defiance in his character that had not been there yesterday and made her immediately afraid the boy was determined to cause great trouble.

Who is this man? the second of the two asked in a voice so disarming it confused her with its veneer of pleasantness.

Which man? she said, struggling to comprehend the obvious.

Him, said the man, smiling, pointing with his stubbled chin at her companion, who stood exposed and rigid as a fence post, sunlit face drained by the pallor of his fallibility.

I don't know, she said, ignoring the shameless tsk of irritation from the tongue of the man in the brown suit.

You don't know? the Partisan said. His smile collapsed into something flat and ominous. Her denial seemed to cue both men to unbuckle the flaps of their holsters; the one who held Stjepan rapped him on the head with the barrel of his gun, not with blatant malice but in the checked way someone would strike the shell of a boiled egg with the edge of a spoon. Stjepan's expression contorted with indignation, a small gash bloomed brightly atop his shaven skull and out crawled worms of blood, and she marveled at his refusal to acknowledge the pain of the blow that had stabbed her own heart.

I don't know, his mother whimpered. She heard the pistol's hammer cocked and watched its barrel nuzzle obscenely in her child's ear and saw the boy breathing fire.

191

The archbishop's envoy, she screamed out. As God is my witness, I don't know his name.

But you are the archbishop's envoy, the Partisan said to her. Step over here with me.

What? she answered weakly. I don't understand.

Step away from that miserable bastard.

Flinging the boy aside, the man pounced forward and she closed her eyes. The blast was so forceful it seemed to lift her off her feet and beyond the deafness ringing in her head the shot repeated itself, echoing in the stony chamber of the square. When she opened her eyes the priest in the brown worsted suit had crumpled to the paving bricks, life bubbling from his forehead and nose, his executioner sweeping the air with the pistol. Go, he said to her with a crazed look of happiness. He brandished the pistol carelessly at the driver. Go, old man.

In This Light
Melanie Rae Thon

PLEASE COME.

Tulanie's trapped: ramp slick with ice, sidewalks crusted deep in snow. He's pulled himself free of the wheelchair and crawled two flights to the attic room.

Now.

He doesn't know who he wants: *God, Kai, Iris, Mother.*

He wants to hear Talia bounding up the stairs—the dog alive, his father mistaken. How slowly does the heart beat under water? If Talia could survive, Kai might follow. Joseph said, *There's no reason why some bodies float and some bodies fail.* Joseph the Jumper, that's what Tulanie called him. He'd been in the spinal care unit at Harborview five months when Tulanie got there. Joseph Trujillo flew from the West Seattle Bridge, snapped three times, and lived—*blessed*, he said, *no reason.*

Tulanie wants the pigeon in the attic to die, or rise up and fly out of here. He's flung the window open wide, but she won't go—she won't leave him. Three days she's stood, trembling in the shadows, refusing to speak, refusing to take the bread crumbs he's tossed her. She's leaking blood and water—clear pink fluid dribbling from wounds he can't see, flesh he can't heal.

Outside, brothers and sisters mourn:

coo–cura–coo

coo–cura–coo

She might be the holy ghost of one he wounded years ago, *before,* when he was fast on his feet, a boy with slingshot and stones, bow and arrows, *so quick*—his limp legs twitch, remembering. He speared lizards and snakes. He shot robins and squirrels. He never considered pain until his body shared their sorrow.

Please.

He wants Neville and Trina and Rikki to blow into his house and steal him. *Now.* Take whiskey and milk, venison and chocolate. You don't need to snatch bones from junkyard dogs or risk your lives eating garbage.

193

coo   ca–doo–ca–doo

Don't sell your skin tonight. The door's unlocked. Lie down in every bed and choose your favorite mattress.

oo–whooo   whoo

Take my mother's clothes—blue nightgown crumpled in a drawer, wool coat hanging in the closet. *Everything, please:* towels, boots, pillows, toothpaste—take my featherbed and all our blankets.

He wants the children warm tonight so he can stop shivering.

Is this love?

Jesus spit in the blind man's eyes, and the man saw the suffering of the world. *So, here, be well, be humbled.*

Neville says, *Everybody's lost, sooner or later.* If he ever had a home, Neville Kane can't remember. He does remember a blue tub and red blanket, a gutted school bus down a ravine, broken glass, no tires—Mother too wasted to work, Mother too sick to keep him—Jessie Kane old at twenty-six, smooth brown skin gone dry and yellow. Neville remembers his uncle's house, a windowless room in a basement, water weeping down the walls, a green sleeping bag, a damp mattress.

So, here, be good. Mother kissed him on the mouth. *I'll come back when I'm better.*

Is this why the bird stays alive, to make Tulanie witness? *Please.* He could ease the pigeon's grief—now, end it—shorten her days, complete her hours.

woof   woof   whoo

The ones outside urge or forbid him. He'd need a rock or a shovel, strength in his hands and heart, unflinching will, absolute focus. He'd have to crawl to her to do it, drag his pitiful legs behind him—Tulanie Rey, down on his belly—humble, yes, bowing down to her.

Not your will. Nothing when you choose it.

It's easy enough for a clever boy to pump pellets from his BB gun—to wound, to maim, to slaughter—but it's not so simple for a cripple to catch and stab, hammer and strangle. You have to love the one you kill—you need to know she wants it.

Who is he to decide? Maybe the pigeon loves her life, *this life,* even now, so diminished. Maybe she waits day by day for the hour when the light reaches her at last, one ray of light, warm and transient.

To kill the bird now, before she chooses, he'd have to frighten her, cause the sudden grief of fear and struggle, the bright stab of pain as she twists and flutters.

oo' koo–koo–koo
whoo–oo   whoo–oo

No wonder the others cry, sensing what he imagines.

Joseph the Survivor said, *You don't know if you want to die until somebody offers to help you.* Joseph Trujillo stood on the West Seattle Bridge leaning out and leaning back again, stalling traffic, in and out—*now, do it*—a dozen times in a dozen minutes, trying to decide: *Is this a good day to jump, or should I wait for another?* How could he know? Even tonight there might be some secret blessing: clouds full of coral light, bright water reflecting them. How can a man think with horns blasting?

Jump. He found the place he wanted—high enough, a way to the water—he wouldn't hit the tangle of roads beneath the bridge, wouldn't fall to Harbor Island. *Do it.* If he waited too long, a fireman would save him. *Now.* The ones stalled in their cars wanted Joseph Trujillo up and over the edge, out of their sight, *gone,* one less heap of trash soiling the world.

Please. He didn't intend to cause them trouble.

That morning, in his tent under the freeway, down deep in the jungle of hemlock and pine, sword fern and maple, Joseph washed his whole body clean with rubbing alcohol. *So I wouldn't smell too bad, so I wouldn't dirty the water.*

Good today not to dig in dumpsters, to stay hungry, to die light and full of God, almost clean, needing no man's mercy.

Blesséd are you who hunger now.

Jump, you idiot.

No human hand will ever hurt me.

raow   raow
gulls cried:
Come to us, now, do it.

He looked back to see the mountain rising out of cloud, disconnected from earth, only the peak of Rainier visible. *How can you bear to leave this world?* Was this the mountain's voice, or had the sturgeons come from the sea to catch him? *Look at you, the light on your hands, just now, so beautiful.*

After the rubbing alcohol, Joseph dusted himself with baby powder. The smell of it kept him on the bridge. *Mother.* Before he had a word for her, he loved the first salty sting, the warm stream from her nipple.

You can die tomorrow.

He heard sirens wail, but the ramp was clogged—the police

195

couldn't get to him. *Joseph.* He could still go home, *please,* one more night, *can I sleep here?*

So kind Mother was the last time, finding his favorite flannel shirt, pulling white towels from the cupboard. He caught a filthy beggar in the mirror—torn trousers creased with mud, black hair hopelessly snarled.

Jump.

The shower burned, hard and hot, tiny pellets. *Please.* He was afraid of the body in the mirror, skin scorched raw, bones chattering. Those clean, quivering hands couldn't hold a razor. *Help me.* Father oiled his face and shaved him smooth. *Why speak now?* Mother took him to the porch and snipped his wild hair down to soft curls. *Home: everyone alive in the merciful light of evening.* Joseph watched fine strands of himself lifted by wind, stolen by sparrows. *May you never die.* Nathan Trujillo smoked a cigar, and Joseph took the smoke of his father into him.

Love. They loved him even now: the birds, the wind, the light, his parents—but the child lost and found and full of smoke slipped free six hours later. *The sheets hurt, too blue and busy.* He stuffed a plastic bag with Spam and tuna, a pint of cream, six oranges.

He stole twenty dollars from his mother's purse. *Please.* He sensed her lying in the dark, holding her breath, breathing only when he did. Mother with her eyes wide: *Anything you want, take it.* She heard the plastic bag crimp and crackle, felt his hand slide into her purse, his fingers slip into her wallet. *I'll weep when I die—a cold, black river.*

Joseph pressed down the keys of the piano so tenderly hammers struck wire but made no sound, left no chord trembling. A cool breeze moved through the house—Joseph gone again—*no matter how much we love you.*

Do it. Were the people on the bridge trying to help him? A woman in a white lab coat floated through the clog of traffic, cloak full of light, long and loose, open in the wind, flapping. *It's only water.* Yes, but the water chopped by waves looked dark and hard, and the gulls cried, *No,* and the snow on the mountain glowed pink, and the sturgeons promised to carry him far, and the wolf-eels promised to eat him.

In and out. Now. Three firemen sprinted between cars, running to push or grab him. *Please.* Two boys leaped from a truck. *Is that a baseball bat? Is that a crowbar?*

coo–ca–doo   ca–doo–ca–doo

One boy wanted to kill, one hoped to save me.
ooo–whoo
Pigeons cried from under the bridge
and Joseph the Flier flung himself free
to be with them.

He heard the song he didn't play, soft as light, light on water. *This can't be death.* He saw the backs of gulls. *So beautiful to soar above them.*

Yes, the water's dark, but the eyes of flounder gaze up at you.

Even if the stunned firemen and curious boys were leaning out to see, even if the woman in white spread her wings and dove to catch him, Joseph Trujillo could not spin fast enough to see his savior. So close now, the water—so cold the air above it—too late not to die, and so he tried to be good, *very good,* forever and ever. Hard, yes, hard as stone, gray as granite, the cold water rose up, and the stone of water broke him.

Did he hear the neck snap? *Three times, but the water never killed me.* Joseph Trujillo lay facedown in the Duwamish River, waiting for rockfish to rise or cormorants to swoop down and take him.

oo' koo–koo–koo

Three hundred pigeons mourned, but he couldn't raise his head even a centimeter to hear them.

Bless you, this body, broken by wave, fractured by water. Lantern fish glowed in the dark. *Don't be afraid.* They'd come from sound to bay to river. *We'll light your path to the bottom.*

So close to life, *all life,* here at the end of it. Mother and Father swam from shore to touch their only son, to witness. *No crying now—you can't weep in water.* They couldn't turn Joseph to the air without severing his spinal cord. He would die this day, *soon,* lungs pierced by splintered ribs, spleen ruptured. *No lullabies—please, I can't hear you.*

He felt clouds watching their backs. *See how small we are?*

Fish, sea, sky, mountain.

His parents were the cold waves so sweetly numbing him. *Now, nothing more—rock me unto death, rock me on the water.*

Something black and terrible rose up. *Not your will.* Three beings came, eyes huge and blind, tanks pumping oxygen. *Don't save me.* They didn't feel the surge of Joseph's thought roaring down the river. *Please.* The lantern fish fled. *We can't help you.* One man swam on each side, one dove under him. This creature had arms strong as a vice—*to clamp my head and flip me over*—one iron arm down the spine, one straight down the sternum. The others slipped a stiff board under him—*stabilized my neck and strapped me tight—head and chest, knees and pelvis.*

Blesséd are you who thirst for air, who gape empty.

Joseph couldn't speak or breathe.

You who died have been delivered.

Two men on the boat raised him up. They had a mask and bag to start his breath, oxygen to flood him. *Don't be afraid.* The divers lifted their own masks and peered at him with human faces. Light slanting through clouds touched the men's hands as they touched him.

Love—no matter what you've done, no matter how dirty.

He tasted blood in his mouth, felt front teeth shattered.

The five prayed to the one broken: *Just stay with us.* And he did stay. *Because they wanted it. They risked their lives to save mine. Who was I to take it from them?*

Blesséd are the broken.

Blesséd are the merciful.

Joseph died three times in the hospital. *And each time Jesus came and laid his hands on my chest and jolted me.* It makes as much sense as any other explanation. Joseph the Jumper, three times dead, three times fractured, arrived in the spinal care unit at Harborview Hospital in early March, and Tulanie Rey arrived from Montana in August. *There's no reason why some bodies float and some bodies fail.* Tulanie was a flier too, nothing spectacular—not a bridge or a cliff—*only a bicycle.*

Joseph should have been paralyzed from the neck down, should have died when he hit, or drowned in the river.

Jump, you idiot.

Blesséd are you when men hate you.

Thirty-eight years old, seventeen years homeless—Joseph Trujillo survived the walk across the bridge, the hundred-and-fifty-foot fall to the water.

Isn't this enough of a miracle?

Jesus held my neck in his hands one night while the rest of you were sleeping.

Joseph whispered in the dark: *If you wish, you can heal me.* And Jesus said, *I do wish it, but I'm old and tired.* It was true: The man's hair was thin and white, his long beard full of feathers. He pulled a chair to the side of Joseph's bed. *I'll just wait with you a while.*

In October, Joseph Trujillo walked on his own two legs out of the hospital—no metal frame to hold him straight, no crutches, no walker—his left leg felt weak, his right hand tingled. *I'm not asking you to believe—I'm asking you to witness.*

Joseph was free to live under the interstate again in a tangle of blackberry bramble, nightshade, and holly—free to build a house with sticks and tarps, cardboard and plastic.

Blesséd are you who live off the trash of the lucky.

Joseph Trujillo was free to dig a pit and line it with rocks and build a fire—free to eat his dinner out there in the wild woods with ten thousand birds singing his name and ten thousand cars roaring above him.

Joseph Trujillo was free to die another day—Tulanie read about it in the paper—not Joseph, but one like him, another scrap of a man doused in kerosene, despised and mocked, set on fire—murdered by boys like Tulanie Rey, fast on their feet, quick and cruel, children who on another day might have gone to the woods to spear snakes and shoot squirrels.

Why does anything die? How can anyone murder?

Are you better than a bird, more clean, more holy?

The pigeon who won't die waits for the light to reveal her luminous body. Tulanie feels it now, her pain, the place he's broken, his own spine stabbed, a fizz and burn down his legs, sharp ribs piercing. He's the one with the knife, and the one in the gravel twisting.

Please come.

You're not going to die today.

Please.

No, I'm going to kill you over and over.

Coo–cura–coo

Now you know.

What?

How it is for all the others.

Please.

And something does come—not God, not his cousin Kai missing now eight hours under the ice in the icy river—not his sister Iris, face burned by cold, fingers half frozen—not his mother who left her voice at the edge of sleep and her smell in every closet—not Trina who let him kiss her naked legs down by the river one holy night last summer. No, none of them come to this room in this hour. Talia doesn't bound up the stairs to shake her wet fur, to spray, to lick, to love him. The pigeon doesn't rise and fly, doesn't offer proof: *Yes,*

even now, all things in me are possible.
Please.

Only the light comes, and the bird who has stood in shadow all day stands in the miraculous light, washed clean, head shimmering bronze and pink, throat flickering green and lavender.

Everything rises up. Everything dies after.

The bird offers herself to him, feathers alive with light, whole body trembling.

Last summer, Rikki and Trina and Neville stole Tulanie's clothes and left him drunk by the river. All night owl spoke to stone, water to willow. Before she ran away, Trina let him kiss the smooth hollow of pale skin between the bones of her pelvis. Never, never will he feel himself moving fast inside her—but when he touches Trina's legs, his own legs shiver.

Is this love?

Every blade of grass leaves its imprint.

Nothing is separate now, nothing outside the mystery—*rock, cloud, tree, river*—Tulanie's body made whole by the bodies of others.

Please.

He didn't want the day to come, didn't want God to find him naked.

You can't say my name softly enough.

Kai helped Tulanie's father lift the broken boy back into the wheelchair.

Your most tender touch destroys me.

Who is he to choose life or death, to imagine Kai on one shore or the other?

Until I see you with my own eyes, until I touch your numb or radiant body.

coo   ca–doo–ca–doo

Blesséd are you who wait, who hope when hope is impossible.

The light holds the bird, and the boy beholds her wonder.

He remembers Dorrie Esteban in the tree house, gold dust swirling in the light, Dorrie's skin sparked with gold fire—one child protected by the light, *Dorrie Esteban*, the first and only girl he and Kai loved together. Impossible to imagine that child not alive, a winter day eight months later.

She pulled her shorts down far enough to reveal the bloom of violet scars high on her hip bones.

Beautiful, he never said, *like flowers.*

What would you give to kneel in that light and touch her?
Heart, hand, eye, liver.
What would you give to raise your cousin to the light and save him?

Dorrie Esteban gave her brother Elia the secret core of herself, bone dreaming bone, sweet marrow.

Please.

If your blood could save this bird, would you open a vein and let her drink you?

Two years after Elia died, Dorrie Esteban flew into the windshield.

What would you give now to touch her wounds, to hear Dorrie whisper a word, to know that secret?

He remembers pounding on her mother's door, circling the little house, throwing rocks at the window. He wanted Oleta to come roaring out, *alive,* fierce with what she'd lost—not one but both her children.

Destroyed and destroyed.

She sat by her son's bed. She drove the car the day Dorrie shattered the windshield.

Please come.

Tulanie hammered hard with both fists. He needed to see Oleta's face, bruises and stitches—as if he sensed the time to come, his own future: legs limp, Kai missing. He needed to understand who to be, how to live, what to love, *after.*

But she refused to show herself to him. Oleta Esteban did not open the door—*no, never*—did not part the red curtain—*not once*—did not press her holy, unhealed face to the glass—did not step into the wild, unbroken light to curse, to love, to bless him.

Death in the Age of Digital Proliferation, and Other Considerations
Christopher Sorrentino

PUBLIC MOURNING: A KIND OF FAST

WE ARE TAUGHT TO respond with mannerly emotion to the inevitably dead—that is, to everyone else's dead, to the dead whom Ernest Hemingway attempted (in the most uncharacteristic of his short stories, "A Natural History of the Dead") to dignify by startling, or disgusting, us out of our misapprehensive complacency, the assimilation that permits us to see "them" (Katrina victims, World Trade Center first responders, US military casualties, etc.) not as graphically *destroyed* but heroically *fallen*. It is a seemly denial of the flesh, like a religious fast. It's hard to say whether Hemingway was more aware of the true conditions under which dead heroes meet their ends or of our own essential ghoulishness: These are the same dead we furtively revel in—the dead of the 3 a.m. Web sites, the secret autopsy reports and police photos, the dead reduced to recovered scraps of DNA, sumptuously interred femurs. These are the public deaths whose smell and feel we seek out privately, to plunge beyond the decorous piety of the news story, to move beyond the taunting simulacra of the movies into wide-open unknowns of anger, velocity, impact, decay. Public mourning says, *I am sad. Now show me the film.*

TRAINING WHEELS

With public mourning, the act to which we are called is the opposite of the grotesque social inappropriateness of true grief (see: keening, rending of flesh, hurling oneself into open coffins to embrace the dead, hurling oneself into open graves, the fulfilled suicide pact, discerning of supernal visitations and signs, etc.). When I was a kid I had a friend who thought that dealing with grief was a little like moving from the bunny hill to the black diamond on the ski slopes.

You started gradually, with a nice, inconsequential death (we do not, as a society, really believe Donne's business about how together we comprise a continent unavoidably diminished by each individual demise), and then moved to the big ones, presumably at last to greet your own death with utter insouciance.

The idea of building up tolerance for grief, for death itself, has its weird appeal. What it overlooks is that there are the deaths that tip you over and those that are no trouble at all. There's a middle ground someplace, I know that: There are the deaths that arouse your hidden fears; there are the deaths that urge forth springlike effulgences of nostalgia; there are the deaths that elicit an unsettled emotional response strangely similar to what I've experienced when the Mets have lost the playoffs. But—to paraphrase Philip Roth—there are some presences whose absence can undo even the strongest people.

I am a middle-class American, so I've managed to remain fairly sheltered from death (despite the invitation to psychological trauma issued jointly some years ago by Al-Qaeda and the New York City Department of Health and Mental Hygiene), and in fact the first death I remember that really startled me was the direct result of class inequality. It was a girl, Juanita, who was in my second-grade class at P.S. 41 and lived at the Broadway Central Hotel, a notorious welfare pit that eventually collapsed but not before claiming her life: She'd fallen down an elevator shaft when the doors had opened on nothing. Lurking somewhere in there is a rueful joke about poverty; one with a punch line that has the landlord saying, "Nu? An elevator too you were expecting at these prices?" My handling of her death was consistent with the macabre norms of American boyhood. In a time before grief counseling was routinely made available to "survivors," my friends and I spent the day speculating luridly on the condition of her body. When I got home from school, I took one of the Magic Markers I was supposed to be drawing smiling suns and rigidly vertical stalks of grass with and drew instead an "X" over her image in the class picture, then crossed her out on the accompanying list of names, writing an explanation within parentheses—"dead."

Then came my grandfather. My mother has always possessed the gift of undaunted candor, a gift bestowed upon her that she, in turn, has liberally bestowed upon all. She always took it upon herself to disabuse me of my illusions—those I might have, for example, concerning any resemblance the movies might bear to real life. So when my grandfather died after losing what an obituary might have described as "a long battle with cancer," while I was away at summer camp, there wasn't any telephone call summoning me from the cacophony of the mess hall or the fellowship of the dingy bunk. There was a matter-of-fact letter, typewritten, composed in my mother's matter-of-fact style.

As if she had planned it thus, there also wasn't a moment when I walked down to the deserted lakeshore "to be alone"; no episode in which I stared at the millions of stars visible in the clear night sky upstate and wondered where in the universe my grandfather had gone. As it happened, when the letter arrived I was laid up in the camp infirmary, aflame with the impetigo that my having been left to my own hygienic devices for over a month had incubated. Every morning a large middle-aged nurse would supervise me as I stripped naked, stepped into a scalding bath, and then scrubbed the crusty scabs off each of the festering pustules using a brush saturated with pHisoHex. It was painful on several levels. The nurse was not attractive. No one visited me. Quarantined without any other reading material, I read the same *MAD* magazine paperback reprint (*Good'n'Mad*) over and over. And of course my mother's letter. In these circumstances I attempted to experience grief for the first time:

> I'm afraid I have some bad news for you, which I hate to have to tell you. Grandpa died last Saturday, and was buried yesterday, Tuesday. It was a very peaceful and a painless death. He really just slipped away, first into a coma, and then very quietly into death. I wish I could have given you the news face to face. If you want to we'll talk about it when you come home. Of course we were all expecting it, and the whole family has reacted very calmly. Grandma will be leaving on Saturday for a trip to Puerto Rico where she can relax and visit with the family.

By my reckoning, Grandpa had been dying practically forever (a variation, I guess, on that idea of building-up-to-it), and the interdiction that took hold, embodied right there in the letter, was that we were all to be relieved that he'd died; to be reassured that it was easier for him to be dead than it was for him to go on living. This myth of the blessed death raises questions, the biggest being: Who and what, exactly, are relieved? Few would argue that leukemia and multiple myeloma are easy, but there is a clear distinction between relief and nonbeing (we are suspicious of precise meanings precisely because of such distinctions). The daily responsibility for dealing with my grandfather's decline was one that my grandmother accepted stoutly (although she enjoyed reminding people of it), and so fully that, having retired in her early sixties after working for decades as a Spanish-language interpreter for the state of New York, she had begun a second career working as a nurse's aide at Montefiore Hospital, encouraged to apply for the job by the staffers to whom her daily visits had made her a familiar presence. But while my grandfather's illness ended with his death, my grandmother's particular hardship—the affliction of the caretaker—ended in full recovery. She "got better." Her duties toward the dead man had been as completely discharged as his duties toward life. She not only went home to San Juan to "relax and visit with the family," but soon was treating her Co-op City apartment (smaller than the place she'd moved out of, near Bronx Park, when it had become apparent that my grandfather wouldn't be coming home again) like a waystation where she dropped her bags and rested between frequent trips to Europe, South America, California, Las Vegas, and pretty much anyplace where some friend or relative would have her, indulging well into her eighties a wanderlust that apparently had built up, unsatisfied, during the years of her marriage.

I believe that some aspect of the relief the new widow felt (along with other conflicts trapped in the opaque amber of the past), or its expression, offended my mother deeply. My mother is like certain cats I have known who ally themselves with and bestow most of their affection on one particular human, tolerate some others, and have little use for the rest. For much of my mother's early life, that human, I think, was my grandfather. She believed that my grandfather was ushered to his grave impatiently, almost gleefully, by my grandmother. As a consequence of this offense, and those other, older, ones, my grandmother became a criminal in our household; she was purged gradually from our emotional lives, and it occurred to me that death could begin an unraveling; that people themselves, their presence, held things together in ways that the memory of them never could.

Let me here append the first paragraph of this essay by suggesting that while another of the emotional purposes of organized mourning is to provide a comforting, if false, sense of death's uniting us, the inherent function of death is to separate us, first from the deceased and then, in a process of extension, from others.

MEMPHIS, SUMMER 2007

A life builds momentum (we hope); we hope that as a product of that momentum the living agency of the people we love persists in the form of their memory: We hope that their influence, the power of their "aura," buoys them, keeps them among the living, an illusion most convincing, I think, with the dead we love with narcissistic force. Last summer we drove into Memphis precisely on the August weekend when the thirtieth anniversary of Elvis Presley's death would be commemorated municipally. It was not a somber occasion, although it wasn't by any means clownish. The city fathers simply recognized that Elvis was and remains the star attraction of a very interesting town. It would have taken a certain mean-spiritedness to point out that in marking Elvis's life with a festive commemoration coinciding with the anniversary of his death, it seemed unavoidably to be celebrating the death itself. Again, the thing wasn't handled for comic effect; no souvenir miniature toilets mounted on pedestals thick with deep shag carpet denoting the place of the King's last act of volition—the attempt to void his narcotics-paralyzed bowels— were on sale. The customary level of vulgarity, and no more, was evident: a sort of polymerized adoration falling somewhere between that accorded JFK and that accorded Padre Pio. There was also the complete elision of the terminal fact itself. An act of self-preservation, surely: "love with narcissistic force" is the phrase I used: because if Elvis lives on, then the corollary to such a formulation must be that when Elvis dies, "a piece of Memphis dies too. . . ." It was, in fact, shortly after Elvis's death that I first heard the now-familiar phrase about the dead—the recorded, published, filmed dead—"living on." "The King may be gone," the announcer's voice said, "but the legend *lives on!*"

DEATH IN THE AGE OF DIGITAL PROLIFERATION

I know I'm supposed to like the idea of a person's living on through some kind of legacy. Nowadays, certainly, with camcorders and

HTML-enabled word-processing software, with Internet access, with free Web pages and blogs, one has tools at hand to extend one's presence, one's utterances and likeness the length and breadth of the world, to be as omnipresent and plentiful as the heavenly stars and grains of sand to which God compared Abraham's posterity—to become, in effect, one's own posterity. The present ability to extend oneself beyond physical limitations as a result of the simplest act of will beggars the imagination; if every citizen of the world had been issued an airplane and a telephone early in the twentieth century it would not have had the same impact. To be everywhere, forever! It's a marvelous thing especially since nothing in particular needs to be achieved in life in order for this eternally globally instantaneously transmitted monument to have a reason to exist. It exists as a universal extension of the brain; as a poignant illustration of our "fixed fantasies" that we carry with us (as the Web presences, publicized by newspapers and other "gatekeeper" media, of various recently dead mass murderers have demonstrated).

If we accept, for the sake of argument, that this is a form of "living" (NB: I don't accept it otherwise), then we need also to acknowledge that such perfected fantasy adumbrations of ourselves as Web sites, Facebook pages, and blogs also have as their corollary, trailing behind them, the inadvertent revenants of our less ideal lives. The best of several examples I saved to draw on for this essay is taken from a Web site called AOLStalker, which purports to preserve, albeit under coded user IDs, the data concerning individuals' Web searches that AOL injudiciously, and somewhat scandalously, released a few years ago. What story, what remainder of a life, are we to infer from the quests of user #672378, lingering there?

curb morning sickness	2006-03-01 18:54:10
get fit while pregnant	2006-03-09 18:49:37
he doesn't want the baby	2006-03-11 03:52:01
you're pregnant he doesn't want the baby	2006-03-11 03:52:58
online degrees theology	2006-03-11 04:05:24
online christian colleges	2006-03-11 04:13:33
barefoot contessa	2006-03-11 11:04:36
nightstand use	2006-03-11 22:09:02
why use a nightstand	2006-03-11 22:09:50
foods to eat when pregnant	2006-03-12 09:38:02
baby names	2006-03-14 19:11:10
baby names and meanings	2006-03-14 19:11:28
la tee da's charlotte nc	2006-03-18 15:57:48

physician search	2006-03-23 10:20:04
taste of charlotte	2006-03-27 15:56:49
best pampering trips	2006-03-27 16:33:26
best spa vacation deals	2006-03-27 20:04:09
maternity clothes	2006-03-28 09:28:25
outlets gaffney sc	2006-03-28 10:44:40
pottery barn furniture outlet	2006-03-28 10:49:09
furniture outlets nc	2006-03-28 11:14:29
pregnancy workout videos	2006-03-29 10:01:39
buns of steel video	2006-03-29 10:12:38
what is yoga	2006-03-29 12:17:31
what is theistic	2006-03-29 12:18:19
what is theism	2006-03-29 12:18:30
hindu religion	2006-03-29 12:18:56
yoga and hindu	2006-03-29 12:32:05
is yoga aligned with christianity	2006-03-29 12:33:18
yoga and christianity	2006-03-29 12:33:42
whitney houston	2006-03-31 11:29:33
www.coffeecup.com	2006-03-31 11:39:45
the coffee cup charlotte nc	2006-03-31 11:40:09
ashley stewart	2006-04-01 13:19:07
lane bryant	2006-04-01 13:22:40
www.patients.digichart.com	2006-04-05 20:04:37
federal government jobs	2006-04-06 18:16:16
jewelry television	2006-04-06 19:06:03
abortion clinics charlotte nc	2006-04-17 11:00:02
greater carolinas womens center	2006-04-17 11:40:22
can christians be forgiven for abortion	2006-04-17 21:14:19
roe vs. wade	2006-04-17 22:22:07
www.livethroughmusic.com	2006-04-17 23:17:41
effects of abortion on fibroids	2006-04-18 06:50:34
effects of fibroids on abortion	2006-04-18 06:55:57
abortion fibroids	2006-04-18 06:59:32
abortion clinic charlotte	2006-04-18 15:14:03
symptoms of miscarriage	2006-04-18 16:14:07
mecklenburg aquatics center	2006-04-18 19:39:00
water aerobics charlotte nc	2006-04-18 19:41:27
abortion clinic charlotte nc	2006-04-18 21:45:49
50th birthday gift	2006-04-20 07:51:19
total woman vitamins	2006-04-20 16:38:16
esteem vitamins	2006-04-20 16:42:42
engagement gifts	2006-04-20 16:57:04
zales outlet	2006-04-20 17:41:03
50th birthday gift ideas	2006-04-20 17:50:16

mom's turning 50	2006-04-20 17:51:13
high risk abortions	2006-04-20 17:53:49
abortion fibroid	2006-04-20 17:55:18
benefits of water aerobics	2006-04-20 23:25:50
new homes charlotte nc	2006-04-24 17:15:05
ethan allen	2006-04-25 15:55:48
wedding gown styles	2006-04-26 19:37:34
hewlitt packard computers	2006-05-05 13:15:15
ibm computers	2006-05-05 13:18:11
dell	2006-05-05 15:28:08
www.gateway	2006-05-05 19:12:13
notebook computer product reviews	2006-05-06 16:19:51
www.wedddingchannel.org	2006-05-06 21:22:18
define - oscillating	2006-05-07 11:21:35
st lawrence homes	2006-05-07 12:21:23
eastwood homes	2006-05-07 12:31:55
ryland homes	2006-05-07 12:41:41
www.substanceabusepreventionservices.org	2006-05-14 13:21:50
virginia credit union	2006-05-14 23:02:46
hgtv	2006-05-16 18:43:34
test taking tips	2006-05-18 14:49:58
northern star credit union	2006-05-19 18:23:08
hotel deals	2006-05-19 21:11:21
courtyard new carrollton	2006-05-19 23:27:55
dead sea scrolls	2006-05-19 23:35:13
dead sea scrolls discovery place	2006-05-19 23:35:44
blueletterbible.org	2006-05-21 07:24:00
recover after miscarriage	2006-05-22 18:17:53
travel deals	2006-05-24 16:27:52
combat uterine fibroids	2006-05-24 16:28:31
degenerative vertebrate	2006-05-25 20:58:19
degenerative disc	2006-05-25 20:59:16
demetrios bridesmaid dresses	2006-05-26 19:32:52
marry your live-in	2006-05-27 07:25:45
juice fasting	2006-05-31 11:54:14
www.healthyliving.com	2006-05-31 12:48:29
community pathways	2006-05-31 13:11:09
carolinas healthcare system	2006-05-31 13:12:48
family specialist	2006-05-31 13:17:29
what is the average merit raise	2006-05-31 13:31:41

The story here is truer than ego would ever permit; as unintended for public scrutiny as the telling gesture of a stranger on the street who believes she is unobserved—is it only the novelist who doesn't

209

require the name to envision the whole person? American dreams and worries are adrift, forever current, within the massive servers that conserve them—672378's dreams of a baby, of a happy father for it, of a wedding; dreams of new furniture, a new home, of a get-away vacation, of a better job, of healthier ways of living; worries about sin, about the emotional and physical impact of medical ordeals; and those strange wild cards (nightstand use?); all will out-last the dark nights and bright days that gave rise to them. And as one reads this plain document, a simple enumeration of the compli-cated things on one woman's mind, it's difficult not to read *into* it—did 672378 look up miscarriage symptoms on May 14 so that she could smoothly lie about having "lost" the baby after having an abor-tion? Did she resolve to have the child with or without "him" only to suffer a miscarriage around May 21? Did she lose the baby because of some substance abuse problem she belatedly sought help with? Did "he" have the substance abuse problem? But as long as it endures, and as true, as minutely real, as it is, this is no second and more durable life, it is only another document positing with each affirmative the expansiveness of the unknown awaiting our inter-pretation, and interpretation is no more than the empty hole we fill with our own reckoning. Elvis does not "live on"; death is that moment when any possibility of learning the unknown is lost, when the inadequate sum of what is known becomes the totality of what there is to know.

Narratologically, this isn't much help. What we like and respond to, in forming the narratives that give our lives and those around us coherent meaning, is something far more than the unadorned accounting of 672378's lonely keystrokes. Think of DePalma's *Black Dahlia,* in which Aaron Eckhart pretending to be a detective watches Mia Kirshner pretending to be the murdered Elizabeth Short pre-tending to be someone else in one of the silent stag movies she made; Eckhart's rapt face is a testament to the phony power of "living on."

MY FATHER

If I seem to be cynical about a perfectly inoffensive way of ordering reality, it may be because of my father. I tried all this business with him (let me say here that the building-up-to-it method I discuss above proved to be of absolutely no help in dealing with his illness and death; the absence of his particular presence ruined who I'd been and made a different man of me) and it made no sense. My father was a wonderful writer (*pace* the blogger—another potential immortal, of course—who wrote that 2006 was turning out to be a great year for literature because Pynchon had published another book and Sorrentino had died), and as such his books leave me with something of considerable substance, but it was as a father that I loved him. Besides, the books make up an artistic legacy, and a public one; there are scores of "sons" out there who can take from those books precisely what I can, and who have no interest in trying to extract from them what I can't, his essence.

That's thorny, isn't it? Another thing we want to believe is that the artist invests himself in his work. Wit, intelligence, facility, profundity, skill, style—all are present, each individually amounts to more than the whole of 672378's found drama, but neither are they life.

I made a Super 8 film of my father once; like nearly everything else from my childhood, it's long gone. It was an actual filmmaking project, titled *Pop on Memorial Day*, which suggests that a suitable subtitle might have indicated that I was home from school, bored, and probably had received the camera about ten days earlier for my birthday. Certainly I wasn't thinking of posterity; I was thinking about getting the developed reel back from the lab and running it through my little Bell & Howell projector. Does he live on in this film in a way that he does not through his books? Certainly, if it were to be restored to me, the film would depict many of the lost corners of my life, because for my parents (unlike for me) only a handful of material things ever accrued sufficient sentimental value to require their preservation, but the film would only confirm the things, in altogether inadequate shadowed blurs, that no document is necessary for me to remember, and the memory of my parents' tables and chairs, appliances and decorations; the combination of the timeless comforts of high bohemia and the dated 1970s particulars is more than enough.

The memory of my father is not enough. When I think abstractly of "my father," the image my mind summons forth is of him at about this time—1973, when he was a year younger than I am now—and of his ultrapredictable habits and mannerisms I would likewise never need a film to remind me of. The only time my father ever surprised me was when he got sick and died.

My father would have ridiculed the suggestion that he'd devoted his life to leaving a record of himself, or of his thoughts, and he would have been especially scornful of the idea that a record of any kind could substitute for, let alone possess, life. He wanted to make things that were beautiful yet, as he put it once, "do not live." He made that clear to me so that I'd always know it. What I always knew I should have known better; I look at the shelves and shelves of books—about twenty-five hundred, I figured during a recent move—everything lying in wait within the dark pages between the two covers, every conceivable situation, and the inconceivable ones, helping not a bit.

Four Poems
Ted Mathys

PAIR OF HOOVES

One began as a front hoof and one began as a rear hoof. As a remedy they were coated in a baking-soda-and-water paste and placed in a plastic bag, frozen overnight. In the morning they were both front hooves, but one was larger than the other. As a remedy they were submerged in isopropyl alcohol and exposed to intense UV rays. They then rivaled each other in size, but one was darker. As a remedy, they were massaged with tea tree and lavender oils. Both attained the color of rust, but then one hoof was to the right of the other, and one hoof was to the left of the other. As a remedy, they were dunked in a bath with a ratio of ten to one water to bleach. They surfaced with a newfound contiguousness, but then one hoof was a deer hoof and one hoof was an ox hoof. As a remedy they were laced with daisies between their Vs and sent down the river. When they arrived, they belonged to the same animal, but one hoof was living and one hoof was dead. And they smelled of the living and of the dead. As a remedy, a toothbrush was used to scrub and scrub until the living one bled and the dead one twitched, both in occlusion to "the nothing that is."

A PLANE OF CONSISTENCY
IN THE EQUIVOCATIONS OF GOD

A horse is a vain hope for deliverance; the vision pertains to the days yet future; in the past was written to each of us; there is a future for a man of peace; there is knowledge in the past, it will pass; they came forward and carried them; startled and bent forward; they will go and fall backward, be injured and snared; for our backsliding is great; fell backward off his chair; his livestock ahead of him; ahead and bowed down to the ground seven times; a hornet ahead; in a pillar of cloud;

work he had been doing; where his tent had been earlier; you have
been set apart; and the owner has been warned; today or tomorrow
we will go to this or that city; with a quota of bricks yesterday or
today, as before; the grass withers and the flowers fall; who can add
a single hour; a man's life does not consist; keep watch over the door
of my lips; yesterday at the seventh hour; to royal position for such
a time; to him for a time, times and half a time.

BICYCLES AND TREES

The question was an oak tree destroying itself. And the answer was
an acorn. Then the question was the acorn destroying itself. And the
answer was another oak tree. In a field of endless green. Then the
question was the right pedal coming up. And the answer was the left
pedal going down. Then the question was the left pedal coming up.
And the answer was the bicycle gliding through lunchtime toward
the oak and the oak gliding through lifetimes toward nothing. In a
field of endless green. Then the bike collided with the tree, and the
oak was destroyed, and the bike was destroyed, and the pedals were
scattered, and the trunk had a gash. Thus began the discussion. In a
field of endless green. Some were collecting reflectors and acorns.
Some were dismayed at the pause. One found the answer to be progression, but what was the damaging question?

A PLANE OF CONSISTENCY
IN THE MISDEEDS OF THE BODY

Come forward, carry your relatives; from that day forward; of those
who shrink back and are destroyed; their horde of faces moves forward; they collect captives like sand; then they walked in backward
and covered their faces; bite the horse's heels so that its rider tum-
bles backward; go ahead and do it; look straight ahead; ahead of time;
I have been commanded; and he has been guilty; ahead in a narrow
place where there is no room to turn; water has been put on the seed
and a carcass falls; do not boast about tomorrow; we were born only
yesterday and know nothing; the same yesterday, today; her unclean-
ness was in her skirts; she did not consider her future; when I see

the blood, I will pass over you; do not dwell on the past; neither present nor future, nor any powers, neither height nor depth; at the appointed time; my times are carried on the pinions of eagle wings; broad is the road; times and half a time, out of reach.

Bayham Street
Robert Clark

I HAD A SISTER WHOM I hardly knew, whose existence I might doubt entirely if it were not for some photographs that show us together. I can see her, you might say, in my mind's eye, but only in one dimension: I'm not sure I can say what she "was like," how her features, bearing, and voice seemed in their entirety. Up to a point, I might have been able to piece her together—to imagine if not a story, at least a character—through the photographs. But a photograph is no more than a refraction in a moment that nothing other than a lens ever saw, scarcely a pinprick in the fabric that veils a life. A photograph seems to contain and to mean much more than that, but perhaps what it does most of all is to induce longing, a hunger for everything—the day and the persons and the place—that it does not contain and which is irretrievably lost to us.

So sensing, perhaps, that it was a dead end, that it would end in bafflement and frustration, I didn't pursue the trail of this sister I'd scarcely even met—I haven't even bothered to mention her name, Patty—but someone sent me another photograph. When my grandparents' house was cleared out, their books were donated to the local library and, sifting through the cartons, a librarian found a photo album. She knew my name and sent it to me.

It was a tiny thing, the pages just big enough to hold one small photo each of me, my siblings, and cousins. It had belonged to my grandmother, and I'd seen pretty much every photo in it, these having been widely circulated among the family; every photo but one, that of a little girl, perhaps four years old, in a green dress on a red sofa against a green wall. She has a fierce look, of insouciance and even defiance. Her arms are crossed in a kind of resigned impatience. She could not care less and yet she insists that you pay attention to her. I thought I knew who it was—the album contained nothing but my grandmother's grandchildren—but the little girl's demeanor threw me off. This child wasn't anything like what I had understood or had remembered Patty to be.

I sent the picture to my other sister, who's five years older than I

and was two years Patty's senior. She didn't recall seeing it before, but she confirmed that it was our sister: Patty, who had been diagnosed as mentally retarded when she was two; confined to an institution; who was put (unlike me and my sister) in my father's custody when my parents divorced; who subsequently developed into a child with normal psychological and cognitive functioning; and who died—by then a bright and vivacious young woman—in a head-on collision during her second year of college.

Her transformation had been dramatic, even miraculous, and no one ever explained quite how it came about. There'd been a psychiatrist in Boston, a Dr. Fleming, but beyond the fact that someone had done some sort of therapy with Patty, the secret, as the cliché says, died with her. But by all reports she was someone else entirely as an infant and small child or, rather, she was almost no one at all. I was an infant then, but my sister remembers Patty's visits home from the institution. She wanted to play with Patty the way a big sister should play with her little sister. But Patty wouldn't play. She sat. Or sat and stared. Sometimes she said strange or incomprehensible things. She said, "Kalifidos," by which my sister eventually figured out she meant "cowboy."

Other people had reported similar things: She was slow, vacant, abstracted. And there were other photos that seemed to corroborate that view. In her baby pictures, she's doughy, ill defined, never quite roused from sleep. In a later photo, she's about two, and she's standing in front of a mirror trying to comb her hair. She's smiling avidly, as if she's amusing herself by combing the hair of this *other* child, the one she sees in the mirror. Either way, she's been photographed unawares—unlike any of her other childhood photos—and, also uniquely, she's smiling. She thinks she's alone, just her and perhaps this other little girl who lives in the mirror. And so she is happy.

That photo was taken on one of Patty's visits home from her institution. My mother and father were still living together, although their marriage was disintegrating. And perhaps Patty—the shame and worry and disappointment of her—was a factor, a shadow cast over their happiness, a vacuum that deprived them of oxygen, that caused the flame between them to die. In any case, it was said that my mother couldn't cope with Patty or, for that matter, very much else.

In fact, the most specific explanation any of us ever heard for Patty's condition had to do with my mother, with something she had done or failed to do for this daughter of hers. Part of the vagueness and mystery surrounding the matter attaches to the fact that none of us is quite sure with whom the story originated. But the gist of it was that my mother had caused Patty to withdraw, to hide or disappear, to annihilate herself.

There's one more photo that perhaps bears out something like this. She's looking at the camera, or at a person near the camera. Her mouth is slightly open, the upper lip just arched upward as though she's about to speak or is beginning to register some surprise. As in the other photos, she's wearing a smocked dress and here she has a little purse slung over her shoulder. But this grown-up accessory doesn't delight her as the comb did in the other photograph: It looks like it's been pasted on her. Alongside the purse, her arm is stretched out, underside up, as though someone's about to draw blood from it. You come to her eyes last, despite the fact that they're dark, shiny, perhaps terrified. They're plangent, but somehow lack the capacity or will to cry. They're bright but stony, anthracite, obsidian. She's terrified or dead or, rather, she's as afraid of dying as she is of living.

I first heard the idea that my mother was the author of Patty's condition when I was perhaps thirteen. Just then, I'd been reading Freud—more accurately, popularizations of Freud—and it seemed quite reasonable to me that a mother might do this to a child, or wish to (and in the Freudian cosmology wishing and doing were much the same thing): It was within a mother's powers of oppression and repression, active or passive, to crush a child or cause her to disappear into herself.

Anyway, it went without saying in the years between, say, 1955 and 1965, that it was at least in large part my mother's fault, and that she would, of course, herself appreciate this fact—she'd majored in child psychology in college—and be ashamed of it. Even without knowing quite why and how, she'd victimized this little girl, and she'd driven her husband away, or he'd left in disgust.

But that is not what struck me in the photograph I'd been sent. Far from being diffident or passive, she is intense, maybe even angry. She dominates the frame that encloses her and the colors that ought to subsume her. Her presence is such that she might almost come out of the photograph, thrust herself before you, and spit, "Kalifidos" in your face.

But, as someone pointed out right away, more than anything, she looks like me, like a shard of my family, like all of us who survived her, who persisted here after she was gone.

I received that photo in the mail perhaps three years ago, and although I felt the imposition, the demand it seemed to make every time I looked at it, I did nothing about it. My other sister, however, was going to pursue the matter: She, after all, had known Patty. She lived in Massachusetts, where Patty had spent most of her life, and she would look into her case. I, meanwhile, was chasing down other things, all of them missing or lost. I went to Bayham Street instead.

Charles Dickens lived on Bayham Street, Camden Town, London, in 1822, age ten, in a house of yellow brick. And there, staring out the window of "the little back garret," commenced the worst period of his life. On account of his family's penury, he was pulled out of school and put to work ten hours a day in a blacking factory under Hungerford Bridge. His father was thrown into the debtors' prison at Marshalsea. Charles lived on Bayham Street scarcely a year—his family moved constantly in order to evade their creditors—but it was the first place he lived in London and in some ways the last; in his imagination, he seemed to inhabit it for the rest of his days.

It was definitely the house of the Cratchits in *A Christmas Carol* and of Mr. Micawber in *David Copperfield.* The view from the garret window of the dome of St. Paul's shrouded in smoke and fog is surely Pip's first vision of London in *Great Expectations.* And it was, for me, the first source of Little Dorrit's view from Southwark

bridge, the panorama she would carry with her to Italy. I felt that in that garret—ashamed, oppressed by his child labor, and half orphaned—Dickens took his emptiness, the void he might have become, and began to make it into art. I wanted to see where this had happened, to see what traces of it might still persist.

I went to London three times over the next two years and on each trip I went to Bayham Street. It's an ugly, straight swatch of row houses, flats, and public housing projects running south from Camden Town underground station. The first time I walked down one side of Bayham Street to its terminus at Crowndale Road—perhaps three-quarters of a mile—and back up the other side, looking for the blue plaque that marks buildings with historical and literary associations in London. But there were no plaques on Bayham Street. It seemed impossible that anyplace in London connected with Dickens wasn't marked in this fashion, least of all his first boyhood home in the city. Perhaps I'd made a mistake about the name of the street.

At home I rechecked the address, and when I returned to London six months later I brought the house number with me. I now knew the address was 16 Bayham Street. But though there were dozens of small brick houses of early nineteenth-century vintage, none of them corresponded to that address. So there was no number 16 and no blue plaque either. It occurred to me that perhaps the house had stood on the site of one of the vast blocks of public housing flats—built, it seemed, in the 1960s or '70s—at the south end of the street, and that in their construction both the houses, the address, and the blue plaque might have vanished. Perhaps I was the only person who had any interest in finding or seeing the house; perhaps I was the only person who understood how important that place had been. And in this thought I took a sort of melancholy pride. But either way, I had to accept that neither the house nor the place where it stood seemed to exist.

The next time I went to London, in the spring of 2005, I had no plans to visit Bayham Street. I'd spent the previous five days in Germany walking for six hours a day, and thanks to a pair of ill-fitting shoes my feet were almost bloody with abrasions and blisters. I was stopping in London for twenty hours to catch my breath and wait until my flight home left the next day.

That next morning I went to Gower Street in Bloomsbury to shop for books. The Dickenses had lived on Gower Street after vacating 16 Bayham Street, after Charles's father had been sent to Marshalsea. I wasn't moved by this fact—I think I'd forgotten it just then—but by a sense almost of dereliction, of having left something that ought to be done undone. So, with a plane to catch in a little over two hours, I took the tube to Camden Town.

I walked quickly over to Bayham Street and started down the west side, no number 16 and no blue plaques visible anywhere. In the distance I could see the end of the street at Crowndale Road, and I asked myself if I was really going to walk the whole way down; if

I really needed to repeat this pointless trek in its entirety a third time. I had a plane to catch and a ten-hour flight to endure. So I compromised. I walked another block to where the modern housing projects began—the point beyond which there were no nineteenth-century buildings—and crossed over to the east side of the street. I swear I surveyed every facade of every house between there and the underground station but I found nothing at all.

I went back to my hotel, got my bag, and rode the train to the airport. I was angry that I'd wasted yet more of my limited time abroad on Bayham Street, but at the same time I felt a kind of guilt, a sense that if I had only tried harder or looked more carefully I would have found Dickens's house. And as stupid and futile as I knew the impulse was, there was no other solution to my disappointment—to ease the longing, to complete the quest—than to go back to Bayham Street another time on another trip.

I was disappointed even before I'd gotten to London. I'd been in Italy for six weeks and then in Germany for a few days afterward. I'd gone to Germany specifically to visit Dresden and then Weimar. From the reading I'd done and the music I'd listened to, it came to seem to me that for one hundred and fifty years—from the late eighteenth through the first third of the twentieth century—Germany had possessed perhaps the most brilliant philosophic, scientific, and creative minds in the western world. Then, in scarcely a decade, it had descended into the deepest barbarity humankind has ever known. This is a now commonplace observation. It wasn't entirely clear to me whether it described a paradox or a necessary relation, an inevitability, but I wanted to see the evidence for it for myself.

For me Weimar and Dresden represented the poles of that history. Bucolic, cobbled, parklike Weimar was the home of Goethe and the Romantic movement, Germany's intellectual and literary heart, and the site of the foundation of its last democratic government before Hitler. Dresden, the baroque capital of the kingdom of Saxony, had once been called "Florence on the Elbe." It was a center of German music and opera and an artists' colony that sheltered Schumann, Wagner, Ibsen, Caspar David Friedrich, and Dostoyevsky. Its museums were the best in Germany, and contained, among other masterpieces, Raphael's *Sistine Madonna*, the painting the nineteenth century considered the most beautiful artwork in the world. In the final months of World War II, Dresden and perhaps fifty thousand of its inhabitants were incinerated in a firestorm of Allied bombing, the greatest conflagration in the western theater of the war. Whether portrayed as an act of slaughter and destruction unjustified by any military need or as a well-deserved retribution for the Nazi horrors, the annihilation of Dresden seemed to me to mark the final extinction of the German genius and civilization born at Weimar.

In Dresden, I'd checked into a postmodern edifice called the ArtHotel. My room was elegantly spare, decorated in black, gray, and blond wood. It overlooked the city soccer stadium, the assembly point over which the British bombers had fanned out on their incendiary runs sixty years before. You would not have known that from looking at it, or by turning in the opposite direction, to the southeast, where the bombs fell. Excepting the city's reconstructed baroque churches and palaces, most of the buildings in Dresden were erected after 1950. The more appealing among them are in the mode of the ArtHotel, but the majority are examples of Soviet Modernism from the era of the German Democratic Republic. The rubble and ruins have been completely vanquished, but a vista of empty form imposed on a waste ground—the ash meadow, the field sown with salt—stands in their place.

But it was ruins, or the remnants of them, I had come to see. I wanted to see cinders and scorched bricks, a baroque statue, perhaps decapitated or armless, tilted at an impossible angle but still standing on a darkling field of debris, a waft of phosphorous on the air. I wanted if not the dead themselves the places in which they died, the stage upon which their holocaust had been acted out.

There are a host of stories about the horror of the firestorm and its aftermath that might drive anyone, man or child, mad, unspeakable things that might turn you to stone were you to see them: cellars, for example, packed with asphyxiated, bloated corpses of mothers and children inside which recovery workers could scarcely keep their footing on account of the carpet of maggots covering the floors. During the bombing Dresdeners instinctively took shelter there but the updraft of the firestorm outside literally sucked the oxygen from the basements.

The air temperature rose into the hundreds of degrees. Many people fled to the bank of the Elbe and immersed themselves in the water. Others tried to evade the heat by hiding in water tanks and fountains. But as the air temperature increased, the water in the fountains heated as well. Those who sheltered in them were boiled alive and then the water itself evaporated, leaving their corpses beached in the empty pools.

There is a photograph I came across that illustrates this phenomenon, and while I found it moving—it shows that there was literally nowhere to go, no escape from the firestorm—I suppose it also exercised a morbid fascination upon me. The fountain was in the Altmarkt or close by it, and I spent some hours scouring the area looking for it in the same hopeful and frustrated manner I'd searched Bayham Street, and to no more avail.

All that, seemingly every trace, has been erased. The past has been carted away, leveled, and paved over. It was not simply that there was no sign of the past—no ruins or reminders—but that even the presence of the past had been obliterated: Even the absence of what once was had been taken away. The past is, of course, dead, but here it had apparently never lived.

The Dresdeners of today are proud of their city, of its flawless replication of historic buildings and the cutting-edge architecture of its new ones. But for me, the excision of the past seemed to spill over into the present. The present too felt empty. That evening, my feet sore from the day's futile reconnaissance, I ate alone in my hotel's chic dining room. For whatever reason—a lack of out-of-town visitors or locals accustomed to dining out—the room seemed a stylish void, its gray walls too gray, the light a little too stark. The waiter stood nervously behind the bar or disappeared into the shelter of the kitchen. Music—the forlorn ranting of Leonard Cohen—echoed from the sound system. I felt lonely and grieving. I missed my family. I missed everyone I'd ever known, or known of.

The next morning I went to see the *Sistine Madonna*, the painting that transfixed the nineteenth century, the golden age of the annihilated Germany that once existed nowhere as much as in Dresden. It had preoccupied the people who preoccupied me: For Ruskin, it was the beginning of the end of art, the triumph of the artificial and the artificer over Gothic faith and naturalism manifested

223

by the anonymous craftsman, but for Dostoyevsky it represented the stunning intersection of the numinous and beautiful. It had been secreted underground outside the city and had survived the firestorm.

I hoped to either love it as much as Dostoyevsky or disdain it as had Ruskin, or at least try to see some of what the past—the dead of one hundred fifty years ago—had seen in it. If nothing else, unlike Dresden, it was present, intact. There's a round banquette placed just in front of the painting, and you can sit before it like a fire or an altar. So I did.

You know it, this painting. Or rather you at least know *them:* the indolent and resigned putti at the bottom of the frame. To us, that tranche of the *Sistine Madonna* is almost an artwork in its own right and—to judge by its constant reproduction on calendars, posters, and consumer whatnot—as much a talisman of art in the late twentieth/early twenty-first century as the entire painting was in the nineteenth. And what makes this image iconic for us is the obvious fact that these angels are a couple of comedians, wiseacres and ironists. The curtains on either side of the frame have been pulled back to reveal Mary, her baby, and their papal attendants. It's—if you will—"The Madonna Show" and those little guys are the stagehands. They're not impressed, they've seen it before, and they're waiting for it to be over. These putti are cute but knowing, even hip. In their recognizance of what's happening they're recognizably us, of our time.

Of course they're really of Raphael's time, but perhaps their seeming membership in ours reveals something about the nature of a work of art: its capacity to project a presence—a transcendent yet objective being—independent of any epoch, including its own. Or perhaps it merely allows for interpretations—projections that come from us rather than the artwork—that our subjective circumstances incline us to make. At any rate, these putti seem themselves to be offering an interpretation of what's going on above them, a sardonic or at least comic commentary on the picture they're a part of.

You might say that what the putti—these moderns with wings—are commenting on is precisely what the nineteenth century loved about this painting: its notion of beauty as spectacle, as a parting of the curtains to reveal a view of the divine, of heaven. The Madonna and her attendants are standing on clouds, and they too are a little vaporous, particularly the Madonna herself, whose tender beauty is somehow unboundaried, as though diffusing the light she contains. In truth, she was, to me, a little vague, not quite present. But the nineteenth century loved words like "diaphanous" and "effusion" and perhaps it loved this painting for so embodying them. For me, however, the Madonna's compassion and illumination did not so much shine as leak from her, puddling in a watery sweetness. In our time, at least, Rothko's layered nimbuses, his lozenges of fulminating color, may seem deeper and truer, may better signify the transcendent.

For all that, she seemed to me the first emphatically real historic presence I'd encountered in Dresden. She wasn't a replica, a reproduction, or a symbol of something missing or lost. But she also wasn't particular to this place. She could project herself—her facticity as art—anywhere. But I had come here to find genuine traces of something I felt I needed to comprehend, markers that were more than symbols or plaques or monuments. I wanted, if not the flames of the firestorm, a whiff of their smoke, a sign of their onetime presence here.

I ate a delicious piece of lemon cake in the reconstructed baroque café near the reconstructed opera house on whose site Wagner and Richard Strauss had premiered their works. I began walking back to the ArtHotel and it was snowing, turning darker and colder. The weather was coming in from the north and the east, from Poland and Russia, from the taiga and the steppes, the deep primal backyard—the shadow self, perhaps—Germany had so many times tried to enslave or destroy.

The avenue that led back to the hotel cut through what had been

225

the royal precincts of the electors of Saxony, the princes who had made this place "Florence on the Elbe." Along one side were several office and apartment blocks from the GDR, and along the other, stretching at least one or more blocks, was a vacant lot, a thicket of trees, brush, and abandoned refuse and junk. At its far corner, jutting out from the tangle of bare trees and shrubs, huddled in the east wind and its scattershot of snow, stood the facade of what once must have been a small but imposing building.

As I came closer, I saw there was an inscription over the portal in the center cut in early nineteenth-century characters. It said ORANGERIE. The gateway was barricaded and braced with wood, as were the windows and the doors to either side. The stone was covered in places with graffiti and posters, and otherwise cracked, pocked, and stained. It might have been due to weathering, subsidence, and vandalism, but also, given its placement directly on the bombers' track, from heat, flame, and shrapnel.

When the building was intact, it must have had an ornate glass carapace beneath which orange and lemon trees were cultivated. Amongst them, in the custom of the time, the elector and his court might have taken tea and imagined themselves on the Bay of Naples. Now the building was pathetic twice over, once as an architectural folly consecrated to growing oranges where oranges could not grow and now as the shabby remnant of a once great but now deposed kingdom and culture. The portal was like the curtain of the *Sistine Madonna,* a hundred-and-fifty-year-old opening onto an ersatz Eden, and today, as the gelid wind blew in from the east, onto a GDR barricade with an overgrown lot behind it.

It was too cold to linger, too cold, in fact, to go out for the rest of the day, and I was catching a train to Weimar the next morning. But in the night, I realized that the Orangerie was what I had come to Dresden to see, or that it was going to be the best I could do—a real sign, a ruined but intact presence of the firestorm and the world it had incinerated. In the morning, on the way to the station, I lugged my bag to the curb opposite and took a picture. The snow had turned to sleet and most of what had fallen the day before was melting beneath a southwest wind, from the direction of Weimar and of Naples.

Weimar was, on its face, everything that Dresden failed to be. There were old burghers' houses, venerable squares, churchyards flocked with birds, and a long park that wended along the river to Goethe's summer cottage, which, even empty, suggested the presence of children, of little girls in pinafores and smocked dresses in some eternal golden past. But most of all there was the light, on that day blue and gold, and you might well imagine why Goethe had become fascinated by optics and the science of color; why, it was said, his last words on his deathbed were *"mehr licht"*—"more light."

The town is built less of stone or brick than plaster and wood, and the predominant colors are pine green, a pale butter yellow, and a deep amber, the hue of the German dying fall, a register removed from the olive, lemon, and russet of Italy. Goethe was, of course, the original northern European Italophile, the author of the verses Schubert set to music in praise of Italy as the antidote to Romantic longing and melancholy.

As the cradle of German Romanticism, Weimar has, of course, a magnificent cemetery, a rolling cavern of conifers and vines. But then perhaps Weimar itself is one vast graveyard that we amicably share with benign ghosts, its muses and geniuses, the dead with

227

whom—having not been annihilated by history and its fires—we live in a parallel dimension, just adjoining theirs.

I got lost in the cemetery and I didn't mind at all. I couldn't find my way out to the southeast exit I believed ought to lead to Nietzsche's house. At last I found a gate that gave onto a street of nineteenth-century houses, the Victorian suburbs of Weimar. Nietzsche's house—or, rather, his sister's house, where, frail and demented, he spent the last thirteen years of life—lay somewhere nearby. I found it on a busy road descending a hill, a garden sloping away from one side of it. It was a boxy, mansard-roofed house, its volume restricted as though by a corset. There was a fussy conservatory porch on one side of it, and I supposed Nietzsche must have been wheeled out here most days to take a little sun. I supposed he stared out into the garden, dozed and muttered to himself, and drooled.

It's a mediocre house of brick, the epitome of the upright bourgeois contentment that Nietzsche held in deepest contempt. Like Goethe, he'd taken shelter in Italy. He wrote his last book, *Ecce Homo*, in Turin, and then he went mad and finished up in this faux villa. If there is any mercy, he never knew where he was. It seemed that the spirit of German genius I'd sought in Dresden was born perhaps three-quarters of a mile away at Goethe's house and had died just here.

I'd come to Germany from Italy myself. Before Dresden, I spent two months in Umbria, writing and teaching American undergraduates. The town was called Orvieto, and it is famous for a crisp white wine and for its Duomo, which contains frescoes by Fra Angelico and Signorelli. It's a big church for such a small town, owing to two facts: that, on a high and secure plateau not far from Rome, the medieval popes frequently took refuge here, and also that it was the locus of the miracle of Bolsena, the event that put the important feast of Corpus Christi on the church calendar.

The miracle takes the substance and form of many such stories—apocryphal hokum frothed up into transcendent epiphany—and goes like this: It seems that a German priest, Peter of Prague, stopped at Bolsena to say his daily mass en route to Rome. He was a good and pious priest but one who found it difficult to believe that Christ was actually present in the consecrated host. On that day, however, as he said the words of the consecration, blood began to seep from the host, to trickle over his hands, to drip onto the altar and the corporal. The priest immediately went to Orvieto, where the pope was then in residence, and the authenticity of the miracle was confirmed. The feast was officially instituted a year later.

I don't know how much this would have normally interested me: I am reserved and a bit cerebral in my Catholicism, and I find myself a little embarrassed by devotions of a too sweaty and visceral sort, those involving relics, flaming hearts, tears, and, as here, blood. But in the miracle of Bolsena there was one more key figure besides Peter of Prague and Pope Urban IV: Thomas Aquinas. Thomas is, of course, *the* great Catholic theologian, utterly devout but rigorously intellectual. He marshaled, as much as anyone ever has, the reasons one ought to believe—the logic and system of God and his creation—and he's deepened, insofar as I understand him, my admittedly shallow faith. He's also "difficult" in the contemporary sense and, in my considerable vainglory, I like the feeling of belonging to the elite who try to take him on.

So I was intrigued to discover that Thomas had been involved in the affair of Bolsena; that he'd been in Orvieto at the time in 1263 and Urban had put him on the case, so to speak, as both an investigator of the miracle and the author of the liturgy in which the feast day was to be formalized. On further investigation, I learned that Thomas's residence in Orvieto was not half a block from the apartment I was living in. Like Bayham Street and the hotels in Rome and Naples my grandfather had stayed in a hundred years ago that I'd also been trying to locate, this was a search, both archaeological and intellectual, I had to undertake.

Thomas's home in Orvieto was on the present-day Piazza XXIX Novembre, where my son had been playing soccer every day with the neighborhood kids. The piazza was dominated by a 1930s-era building used as a military barracks, but in one corner stood the church of San Domenico. I'd been looking at it as I oversaw Andrew's play in the center of the square. On its flank, adjacent to the barracks, the exterior wall of the nave showed signs of what once must have been another wing of the building just as tall as the rest of the church: the shadow of an enormous arch, of buttresses removed, of truncated columns, of an open space now sealed with stone. I spent some time trying to figure out what this signified. I went inside the church, both at mass (the parish was one of the most vibrant of the town) and afterward, and what I saw inside was as confusing as the outside: columns with one side stripped away as though by a cleaver, and others whose feet didn't align with their trunks or that terminated halfway up the wall for no reason. More happily, there were also some signs of Thomas here: a patch of thirteenth-century fresco and, more substantially, an oak box said to contain the chair in which he wrote, taught, and prayed.

In those two materials, the wood and the paint on the wall, Thomas was, I felt, still vaguely present in the church of San Domenico, although perhaps only he could tell you precisely to what extent and in what manner. Thomas's great preoccupation was the relation between the seen and the unseen, between things and their sources, between their material substance and the form in which they appear, contained in the flux of time and space. In this, he was attempting to fit the philosophical realism of Aristotle (whose writings had just been rediscovered by medievals) to Christian theology and revelation. You might say he was trying to square matter with spirit, no easy task, then or now.

Thomas was particularly well suited to investigate the miracle at Bolsena. What had transpired with Peter of Prague represented a momentary tear in the veil separating the physical and spiritual aspects of the sacrament of the Eucharist. One definition of a sacrament is "an outward and visible sign of an inward and invisible grace," but in this case the unseen—the actual transformation of bread and wine into Christ's body and blood—had become utterly tangible.

Admittedly, this notion of the "real presence" is one of the more difficult—not to say, for some, incredible—doctrines of the church. Christians intuited it from Christ's words at the Last Supper ("This is my body"), but it was Thomas, with help from Aristotle, who worked out its underlying logic. Things, according to Aristotle, consist of substances and "accidents," their essential matter and the visible form in which that matter manifests itself. For example, you might say that ice, liquid water, and vapor are all accidents of the substance H_2O. In the Mass, the substances of bread and wine are transformed into Christ's body and blood while retaining their original outward accidents.

This is still a miracle—it transcends what seem to us the laws of science—but by Thomas's lights it is a logical and explicable one. It's also consistent with Thomas's Aristotelian realism, his understanding of the independent, objective existence of the world and the things in it that present themselves to us. As against Platonic idealism, in which sense impressions are formed not from things themselves but from imperfect replicas of them, created things are what they appear to be and in being created imply a creator. Since prior to creation nothing exists but the creator—the unmoved mover, the first cause—that creator creates through the pouring out of his own essential being. Thus Thomas maintained that "God is in all things, and intimately so": Created things are not "just" things but partake of their creator. He is present in everything, so for him to be present in the forms of bread and wine is not so great a leap after all.

There's a kind of wholehearted optimism in Thomas's thought: Created things are both real and good rather than defective or false. Thomas insisted on the real presence not only of the Eucharist but the real presence of objects and persons and therefore of their value, their worthiness to be attended and loved. For Thomas, Paul of Prague's inability to believe in the real presence was a refusal to see the reality of the real at its most profound, the indwelling of God in his creation.

To me, in Orvieto, it also seemed that Thomas must be insisting on his own presence—signs of himself—here and now that I might see. But I couldn't puzzle out the church of San Domenico, still less locate the place where Thomas had done his writing and thinking. Yet it was that trace of his presence that I really wanted to find. Meanwhile, I'd gone down to Rome to visit the Ambasciatori Palace Hotel, where my grandfather had lodged some dozen times in the 1920s and 1930s.

The Ambasciatori had been remodeled three or four times since then, most recently in the nineties *"nel rispetto dell'originaria fisionomia degli ambienti,"* "in keeping with the original appearance of the surroundings." But other than the grand staircase in the lobby, which might have contained some elements from eighty years ago, it seemed that not a single surface present in my grandfather's time had survived.

In 1934 he'd brought my father with him here as a young adolescent. Apparently my father had not been impressed by the Ambasciatori Palace either. In a letter home on hotel stationery he only complained that "I don't like speagete" and that "I never can understand what they are talking about when they try to tell us what there is to eat." He also wrote that he hoped to see Mussolini "some day when he comes out of his house," although I never knew if this wish was granted. He can't understand the things he wants to know. He can't see what he wants to see. He's unmistakably my father, and Patty's father too.

That same year, Mussolini had been at work in Orvieto, and what he did there had a bearing on the Piazza XXIX Novembre and the church of San Domenico. As in other such regimes, the Italian Fascists promoted "physical culture"—a cult of the body founded on notions of the Italian nation and race—and they wanted to establish an "Accademia Femminile di Educazione Fisica," a woman's athletic academy. The chosen location was Orvieto and the building then occupying the prospective construction site was the church of San Domenico and its cloister.

I'd learned this after my return from Rome and the Ambasciatori. Our apartment was in a palazzo belonging to an elderly couple who were natives of Orvieto. Signora Petinelli was an elegant woman in her late sixties, a skilled cook and a font of Orvietan history and culture going back to the middle ages. Her husband, *"il dottore,"* was a nattily dressed retired surgeon and art connoisseur who, that autumn, recited Catullus in Latin as he gave me a flu shot.

They knew all about San Domenico and the Accademia Femminile: It had all happened while they were children living in this neighborhood. A controversial project at the time, it pitted civic boosters who welcomed the largesse from Rome against preservationists and clergy and the congregation of San Domenico. The Fascists and the boosters won out, of course but, in a sop to the parish, a portion of the church was allowed to stand. The entire nave—the church's larger, main axis in which the congregation sat—was demolished and the transept—the church's shorter, smaller crossing axis—was transformed into a nave with a new altar at one end. The truncated pillars I'd seen inside and outside were the scars from the amputation of the original nave.

Until then San Domenico had consisted not only of the church but of gardens, a dormitory, a cloister, and a refectory where the brothers—among them Thomas—worked, ate, and slept. All that was gone, save for the rump of the transept. It did not seem enough, not as much as I wanted of Thomas's residual presence, of real signs of the reality of the great architect of realism, of the real presence.

Any Orvietan over the age of sixty-five could probably have told me what I'd wanted to know. But I didn't speak Italian well enough to form the question or, without several slow repetitions, to understand the answer. More crucially, I felt driven—perhaps almost to the point of obsession—to use only the evidence of my own eyes, however uninformed my capacity to perceive the reality of the things I was looking at. I was twice blind, both to words and to the realities of things seen and unseen.

Sigmund Freud, I later learned, had also been to Orvieto. In fact, he based the first chapter of one of his key works, *The Psychopathology of Everyday Life,* on an incident connected to Orvieto's duomo, the great church raised in response to the revelation of the real presence to Peter of Prague. On a train, Freud wanted to talk about the frescoes in the duomo, but he could not for the life of him recall the name of one of their two principal creators—Signorelli—despite having seen them on several visits. Analyzing this inexplicable lapse of memory, Freud recollected that just prior to his attempt to talk about the frescoes, he had been preoccupied with the suicide of one of his patients whose problems Freud traced to "an incurable sexual disturbance," undoubtedly homosexuality. He decided that the troubling nature of these thoughts—of sexuality and death—had caused him to forget the name of Signorelli, and upon this incident Freud subsequently formulated one of his principal discoveries, repression.

The notion that wishes, intentions, and purposes run deep within us like underground rivers is key to Freud's view of the soul. We both know and do not know what we are doing, and repression is the device whereby we square that contradiction. It's what enabled that unknown diagnostician in the 1950s to conclude that my mother might both want to drive Patty mad—withdrawing her love in such a way that Patty in turn withdrew herself entirely from the world— and yet feel she would never, ever want to do such a thing to her child; that her maternal love was double-edged, that its presence was a kind of void into which Patty might fall and disappear, consumed.

That is Freud in extreme form, Freud forgetting Signorelli's name almost as if he wished the duomo frescoes destroyed. For me, in Orvieto, I can't say that I in some way avoided the facts I thought I wanted to know. But I would say that my own preoccupations and needs prevented me from finding what I sought, from hearing and seeing what was before me, from translating the words and images correctly. Sometimes things may indeed look or sound absurd but still in fact represent the truth. Sometimes kalifidos does mean cowboy.

To find what I wanted to find, I needed help, and Signora Petinelli gave it to me. Presence doesn't always make itself present simply because we desire it to be. And perhaps the presence we seek— however sure we are that it is other persons and things, the presence of the past—is actually our own presence, the reality of ourselves standing in relation to all reality, to the real presence. Maybe I needed Bayham Street, Dresden, Weimar, and Rome for that purpose, and now Orvieto too.

I'd been a little dejected by the discovery of the almost total destruction of signs of Thomas Aquinas in Orvieto. Then, in scarcely an aside, Signora Petinelli mentioned there was a little more, *"poche piccole tracce"*—a few small traces—inside the academy, now the military barracks, into which the priory had originally extended. She would try to get me inside: She knew people, calls could be made.

A few days later, Signora Petinelli knocked on our apartment door. Was I ready to go? She had talked to the *commandante.* We could come if we went right now. She and I walked down the block and across the Piazza XXIX Novembre. Buttons were pushed, speaker-phones addressed, and buzzers sounded. The metal gates swung open. A young officer escorted us through a vestibule and through a second gate.

We were outside again in a vast courtyard enclosed by walls in the same Mussolini-modernist style as the facade, an arena in which I supposed the flower of fascist womanhood performed their calisthenics. But on one wall, along the bottom, something entirely different stood out in relief: an arcade—a series of open arches separated by Romanesque columns atop a wide, level balustrade—of dark amber stone. It was a section of cloister, cut off above and on both sides and incorporated into the fourth fascist wall, left intact on an architect's whim or in a perverse attempt at recycling or cost control or maybe because of some inchoate sense that, yes, the Accademia Femminile di Educazione Fisica ought to contain a little fragment of San Domenico.

"It's thirteenth century," Signora Petinelli said with confidence. That meant this was Thomas's cloister, that he would have worked and written here; would have paced circuits though this corridor and around the other three sides—now vanished—of the cloister.

Signora Petinelli was talking rapidly in Italian about Thomas and the priory, apparently for the officer's benefit. Most of what she was saying was going past me. I thought the officer could not possibly know who she was talking about or take any interest in it, but it seemed that he did. He nodded assent or expressed surprise with genuine enthusiasm and curiosity. Or so it seemed to me, since he spoke English even more poorly than I spoke Italian.

As Signora Petinelli continued recounting the history of the priory,

Corpus Christi, the real presence, and this *fratre, scrittore,* and *grande filosofo* who had lived just here three-quarters of a millennium ago, I simply stood looking at the stratum of cloister frozen in Mussolini's wall. This, somehow, was the trace of Thomas I had been after, the real presence of him, caught unmistakably here. And to record and mark it—just to make sure of what I was seeing—I wanted to take a picture.

As soon as I lifted my camera, the officer raised his hand and gestured an emphatic no. Signora Petinelli protested that surely there was no harm in photographing an old section of wall. But it was absolutely forbidden, the officer said apologetically. No photography whatsoever was permitted in a military installation. He turned to me and spoke half in Italian, half in English. Surely I understood the reasons, after "il undici Settembre." "All this must stay . . . lost, secret," he said.

So there could be no photo. I would have to accept what I had seen on faith, to keep it present before my eyes through trust and hope. Once past the gate, I did take a picture of the children—Andrew's soccer friends—on the piazza, and they, present there, will have to stand as the outward sign of what is inside, of what Thomas and his God are making real, putting us in the presence of, realizing in and through us.

When I came back from Italy, Weimar, Dresden, and London, I hoped there might be some word about my sister Patty. We'd tracked down her psychiatrist, Dr. Fleming, who had apparently effected or at least witnessed her transformation. But we were too late. After a distinguished career at Massachusetts General, Children's Hospital, the Judge Baker Clinic, and Harvard Medical School, she'd died four years before at the age of eighty-nine.

We'd also tried to locate Patty's medical records. Someone in our family had dimly remembered that there was supposed to have been a case history published that was based on her. The name had been changed but we would surely recognize her by the details. I went to the medical school library near my home and scavenged the indexes and databases. I found two articles by Dr. Fleming, one on a medication used in the treatment of schizophrenia, the other on the families of juvenile offenders. Neither had anything to do with Patty.

The hunt for medical records was still continuing. All the institutions Patty's doctor had been associated with were helpful, but one by one they reported they had found nothing. Perhaps Dr. Fleming had treated Patty as a private patient, in which case a relative might know the location of her papers. But Dr. Fleming had left no survivors, and it seemed unlikely that files and paperwork from forty years past would have survived her.

So my family and I are left where we began, with the vague impressions and hunches of people now dead whom we heard speak long ago, of whom our own memories have begun to fade. My mother too is gone. She spent the last year of her life in a nursing home, all the day lying flat on her back with her hands folded over her stomach, staring at the ceiling and now and again dozing off. She'd laid herself out like a corpse. When she did die, without so much as a gasp, just before dawn on a morning in March, it took the nurse and orderly some time to realize she'd undergone any alteration at all.

I wish I'd asked her about Patty. But neither I nor my other sister had ever devised a way to bring up the subject without its leading to a discussion of Patty's specific pathology and thence, inevitably, to my mother's part in it; to her role as the "rejecting" or "emotionally absent" mother who induced "infantile schizophrenia" in her child as surely as if she'd throttled her or scalded her with boiling water. Looked upon now from an age less certain of Freud's intuitions on repression and unconscious wishes—of the inexplicable absence in the mind of a name connected to a fresco cycle in a church in Orvieto—it seems a little too dramatic, too determined to find the fatal deeds and outsized personalities of the Greek tragedies Freud loved in a smallish mock-Tudor bungalow in the Midwest of the early 1950s. I suppose that in practical terms it's also a calumny against my mother that provides an answer to the mystery of Patty at the cost of raising, for me, an unacceptable question.

So barring that explanation, here is what I know about Patty: She was born, she vanished into a state a little like autism or retardation or catatonia, she reemerged as a person pretty much like anyone else, and then she died. She was not here, then she was here, and then she was gone again: absence, presence, absence. Or so it seems.

I wonder about the moment she died, the cars hurtling toward one another, fusing, separating, and coming to rest, steaming, burning, exhausted. After the alarm, the terror, perhaps the flare of images as every instant of her life—the secret, hidden parts none of us ever saw—passed through her mind's eye, what happened, where was she? As the impact came, as she dove into the firestorm, through that veil that hung before her like the windshield toward which the oncoming car was pressing, did she disappear? Did her soul and the soul of the old woman in the other vehicle wheel past one another, above the smoldering thicket of the wreck? When did she leave the scene, when was she no longer present there or in any other place to which we, the living, can go?

Thomas said that the soul is "substantial form," an immaterial matter that shapes and integrates all the parts and aspects of the human person. A person is not a person without a soul or without a body, and it is the presence of this substantial form that makes a body a person rather than a corpse. I am not sure I know what Thomas meant by this, although I am sure he did. I wonder if it was necessary that every trace of life—like the cooling metal of the engine and the condensation of radiator water on the asphalt—be stopped and still before her soul could take its leave. So perhaps she lingered in that place long after the state troopers arrived and the spinning red and blue lights were extinguished and the ambulances departed with their cargo.

I don't know. I can't see any sign of it. The picture of the soul—the psyche—I grew up with is closer to Freud's than Thomas's, a chasm of fractured strata through which one descends into ever-deepening and incomprehensible darkness, far from any unifying form, still less the presence of its creator. But faith—my faith and Thomas's—the one that I attempt to maintain a grasp upon despite the evidence of so much of my senses, the glaring absences that seem so often to make proofs, says it is otherwise: that Patty is present to God and God is present to her, not by signs or traces, through memory or hope, but in fact, in full view. I would like, as Thomas described, God to make me present to himself, and to her, and to everything I thought was lost or missing.

I don't, of course, know how or if that will happen. I may go back to Bayham Street. After I came home, after it was clear there were no records, no signs or explanations of Patty—after I learned she might have been as imaginary or as real as Little Dorrit—I found out that Bayham Street had been renumbered late in the nineteenth century. Number 16 is now number 141. There is also, somewhere, a plaque, and I found a picture—a little hazy and ill focused—of it. It isn't blue at all. I am looking for the boy in the garret looking out onto the fulminating world, calculating how he might make his way in it, how he could leave a mark upon it that someone much later, someone like me, might find.

Another Modest Proposal
Doris Betts

—In memory of Ronnie Frye, killed by lethal injection, Central Prison, Raleigh, North Carolina, August 31, 2001

WHENEVER I HEAR TALK of table tipping, crystal balls, channeling, ecto-plasmic appearances, squeaky tape recordings of ghostly moans in graveyards, I give off an eerie cackling laugh that no living human can hear.

Humans don't hear because the so-called "Other Side" is a one-way trip.

Everybody goes. Nobody comes back.

Trust me. I know.

I, Jack McCall, have been dead since March 1, 1871, hanged in Yankton, South Dakota, after shooting Wild Bill Hickok in the back as he deserved, then buried with the rope still embedded around my neck. So I've been dead a long time; all my neighbors, friends, enemies, and strangers are dead, and I can testify that not a single one of us has ever haunted a single house or castle or tomb anywhere in the living world.

Nor do the living make contact with us. Not at all.

We don't do automatic writing. We never attend séances. Nobody but the owner of the Ouija board ever slides that pointer. If those who killed us later suffered from bad conscience, that wasn't our doing.

The Greeks came closest to imagining the realm of the dead: flat, gray, boring.

To relieve eternal boredom, we have developed two forms of entertainment.

Call the first Look But Don't Touch. This spectator sport allows the dead to see into the world we left through a translucent barrier—like one-way glass—an impervious force field behind which even if we did clank chains, the living would not hear, beyond which even if the living wept, no touch or whisper of ours would penetrate.

Once we've seen how children and grandchildren have turned out, we're primed for the ultimate in family quarrels, angrily postponed

238

until our descendants join us over here.

For the childless dead, like me, or for those whose offspring are themselves boring, our second entertainment is a myriad of clubs. These elect officers, take minutes, and take themselves seriously. After aeons spent in endless meetings with one's betters, it's possible to get quite a postlife education here. Notice, for example, my vocabulary? As a living outlaw, I doubt I knew as many words as my horse.

Our first groups had only one gross division into large blocks of lived time, since Galileo would have little in common with those astronauts from the *Challenger*.

Then the organization chart expanded; we needed more ways to, well, kill time, and our clubs broke down further by national origin because dead Eskimos were not interested in dead Pygmies.

Smaller and smaller categories soon proliferated in more and more specialized clubs. Americans, especially, will split their groups down and down until only a handful could even qualify for the narrowest, most elite membership, with passwords and a flaccid attempt at secret handshakes. There are now so many tiny clubs that dead men and dead women can belong to dozens, keeping their eternal calendars eternally filled as they assemble by gender, profession, hobby, hometown, civic club, sport, political party, and so on. If you miss your dog, there's a club to share pet memories, with subdivisions, of course, into breeds, Westminster champions. The Nobel scientists meet in seclusion. Beekeepers, Mafia, whalers, violinists separated from fiddle players, Oscar winners, the Catholic saints? There's something for every (dead) body, including those who appreciate a witty parenthesis like that one.

To look but not touch, to meet without ever finishing, not only staves off boredom but members can take their specialized views of the inaccessible world. Dead politicians spy through the glaze at government and argue here just as they did in Congress. The stamp collectors add up postage sightings. And for widowed spouses forced to observe how well life now proceeds without them, our dead lawyers enjoy practicing postmortem suits, retroactive divorces.

Since as a saddletramp I never knew what a hobby *was*, I concentrate in the group that reflects my own specialty: the US Chapter, Centuries Nineteen and Twenty, of killers who were executed.

Our murder club is tightly organized with membership rules so specific that we are seldom pestered by dead lawyers suing over applications we've denied. Executed murderers are not a peaceful group and all have had to be trained in Robert's Rules of Order. As our bylaws make clear, execution is not the same as martyrdom, though the Salem Witch Trials were problematic before we cut off members from the seventeenth century. The way we're set up, we also won't accept victims of lynch mobs or assassins whose bad luck got them killed in the act. We long ago eliminated those executed but innocent, since they endlessly stated and restated their innocence until expelled to convene a rather large and noisy club of their own. So we turned down John Wilkes Booth but took in Mr. Rosenberg (Ethel defected to the Innocents), Bruno Hauptmann, Ted Bundy, Caryl Chessman. When Jeffrey Dahmer was murdered in prison, we were glad to be spared his company; we have *some* standards, and I don't know where his like hold their meetings. We're stuck with Albert Fish, however, but he rarely attends.

No member can filibuster against his defense lawyer, judge, or trial. At meetings, I can't even make clear that Wild Bill Hickok shot men in the back himself (Dick McCanles, for one) or explain how drunk I was at the time. Still, I hear that in the Western Lawmen's Group (much more carelessly run) Hickok berates me constantly. They let him into that inferior outfit where Bat Masterson is still claiming he killed a man for every year of his life and John Selam—who himself shot Wes Hardin in the back of the neck—got away with murder and still pleads self-defense.

But our organization maintains high standards. We won't even schedule joint meetings with related groups, like the one—for example—that has Lizzie Borden for president and O.J. Simpson on the waiting list.

Nobody from other clubs is invited to travel with us on our field trips. Though restrained behind that barrier, our observers have gone to every legal execution in the United States from 1800 to now, and not merely to recruit new members. Instead, we like to test their dying against our own, which in the good old days was naturally worse.

Such field trips are a lot more educational for us than for the fifty thousand spectators who watched John Johnson swing at Thirteenth and Second Avenue, New York City, in 1824; he still brags about drawing the crowd. It's the modern niceties we find upsetting— the final meal, the final medicated sleep. Had we not seen for ourselves, we'd never have believed that family members of the victim along with family members who come to see Junior killed are served snack refreshments beforehand by the state, at the same table, cafeteria style.

*

After one recent meeting I didn't sign up to take the next trip so the chairman asked if I planned to go inactive.

In this place, my shrug makes gray strips of what used to be shoulders fly up, then settle. I still wear what used to be rope around where my neck is remembered.

"We'll need your perspective," our chairman said.

I gave in, though lately the executions have been boring and those singing people with their candles sometimes block my view.

I seem to enjoy our death-row visits less and less. In my day, hanging was how we all died, a common experience that bonded us when we reassembled here. Under the black hood we all had gone, had felt the noose adjusted so its hard knot pushed the left ear forward. Our legs, sometimes the arms as well, were then tied down. At a signal, three unknown men hidden in their small raw-wood booth on the raw-wood platform would cut three simultaneous strings, one of which made the trapdoor drop.

I did not benefit from that particular nicety in South Dakota, though; one hangman was all the cheapskates hired. The hidden three again remind me of the three Graces from Greek myth, this tender protection of the feelings of those who live on. Not that I'd ever heard of Graces back when I galloped across Nebraska and Dakota, cross-eyed, my broken nose in between, looking in the wrong direction for trouble. Back then I hadn't even heard of firing squads where only one gun is loaded with real bullets.

Of course there are Executioners' Clubs over here, but we've always voted down hotheaded motions to wreck their meetings. I hear they every one got paid in cash, that nobody wanted his name tied to the job.

Our brotherhood of hanged men (always at risk of seceding into a smaller club of our own) maintains stringent criteria to evaluate those later hangings we witness as unseen tourists. Was the knot expertly placed so it knocked the man unconscious right away while his neck bones broke? Set that knot wrong and the head itself might come part, even *all* the way off—a bloody mess. (Over here, such clumsily decapitated men stay in our club with us as if routinely executed, since they've been blackballed by the subunit of those who were neatly guillotined.)

The last thing I told the marshal was to make the knot tighter. And he did.

In a clean hanging, the criminal's backbone will snap just right; he's paralyzed, and with his brain shut off from oxygen, there's less gasping and flopping about while the guts open so shit and then piss and maybe even sperm run down both legs. They did on mine but I couldn't smell or feel wet by then.

In a well-managed hanging, there comes one last dead man's leap of the body. If it's badly managed, though, he'll keep on making an awful noise while he slowly chokes to death for ten minutes, fifteen, even twenty. They checked me at twelve, left me for ten more.

We who have, well, lived through it ourselves judge each execution much as a theater critic might judge a particular play. When a prisoner kicks so hard that someone must grab his tied legs, drag him down, and get washed by the final expulsion of waste, that's a bad hanging, though we agree it serves the assistant right.

Hanging has lately gone out of style, Delaware being the last state to use it. Some twenty years after my own unjust hanging, they invented the electric chair. At first we who are products of the noose found it a novelty to watch. I'll never forget those picnic trips to Mississippi where we followed guards as they drove their portable chair in a van from courtroom to courtroom, so sentence could be promptly carried out.

So much for the slowed-down South.

The electric chair caused a new hierarchy in our club. We no longer had just the hanged vs. the fried, but the old-timer-fried outdoing the new-arrival-fried, going on and on about how much worse their own executions had been. Even the two hundred who came over from Sing Sing went out both hard and easy, and competed with one another.

"Back then, they turned on the juice? Maybe three or four thousand volts in my day! Both my eyeballs popped right out!"

To which a later arrival might say defensively, "Well, mine *would* have, but nowadays this mask is so tight that it holds them in."

Cooked meat, both of them. Well-done or rare. A dentist invented the thing, wouldn't you know? The body temperature hits 138 degrees. There's usually room for us tourists to mill around behind the official witnesses, who gaze through a barrier themselves—sometimes it's one-way glass, in other chambers the man strapped to Ol' Sparky can see who's crying and who's waving goodbye with his middle finger. They've shaved his right leg and the crown of his head where the wet sponge rests on white soapsuds to help conduct electricity; sometimes the leg splits open when the power runs down to the floor and it snaps and snaps, sounding so much like gunshots that old cowboys like me will duck and grab and then get embarrassed.

I can't say much for the gas chamber, first used in Nevada in 1924; we had so many no-shows for those dull trips that now only new members bother. Do three executioners drop different pills into the sulfuric acid so everybody's conscience is clear? They tell the man in the chair to breathe deep so he dies fast, but all of them hold their breaths as long as they can. And there's the distant doctor with a stethoscope hooked up to another room so he can hear the heart stop long-distance. If an electrocuted man is red and so hot that his corpse will blister you, the cyanide man is purple, and has to be sprayed with ammonia before men in gas masks and rubber gloves can haul him away.

And our attendance at club field trips continues to drop. You can't tell an execution chamber from an operating room these days. He's strapped on a hospital gurney with an IV drip in either arm, and while there's nothing but saline coming in, he can sit up and make some final statement. He's dressed like a boy who's having his tonsils out. All the people who couldn't get close to see him die watch from another room on closed-circuit TV. Then something new goes into a vein and he sleeps, and something worse paralyzes the lungs, and at last the worst injection hits his heart and it quits. He's hooked to a monitor everybody's seen on doctor shows with its peaks and drops; now the bright line goes flat. That's it. Five minutes, ten, never as much as twenty.

For a veteran, it's hardly worth the trip.

Our club has several motions on the floor to send these sissies off to their own low-standards club, where they'll act like it's a recovery room instead of death.

But meantime, if I could just get through the barrier, if I could slide paper underneath or fly it overhead, I know what they need to do with convicts condemned to die.

First they expand the television coverage from closed to open circuit, and try it pay-per-view to build a core clientele. Everybody knows that execution is not about justice but revenge; it's payback, not deterrence. And that has entertainment value.

Soon my own boredom will surface afresh in those viewers as the event becomes so sterile as to disappoint, especially as the show acquires prime time and mass audience. What's all this going-to-sleep business? Did the store clerk sleep, the rape victim, the policeman, the troublesome poisoned wife? By public demand there will be extra injections added for pain, a neurotoxin some new Edison will brew in his basement. Then that form of killing will acquire familiarity and wane; states will move back to the gas, not cyanide but another and slower-acting vapor now, producing long spasms, full-body convulsions, vomit. Viewers will recoil but they will not turn off their sets. In time even that extremity will seem insufficient for multiple killings and child murderers. Technology will make possible a newly designed electrical bed that gives shorter intense bursts, and localized, so one part of the body burns crisply alone, prolonged, then sears at another new place and moves again.

That'll serve him right!

The trend to impose more and more justifiable punishment that fits the crime will not regress so far as fire at the stake or drawing and quartering, not in these civilized times.

And civilized beings will watch through their own transparent boundaries, on screen, from their living rooms, with snacks prepared in their own kitchens, while I and club members make more and more field trips to study through our barrier both the executed and their executioners.

Bijou

Mark Doty

THE MOVIE I'M WATCHING—I'm hesitant to call it porn, since its intentions are less obvious than that—was made in 1972, and couldn't have been produced in any other era. A construction worker is walking home from work in Manhattan when he sees a woman in a short fake fur coat knocked over by a car when she's crossing an intersection. The driver leaps out to help her up, but the construction worker—played by an actor named Bill—picks up her purse and tucks it in his jacket. He takes the subway to a banged-up-looking block, maybe in Hell's Kitchen, climbs up to his tiny, soiled apartment, nothing on the walls but a few pinups, women torn from magazines. On his bed, he opens the purse, looks at its spare contents, keys and a few dollars. He opens a lipstick and touches it to his tongue, tastes it, does it again, something about his extended tongue touching the extended lipstick . . . Then he's lying back, stroking himself through his jeans, getting out of his clothes; he's an archetypal seventies porn guy, lean, with thick red hair and a thick red mustache, a little trail of hair on his wiry belly. Then he's in the shower, continuing his solo scene, and he begins to flash on images of women, quick jump cuts, but just as he's about to come he sees the woman in fur falling when the bumper of the car strikes her. That's the end of that; the erotic moment is over, for him and for the viewer, once that image returns.

Chastened, toweling off, he's back in the bedroom, looking again at what spilled from her purse. There's an invitation, something telling her about—a party? an event? someplace called Bijou at 7 p.m.

Then he's walking in Soho—the old Soho, long before the art glamour and even longer before the Euro-tourist-meets-North-Jersey shopping district: garbage in the streets, cardboard boxes in front of shuttered cast-iron facades without windows. He finds the address, goes in and up, and the movie shifts from the gritty Warholian vocabulary it's trafficked in thus far to another cinematic tongue. An indifferent woman in a lot of eye makeup sits in a glass booth; Bill proffers the invite; she gestures toward a door and utters the movie's only line of dialogue: *Right through there.*

Mark Doty

"There" turns out to be a hallucinatory space, its dominant hue a solarized, acidy green. Within that color, Bill moves forward. He confronts the image of his own body in one mirror and then in many, reaches out to touch his own form with pleasure. Time dilates, each gesture extended, no rush to get anywhere, only a little sense of forwardness. In a while there's another body—man or woman?—prone, facedown, and Bill's on top of him or her, they're fucking in a sea of all that green. In a while we can see the person beneath Bill is definitely a man. Then, much later, Bill's alone, lying prone on the floor as if now he's let go, all his boundaries relinquished, and one man comes to him and begins to blow him. Bill lies there and accepts it. In a while another man enters the scene, and begins to touch and cradle Bill's head, and then—no hurry here, no hurry in all the world—there's another. Now the pattern is clear, one man after another enters the liquid field of green that sometimes frames and sometimes obscures—and they are all reverently, calmly touching Bill. They have no end save to give him pleasure, to make Bill's body entirely, attentively, completely loved.

This is the spiritualized eroticism of 1972 made flesh, more sensuous and diffuse than pointedly hot, a brotherhood of eros, a Whitmanian democracy. It makes the viewer feel suspended in a sort of erotic haze, but whatever arousal I feel in imagining Bill's complete submission to pleasure suddenly comes to a halt, as surely as if I'd seen that woman struck down in the crosswalk again, because I realize that all the men in the scene I'm watching are dead. Every one of them, and the vision they embodied, the idea they incarnated gone up in the smoke and ashes of the crematoriums, scattered now in the dunes of Provincetown and Fire Island.

Or that's one version of what I felt, watching *Bijou*, Wakefield Poole's weird period piece of art porn. Of course it is not news that the players are all gone now. How beautiful they look, the guys in the movie, or the men in the documentary *Gay Sex in the 70s*, posing on the decks in the Pines or on the porches of houses in San Francisco, eager for brotherhood and for knowledge of one another. That is a phrase I would like to revive: to *have knowledge* of someone. It suggests that sex is, or can be, a process of inquiry, an idea that Poole would certainly have embraced.

Watching the movie is just one of countless experiences in which the fact of the AIDS epidemic is accommodated somehow. *Accommodated* doesn't mean understood, assimilated, digested, interpreted, or integrated. Accommodated: We just make room for it

246

because it won't go away.

I don't know what else I expect. What could lend meaning to the AIDS crisis in America? Hundreds of thousands perished because there was no medical model for understanding what was wrong with them, and no money or concerted effort offered soon enough to change the course of things in time to save their lives. They died of a virus, and they died of homophobia. But this understanding is an entirely social one, and it doesn't do much to help the soul make meaning of it all. I have no answer to this problem save to suggest that a kind of doubling of perspective—an embracing of the layered nature of the world—is one thing one could carry, or be forced to carry, from such a shattering encounter. AIDS makes the experience of the body, a locus of pleasure and satisfaction, almost simultaneously the site of destruction and limit. What if, from here on out, for those burned in that fire, the knowledge of another body is always a way of acknowledging mortal beauty, and any moment of mutual vivacity understood as existing against an absence to come? Presence made more poignant, and more desirable, even sexier by that void, intensified by it.

Maybe the viewer's involuntary gasp, when Bill thinks of the woman hit by the car as he's jerking off, is two-fold—first, the shock of the inappropriateness of it, and then the secondary, deeper shock—that the particular fact of her body is differently understood, differently longed for, when it is seen where it really is, in the world of danger—and that such a perception shakes the desirer out of simple lust and into some larger, more profound realm of eros.

I used to like to go to a sex club in the East Village, a place now closed through some combination of pressures from the Health Department, the police, the IRS, and the real estate developers who are remaking Manhattan as a squeaky-clean retail zone. A combination Whole Foods/condo development has opened right down the block.

Beyond a nearly invisible doorway (shades of the one Bill entered in Soho, long ago), there was a bouncer inside the door, a flirty man who loved jazz music, and then an attendant in the ticket booth ("Right through there . . .") and then a sort of living room where you could check your clothes with the two attendant angels, one black and startlingly shapely, one blond and ethereally thin. They were loving, kind, and funny boys; they looked at the goings-on before them with a sly combination of blessing and good humor, which is just what you'd want in an angel.

Then, beyond a black vinyl curtain shredded so that you could part it dramatically with a swipe of the hand, were two floors, with a kind of stripped industrial look to them—bare brick and cement, a certain rawness, and structures of wood and metal in which to wander or hide, all very plain the first year I went there, and later redone with branches and dried leaves everywhere, as if an autumn forest had sprouted in the ruins of a factory.

Sometimes it was a palace of pleasure, sometimes it was a hall of doom. Sometimes when you thought you wanted to be there, you'd discover you just couldn't get into the swing of it. Sometimes you weren't sure you'd wanted to go and it was marvelous. Often it felt as if whatever transpired had little to do with any individual state of mind, but rather with the tone of the collective life, whatever kind of spirit was or wasn't generated by the men in attendance that night, or by the city outside busily thinking through the poem of this particular evening. There were regulars who became acquaintances and comrades. There were visitors who became dear friends. There was a world of people I never saw again, once the doors closed.

Whoever made the decisions about what music to play preferred a kind of sludgy, druggy trance, often with classical or operatic flourishes about it. The tune I'll never forget was a remixed version of Dido's great aria from Purcell's *Dido and Aeneas*. It's the scene where the Queen of Carthage, having been abandoned by the man she's allowed to wreck her kingdom, watches his sails disappear out to sea and resolves to end her life. As she prepares to bury a knife in her breast, she sings, unforgettably: *Remember me, but—ah!—forget my fate.*

It seems, in my memory, that they would play this song every night I attended, always late, as the evening's brighter promises dimmed. There was a bit of a backbeat thrown in that would come and go, in between the soprano's great controlled heaves of farewell and resignation, but the music always had the same effect. I'd take myself off to the sidelines, to one of the benches poised on the edges of the room for this purpose, lean back into the swelling melancholy of the score, and watch the men moving to it as though they'd been choreographed, in some dance of longing held up, for a moment, to the light of examination, the perennial hungry quest for whatever deliverance or release it is that sex brings us. It was both sad and astonishingly beautiful and now it seems to me something like the fusing of those layers I mentioned above: the experience of desire and the awareness of death become contiguous—*remember me*—one not-quite-differentiated experience.

My partner Paul's mother has Alzheimer's, or senile dementia. The first sign of it he saw was one morning when, for about a forty-five-minute period, she didn't know who he was. Now she doesn't know who anyone is, or if she does it's for seconds at a time. I was sitting beside the condo pool with her—the Intercoastal Waterway behind us, so that we sat on delicate chairs on a small strand of concrete between two moving bodies of water—along with one of her other sons. *Who are you,* she said to him. *I'm Michael, your son,* he said. She laughed, the kind of humorless snort that means, *As if . . .* Then he said back to her, *Who are you?* And she answered, *I watch.*

That's what's left for her, the subjectivity that looks out at the world without clear attachments or defined relations. She is completely obsessed with who everyone is; she is always asking. I wonder if this has to do with her character, or if it's simple human need; do we need to know, before we can do or say anything else, who people are to us?

Not in *Bijou;* abstracted subjectivities meet one another in the sheer iridescent green space of sex. They morph together in patterns, they lose boundary; they go at it so long, in such fluid ways, that the viewer does too.

Paul's mother's state is not, plainly, ecstatic; she wants to know where she ends and others begin. The desire to merge is only erotic to the bound.

The other day my friend Luis asked me if I thought there was anything spiritual about sex. We happened to be walking in Soho at the time, on our way back from some stores in the Bowery, so we might have passed the very door through which Bill long ago entered into his acidulated paradise. That prompted me to tell my friend about the movie, and my description prompted Luis's question. Luis has a way of asking questions that seems to say, *You really think* that?

I am not ready to give up on Whitman's vision of erotic communion, or its more recent incarnation in Wakefield Poole's pornographic urban utopia. But the oddest thing about Poole's film, finally, is that woman knocked down by the car; why on earth was she

249

necessary to the tale? I suspect it's because even in the imagined paradise of limitless eros, there must be room for death; otherwise the endlessness of it, the lack of limit or of boundary, finally drains things of their tension, removes all edges. Poole can almost do this—create a floating, diffuse, subject-and-object-less field of eros. But not quite; the same body that strains toward freedom and escape also has outer edges, also exists in time, and it's that doubling that makes the body the sexy and troubling thing it is. *O taste and see.* Isn't the flesh a way to drink of the fountain of otherhood, a way to taste the not-I, a way to blur the edges and thus feel the fact of them? Cue the aria here: *Remember me,* sings Dido, *but—ah—forget my fate!* That is, she counsels, you need to both remember where love leads and love anyway; you can both see the end of desire and be consumed by it all at once. The ecstatic body's a place to feel timelessness and to hear, ear held close to the chest of another, the wind that blows in there, hurrying us ahead and away, and to understand that this awareness does not put an end to longing but lends to it a shadow that is, in the late hour, beautiful.

Shadows, of course, lend objects gravity, attaching them to earth.

Luis is right, sex isn't spiritual. The spirit wants to go up and out; it rises above, transcends, flies on dove wings up to the rafters and spies below it the form-bound world. Who was that peculiar French saint who died briefly, returned to life, and then could not bear the smell of human flesh? She used to soar up to the rafters in church, just to get away from the stench of it. Sex is soulful; sex wants the soul-rich communion of other bodies. The sex of *Bijou* isn't really erotic because what it wants is to slip the body's harness and merge in the lightshow of play, the slippery forms of radiance. That's the aspect of the film that's more dated than its hairstyles, as if it were desirable for sex to take us up out of our bodies, rather than further in. That distance is a removal from knowledge; the guys who are pleasuring Bill aren't anyone in particular, and do not need to be individuated. But that's not soul's interest. Back in the sex club in the East Village, soul wants to know this body and this, to seek the embodied essence of one man after another, to touch and mouth the world's astonishing variety of forms. Spirit says, I watch. Soul says, Time enough to be out of the body later on, the veil of flesh won't be set aside, not tonight; better to feel the heat shining through the veil.

My Brother's Dust
Terese Svoboda

1.

OUT OF A STORM SO thick with dust, a storm so charged with first-rate prelightning ions that the grit flashes and the car dials suffer fades, a storm so dark no taillight shines through, though drivers have flicked on every emergency switch vehicles operate with as soon as the wind begins pushing hard at their rears, and boughs from trees who can see skitter like so much packing shred across this shortcut, out of a storm even this dustbowl state stops for, out of a storm of wild dust and wind and electricity, I spot my brother with a shovel.

Men who toe shovels look alike. They all face where the wood joins the metal or at least their glance grazes there on its way to the shovel tip so all you see is head or hat, in this case, a cap brim, most likely lettered FEED AND SEED if I know my brother, tilted at some unreadable angle. What I can read while I creep the car forward, seeing and not seeing, is that he is not about to dig, he has dug. What he has dug swirls around us—me, in my car creeping through all this flying grit—and him, seen just in the time it takes to see, where lightning now laves and leaves.

How do I know it's him in all this dust? Only my brother would dig in this dust, because he is a digger. He has even dug graves as a gravedigger. Then again, he could be digging just for the hell of it.

I guess that last is what he is doing, with emphasis on the *hell*. Just the way our cousin in another state was caught outside her parked vehicle, holding up her unwrapped baby to a tornado—was caught more than once—my brother digs for himself, he digs that deep.

But even if I park here—which I should, given I can't see a damn thing, and can hear only some semi shortcutting its own way right behind me, honking now and then like a boat lost in fog, the sound a semi too close would make that could smack right into me, especially if I stop—even if I do stop and park and get out and walk over to the field where he must be, he will not be there.

251

Of course, not all the dust is from his digging graves, just as why I won't find him is not all because that's what he did. Certainly flesh and blood dig, certainly a man standing by the road at the lip of a ditch could dig, and dig anything and be found. But not my brother now. My brother's gone graveside, my flesh and blood's gone down into his place of work. He can no longer dig, he's dead.

I tap on my brakes. I make the tapping lively, not nervous, as I go by so slowly, it's really an SOS for the semi to think over, not a signal to my brother. I push my roll-up-windows button again just to hear my windows roll even tighter. I don't want to breathe his dirt in, all that grit that could be his it's so close. We're already close, too close, eleven months, one foot in the womb, the other in the—

I tap it out.

If I could Morse code a real message to him with these taps it would be: I'm not stopping now the way I never stopped for you before. But there can be no *ifs* to think about with the foghorn of the semi rattling my car. Or is it something else? Some other moan? Some way I bypass him that is deeper, that I can't get around at all or hear right.

The dust everywhere is so charged the radio has gone static. This charge is my brother's fault too, a charge he gives off even when he's behind me and dead, being someone with too much electricity in his head that will forever discharge. He had spells. All that electricity he had in his head, *petit* and *grand mal*, is probably all still around here. Or have I come to where the meteor landed, that dark spot on the windshield, that break it makes in the land that's a giant pock all alive, all glittery with electricity, its dirt dancing up and down on the radio waves and having a day?

Don't stop, moans the semi.

The dark spot on the windshield could be the slag side of the meteor but it could just as well be a rundown Chevy pickup in dirt and blue. Yes, it is some sort of vehicle and one thin wipe of the wind shows no one's in it. Whoever drove it to the shoulder is gone, maybe out walking into the plowed field, or else chest down in the meteor cut, away from this weather of lightning and dust. Or gone to stand with a shovel? I don't know what kind of vehicle my brother would drive now that he's dead but I don't want to find out or find him on the road moved, with his shovel.

Though maybe that Chevy is on the road and I'm not. The land here, if it is land I'm on, is both flat and bumpy like the road. I am leaning into the wheel, my arms ache trying to lean it right and straight. At least here the roads are straight. If I am really off the road, then that meteor hole is around here somewhere and I will fall into it if I don't drive straight enough. I glimpse the pasture's crewcut through the dust, that is, the crewcut that should *sh-sh* my car's underside if I'm on the pasture, the crewcut that disappears in another woof of dust into where I think might be the hole but then all that dust shimmies up again and takes over. No *sh-sh*.

At least the semi still calls. As long as I can hear it, I know I am here and not where my brother stands, so to speak. It's all my brother's dirt now, I'm sure it is—his disturbance, his unquiet, his dug dirt whipping up the storm's storm. The semi calls again and this time the lightning answers it, about the fanciest electricity yet, a tree of it not three feet from my hood.

Where I once again see him.

He's in the same position. But I don't really expect him to be standing there different—he's dead, after all. It's me who should be moving. Or do I just circle him with all my straight driving?

I turn on the AC because of sweat, the kind that comes when all the windows are up, and so is fear.

I need someone, or just someone's cell phone, to swear into now, talk to take place outside of this dust- and lightning-blinded shortcut, the solace of company or fear shared, and not just this silly moaning semi that's obviously more lost than me, that has obviously driven way off the road and is hoping to make its way back via some answering moan before it hits the meteor hole, that is, if the driver knows about the hole and doesn't think that land is all flat here with no lessons to be learned.

There are lessons to be learned is what seeing him twice in the dust says to me.

Sweat runs into the lifelines of my palms where the dirt collects, where I grip the car's plastic. His lifelines are dust. What about mine, my future? I just want to push down on the pedal and arrive. If I accelerate now I'll be there, I'll be out of this brother-ridden storm. I honk as if my brother will hear me, I honk back at the semi as if it can hear and avoid me, but there's no more moaning.

That's not good.

If someone rich drives into a storm like this, does he stop and let someone else finish the shortcut, are the rich rich enough to buy off this kind of problem? Or blame? Or even fear? Which of the hard things do they get to buy off? Not that many, I decide, staring into the dull screen of my side mirror that the semi is moving by, one wheel at a time, the dirt swirling over and around us, sucking at us together, dirtying us.

I want to see my brother again.

2.

I am still shaking from my long tight grip on the wheel when I cross the lot over to the grain elevator.

Today my wee fifteen-year-old son has squeezed his six-one frame into the elevator's afterthought office, trailer squat and fiercely air-conditioned, to tend my screen after the workday has blanked it, a summer job I made up for any adolescent but one I filled with him. I help out at the elevator for money. I track sales, register the loads, pay the slips, and get the phone when it needs getting. It's a good job for a grass widow, my father says, somebody whose husband's slid back into the grass and down some hole. I left home for that husband and came back years lighter, my mothering career almost over, my wifing best forgotten, and a humanities degree that makes me human and jobless. I help out sometimes seven days a week at the elevator when there's lots of grain to be shipped or stored.

Today something has interfered with my screen that my son has to fix. The dust? My son laughs.

I take a cold folding chair and wait.

With Aphra.

Some storm, I say to her. I don't say my brother was in it; no, I would never say that, I would never mention him to her.

I love all that dust, she says. It reminds me of him.

My brother learned what he learned about girls from Aphra, and not without protest. She circled our place all throughout high school, yelling plaintive *OKs!* then throwing her shoes at our door with an even more coquettish *Please!* A parody *Please* to everyone else. Every male of any age in our small town of high-school track-star cops and crooks had taken time with her in the dark where one noticed less the harsh arrangement of her features, and the limbs so generously pillowed. My brother, while being not as comely as said track stars but of soft heart, made the mistake of giving a *Thank you* to her *Please.*

Aphra holds up her disk to be fixed.

My son holds up his hand in *Not yet.*

She is the one who found my brother first, nude and dead and not a mark on him. Maybe he shouted for help and she heard him.

254

Maybe she was there all the time. She was unclear and distraught and evasive after, but no one in this small town thinks that she killed him.

He ascended, she says to me.

My brother's bell has begun ringing, among others. My ancient forebear bought church bells for the males, only the males. She wanted a secure slot for her postpeasant descendants, good farmers, good lawyers, good candlestick makers, and what better way to start than from above, with a clapper? The sex of these bells stopped swinging when their innards were remade with a recording that plays on remote but they still release the proper male peals on time for the Virgin's six o'clock notice. I have bell envy.

Ascended? I say, although I know who *he* is.

The Ascension—only him, not the Virgin. She leans toward me, her breasts rippling like loose muscles in her scoop neck. Remember Charlton Heston in a white robe and sandals? The bells reminded me. I'll bet they had wine waiting for him. No, wait—a nice cold beer. He never liked wine.

Right, I say.

I went to check on him three days after, she says, moving a second chair closer, rearranging her large rear for both. Floating, for her, is the only exit.

And? I brush off dust. His dust? I wonder. I have my own visions.

My legs went light.

I nod. About a week ago, I noticed footprints where the sod was soft.

That could've been anybody, she snaps.

All through high school my brother tried to shake Aphra by walking there instead of driving, a setup more loathsome to a teenager than being greeted by a sibling in study hall. He would hide in a Mrs.' spiked bushes and sprint through backyards patrolled by craven dogs on long chains. He was not saving himself for a prom queen or even Ivy Jones, the girl with the pointy red glasses, the one Aphra suspected, but saving himself in the more literal sense.

I have decided she smothered him.

He would have had to suck air between breasts in any act done to completion. She did find him nude in the kitchen, a place where sex and food might intersect. But the premeditated seems to lie outside her circle of meditation. She is of the minute as much as a model because her hungers overwhelm the moment, they occupy her future so far as her mind can stretch and this hunger blankets every second, fully obliterating the deliberate.

She is opening a snack, its bag so small as to seem part of the snack, wrenching the pressed-together bits of cellophane apart with her worn teeth.

She offers me the first dive, she shakes the bag so I know I have to take one, at least one with her big *Or else* self at the other end of it. Or is this my prejudice of the calorie challenged? She radiates a toxic you-can-catch-this-from-me anger. It could be grief. My anger is with my brother for having died where she could find him. I don't want her chip. To take her chip and eat it would be sharing grief.

They're cheese sprayed, she says, and smiles, showing their orange.

I eat her chip and wonder how long my son will take. Then I imagine Aphra undressed. Then I imagine a book, some kind of operating manual for women, the kind with charts that you are led to believe correspond. I can see my brother leafing through it, one hand searching for the parts as if in the dark of a tool chest, the other pressing the paperback open, breaking its back.

Ascension is much like sex, I decide. You're allowed your own body while you ascend and surely the release from gravity is the release the sun and yourself touching each other get. Then birds towing welcome ribbons rush over to cover your nakedness, all that body. Then maybe the wine.

She finishes her bag.

My son slowly taps the computer keys. I sidle over to check my screen. He's not really slow, he is just hoping Aphra will move on, that whatever she needs she will find somewhere else. Cosmically, he says.

Comically, I whisper. A sense of humor is all you need, I say. We have to be nice. Remember, she dogs you only because you look like him.

He shrugs. All my life? I have to look like him every day? He can barely get out the words, he is so angry.

Aphra hoists herself to her feet, wields her disk six feet away.

My son stays reasonable with her. No, he can't repair the crack that perhaps she herself put in so she could wait here for him.

She titters and tosses the disk in the trash beside the desk, then steps closer. Oh, that's too bad. I needed it a lot. She clears phlegm from somewhere. Could you please move a little to the left?

I go over and tidy my files.

My son pretends my tidying makes it too noisy to hear.

She wants him to move in front of the fan and she has it in her to insist. Genes or chemistry under the sway of genes must force her. She will sink to her knees for this, she says, it is only a small, small thing you understand—smell, his uncle's smell. Her voice drops sadly.

When she falls to her knees, he gets up and goes to stand in front of the fan the way she wants. She inhales deep and long. But she is not greedy, inhaling over and over. She starts at once to get up. But it will take her another ten minutes to haul herself off those knees and once the fire department had to come, Joe Broward and the other big guy, the only ones who can lever her back to standing without compromising themselves, without her sniffing at them like some kind of loose bear, heat-struck and lonely.

I am the one to telephone these volunteers.

3.

Don't you see how I loosen my hands around the spoon so they don't look like his? asks my son. He is draped, as only adolescents drape, over a mostly flattened piece of furniture on wheels he's rolled into the kitchen, holding a spoon. I'm blowing my still dirt-filled nose.

You just look like you eat with gloves, I say. Don't all teenagers?

No. He flips to his stomach and propels the furniture crablike along one wall, spoon out. Sir Real, he says, very carefully. How we had to use the motherboard. Get it—Mr. Real?

I agree. It was definitely surreal to use the computer part to lever Aphra's behind off the floor. You're a genius, I say. Thank God I didn't have to call the fire department.

My son begins to do push-ups with the furniture for balance, his legs hooked impossibly over the side.

Even as a teenager, my brother didn't do things like that. The electricity in his head might go off. It went off in stores and parking lots and museums and communion rails and in front of any best friend. He took medicine for it that was never right, that changed his face into someone else's and after a while, he was that someone else, and mean. He would corner me in a room and Indian-burn me, punch me in the stomach and laugh. I clawed and bit back and got punished but he was never caught with a mark, and if he was caught, well, he had spells. Did he have those spells in front of everyone to spite me, the spiteful?

I shower and scrub at the dirt but the dirt grit is everywhere. Eyelid grit, towel grit, toe grit, grit that makes me feel so alive I could kiss it. Kiss grit.

I don't say kiss grit to my son when I come out of the shower. Kissing isn't something you discuss with someone as old as he is. VD you could discuss or even more likely AIDS, something they learn about in class. Kissing is too personal, something that they learn about outside class that they could be seen learning.

My son is already working over a large mound of flakes or chex, his stopgap snack. I insert things frozen into the oven. While he eats, he exudes charm. By this, I mean he takes a sudden interest in my money, an interest he began to make clear during our drive home from the elevator, wanting the purchase of a cord or a widget or a new motherboard for his own computer. The specific charm he exudes consists of watching me while he discusses this interest. Boys his age ordinarily regard their mothers without regard or discussion, so watching me is charming. I know I am doing nothing a boy would find watchable. I am not lighting a match, for instance, or inspecting my bra. I am now throwing away the coupons my brother collected and my father gave me to sort, my mother not having the interest in my father's theories that I do. I am throwing them out by date of expiration the way my father can't—the print is too fine—because that last date might tell us something.

He needs a clue.

My brother's body across the clean kitchen floor.

I am not the one to wonder, to pick and to pry. I can watch a big bird settle on a dusty leaf and not crane or open a window to crane. But my brother was way too close to me in age and of course, with his dying for no reason, really much too close not to wonder.

It wasn't a spell.

I'll think about it, I tell my son.

He redoubles his watching.

My father enters and he too is struck by my son's sudden hunger. He pours out the few chex or flakes we have left for him, the frozen food still being, for the most part, frozen. The dust storm he has only heard about, office-bound as he was at the bank, struggling with an officer over a tithing arrangement for his French sunflower crop, an arrangement he says is as inaccessible as a calendar girl, and he sighs, hearing of Aphra and her disk, my son's lack of money, and then all about my brother turning up at the shortcut.

I don't remember your brother the way you do, he says between bites. He made a good banana bread. Your mother gave his crockpot to the poor.

I chew on the cereal too. My son chews louder. What if it's like

Hamlet and I'm supposed to do something? I ask over all this chewing.

I know that one, says my son, and gives us his best soliloquy.

The play within the play that reveals all, adds my father, the sword through the curtain, that blood-soaked curtain.

The ruined curtain, says my son, pointing to a spot on the wall beside our food, and burping.

Finish your food, I say.

My son goes back to watching me. My brother would chew loudly and watch and then I'd find gum stuck to the inside of my bowl or a fake thumb in the milk. I move slowly even now, under such watching.

Did Great-Uncle Beck actually invent Jell-O? my son asks, flourishing the emptiness of his bowl.

He did not claim that often, I say. I mean he sometimes did say something like that but as to the actually, I don't think so or somebody else held the patent on it or else nobody could hold it because ladies all over the world already knew about it. Your uncle, however, had his own Jell-O ideas.

I know, I know, sighs my son, against the tedium of familial recitation. Only two people bought his Jell-O cushion: the high-school teacher whose wife threw it out, thinking he was endangering his privates, and the lady with the old dog that liked the taste of it. How could he have good ideas? He lived around here.

You need more pavement for good ideas? says my father. More trouble and people to dish it out to? A lot of rooms full of pictures painted by the dead with their troubles on their brushes—museums—and graffiti on the buildings to boot? A city?

Jeez, Gramps.

He's probably right is the long and short of it, I say. Your uncle did live somewhere else for a while, like you will.

I will, Mom. Somewhere closer to the milk.

He offers me the carton. I look inside it as if he has slipped between the lips and drowned or as if he will step out of the bottom, all grown. Of course it's empty. He's all smiles, having tricked me into the disposing of it. Ha, he says and begins singing, "Home, home on the deranged," and my father knows even better words than he does.

I wasn't home when my brother left, I was elsewhere, propelled there as far as that kind of away-from-home propulsion takes you, and in and out of marriage. He wasn't away far or long. After a brief battle with a baccalaureate, he found a town that let him pick up boards, picking them up from sites that weren't built yet. People came at night with pickups to steal these boards if he didn't stow them. He did his pick-up work after the site was closed and then put the boards behind cable or Sheetrock in the lockup. Who knows how many boards you have to pick up in a place like that in order to keep visiting the grocer's, to pay for NyQuil, to stand in a mall now and then and ask directions. He was as thin as a board after.

Maybe he dug a little between boards.

Where he had gone to live must have been like here, or anywhere else where they have those building sites, where you don't know why all the stores close at three on the first Monday of the month, why the pastor drives a cut-down Chevy, why the cinnamon buns unwind backward, or the water tastes like a chemical no one can name.

He brought back mystery. Before he left, there was nothing outside of where he went during his spells that he could tell without us already knowing it. Now there was so much he could not tell us.

They had birds there, he said when he returned, after my father bought the garage like a house for my brother and he moved in. Birds? my father asked. He meant birds you could buy, not that he bought one, those birds in cages built out of thin boards, slats really, to keep the birds in. An old lady had them. These birds were not strong enough to break out of their cages, though, he said. They beat their wings against those slats. He came back because those birds reminded him of the birds in cages that can't breathe after you dig to the bottom of one of those mines that need them.

Birds? we repeated. Mines?

My son is digging for pennies in the bottom of a creamer the shape of a bronco. It is habit, it is a signal of money-want. My brother did not like him digging in the creamer that was his, and probably filled with his pennies. He did not like him looking so much like him. I think he thought it wiped out his mystery. Where was that creamer from? Not from Reno, which was stamped on its bottom, according to my brother. My son would guess where else and he didn't like that either.

The creamer was last emptied of pennies when my brother was a year or so older than my son is now. With them and car-wash money, movie-candy-saved money, and gambling profits—will this fluff fall first for a quarter?—he bought himself a car, a seriously dull cheap car that he paid for in full and then crashed just a year later in a spell, and then had to be driven around by Aphra because they took so many points off for what my father decided had better be called speed instead of a spell.

Before his crash, my brother invented the Jell-O cushion. After his crash, he was working on Jell-O-as-airbag. Who was ready for either?

Boys are always ready. I hand my son some milk money and tell him to buy more and bring home the change. I see him pocket the bill and smile, the way only he would.

4.

Graves are what founded our town, not a brand of tires or a confluence of water or an aneurysm of oil. Here graves shot up out of opportunity—too much speculating and people got shot, or too little opportunity, a lack of food. Pretty soon, people passing by started to think of this place as where to dig a grave and they started to save up their dead just to stop here and dig. After people started burying here whomever they had because someone else had buried here, people started to stay and bury more and after a while, people couldn't move, out of either or both so much mourning or so much need, since people are needed to haul lumber for what graves contain and the usual appurtenances, meaning not only the boxes but the crosses too, and the fence. And, of course, soon some professional is needed to hammer things together better than the others and someone else is needed to sell the nails for that hammer and the coffee it takes to get that hammering good and loud and someone has to say something better than the others to keep the dead down and all of them need wives who soon need a little something extra for the children.

I am in the library looking it up because TV shows, I discover, are mostly about death. Here I have found fiction dwells on it too. The classics reek of it, the trashy novels are simply light in motivation. I despair of any lunch-hour distraction at all until I come upon this history of the town, sure it will be just a boring recitation of begats and swindles.

Graves.

It is just a place between places where people could bury, right? People don't die here on purpose, just to get buried. Lots of towns must have extra space for graves. But still I see all that digging. Backhoes do most of the digging now when they need it. I don't know exactly what kind of digging my brother did but it was not often. The town didn't need more than one digger, at least not anymore.

He looked like someone who dug. Gray was his color, the color rocks get a second after they're spit on. He was a rock that had been spit on, shiny enough, but frozen good and gray in life, with the dates already cut in him. As regular in size as a stone in a row, with dark any-color eyes caught in a face that was always turning away—or yours was, from his meanness.

I wander into the children's section, avoid Grimms' for the title, and pick up *The Snow Queen*.

Here's the two who can't be anything but brother and sister, who hold hands the way a sister and brother want to when they're close but can't be. The Snow Queen spits in the boy's eye and leaves sand or grit or glass or dust in it that changes how he sees and becomes a kind of bad-contact-lens way of seeing, not the way anybody would see. No matter how often the sister wipes his eyes after he's spit on, this dust or grit in the brother's eye sticks tighter and makes him mean. He goes gray with his meanness, and I don't think just in the eye, that kind of gray, but a gray that tows the whole face and body with it into the grayness of old mean—no, a dead, mean gray.

So much for fairy tales.

I had forgotten my brother was the boy whose hand I held first. He forgot me so easily, falling to the ground in a spell, his eyes rolled in white-out, babbling words like *pancake, where, if.* He often didn't know who I was after he recovered, at least not for a minute. When he spoke after a spell, it was slow, a gradual drift into what needed saying and then all at once too much of it, talk that ran on like a fear, into dark muttered corners. A spell.

Thanks, I tell the librarian. Maybe I'll just get some music. An instrumental.

Although the library's not far from our place, I drive. I like being inside a car where I can't be asked how I am, or squinted at with *Lovely day?* I like the driving part of grieving, its privacy. But on my way home there's the light.

There's only one in town. Every time I stop I think, *Here's where Aphra pulled up next to me.* She was driving my brother after he lost his license and I drove up next to them. He didn't travel often with her but would call us first, so this must have been some emergency, like a stitch at the hospital from a shovel cut. I did not wave. I did not glance over at her or him during the light's long two minutes even though it might have been an emergency.

She shamed me.

When he turned his face to me it wasn't to see why I didn't wave, he knew why. He was me too, he wore my face of shame. I never saw it for sure because I never looked but I know it was there. He was her captive. Why didn't he leap out of the car and into mine is the question. That was the kind of love they had is the answer, the caught kind, a webby one, where feelings no one would have thought unwound and stuck while other kinds went on playing. I have had some experience with the caught kind myself that I have had to leave so far as to come here and help out at the elevator. So maybe it is my own shame too that shamed me that I was so busy not looking while Aphra talked to him at the light.

You can't die of shame. Shame might blaze up across the sky of your life but you can't die of it.

Some say Aphra had something to do with the crash that caused him to have her take over driving. I'm not saying who. Of course Aphra brought on a spell and caused the accident. She loved to drive for him. Some say those emergencies he had happened on a schedule, and it wasn't his but hers.

When he came back from that other place, his face was pinched thin and brown. Did he fear Aphra even then, did he move to get away from her and then return in fear of her? The brown part I had figured out: It wasn't that he was digging at night in our town like some legend or anything, but that board picking up gave no shade, no willow weeping that his usual place provided. It was the pinched part I wondered over.

Mostly he didn't drive, he stayed home and had the grocer deliver, a service so rare in our small town that it added to the caution of even the larger children crossing his kicked-up yard. But there were still boys who shot BBs into his windows and laid dead cats on his doorstep and filled his yard with fill because they could, boys who climbed into a parked truck there at the end of the road and shoveled fill all over it for fun. Not a hill of fill but something of an incline to where you would think a walkway might start. A lot of fill. Well, he couldn't shovel it off, could he? He had pride enough in his work but a yard full of fill wasn't going to make him dig at home. The dirt blew and the filled yard made him look even more like a Shove, which is what the boys called him. Hey, Shove, I heard them yell, Shove it.

These Shove-it boys were not my boy's friends. He didn't have many friends yet but these were not his. I think it was Aphra who scared them away from my brother's, coming around so often the way she did. It could have been. But despite all her drive-by intentions, my

263

brother lived alone. So alone he lived, with junk mail in mounds as if it would be answered, the smell of boxed food, and a too-clean floor in a house the size of a garage with garage stains on the floor and walls, a house without so much as a crawl space. A house the size of a rocket ship, said my father when he was trying to sound up.

It was my son on a visit who guessed what my brother had hidden under a tarp around the side of his house. Even though the delivery van bore out-of-town plates and had the scion of a washer-maker painted on its side, it wasn't a washer. Too round. Plenty of us guessed planter but the why of that made us stupid with more guessing. Plants of that size? Him, a waterer? He laughed at us but didn't call us nosy idiots. He just didn't confess. Until the neighbors called the firemen to investigate the steam rising from under the tarp, my son's guess wasn't any more right than the others'.

It couldn't be that, not him. Hot tub?

No, I really never knew what my brother was thinking. We weren't really close, except in age. Irish twins, they used to call us, born so few months apart. Such proximity didn't help. Why did he dig? Why did he stay in this town to do it?

I'm back because there's room to park. I can leave the car two feet from the curb or at the wrong angle. Nobody questions anybody.

Except Aphra.

5.

Aphra made a fuss at the funeral. License plates from here to here lined the lot, enough hind ends of cars with county numbers to make the funeral decent, which is what it was, with enough people to sign the guestbook, names that certified a crowd had come to watch. But lining up that clutch of plates beside the book, well, it seems there must have been some names that weren't written in, that had just had license plates behind them that we knew but couldn't place, or faces that stared back from people we didn't know who did not feel her lack of explanation, who had read the paper that said sudden but natural death and they thought, *What's natural at his age?* A lot of people came just to look at what the casket cradled, knowing full well how unnatural in general death is, over and over, whatever the cause. A stopped heart? Doesn't everyone get a stopped heart? Or maybe they came to shake their heads because of how few names in the end got written in the book.

That's why Aphra made her fuss. She said no one should leave who

264

hadn't signed in. She whispered it so loud in the direction of the family that we looked down as a family toward the casket, the only other area her large self did not yet occupy and command.

Grief was fuss enough.

It was why we looked anywhere at all that day. Before they closed him in, we had to bring over our grief and look in and look hard. To do this, we were standing in line, more or less, the line-ness being often lost and listless, slack in its fearful disinterest for a closer look while Aphra hissed her fussiness and we ignored her.

On my turn I peered in the way you do, with your eyes protruding as if to see all that's inside without moving any closer but even that far away I saw it wasn't him, that the sinuses that backed his eyebags and cheekducts in allergy had been drained, and that the medicine for his spells was gone too, unpuffing his lips. Without these, his face was changed into not so much a sleeping stranger but into someone who could get up and start a new life incognito. Later I could tell it was him in a dust storm but then, in repose, who knew? Not the funeral director with his smile so smothered you couldn't be sure he wasn't frowning.

We left, signed or unsigned.

Police with hats off stopped the traffic when we met red lights on our slowed-down drive to the plot. Who cares about robbers or con artists or interstate speeders were what those hats off said, with respect I hadn't suspected from that lot of ex-football ends. Aphra went through twice, herding in the few cars that hadn't shown up for the funeral, let alone signed in. Being helpless to control the signers must have left room for her to consider controlling the cars, cars I saw that contained just kids, nobody who would come.

Even they plodded across the unsold stretch to where the director waited. Then, after what he said and the clergy said and the family said what you say over such a hole, and after we had all thrown in our bits of dirt, Aphra had to throw in a peach pit. Dead silence met that. The director did cough but said zilch. You know it will sprout and be trouble to the mower. She would do such a thing after she had done all the others.

Weeping, weeping, she turned from the pit and its pit, and careened like a storm in the Gulf through all of us, coming adrift of my son, where she put her hand on his shoulder, surely trying her best to mistake him, as grief-filled and tear-blind as she was, for my brother.

It was then that we all saw how my son did have his exact look.

Helping was a fresh haircut and the two inches he had stretched in the last two months. Of course, the hand-me-down suit he stood in, handed down straight out of his uncle's closet since nobody wore a suit around here except at funerals and never wore one out and what would you get for it but a quarter at the Jumble Shop and there wasn't a thing in town in his size anyway unless it was ordered—that suit made a real difference in the resemblance, especially for those few who had ever seen my brother in a suit, or could imagine it.

I stepped between the two of them, my son still in Aphra's grip and his head down the way only an adolescent can tuck into a neck, and I told her that we were going now and would she follow us because we had so many hams and cinnamon buns given to us in our grief that the freezer wouldn't close. We wanted her with us, I said. She pulled herself off him—hand over hand—and she said, Why, how kind. We all watched as she swayed her big self over to where she was parked, over the too smooth grass with its flat-to-the-ground markers just far enough apart to be side tables, places to rest your drink of water or a rubber on, with a plush of grass between them in a plot so bedlike even I wanted to peel down the sod and crawl under.

But my brother is dead is what I remember and I cry instead, a little the way a car does when the ignition's gone, a click and a grind, something that needs something, that can be stopped only by stopping.

Aphra didn't appear at the wake, she got lost driving over or she followed some of those uninvited, unsigned in elsewhere for a wake of her own. Maybe her car didn't start. Waiting for her—we did wait—the tidbits cooling and the punch warming, my grief balled up into anger, a ball that could be thrown quite a ways.

6.

The meteor fell aeons ago. There's no other depression around like it for a hundred miles. Of course you never see the actual meteor, just a pocked hole with rocks all around it, rocks that drive a compass wild. The meteor itself, all dust or pebbles from its splash that long ago, made that hole with its drop, the hole that holds the trash of time on top of it, bones and arrowheads, and weed remains. But that meteor's hole still doesn't fill up, that's how big a hole it is. Other holes farmers, even ranchers, bulldoze flat, it's good for their operations. But some holes are too low and depressed to bulldoze, and some are even more meteored.

Do you have to wake me up to tell me this? my father groans from in front of the gray TV, where I too sit, paging through the nice, dull encyclopedia, having found the meteor entry and talked out loud about it, thinking he has an interest since he hadn't filled in his meteor hole, thinking he was awake.

It's just like his death, I go on anyway. A meteor blazes across the blue of an evening or a morning the world is not ready for, a meteor that is just junk from some other blaze or maybe not, maybe it is thrown by a baseball-capped god out of telescopic range—and that's that, impact. Nobody goes in looking for a black box to answer why it crashes unless it's a fat-cat scientist on a government grant somehow relating it to usefulness, the trajectory of hand grenades. Nobody's investigating his death.

My father looks into my teacup at that drowned thing, the bag. You didn't think that much about him when he was alive, he says.

I close the book and see a star already lights the back window. I'm going to sleep, I say. Good night.

I can't say more or I would say, *What did you care then too?* But who shows how much worry goes into care or even a lack of care, how much *Hands off* is caring. I have a child now too.

I walk back to my room without turning on lights to make him think, half asleep, that what I said was a dream of his, and not me talking.

It's not true that scientists don't want to know why things fall from the sky. Scientists are always wanting to know about what happened, especially if what comes is from other places, alien places. I tell my son aliens are just people who haven't yet been introduced or pay taxes but most people who live on this flat land here don't say that, they say meteors are vehicles for aliens and that aliens have landed with them and probably killed a lot of people in doing so, not to mention while wandering the world after. If scientists don't want to know what happened with regard to a hole like this, these people do and will tell them.

What happened to my brother?

My father thinks aliens.

Years ago, my father drives his pickup straight across some snow-blown flat ground that the land has here, as much white land as you can squint into at one time, and my brother rides with him, eating peanuts instead of breakfast, which is what you do if you haven't been on the inside of a grocery store for the last goddamn week because you're working late digging postholes the way your father likes you to because it is winter and no grocery is open at that hour except peanut dispensers around the gas-up. The way my father tells it, they are driving along a fence line eating peanuts and checking posts when a cigar-shaped something comes hovering not a hundred feet away, hovers, and zips off.

My brother, to the day he died, did not contradict him.

My father says, did say, the government is up to something, it's one of those scientific tests they like to make, with dummies at the cockpit or helm, and barrels of taxpayers' money get burnt to a crisp in the flash the cigarshape makes exiting, he would say that and swear by it and forget it except that afterward, the waitress at the Snake House—what they call it instead of the Steak House because of the can curlings you get in the soup if you aren't looking close—after she seats them where the light is great for pitch, but a little low for newspaper reading although my father does try to read one right off, to see if there are any articles about government waste-of-money testing publicized in any of the back pages where they like to hide those things and say, See, we published it, then she seats two complete strangers in the booth behind them.

He doesn't say anything about the strangers at first, just sips the grindy coffee very quietly, just says, *Pass* a couple of times, putting his paper down since it is dummy bridge they have taken to playing instead of pitch between newspapers. He listens and my brother begins to listen too because when do two total strangers ever come to the Snake House if they don't have to, if they can drive on by and eat anywhere else. These two are talking about government testing.

Swear to God.

They say, stiff as anything, What did you think of it, Herb? or someone else's made-up name. And the second guy says, kind of loud but everyone is quiet so it could have been in a reasonable tone, just regular talking, They're going to test five more like that this winter.

Then the two men go quiet too, eating the special that makes everyone quiet, looking for what might not be so special in it, and the waitress gets their desserts that the special requires although she gets them mixed up so they have to talk again in their strangers' voices and then they stand up to pay, reaching for their wallets in their behind pockets.

That's when everyone turns to get a good look at them.

My father anyway, and my brother.

They were just two strangers, says my father and my brother who used to nod there too in his retelling as if why wouldn't they be,

268

given what they saw that morning? Then the strangers walk out and are never seen again.

And why would they be seen again? asks my father. They came to the Snake House to allay fear, to stop rumors. My father is sure they are not government plants, he is sure they are aliens trying to cover up. As my brother's death has to be covered up. So many strangers come to the funeral, that's another sign, says my father, sure after seeing that takeoff that he and my brother were always in great danger and that aliens would come to check if he was really dead. My father wears a copper bracelet to protect himself—from arthritis according to the quack he met who sold it to him but my father swears it also works to keep off the intense radiation that sometimes aliens beam.

My brother would never wear one.

Took it upon himself, says my father.

There wasn't a mark on him and the autopsy rang up zilch. Not even a fried brain.

Those aliens have long memories, says my father. Time isn't the same for them as for us. They have accordion time.

Whenever he gets to this part, he pretends to play an accordion and it is some sweet sad Bohemian song that has a polka inside it that no one can resist, especially since time and death are all that's worth singing about even if you can't sing. He hums and we hum, the accordions of our lungs living synchronous and no doubt on the wane.

This is how he sees it:

An alien like some big ugly guardian angel has been lurking around my brother for some time, long enough so nobody's bothered, nobody notices anymore, least of all my brother. My brother goes to sleep fine one day to the next then my brother does something stupid—or doesn't, like he stops going to the irrigation ditch, which we know he does for no reason that we know of, except to pee, where he could be offering gin or food to the aliens or even to a god who, it must be said, like all gods, carries the odor of the alien on him, being that no one ever sees them or knows them too well. Or else he pickles an offering and eats it instead of leaving it or drinks one of the beers he puts in the sand to cool. Or he just pees there and that is the wrong place.

Anyway, my brother does something stupid and they pull the plug on him.

Not a mark on him.

269

It was a dark day, says my father.

It was winter, I remind my father. No moon had crossed the sun nor was anything else blocking it. It was seasonal.

Time is all you need, all you have, says my father. That's what they wanted from him.

Little Sister
Mary Gordon

"YOU MUST UNDERSTAND that Nathan is ill, very ill. The doctors do not give much hope."

Susanna heard the words, but tried to sift the meaning from the heaviness of her sister-in-law's tone. Lena had been married to her brother for more than fifty years; it had taken a while for Susanna to feel comfortable with her, but she had grown to respect and even to depend on her—perhaps that was a kind of love.

Lena and Nathan thought of themselves as scientists, rational people who knew the ways of the world and how to go about them. For them, Susanna was always the little sister, the poet; Nathan's impulse was to protect her, but Susanna suspected that Lena often wanted to shake her, to wake her up. For her own good, she would have said. Nathan seemed to enjoy hearing his wife and his sister argue, arguments that were on the surface about the uselessness of poetry but were really about what was important in the world.

Lena would speak out in favor of plain language, of facts, of information communicated simply and straightforwardly, as quickly as was possible, and quite without embellishment. And Susanna would say: But how do we understand facts so that they are of use? The understanding has many parts, and poetry completes the process. There is the observation of facts, the recording of facts, the interpretation of facts, the finding of the right language so that facts can resonate in the body and the heart. I rely on you and Nathan for observation and recording—but that is not all there is. The rest—the portion that is mine—is what is known as poetry.

So perhaps Lena, with her crude grasp of language, hadn't understood what the doctors really meant. And then there was her habit of putting the worst slant on things— "the dark lady," Susanna's husband, Michael, called her. It was a kind of vanity, her conviction: that she would never be surprised, never caught out, never be made a fool of by hope. Even if the doctors had offered hope, even invoking the most scientific terms, Lena wouldn't have accepted it, would have rejected it as a bad bargain, shoddy goods offered at too high a

271

price by an untrustworthy merchant.

Lena's hardness, her pessimism, surprised Susanna: It would have been more likely, more explicable or justifiable, if she and Nathan had been the hopeless ones. They were the ones who had lived the nightmare: two children hidden in a barn for ten months from the Nazis, saved through the kindness or the greed of strangers. Lena had been brought up in the safety of Detroit, the child of Socialist Zionists; she had come to Israel in its first dangerous years; she and Nathan had met on a kibbutz; "My first sight of her was on a tractor," Nathan liked to say. But it was he who was hopeful, open to new ideas, new people, new experiences. Sometimes Susanna wondered if he had married Lena so that she could take on and carry the darkness for both of them. She would carry the child that was really both of theirs, the hopeless one, the pessimistic one, and when it was born it would have her features only: He could deny its paternity, and run off, free.

Lena said that the Lowensteins were all dreamers, all idealists: She was the only practical one of the bunch. It was true; it was because of her that Nathan had left the kibbutz to come to Indiana for his PhD in biochemistry. And then the good luck: meeting another foreigner, Sven Torveson from Stockholm, who invited him to come to Sweden, where they would start a company devoted to desalinization of seawater. So they had lived in Stockholm for forty years. Lena had got a job as an electrical engineer. Nathan had become prominent in the Stockholm synagogue—"I like a place where I am the first one they think of when they hear the word Jew," he said. Their lives were prosperous, their children healthy and successful; Nathan spoke often about his gratitude for their good lives.

Nathan's optimism was an offense to Lena, who would accuse him of refusing to face things, of repression and denial. Once, after someone had used some of his research and presented it as his own, she had insisted that Nathan make a public accusation and Nathan refused, saying he was sure the man didn't mean it, didn't realize what he was doing. "I don't understand you, your willful blindness. After what you saw the Germans do in your town, how can you refuse to see what the world is really like? Your hopefulness is a kind of blindness. You won't admit that you have seen what you have seen."

"I know what I have seen, and some of it has been more terrible than you imagine. But I have seen other things as well," Nathan said.

They were silent then, all of them: Lena and Michael and Susanna, because whatever they had been thinking, and they had all thought differently, was of no moment now. They all understood that after what Nathan had said there was nothing left to say.

Susanna adored her brother; she had adored him all her life, and their time in hiding had only been a deepening of her adoration. Sometimes when people asked her why her experience hadn't damaged her more, she explained, "Well, I was very young. Four years old. And for me, it was a time when I could have my brother all to myself. Before that, he saw me as just a nuisance—he was five years older. He used to call me the little imbecile. He trained me to say, 'Hello, my name is Susanna and I am a little imbecile.' But when we were in hiding, he had no one but me and he made a magic world for me. And nothing has ever been able to destroy it."

Would death destroy it now? How could she be the little sister (*kleine Schwester,* he called her, using the Yiddish words) if the big brother was no longer in the world?

Little sister—that was who she was to him. Always he held her hand when they crossed the street, always he ordered for her in restaurants . . . even when they were traveling in Europe and it was ridiculous—she had Italian and he had none and her French was a hundred times better than his. But it pleased her to return to that place where she could look up at him and feel safe, prized, miraculous.

It was not possible that Nathan was dying. She was certain that when she told Michael about Lena's call, they would joke about her forebodings and that would make her words less real. She would ask Michael what the real prospects were; Michael was a physician, a neurologist: He would be able to interpret the words in a way that Lena, who was only an engineer, would not. He would call his friends; they would explain things in detail to him. And in the end they would determine that Lena had been wrong, that Nathan would be all right.

Susanna sat next to him when Michael phoned Lena later that evening; she didn't move during all the calls he made to his doctor friends. She studied his face, that face that she had known so well, loved so well for forty-six years, the face of the nineteen-year-old boy whom she had sat next to in American history class in college, and had married a year later. He could never keep things from her; it was how she knew he had never been unfaithful—he would never have been able to hide it. Even a little light flirtation at a party caused him to blush and stammer—it was she who could toss her hair and look a handsome man in the eyes and offer up extravagant compliments, without the slightest hint of unease. So when she saw him take his glasses off and rub his hands over his eyes, she understood for the first time that the danger to her brother's life was real.

"Pancreatic cancer," he said. "It's a death sentence, a time bomb. There are experimental protocols—we'll try everything. But it could be a matter of a few months."

The hammer fell on her head, she felt the wounding in her brain, and the impairment of her understanding when what she most needed now was the correct understanding, the discernment: above all, since her brother had left the realm of words to her, the right words. But there were no right words. To imagine there might be was the worst sort of vanity.

Michael had arranged for Nathan to see a friend of his, a specialist in pancreatic cancer. He picked Nathan up from the airport and brought him right to their apartment. It was very convenient; four blocks from Mount Sinai, where the doctor had his office. When Susanna came in from teaching her class she could hear Nathan and Michael in the kitchen talking about baseball. Nathan had only lived in America for three years, his years of graduate study, but he was obsessed with baseball—even from Sweden he had followed the Yankees' progress. It was a mystery to her that two men so intelligent as Michael and Nathan could spend so much time and mental energy on something that she thought not only irrelevant but boring and ridiculous as well.

"I know the Yankees are winning and will win; what else is new?"

Nathan turned around. She was shocked at how thin he had become, how he had aged, and she knew he saw it on her face. In all her life she had never been able to hide anything from him. Sixty years of a life and not one lie, no secrets, nothing hidden, blocked, or prettied up.

"You don't find me fashionably thin? Like one of those boys with the hairless chests and the five o'clock shadow modeling Italian suits?"

"Since when would you spend the money on an Italian suit? I don't think you even own a suit. I haven't seen you in a suit since my wedding."

"Well, since I'm in New York I'll have to buy one. Tomorrow you'll take me shopping."

"Right now I'll have to cook supper for the two of you. Put some meat on your bones."

She walked quickly into the kitchen so that Nathan wouldn't see her tears. She made exaggerated noises, banging pots, pounding meat on the cutting board to discourage the men from coming in to join her. Her hands were shaking and she cut her finger chopping a carrot. Both men ran into the kitchen when they heard her cry out.

"I'll let the doctor do first aid," Nathan said, and pushed Michael out of the room to gather bandages and antiseptics. But he stood only six inches from Michael's elbow as he spread antiseptic ointment on her finger. "Careful now, do it gently."

"I think I can handle it, Nat," Michael said.

"She's very sensitive. She feels things more than most people. She isn't very tough."

"I know her pretty well after forty-five years of marriage."

"But I know her better. I held her in my arms when she was five hours old."

"OK, Nat, you win," said Michael, snapping shut the tin lid of the Band-Aid box.

"Of course I win," said Nathan. "Don't you know? I am always the big winner."

"How will I talk to him, what will I say? We aren't a family who talk about things. I know you'll say that I'm a talker, but not to my family. We never talked about the war; sometimes I force something out of Nathan. But my parents, never. Not a word to the day they died."

Susanna understood the way her parents thought that putting memories into words would make them real, and the important thing was to get on with life. They had been spared, they had been blessed with more life, and their responsibility was to take the gift they had been given and make the most of it. Thinking about the past was for them like soiling the gift with the mud of the road instead of walking barefoot in the presence of the face of God.

Even she, whose life had always been in words, had kept the silence. "A forty-year silence," she said once. "Silence in a sea of words—for I was always writing, ever since I was tiny. I could read at three and write at four"—she said this to explain to an interviewer why it had taken her forty years to include her wartime experience in her poetry. "Like Moses wandering with the Jews in the desert. Forty years. Sometimes that is just the time required. And then, after the wandering, the sea is parted, and you can walk through something you wouldn't have even been able to imagine."

One reason she didn't like to talk about her experience was that she didn't want to talk about it wrongly. How to convey what had happened to them simply, plainly, without making an exotic tale of it, or falling into self-pity, or making it a species of special pleading? How to say, across a dinner table, walking in the woods, sitting in a chair beside the ocean, "This is what happened to my family. We lived in a little town not far from Bratislava. My father was a merchant: He imported and exported china. We were comfortably off. My mother had gone to a very good finishing school and was very intelligent; both my parents were devoted to the arts. They would often go to Vienna for the opera. We had several servants, and a large house. Then the war came. Things happened gradually. We couldn't imagine that the people in our town who had been our friends would not protect us. Then it became clear. At first, Jews were forced to give up their businesses—it was called the Aryanization, the de-Judification of the economy. In this my father, my whole family, were lucky.

My father had a very good friend, a non-Jew, quite a religious Catholic actually, who kept telling the Nazis that he was taking over my father's business, but he had to keep him around for a while longer, to get the benefit of his expertise. This man, he was a hero, was holding on to my father's money and he had arranged for us to be hidden in the house of a local farmer whom he trusted. And one day, the Jews in the town were rounded up and taken away—all our friends, everyone we knew, and you must understand that until the Nazis took over, all of us believed we had a home in the town, that we were perfectly accepted. But one day everyone was put on a train, every Jew except for my family and the doctor of the town and the dentist. I don't know where they went. My father's friend took us in the dead of night into the countryside. And we were hidden in this big barn, really an outbuilding where hay and machinery were stored. There were no animals there, but there was a smell as if there had been animals—horses or cows, I didn't know, I couldn't tell: I was a city child. For ten months we never went outside—the only way we could see out was by removing a loose brick and seeing just what could be seen in the few inches of space. A few inches; the color was everything; the weather, the whole outside world concentrated itself into a rectangle of color. Blue or gray or white: That was the extent of our knowledge of the outside world.

"Actually we did go outside once. One night my brother and I sneaked out because it was snowing: We felt we had to taste the snowflakes on our tongues. And our father, who was the most gentle man in the world, beat my brother, because he said we had jeopardized all our lives. Then the war was over, and the Russians came and we could come out again."

When she talked about it, she tried to speak flatly, neutrally. Plain words, no figures of speech. And this effort at plainness made it impossible that she could put these things into her poetry.

It happened in a way by accident, the breaking of her silence, the breaking through it into poetry. All the adjuncts at Hunter, where she taught, shared an office, and on the desk that she used on the Tuesday and Thursday nights when she was there she saw a book she didn't know that belonged to one of the other instructors. *O the Chimneys*, it was called; the poet was Nelly Sachs. The name was unfamiliar to her but she was always eager to discover a woman poet she hadn't known of.

The first poem hit her like a blow to the mouth.

> O the night of weeping children!
> O the night of the children branded for death
> Sleep may not enter here.
> Terrible nurse maids
> Have usurped the place of mothers.
> Have tautened their tendons with the false death,
> Sewn it on to the walls and into the beams—
> Everywhere it is hatched in the nests of horror.
> Instead of mother's milk, panic suckles those little ones.

She had never been able to explain to anyone what had happened to her when she read those lines. What happened, the experience of it, would be turned into language but it had nothing to do with language, it was anterior to language or beyond it. She read: "O the night of weeping children! / O the night of the children branded for death," and she knew it was herself that was being spoken of, she was the weeping child, although she had not wept, the child branded for death, although she had not died, and she was back again in the barn, the outbuilding where they were hidden, the enclosure they had not dared go outside for ten months, and she was with her brother kneeling to peer out of the chink in the wall, the rectangle of light allowed in by the single loosened brick. It was May, May of 1945; full spring; through the rectangle they could see the leaves turning from green to yellow-green to what would be their full and final greenness; the

277

leaves made a net through which the sun fell, and in the darkness when the moon was full, its silver. Sitting at the metal desk, below the fluorescent lights that hissed and buzzed and did their job of partial and unsatisfactory illumination, she was seeing it again, something so strange, so improbable, such an unlikely sight to be seen through a rectangle of five inches by three.

He came like a figure from a tale, or from a dream, a story by Tolstoy or a pogrom nightmare. Yet she knew not to be frightened, but elated, by the vision of this man, a man on a white horse, dressed in leather—dark brown or black, she could not quite be sure—a leather coat or singlet that went down to his ankles. He was too far away for anything to be made out about his face, but she could see his hat, a fur hat, black, the black fur glistening in the sun like the flank of a healthy animal, and on the front of the hat, a red star blazoned. And he was not sitting in the saddle, the man, the man in dark leather on the white, white horse, he was standing in the stirrups urging the horse faster, faster, toward them. How clear the colors were: the slate blue of the May sky, the yellow-green of the new leaves. The milk white of the horse's coat, the black fur of the hat, the dull earth– or night-toned leather. He was eating up the distance, all that came between them, and as he became closer and closer he seemed more and more glorious and Nathan said, "He has come to free us, this Russian soldier, he will save us. We will soon be free." But before he came to where they were he turned his horse and rode away. It was nearly a week later that the real liberators came, ordinary young men, ordinary soldiers. One tried to run away when he saw them; "They are as white as devils. They are devils," he said. Her father explained to him that they were very pale because for nearly a year they had not seen the sun.

The memory, the image of the memory came to her rapidly, steadily, like a horse galloping closer, closer, until it was breathing its hot breath into her, and the image grew in her until it was full grown and she could turn it into words, bring it from her mind to paper. Right there, on the ugly table, underneath the loud and ugly light, she wrote the first draft of the poem about the children kneeling and the chink of light and the miraculous Cossack riding to them, then turning away. For a month, she showed it to no one. It frightened her. What frightened her most was that she didn't know whether she was describing something real or something she had invented. And it was essential to her that she knew which.

She phoned Nathan in Sweden. "Of course it happened, little

278

imbecile. Did you think your imagination, even yours, was able for the likes of that? And what does it matter, if it happened, or if you made it up? If people read it, they will understand something, and that is a good thing in the world."

"No, Nathan," she said, "it's essential that there be a difference, that I make the difference, between what happened in reality and in my imagination. To deny the difference between the real and the imaginary—that is to betray. There is a difference, Nathan, between words and flesh. Words are replicable; when I'm writing I can substitute one word for another, it is what I do, substitute, discarding one, finding a better one, it is what I must do, Nathan, and if I substitute one word for another neither suffers. But the people who lost their lives, they only had the one life, and it was irreplaceable. There is a difference between words and flesh."

"Well, I am very lucky then, that I live in the world of solid things, and I don't have the thoughts you have. I think that if I did I would be very miserable. I have always told you, *kleine Schwester*, I am the lucky one."

"So it did happen, Nathan, you saw it too. The Cossack on the white horse. You remember."

"Yes, of course," he said. "Some things no one forgets."

After the first poem, she wrote a series of poems called "In Hiding," and they made her a minor celebrity in the poetry world. She no longer had to scrounge courses as an adjunct; she was given tenure, a full professorship. Nathan had had a friend of his translate the poems into Swedish; she believed that he had paid for the publication, but when she asked him he said, "Who pays attention to things like that? This sort of thing has no place in the minds of poets." And at the party that he threw for the book, renting a room in an old hotel overlooking the river, he nearly carried her in his arms from friend to friend saying, "My little sister, she got all the family brains. I'm only a technician. But she is brilliant. And to think I called her all those years 'my little imbecile.'" And the friends, who loved Nathan, and before that had no understanding of his past, friends who had probably never before read poetry, gathered around her shyly, as if she were a brightly colored tropical bird who had landed in their sensible and sturdy nests.

When Nathan was no longer in the world, there would be no one to ask if her memories were real or her own invention. She would be alone in a way that she had never been.

He slept late the next morning, later than she'd ever known him to sleep. "How is your finger?" he said, taking the mug of coffee from her hand, as if he were afraid she was too weak, too wounded, to hold it for more than a second.

"Stupid carrot," she said.

"Stupid disease," he said. "I know that's why you cut yourself. You were upset at my disease. But listen, my little Susanna, *kleine Schwester,* we are rational people. We can't pretend that I'm not sick. That I may be dying. But we have no right to tears. We got fifty more years of life than our schoolmates. We are the lucky ones: Did you think we would cheat death forever?"

"No, for a few more years," she said. "I want a few more years with you."

"A greedy girl. You always were a greedy girl. We each owe God a death; I think it was a Spaniard who said that. But they are a people in love with death, and we, thank God, are not. Nevertheless this particular Spaniard was right and I must pay my debt to death."

She heard him say the word death and she disliked the sound of it. Death to rhyme with breath. It was stupid, it was wrong that there should be only one word for it. One word to stand for what happened to the other children in her town, and what had happened to their father, an old man, as he slept, and what was happening to Nathan, his body consuming itself, and what might happen to her: run down by a truck, or garroted by a madman, or skiing into a tree on a night when the moon fell on the snow like a silver disc. Poetry makes nothing happen, one poet had said; no poem has ever changed anything, said another: They both were right.

When Nathan died would she want to write a poem about it? The thought disgusted her. But even in her disgust, an image came to her, an image from the war. And this one she would not ask Nathan about, whether it was invented or real. She would not ask him about it because it was a way of making a figure for his death, of making it more real, more palpable, and how could she do this? How could she use words to make death more real for one of the living who was about to enter it forever? One of the living whom she thought would never die, because he was so full of life and because her love for him was so strong it must be stronger than death.

But that was a lie, a stupid lie, not a beautiful lie, like the lies of poetry: All metaphor is a lie; it says something is what it is not. Her brother would die. The beautiful loved face would no longer be in the world. That was what death was: the disappearance of a face, a body.

The image kept coming back to her—the image from the war that she would not ask Nathan about. Her mother had buried their jewels and silver in the back garden. And while she watched her mother doing that, she buried her own dolls: the most precious things she had, as precious to her as the jewels and silver were to her mother. She had named them: Bella and Natasha; one had blonde hair, one dark brown, surrounding their porcelain faces like halos. When the war was over, and they went back to their house, their mother dug up the jewels and the silver. And Susanna dug up her dolls. But their bodies had disintegrated; made of cloth, unlike their heads, which were porcelain, they had been absorbed into the earth. Imagining she would recover her beloved toys, the companions of her secret fears, her most complicated conversations, she found only bodiless heads. Grinning up at her, as if what had happened was a joke that only they could get, their once pristine whiteness smeared with brown, what they suggested about human fate was worse than anything she had yet been forced to imagine. The sight enraged her. With two fingers, as if they were diseased things, she picked each head up, put it in her skirt, and then carried the lot to the strip of pavement that bordered the garden. She stomped on them then, crushing them into smithereens, a pile of shards she stomped on again and again to make smaller and smaller till they were almost powder. She pushed them under a tree with the side of her boot, not even bothering to bury them, not even wanting to do them that honor. And ever since then the sight of a doll had filled her with rage. She was fortunate, she often thought, that she had had only sons.

She would not put this image into a poem, she would not. She refused it admittance into the part of her mind that made poetry. She would not liken her beloved brother's face, which would also be absorbed into the earth, to the porcelain face of a doll.

The old rabbis were right, she thought, to forbid images. No image could honor God or death. The Cossack on the horse, the dolls and their grinning faces, these were about life, even if it was horror that they invoked. But horror was still a property of the living. The dead lost all their properties.

What poems could she write that would mark her brother's death? What image could there be for the ending of a life? For the nothing made of the everything that was? It had taken her forty years to write about the war dead, but she did not have forty more years of life for the right words to come to her for the death of her brother. And it seemed more possible to write of the deaths of those she had not known, a larger death, a death that could be written with a capital D, death that seemed to have some significance or lesson, death that was a sign of something: cruelty or courage or despair. But Nathan's death was singular, it pointed to nothing but itself, and at the same time it was anything but singular, because, as Nathan had said, we all owe God a death, but not just one, what is owed is our own death and the deaths of all that we have loved.

She stood beside her brother at the window. His illness had not diminished him entirely; he was still much taller than she. She put her head on his shoulder, and he put his arm around her and patted it three, four, five times, then stroked the area above her elbow in a circular motion that she knew was meant to soothe. But she could not be soothed; she thought perhaps this was a loss she would not bear.

And she thought of all the things borne by people: her parents, her parents' friends. How strange, their insistence on life, on going on being among the living. She looked across the street at the dark trees of the park; she saw the lights on Central Park West, and the people, going about their lives, walking beneath them. What should be marked of all this, what saved from loss, what commemorated?

"How fortunate you are," Nathan said, "to see everything that from this window can be seen."

Outside, a taxi stopped in front of their building. The doorman with white gloves opened the door for a man and a woman, and across the street, a dog barked and the moon, made insignificant by the lights of the lively city, shone from behind a cloud that soon the wind would turn to nothing.

What would be the right thing, when her brother died: to mark his death with silence, because the language of the dead was silence, or with images and words, as if to join him to the world of the living, and what they saw and heard?

She hoped that when the time came she would know.

For now, she hoped only that she would have the courage to say, if only in silence, if only to herself, the simplest words, the words she knew were true: "I love my brother; he is dying."

And one day to say the other words, as simple and as necessary, "I loved my brother; he is dead."

St. Francis Preaches to the Birds
a short comedy
David Ives

Characters:

MIKE
ANGELA
ST. FRANCIS
GRANDMOTHER
CACTUS

(*A desert, defined by: a rock, a cow skull, and a human-sized, two-armed cactus. Hunkered down center are two vultures, named* MIKE *and* ANGELA. *They have sharp talons and long, curving beaks, bald heads and a ruffle of feathers around their necks.*

At lights-up, the birds are feasting on the body of ST. FRANCIS, *which lies between them, its stomach gaping open. The body is dressed in a rough brown robe bound at the waist with rope.* FRANCIS *also wears sandals and a golden halo on a wire.*

The birds eat for a while, digging into the cavity with their beaks and talons, and vocally appreciating the meal.)

MIKE. (*Appreciating the food vocally.*) Mmmmmmm. Mmmmmm-mm. Mmmmmmm. (*Takes some bloody pieces of meat out of the cavity.*) Giblets. I love giblets! (*Gulps, loudly, with a slurping sound.*) Gimme more. Gimme more. What is that? (*Stretches a long rubber band out of the cavity.*) Intestine? Aaah. Too stringy. (*Lets it snap back.*) Where's the good stuff? Where's the liver? Angela, did you take all the good stuff?

ANGELA. I'm not talkin' to you, and I'm eatin' my dinna, do you mind?

MIKE. (*Takes some vegetables out of the body.*) The hell is this? A carrot? Eggplant? Zucchini? I think this creature was a vegetarian! Disgusting! (*Tosses away the vegetables, takes out a rack of ribs.*) OK, here's some good stuff. Ribs! I love ribs! Mmmmmmmmm. Mmmm-hmmmm. Mmmm-hmmmm . . .

ANGELA. Michael, could you please not eat wit' your beak open?

MIKE. Angela, va fungoo. Do not interfere wit' how I eat. OK?

ANGELA. You are so uncouth. I ain't flyin' noplace witchoo no more.

MIKE. Aw, please, Angela. (*Takes a heart out of the body and holds it up.*) Have a heart! (*He squawk-laughs.*)

ANGELA. (*Deadpan.*) That's real funny, Mikey. Real, real funny.

MIKE. Yeah, well, I have a "talon" to amuse.

ANGELA. Very humoriferous.

MIKE. Angela, do you wanna tour the bottom of the Mediterranean? The hard way?

ANGELA. Yeah, yeah. . . . You don't say that on a Friday night when you want a piece of tail feather. Do I have spleen in my teeth?

MIKE. You don't have teeth, Angela. You're a vulture.

ANGELA. So this is the desert all your relatives been squawkin' about, huh? (*She squawks raucously.*)

MIKE. OK, so I was misinformed.

ANGELA. Lookit this decor. It's a friggin' wasteland out here!

MIKE. I did not create this desert, Angela.

ANGELA. I'm sorry, but I say overrated.

MIKE. OK, OK, I gotta say definitely overrated.

ANGELA. And two claws down on the food. This corpus is not as delicti as that Chinese we had last week.

MIKE. Aw, now that was a body of work. Nice and putrid.

(*They slurp their tongues loudly, remembering the taste.*)

ANGELA. This carcass is not nearly as lyrical. It's not as light. The blood is bland. And altogether it does not have a warm and welcoming aroma of decay.

MIKE. Personally, I think this repast is gonna repeat on me.

ANGELA. That's because it's O-F-F-A-L awful. This is a dish that usually turns my stomach anyways.

MIKE. Homo sapiens? Eugh.

ANGELA. Filthy scavengers.

MIKE. And they're stupid. Wandering around in the middle o' nowhere. For *what*? "Let's go to the desert! Let's go to the desert!" Yeah. And *DIE*. (*Squawks.*) I'll tell you what *I* think about this species.

ANGELA. It's overrated.

MIKE. I would say definitely overrated.

(FRANCIS *lifts his head and looks at them.*)

FRANCIS. (*Cheerily.*) Hello, Mr. and Mrs. Bird!

MIKE & ANGELA. *IT'S ALIIIIIIIIIIIVE!* (*They squawk around the stage, waddling in a panic, fluttering their "wings."*) Brrwaaak! Brrwaaak! Brrwaaak! It's alive! It's alive! It's alive! It's alive! It's alive . . . !

FRANCIS. Excuse me. Excuse me. Hello? Mr. and Mrs. Bird? Hello?

(*They stop squawking around the stage.* FRANCIS *rests himself against the rock.*)

MIKE. Did I not say he shoulda baked longer?

ANGELA. Oh, I see, I see, this is all my fault.

MIKE. Keep 'em bakin' in the sun an extra ten-twelve minutes! But no, you gotta have it medium rare. 'Cuz that's how you always ate it back in *the nest*. With *Mom*.

FRANCIS. Excuse me . . .

ANGELA. Why do I stay witchoo, huh? Why, why, why?

MIKE. Did I not say we shoulda stopped at that dumpster and had the smorgasbord?

David Ives

ANGELA. I did not want smorgasbord. I wanted a squat-down dinner.

MIKE. Yaak, yaak, yaak . . .

FRANCIS. I think you're both being rather harsh to each other, Mr. and Mrs. Buzzard.

ANGELA. Hey, hey, hey! We are *not BUZZARDS.*

FRANCIS. I'm sorry.

ANGELA. We are *vultures.* You got it?

FRANCIS. I'm sorry. I'm sorry. I'm sorry. I'm sorry.

MIKE. Didn't I tell you he was gonna repeat on me? Anyway, Signore, we apologize for this little snafu.

FRANCIS. Snafu?

ANGELA. Yeah, please forgive us for digging in slightly premature. Now DIE, YOU BASTARD! *DIE! DIE! DIE!* (*Stops.*) Hey, wait a minute. . . . We understand what you're saying!

FRANCIS. Of course you do. I'm St. Francis. I speak to birds and animals. It's sort of a special skill of mine. I also speak to quite a few of the insect species and many fish, justifying the ways of God to minnows.

MIKE. Oh. A novelty act.

FRANCIS. Lately, I've been talking to plants as well. Hello, Mr. Cactus! Hello! Hello, Mr. Cactus! Hello! Hello, Mr. Cactus!

(*No response from the* CACTUS.)

Have a nice day, Mr. Cactus!

MIKE. Mr. Cactus ain't too talkative.

FRANCIS. Yes, I haven't quite gotten the hang of plant language yet.

MIKE. Yeah, me neither.

FRANCIS. Oh, have you tried too?

MIKE. Aw, I'm chattering with the dandelions all the time. Ain't that right, Angela?

ANGELA. Can't shut him up.

FRANCIS. I'd love to learn to talk to dandelions.

MIKE. You *better* learn how. You're gonna be pushin' 'em up soon enough!

(*They find that funny.*)

ANGELA. Questionay, Signore: Who the hell are you?

FRANCIS. (*Digging around.*) I think I have a holy card here somewhere. . . .

MIKE. A "holy card"?

FRANCIS. Yes, it's sort of a Catholic headshot.

ANGELA. He's prob'ly sellin' something.

FRANCIS. (*Takes out holy card.*) There you go.

MIKE. (*Looking at it.*) Whoo, that's gaudy. Kinda 3-D, huh.

FRANCIS. The bright colors are sort of traditional.

MIKE. So lemme see, what we got here is a picture of you covered in pigeons.

FRANCIS. It sure was hard getting them to keep still.

ANGELA. Musta crapped all over you too.

FRANCIS. Oh, I'm used to that.

MIKE. They don't show that here.

FRANCIS. They airbrushed it out. My bio's on the back.

MIKE. (*Turns the card over.*) What. I can't read this. It's written in buzzard!

ANGELA. Didn't I tell you, we are *not BUZZARDS!*

FRANCIS. I'm sorry. I'm so sorry. (*Flips through his other holy cards.*) Japanese . . . Polish . . . Esperanto . . . Yes, here's a card in vulture.

MIKE. I can't read that. I'm *illiterate.* I'm a friggin' *vulture.*

FRANCIS. I can read it to you, if you'll forgive my pronunciation. (*Reads.*) "Brrwaak, brrwaak, brrwaak . . ."

ANGELA. (*Translating.*) "St. Francis was born to a wealthy family . . ."

287

FRANCIS. "Brrwaak, brrwaak, brrwaak . . ."

ANGELA. "In the town of A-Sissy. . . ."

MIKE. Rich kid, huh. No wonder he's wandering around. Prob'ly on spring break.

ANGELA. Hey, Mike, ain't A-Sissy where we had that sheepdog?

MIKE. Ooh, that dog was bad.

ANGELA. Bad.

MIKE. Bad. Bad. Bad.

ANGELA. Very bad.

MIKE. Very bad. Very bad.

FRANCIS. Actually, you know, it's not "A-Sissy." It's "A-*See*-see."

MIKE. Oh, pardonay mwah. Not "A-Sissy." *Aseesee.*

FRANCIS. A-*see*-see.

MIKE. Can I tell you my frank assessment of A-*see*-see?

ANGELA. I say overrated.

MIKE. I would say *highly* overrated.

ANGELA. You remember the fur on that sheepdog?

MIKE. I still get hairballs from it. *Bad.*

ANGELA. Very bad.

MIKE. Very bad. Very bad.

FRANCIS. Now that I think of it, there was a sheepdog around there I used to converse with. . . .

MIKE. In Aseesee?

FRANCIS. In Aseesee. Was he very cuddly, with a cute brown spot behind the ear?

MIKE. That was him. Tasted kinda like . . .

ANGELA. Chicken.

MIKE. Like chicken. But bad.

ANGELA. Very bad.

MIKE. Bad dog. Bad dog.

FRANCIS. (*Clears his throat to get their attention.*)

MIKE. Oh, I'm sorry. Did we interrupt you?

FRANCIS. Do you mind if I continue with the bio on my holy card? (*Reads from holy card.*) "Brrwaaaak, brrrrwaaaaa, brrrr-wwwakkk . . ."

ANGELA. "St. Francis gave away all his riches . . ."

FRANCIS. "Brrwaaaak, brrrrwaaaaa, brrrrwwwakkk . . ."

ANGELA. "And left home to help the poor . . ."

FRANCIS. "Brwaaaak, brrwaaak . . ."

ANGELA. "Taking a vow of . . ."

FRANCIS. (*Honk.*)

ANGELA. "Chastity." What was that again?

FRANCIS. "Brwaaaak, brrwaaak." (*Honk.*)

ANGELA. Yeah, "taking a vow of chastity." What is that, "chastity"?

FRANCIS. Well, chastity means I'm not allowed to, ahh . . . How shall I put this? I'm not allowed to, ahh . . . utilize my, umm, more private areas. . . .

MIKE. Not allowed to utilize . . .

ANGELA. His more private areas. . . .

MIKE. Hey, wait a minute. This vow of "chastity." Are you telling me . . . ?

FRANCIS. Yes.

MIKE. Are you saying . . . ?

FRANCIS. Yes.

MIKE. Are you telling me you can't (*Pumps his fist back and forth horizontally, making a suction sound.*)—?

FRANCIS. Exactly. I'm sorry?

MIKE. You never (*Pumps fist and makes suction sound.*)—?

(*He keeps that up while* FRANCIS *tries to figure out what that means.*)

FRANCIS. I never . . . polish the silver? Never . . . pump a kerosene lantern . . . ? Oh, *that.*

MIKE. Yeah, *that.* You tellin' me you gave it UP?

FRANCIS. That's right. But anyway, is (*Pumps fist and makes suction sound.*) really important in the great scheme of things?

MIKE. Well, it sure is fun on a Saturday night!

ANGELA. OK, so you don't (*Pumps fist and makes suction sound.*)— What else don't you do?

FRANCIS. Well, I don't lie, or cheat, or steal, or use dirty language or cause harm or covet anything. I don't bear false witness. I don't commit adultery, whatever that is.

MIKE. Dj'ever put somebody's feet in cement and drop 'em in a river?

FRANCIS. Um, no.

MIKE. So, like, what does that *leave?*

FRANCIS. Well, I preach. I wander the desert. I do miracles. I'm a saint. You see? (*Back to holy card.*) "Brwak, brwak . . ."

ANGELA. "Because he was a saint . . ."

FRANCIS. "Brwak, brwak, brwak . . ."

ANGELA. "Francis had a remarkable gift for talking to animals . . ."

FRANCIS. (*Cheep!*)

ANGELA. ". . . though some say this is merely a colorful legend."

FRANCIS. Wait a minute. It says legend? "Brwak, brwak, brwak." (*Cheep!*)

ANGELA. "Colorful legend." That's what it says.

FRANCIS. Well, golly! All those years I thought I was actually talking to animals.

MIKE. Well, obviously we're talking so obviously it's not a legend.

FRANCIS. Oh. That's true. Phew! Thank you, Mr. Vulture!

MIKE. Whoo, he's dim.

ANGELA. When is he gonna die?

MIKE. Shh, shh . . .

ANGELA. *I'm gettin' peckish again.*

MIKE. So you're a, what did you call it, a "saint"? What is that?

FRANCIS. Oh, it's just a job, really. My own particular area is telling my bestial brothers and sisters about the miracle of creation.

MIKE. "Miracle of creation . . ."

ANGELA. "Miracle of creation . . ."

MIKE. And what is that exactly?

FRANCIS. Actually, I was walking along contemplating the miracle of creation when I fell into this gully. I must've twisted an ankle or something. Nothing too serious.

MIKE. Nope. Nothing serious.

ANGELA. Only total extinction.

(*The two of them snicker and high-five.*)

Does any of this saint stuff explain the antenna on your head?

MIKE. (*"Mafioso."*) Hey! Hey! Gumba! Are you wearin' a *wire*? (*He finds that very funny.*) "Are you wearin' a wire?"

ANGELA. Funny, Mike.

MIKE. (*Readjusting* FRANCIS's *halo.*) How's the reception with that thing? Look in his eyes. I think I'm gettin' the Food Channel.

FRANCIS. It's called a halo. It wasn't my choice. They just sort of issue you one after a while. Standard issue, really. You might call it a metaphysical good-conduct medal.

ANGELA. Is it edible?

FRANCIS. I don't honestly know.

ANGELA. We'll find out soon enough!

(*The birds slurp their tongues.*)

291

MIKE. There's always room for halo!

(*They find that funny.*)

ANGELA. You say goodbye, I say *ha-lo!*

MIKE. ("Hel-*lo*-oh!") Ha-*lo*-oh!

FRANCIS. Anyway, the glow sure makes it great for reading in bed. You can turn it up too. And if you put a pot on it? It boils water for pasta.

MIKE. Pasta? What is that?

ANGELA. You know.

MIKE. What, that stuff? Don't get me started.

ANGELA. Not unless it's got a meat sauce.

MIKE. Not unless it *is* a meat sauce.

ANGELA. So why do you do all this saint stuff? Or should I say, *don't* do all this stuff?

FRANCIS. So that I can meet God.

MIKE. Oh, uh-huh. "God." God . . . ?

(ANGELA *shrugs.*)

God . . .

FRANCIS. *You* know. The highest power in the universe.

MIKE. Oh, the *highest power in the universe.*

ANGELA. "God," remember?

MIKE. Sure. "*God.*" You go around not doin' this and not doin' that so you can meet *God.*

FRANCIS. That's right. And so that I can get to paradise, where God is.

MIKE. Whoa, whoa, slow down, Frank. You're throwin' around a lotta technical terms here.

FRANCIS. Paradise is where you go after you die.

ANGELA. Oh, you mean like six feet under.

FRANCIS. No . . .

ANGELA. You mean nowhere.

FRANCIS. No . . .

MIKE. You mean dumped in a river.

FRANCIS. No, *paradise.* Traditionally paradise is up in the sky.

ANGELA. Oh yeah? I frequent the sky and I'm a stranger to paradise.

(*The birds hum the "Stranger in Paradise" theme.*)

FRANCIS. Ha, ha, ha. Paradise is invisible, of course.

ANGELA. Oh, it's *invisible.*

MIKE. "Of course."

ANGELA. Well, this explains everything.

MIKE. Small wonder my confusion.

ANGELA. And you yourself have talked to this higher power? Person to highest person?

FRANCIS. Not exactly talked, as such. I once got a stuffed turtle I wanted, named Mr. Murphy.

MIKE. OK, so the highest power in the universe lives in a garden in the sky and he dispenses toys.

ANGELA. This is possible.

MIKE. And what do you do once you get there? (*To* ANGELA.) I can't wait.

FRANCIS. Well, many people claim you sit on a cloud and play the harp.

ANGELA. Mm-hm.

MIKE. You sit on a cloud and play a *harp.* . . .

FRANCIS. The sitting on clouds has caused some discussion. But don't forget that a spirit is lighter than the water droplets that make up a cloud, so it actually is physically possible for a spirit to sit on, or at least, hover over a cloud.

MIKE. And these harps are *helium* harps?

293

FRANCIS. The harps are a bit sticky, scientifically. These days some theologians say it's not harps, it's guitars.

ANGELA. Yeah. *Air* guitars.

FRANCIS. I have my own theory, taken from scripture, that Hawaiian luau music is quite popular Up There.

MIKE. Francis, lemme get this straight. You spent your life talking to raccoons and you gave up (*Pumps his fist horizontally and makes a suction sound.*) for Waikiki in space?

FRANCIS. Uh-huh.

MIKE. Luau music?!

(*The birds collapse in laughter.*)

FRANCIS. Anything is possible.

ANGELA. Yeah, anything is possible—including zip zero nada *nothin'*. Which is slightly more probable.

MIKE. May I speak frankly, Frankie? You ain't headed for the clouds. You're *living* in 'em.

ANGELA. Is this a rich kid talkin', or what?

MIKE. "Anything is possible." Wake up to social conditions, brother. Think about *this* world for a change.

ANGELA. You coulda been anything, and you picked what? Idiocy. You're a loon! You're a kook! You're a fruitcake!

FRANCIS. We all have our beliefs.

MIKE. Yeah, some of us have the *leisure* to have beliefs. You get to sit on your apse and contemplate cloudlife, *we* have to move from place to place and feed off rotten, stinking, putrescent carcasses. Not that we don't *like* rotten, stinking, putrescent carcasses. . . .

ANGELA. But we didn't have any choice in the matter. We *had* to eat rotten, stinking, putrescent carcasses.

MIKE. I didn't want to be a vulture. I wanted to be a director.

FRANCIS. Film director?

MIKE. Funeral director. My mother says to me, You're a vulture, Mighaele, you eat carrion and fertilize the desert with your shit, so siddown and take your place in the food chain. My sister wants to study French, that's OK. Spring at the Sorbonne, that's *fine*. Reading dead authors instead of eating 'em. *That's* purposeful. I go to Avis with a fresh concept. Avis-Rent-a-Carcass. Do they bite? No. Can I get financing? No. Why?

FRANCIS. Because you're a vulture?

MIKE. Because I'm a vulture. I shoulda been *capo di capo* and soared with the eagles. Instead I got life as a buzzard and I flew with the sparrows.

FRANCIS. Well, you're a vulture.

MIKE. Actually, I'm only one thirty-second vulture. The rest? Pedigreed buzzard. (*Weeps.*)

ANGELA. No!

MIKE. *Si!*

ANGELA. *No!*

MIKE. *Si!*

ANGELA. NO!

MIKE. *Si!* It's true! It's true! I'm a miserable friggin' lowlife buzzard! (*Abruptly snaps out of it.*) But what's the difference. Buzzard or vulture, did I ever have any options? You had everything and you threw it all away!

FRANCIS. But I wanted to help the poor.

MIKE. You didn't help the poor. You *joined* the poor. You *are* the poor. You spent your whole life as a scavenger on creatures who *work* for what they have. You're pathetic. You're a loser. You're a dickhead. And what have you done? Nothin'! You fell sucker for a concept, Frankerino. For a line. I say there's nothin' out there but oxygen, so gulp it while ya can.

FRANCIS. A fairly bleak world view. . . .

MIKE. Us vultures at least got a purpose. We fertilize the earth. We excrete nitrogen-rich turds. What did *you* ever do?

FRANCIS. Well, maybe nothing as tangible . . .

ANGELA. You done zip zero nada nothin'.

MIKE. Period!

FRANCIS. Well, listen, I'd love to stop and talk some more, but I've got a bullfrog waiting down the road for confession. (*Tries to get up, but can't.*) It was really nice meeting you two. Mike. Angela. (*Tries to get up, but can't.*) Arrivederci. (*Tries to rise, but can't.*) Whoo, hey, am I stiff.

MIKE. "Stiff" is the word all right.

(*The birds find that funny.*)

ANGELA. Is that rigor mortis, or are you just glad to see me?

(*Even funnier.*)

MIKE. So how do you say "croak" in bullfrog?

(*Even funnier.*)

FRANCIS. I see I have a slight stomach wound here . . . (*Takes a lamb chop out of the wound.*) Maybe I'd better have that looked at.

ANGELA. (*Taking the meat from him.*) Thank you. I'll just pick.

MIKE. (*Holds out a "microphone," talk show–host style.*) So tell the folks at home, Frankie. Any near-death experiences? Do you see a long tunnel of light with your dead grandmother at the end of it?

FRANCIS. A long tunnel with my dead grandmother . . . ? No. Should I? Where is it?

ANGELA. "Answer your beeper! It's the Reaper!"

FRANCIS. Reaper . . . My dead grandmother . . .

MIKE. You oughta be seeing her in about I'd say six minutes.

FRANCIS. I'd love to see her. She used to make the most wonderful Jell-O molds.

MIKE. Mm-hm. Really.

FRANCIS. Lime on the bottom, orange on top, with these teeny-tiny marshmallows floating inside.

ANGELA. Fantastic.

MIKE. You oughta be tastin' that Jell-O anytime soon.

FRANCIS. (*Realization.*) Oh. *Ohhhhh . . .* You're not implying that I'm about to, um . . . ?

MIKE. Die? Yes. Bingo!

(T*he two birds start filing their beaks.*)

FRANCIS. Ah. Oh. Mm-hm. Yes. Is that what this is. Right, of course. I'm in the middle of the desert with a gaping stomach wound and there's nobody for miles. A few major organs missing. Death would certainly seem inevitable. Ah, well. Comes to us all, doesn't it. (*Suddenly screams.*) HELP! HELP! I HAVE A GAPING STOM-ACH WOUND AND I'M MISSING SEVERAL MAJOR ORGANS! I'VE ONLY GOT SIX MINUTES TO LIVE!

MIKE. Tops.

FRANCIS. *TOPS!* I'M GOING TO DIE AND BE EATEN BY BUZ-ZARDS!

ANGELA. We are *not BUZZARDS!*

FRANCIS. Who GIVES A SHIT what you are?! AND YOU ATE MY FAVORITE SHEEPDOG!

MIKE. I hope you're tastier.

FRANCIS. Why I oughta . . . I'M DYING UP HERE! HELP ME! HELP! HELP!

ANGELA. Sure took him long enough.

FRANCIS. IS ANYBODY OUT THERE? IS THERE ANYBODY OUT THERE? HELLO!

MIKE. Now who is gonna respond to a scream like that?

ANGELA. Too much vibrato.

MIKE. Narrow range.

ANGELA. Nobody's got a good scream anymore.

MIKE. Sure sounds like "a sissy" to me!

FRANCIS. WILL SOMEBODY HELP ME? I'M A DICKHEAD! I'M A TOTAL DICKHEAD! AND I'VE DONE NOTHING WITH MY LIFE! NOTHING! NOTHING!

ANGELA. Zip zero . . .

FRANCIS. ZIP ZERO NADA NOTHIN'! I HAVEN'T LIED OR CHEATED OR STOLEN OR COMMITTED ADULTERY! WHATEVER THAT IS! Oh God, oh, God! What God? There is no God. There's nothing. Nothing! NOTHING!

MIKE. He's good.

ANGELA. Now watch, here's where he begs us for help. Watch this.

FRANCIS. Won't you help me, please, please, pretty please with sugar on top? Help me live! Please! Don't let me die! Help me LIVE! *I WANT TO LIVE!*

MIKE. Um. Sorry.

FRANCIS. (*A cry of total despair.*)

ANGELA. Now the weeping.

> (FRANCIS *weeps.*)

Now the gnashing of teeth.

> (FRANCIS *gnashes his teeth.*)

Now the tearing the hair.

> (FRANCIS *starts tearing his hair.*)

Right. Good. Biting the knuckles.

> (FRANCIS *bites his knuckles.*)

Uh-huh. Now the rocking and moaning.

> (FRANCIS *rocks and moans.*)

Very well done. Now the fast breathing and the sweating and the panic attack.

> (FRANCIS *has a panic attack.*)

Good one. Now the calling for Momma.

FRANCIS. *UNCLE BRUNO!*

ANGELA. A variation.

MIKE. Now here's where he gives up all hope. Total panic and despair. I love this part.

> (*They wait for it. Instead*—FRANCIS *stands up.*)

FRANCIS. *WOW!*

MIKE & ANGELA. (*Fluttering around, flapping their wings in fear.*)
Brrrrwaaaaak! Brrrrwaaaak! Brrrrwaaaak!

FRANCIS. Wow! Is this not the most spectacular day you've ever
seen? *Shazam!*

ANGELA. Am I on peyote, or did he just stand up?

FRANCIS. Will you look at this place? Is this gorgeous? I mean, the
rock, the cactus, the *skull*. Kazowie! Guess I went through a bad
patch there for a second. Sorry about that.

MIKE. Must be hysteria.

ANGELA. This too will pass.

MIKE. Yeah, and so will he. Any second.

FRANCIS. Five minutes to live, huh. Isn't that something. Five whole
minutes to enjoy all this. And then—*PSHOO!*—blast off!

MIKE. Yeah, blast off, all right. To *nowhere*.

FRANCIS. All right, so I'm going nowhere! There's nothing waiting
out there for me? Fine. No higher power in the universe? I'm all
right with that. But even the chance to have experienced nothing
is not nothing. It is not nothing to have seen this desert. It is not
nothing to have tasted a purple plum plucked from a bough in
Tuscany. It is not nothing to have met two creatures as glorious as
you on this, the final day of my life.

ANGELA. Glorious creatures . . . ?

FRANCIS. Yes, you are two beautiful, radiant creatures. And I say it
is not nothing for us three to be here together on a great round rock
flying through a void a trillion light years wide. I say that is a miracle. And we are standing on that rock right now, not another
time, right now, not some other time, but now. This very moment.
When I am filled with joy, even awaiting annihilation.

(*Hawaiian luau music is heard.*)

It's sort of too bad there's no higher power. And I did sort of have
my heart set on an afterlife . . . but hey. Them's the breaks, right?
Maybe another time. Do you hear something?

David Ives

MIKE. Is somebody holding a *luau* near here?

FRANCIS. You know, it's funny but . . . I could swear I see a long tunnel of light with my dead grandmother at the end of it.

> (*His* GRANDMOTHER *appears on a cloud, holding a plate of Jell-O.*)

Yes! She's waving to me! And she's holding a plate of Jell-O with the teeny-tiny marshmallows floating inside! Hello, Babba! Hello, Babba!

GRANDMOTHER. (*Italian accent.*) Francesco! Francesco! Long time-a no see!

FRANCIS. Babba, you're standing on a cloud!

GRANDMOTHER. This is because I am spirit, lighter than the water droplets I am-a standing on! But come, there are all these beautiful people here! All day we go (*Pumps fist and makes suction sound.*)—But *viene! Viene!* Your Jell-O she's-a melting! (GRANDMOTHER *disappears.*)

FRANCIS. Isn't this cool? Well, aloha, Mike. That's Hawaiian for "hello" and "goodbye."

MIKE. Yeah, yeah, yeah. I know what aloha means.

FRANCIS. Will you give me a hug? Come on.

MIKE. Goodbye, Francis.

> (*They hug.*)

FRANCIS. Aloha, Angela.

ANGELA. Aloha, Francis.

> (*They hug.*)

FRANCIS. Thank you for keeping me company today, you two. And hey—keep those nitrogen-rich turds coming! You're doing a fantastic job!

CACTUS. (*Voice from behind the stage.*) Goodbye, Francis!

FRANCIS. Goodbye, Mr. Cactus! Isn't that wonderful? I finally learned cactus! Goodbye, Mr. Rock! Goodbye, Mr. Skull! I love you! Aloha, everybody! Aloha, world! Aloha! (FRANCIS *disap-pears. Hawaiian music fades. All quiet.*)

MIKE. I knew we shoulda had the smorgasbord. So you think there's really . . . *you* know . . . after we die?

ANGELA. Anything is possible.

MIKE. Obviously.

ANGELA. Obviously. I tell you this, though: I'm goin' on pasta *tomorrow.*

MIKE. So, Ange, you forgive me for bein' a miserable, lowlife buzzard?

ANGELA. Yeah, I forgive you the buzzard. I do not forgive you the green wall-to-wall shag you put in the nest.

MIKE. I'll change it soon as we're home. I swear to (*Points upward.*)— even if there ain't one.

ANGELA. *Caro bellissimo!*

MIKE. *Mio tesoro!*

(*They join talons.*)

ANGELA. Y'know, honey, I think this desert is slightly underrated.

MIKE. I would say highly.

ANGELA. I would say highly, vastly underrated.

MIKE. Looks like it's gonna be quite a night, huh. Lotta stars . . .

ANGELA. Yeah. And you know what I say? I say: *Delicious.*

(*We hear birds and crickets and tree frogs as the sun sets in a gorgeous array of reds and golds. The stars come out.*

The lights fade.)

Toxicology
Jessica Hagedorn

MIMI CONTEMPLATES THE word *fame* while pouring herself the second-to-last bit of precious fuel from her stash in the freezer. On the rocks, garnished with a twist, the premium blend tastes dangerous and smooth. Mimi relishes each oily sip of her cocktail, fights the urge to guzzle it down. Cost of gas rising, prices highest they've ever been on the day the gorgeous young actor decides to kill himself, the same day Mimi filches the shipping box from Mrs. Schnabel's recycling bin and makes a bed for the dying animal. The dead actor is famous. The dying animal in Mimi's overheated apartment is not.

There is no product to be found in all of Manhattan or Brooklyn, or any other borough, for that matter. One shimmering drop left in the humming fridge. Mimi licks her lips, fights the urge to swoon. She flips open her cell, rereads last week's text message from Bobby:

> Bitch b cool
> Cuzn of mines 2 fuckin bad.
> Bad bad not good bad.
> Fnd nu srs. Dnt panic

Then he sent one more, seconds later, before disappearing for good:

> I wl mis u

The days fly by. So much work and nothing to do.

Mimi lights up one of those small Cuban girlie cigars, a cherished souvenir from Bobby's many clandestine trips to Bobby-wouldn't-say-where. Even after all these months, the cigar tastes fresh. She stares out the window at the shell of a high-rise luxury-loft condo being built across the street. Each floor starting at six point six. Rooftop gym, spa, pool, garage, natch. Doorman, valet service, twenty-four-hour concierge, no brainer. The architect's famous and Dutch.

Mimi's view of the river's now blocked, but so what? Mimi's always avoided looking at that river; the river reminds her too much

302

of the greasy oceans beyond. Mimi chides herself for getting morose. One shimmering drop left in the humming fridge; take it slow and easy, Mimi. And speaking of fame, just like that most famous of famous Lorca poems about death—Mimi glances at the clock and cheers up. Five in the afternoon. At *five in the afternoon, exactly five in the afternoon* . . . Lorca's hypnotic lament conjures the image of a young matador being gored by a Lydian bull. Five in the afternoon. Mimi takes another hit off the dainty cigar and wonders why she can't remember any other lines from the poem.

Five in the afternoon. At exactly five in the afternoon! You're such a drama queen, Mimi. Mimi It's All About Me-Me! Why the tears? You don't know any matadors. You never knew that poor, dead actor.

Cost of gas rising. And rising.

The animal crawls out of the shipping box, huge glassy eyes fixed on Mimi. It howls. It stinks. It's time. It's really dying.

I can't help you, Mimi says.

She's the squeamish type. Never mind the low-budget slasher films she concocts with such glee. You've seen the trailers. Supermodels trapped in desolate hostels in the Black Forest. Trembling jocks strapped down and eviscerated. Mimi's an auteur, so good at dreaming up genius scenarios. Next time you invite her to a dinner party? Watch the way she suddenly stops eating. Watch the way she flings her knife and fork, aiming straight for your face. The cutlery flung with such élan!

But when it comes to a suffering animal, the chick's a wuss.

Mimi stubs the cigar out in the sink. Restarts her computer. DISCUSS. SHARE YOUR THOUGHTS, urge the online bulletin boards. Sad. Tragic actor guy. So young! RIP. How could you? Oh, man. You were the source of our national pride.

LIKELY A SUICIDE OR ACCIDENTAL OVERDOSE. The headlines confuse and contradict just minutes and seconds after the famous actor's corpse is discovered by his Tantric masseuse. Mimi turns the flat-screen TV on, turns up the volume to drown out the sounds of the dying animal. Apparently, the actor's body has not been removed from the building. Apparently, the Tantric masseuse had a key. Apparently, the Tantric masseuse, the one carrying an umbrella and a set of keys, slips out the side exit while no one is looking and hails the first available taxi.

Police barricades hold back the growing mob of grieving fans. Hundreds and thousands of them, patient and determined. I am here to bear witness, a woman announces for the cameras. A man dressed like an Arctic explorer shakes his head and murmurs, Unreal. This is so unreal.

At five in the afternoon. At exactly five in the afternoon. Mimi's gaze wanders past the dying animal, the ticking clock, over to the ancient, humming fridge. That last, odorless, shimmering teardrop, waiting. Mimi must decide. And soon.

After Tourism
Ann Lauterbach

Disturbed over her marvel I heard her say
something nocturnal I saw
mystery as merely change I saw
envy and the illegitimate mile I saw
under the formal atrocity at the messy embankment
all these and vocabulary lagging behind its science
tramp unknown soldier cop
talking strange talk
under an altered light under daze
I heard her say *tomorrow* as if she knew
I heard her say *come back*
and I choose you
as analogue of the yet to be.
Do not foreclose
investigation, but come along I will
try not to protract my look into
now I will continue as if
you were next if you will I heard a man say
on the radio the other day, well, yesterday
talking about headaches
if you will
and today I had a look at
a Chinese cabinet, only it is not clear
it was Chinese it
may have been from another country I took
measurements nevertheless

Ann Lauterbach

    for my next life I am thinking of requesting librarian
    although I am as yet not on a list
    of possible survivors I am
    thinking of erasing the word sorrow from
    the world hurting under an illusory pennant
    master of ceremonies hidden behind its junk
    I am thinking of coming back as
    part of your coat as a tree is part wind.

Cézanne's Colors
Brenda Hillman

MY SECOND HUSBAND is writing an obituary of my first husband for
the U.C. Berkeley English Department archives. Rain runs past spiky
succulents & roses into storm drains near where we all stood together once, laughing & chatting by the gate. Lenny thinks this is
hilarious and is telling jokes in heaven. Whatever heaven is for him.
Or us.

*

I have been thinking about the nature of abstraction, about rivers in
California, and the way water molecules attach themselves in a completely generous fashion. I've been thinking about Cézanne going
back to fetch the paints he'd left on Monte Saint-Victoire. Some say
this trip back up the mountain made the painter ill. He had by then
combined shapes that could withstand the retreat of color—cylinder,
cone, & sphere. Perhaps the people standing before his paintings
helped them breathe at night.

*

Shortly after the Iraq War began, we lost three loved ones in our circle of family and friends. Each death seemed the opposite of the previous death yet they are connected somehow. Each person died in a
way that made no sense. Our friend Carol Thigpen Milosz had come
from Poland with an undiagnosed blood disorder. We stood next to
her bed daily at UCSF for a few weeks, watching her body be inhab-
ited by a spreading of red. I fixated on the monitors and her medication schedules, on things she said and scrawled on her paper, on the
cycles of relief from Ativan. I came to hate the morphine drip, the
thought of all the opium fields controlled by the CIA. The morphine
drip, like the Internet, protecting the traveler from the other senses.
Hemoccult. Tubes with their entrances.

*

Rainer Maria Rilke took a great interest in Cézanne's work and process, and for several weeks in 1907 while living in Paris wrote a series of impressionistic letters to his wife about the painter. The letters are remarkable for their accuracy about existence and the suffering of the soul. Rilke was not interested so much in the technique of the paintings—though craft was always of interest to him—as he was in the approach of the materials to the brink of being. As usual, Rilke wanted to see artists demonstrate an ability to live in an absolutely uncompromised manner; he looked to visual artists—particularly to Cézanne and the late impressionists—to help him on his way: "Here, all of reality is on his side in this dense quilted blue of his, in his red and his shadowless green and the reddish black of his wine bottles." The letters track Rilke's quest for pushing language through to the edge; he studies the paintings in which Cézanne foregrounds shapes and volume over luminescent color. Cézanne is not like other painters who are trying to perfect the drop of water, the virgin's smile, the slain rabbit beside a cornucopia of autumn vegetables, or (after all of these things) the release of light into impression. Cézanne is trying to release color from shape, and then to give shape abstract volume—and Rilke tries to track Cézanne's unmanageable blue from its sources.

*

Referring in contemporary conversations to the busyness of a spirit in afterlife does almost nothing but send horror and nervous panic onto the faces of what used to be called "the intelligentsia." When I start talking about the spirit on a bardo journey, friends want to know if I "really" "mean it." I have never thought my belief in the animating spirit world does any harm whatsoever to my daily life. I do not try to convert others to my belief, and it does not stop me from being a fairly high-functioning, occasionally rational adult. I haven't ceased to be interested in the facts of daily existence, in the well-being of family and friends, in poetry, in politics. The notion of a highly populated, invisible world seems one of the best metaphors for meaning-beside-the-meaningless. *Do you believe that with a straight face,* asked another friend. *I mean, do you believe she is floating around in some invisible world?* Let me say I refuse to limit my experience by not including this possible reality.

*

Carol Milosz suffered her death in a way that emptied the world of meaning and color. She bargained and pled with her loved ones to stay all night. We were not allowed to stay as long as she would have preferred us to stay. The doctors were unable to diagnose her blood disorder, and when her elderly poet husband arrived from Kraków to see her, she was about to be transported "upstairs to hospice," we were told one day. At the end of an illness when the body is undergoing radical change, its transfer of color is, at the very least, amazing. Her legs filled with red as they changed and swelled and became streaked. We ceased to understand color as a form of familiar experience; the varieties of red in her legs were in a realm between familiarity and terror. We could not contact Carol, a somewhat religious person, but kept her company by her bed, as a stay against the utter meaningless of her torment. "The new drugs are helping," she reported to us, for the dying are some of the best reporters. I think we stood there as much from duty and curiosity as from love, though it is shameful to admit. Each night we went back to our bed across the bay, to sleep and to wake in torpor. My husband's mammal body, turned away from me in the dark, kept meaninglessness away.

*

A spider bundles up a blond caterpillar, hanging deftly outside our kitchen window in the rain, and it is placed against the dewy morning as a constellation stands against the void; the caterpillar continues to squirm back and forth for hours, and when it is no longer mobile, is poised in relief, an inch-and-a-half pellet of matter with knobs protruding from other knobs, head facing down. Is its death just part of nature as a mere event in the morning? For maybe it has a grand meaning somehow, traced in some other realm.

*

Using an image system from trance work, I envisioned white figures at the edges of the field. One day when we went back to the hospital I felt the figures waiting for Carol across a river while resting my chin on the bed rail; I couldn't see them exactly, I simply experienced them at the periphery of the scene and supposed someone had

309

extended a hand. I said to the spirits, Take her with no clothes; the clothes are bothering her. I stood on this side of the river; they stood on the other. I knew it was my brain but our river.

*

In the late eighties, I worked on a series of pastoral elegies I called "Tractates," after some Gnostic Christian texts I was reading at the time; in my poems, a grieving person seeks to contact the mourned presence by looking sideways, rather than up or down, into death. What lived/lived on both sides. The loved one's soul floated next to me, in bushes, in streams.

The diagnosis for everyone is death, yet even in times of thinking about the afterlife, I've thought of being part of an endless system of metaphors, and imagine consciousness as something like a very large state-run park near our home, next to a petite lake called "Jewel" in which turtles are lined up like shallow helmets, and where benefi-cent rangers are in charge. A phoebe; a blue heron stimulates its oil glands with its long beak; and even in the driest time, murky green water is full of infinitely interesting wildlife, inch-long minnows, frogs about to be ingested by the heron. But not just being that, a part of that, but being conscious of being that. Of its being all right.

*

About half a year after Carol's death, we received news of the suicide of a friend J. J and I had lunch the year before, and she had told me she felt incurably depressed. J had a very good support network and plenty of resources for medical care, and I always felt reassured by the fact that she could get the care she needed. She was leading a vital, useful life, full of activity, and was much loved by her husband and friends. So it was with horror that we learned of her suicide out-side her home. I imagined on the leaves that had breathed in and out with her daily, an inappropriate, unmanageable red. On the backs of them, intricate veins, having evolved . . . not *toward* anything, exactly. Suicide removes "the plan."

*

A life plan. In the Greek pantheon, the Fates trumped Zeus. Even as the sky gods win out over the earth gods, and Zeus becomes the head of the Eumenides, the Furies, what trumps them all is the unknown that seems to be based on a series of whims of unknown origins. I shall consult the Fates, says Zeus. Having a life plan might be a lottery ticket scratched off by the desperate being who stands at the checkout counter of the convenience store.

For months the first thing I thought of each day was bright red among the green plants. I kept saying to J in the bright red: "You have misunderstood. We had a contract. We stay here for each other till fate removes us. You don't get to do this." I said it in my selfishness—the selfishness of the living.

*

I refuse to rule out the opening of the senses, which can make of death an entrance—not in any happy American way, but an entrance that might fill the dying brain with unmatchable awe. This sense of irrational commerce between living and dead—something that began when I was a child in the desert—derives from an energy experienced in dirt and plants and energy, an energy that is in itself the greatest thing, and is absolutely outside of anyone's control. Our senses are simply not tuned enough to perceive all there is to perceive, as William Blake observed ("If the doors of perception . . ."). If the mapping of knowledge includes a panoply of physical facts that have not been completely accounted for, based on laws of nature that are ceaselessly revised, if dogs and elephants have a larger range of senses than we, if certain forms of life are able to exist at temperatures that would make our blood boil, why is it not possible that there are other forms of matter in which consciousness, as puffs of otherness, carries on beside bodies enclosed in skin?

*

One of Rilke's most intense letters to Clara about Cézanne concerns the painter's late years when he is working, old and sick, nearly exhausted, by himself, yet attending mass and trying to find redemption by driving himself to work. Rilke writes: "Beginning with the darkest tones, he would cover their depth with a layer of color that led a little beyond them, and keep going, expanding outward from color to color, until gradually he reached another, contrasting pictorial element, where, beginning at a new center, he would proceed in a similar way." He writes of Cézanne's struggle to make the most of what is perceived, as if it is all, always, a process. This has reminded me also of Rilke's search in his own poetry for the relationship between the symbolic figure and the general matrix of the search, the background of the search, as it were. It is in this hall between being and nonbeing that both poetry and art have always been of most interest. Dying people are some of the best reporters.

*

I know little about J's last days except that it seems she left many writings. She and I had had many arguments about whether modernist poetry in fragmentary form can address suffering. I argued that the sentence is not a requirement for thought, and in fact, sometimes the brief spurts, the more abstract or difficult fragments can speak to conditions of human suffering in ways that are useful to the average person because they are brief and pure. Floating shards of a wreck that are whole. (Microsoft Word's squiggly green line recognizes I have written a fragment—it calls on me to complete it.) In the mystery of suffering, that tiny biochemical ability either not being able to look forward to living a day, or being able to.

Even if meaning is not a net, the search for meaning is something like a net; the suicide forcibly withdraws it. It is unfair to say, but suicide changes the possibility of grief in the same way that sudden death by unwillingness allows. In that hall between being and nonbeing there is neither ignorance nor knowledge. The splatter of red in the garden. The degree to which living from moment to moment can both sabotage and save. . . . Our friend's husband said at the memorial that J was only able to hold onto herself for a minute at a time. I think of this quite often now: the idea that the suffering of a particular kind is about finding a momentary accommodation to one's ego deficiencies. I will never get over thinking I should have done more for J—

Here is a poem I wrote for a suicide some years later:

DECEMBER MOON

Suppose you are the secret
of the shore—a strong wave
lying on its side—

you'd come to earth again

(as if joy's understudy
would appear) & you
could live one more bold

day without meaning to,
afresh, on winter's piney floor;

you say, I've been
to the door & wept;
it says, what door

*

Cézanne's suffering seems to have interested Rilke in part for the overlapping ways complex emotions inform abstract decisions in an art. Rilke admired the sacrifice of the artist and the suffering when faced with the unknown, having absorbed Nietzsche's fierce Übermensch philosophy in an odd way. In October of 1907, he writes to Clara about Cézanne's days: "To achieve the conviction and substantiality of things, a reality intensified and potentiated to the point of indestructibility by his experience of the object, this seems to him to be the purpose of his innermost work: old, sick, exhausted every evening to the edge of collapse by the regular course of the day's work (often he would go to bed at six, before dark, after a senselessly ingested meal), angry, mistrustful, ridiculed, and mocked and mistreated each time he went to his studio—. . . hoping nevertheless from day to day that he might reach that achievement which he felt was the only thing that mattered."

*

In the spring of 2003, my first husband, Lenny Michaels— in a somewhat similar manner as Carol Milosz—came back from Europe with cancer of the blood. He had been diagnosed with lymphoma, although doctors were not sure what sort. Those of us who loved him—and who lived with his particular brilliance and craziness—know that he did not always "embrace death" as many people learn to do; when I lived with him, he feared death absolutely and thought the death of any individual human was an outrage. With little warning about his own, he had fought death in his life and writings. And when he was in the hospital, his body, like Carol's, exchanged colors with the world's colors. He made jokes under the morphine, and laughed. We tried to laugh back because it was Lenny. Our daughter stood at the door daily, waiting for reports from the doctors, and the doctors went in and out. His children and his wife, Katharine, and friends stayed beside him day and night.

When he was moved to Intensive Care, several of us slept in the waiting room, and when we were told he would die that day, we gathered. Many were called to his side: his wife, children, ex-wife, former lovers—we held his feet and hands and begged him to stay. We told him it wasn't time yet. I can almost compose a Lenny sentence about this, even now: "They held Ickstein's feet." Not only did he not die that day, he rallied. He lived several days after that, as if he would be able to fight what was absolutely not negotiable. We were almost powerful enough to hold him, and Lenny knew this. When his mother arrived a few days after the rally, he was able to say goodbye.

*

Not a day goes by that I don't think of Lenny being here in some form still, laughing over something ridiculous. There are aspects of the physical universe we do not understand; far from imposing the notion of the spirit world on civilization, my own confusion carries me into places in the afterlife that do not seem forward or backward, nor do they seem like personal memories of the dead, of Carol or J or Lenny. In culture after culture in which such a fringe of entities have access to another reality, our great dead help us, and they are far more numerous than are our present bodies. This makes sense, for the world of the dead is very populated and they are helping us be wise; those extra realms have far more cumulative consciousness than just my own.

My husband, Bob, and I have experienced several other deaths since then, and in all the states between consciousness and unconsciousness—these states in which one is loved, but in which one must go to the great sea, not to be particular. We want unbearably much for these loved ones to feel at peace with their fate. I do not think human memory is the only form of "theoretical immortality"; works of art and aspen trees are other forms.

*

Years later, I dream my second husband and I are taking my first husband to the Louvre. Eager as a nuthatch, packed and solid, Lenny looks for the things he agrees with, or that his body might be comforted by—the colors of Cézanne, for example.

*

When I see Cézanne's last paintings I think of the bodies standing before them during the so-called Great War, and the way the warmth of bodies met the warmth of the colors. As people stood admiring them, the heat of bodies entered the paintings. Their edges did not beat antique drums for the coming violence yet the edges accompany whirlwinds in the terrible war. The paintings are free & do not grasp; their abstract logic, hovering at the boundaries of meaning, never eclipses the reason of atoms.

Shilling Life
Thomas Lynch

MOSTLY I REMEMBER the quick pearlescent cloud, the milky stain it made in the rush of current, when I dumped Hughie's ashes in the water. Watching what remained of him disappear downstream, the thing that I thought of was that thing they said whenever the big music gathered and the masked man rode off at the end of that cowboy show I watched as a boy, "A fiery horse, with the speed of light and a cloud of dust, and a hearty 'Hi-Yo Silver, Away!' The Lone Ranger!"

There goes Hughie now, I thought, that big music racing in my brain. Hi-Yo Silver, Away!

The little bone fragments, bits and pieces of him, glistened in the gravel bed of the Waters of Leith whilst his cloud of dust quickly worked its way in the current downstream to the eventual river mouth and out, I supposed, into the Firth of Forth and the North Sea and the diasporic waters of the world. I dipped the little metal disc I'd picked out of his ashes into the water, washing the dust of him off of it, and held it up like a silver bullet. "Who was that masked man?" I said to myself and slipped it into my pocket with the other foreign coins.

I wiped my eyes and focused on the water. I was not weeping but I could feel it—like abundance, overflow, spillage, real.

I pulled a camera from my pocket and snapped a photo on the off chance that any of his family would want to see the little waterfall and the leafy banks of the river tucked into the west end of the distant city that had become, if not his final resting place, his launching place, his headwater.

In my notebook I wrote, *13 August 2000, dumped Hugh Mac-Swiggan's ashes in the Waters of Leith near Dean Parish Church and Cemetery, Edinburgh.* Whether for the file back at the office or my own uncertain purposes, it's hard to say. I'd only started carrying a notebook again in the weeks since Hughie died. For the first time in years I was keeping track of things again, making notes, writing down oddments and loose ends. *Hi-Yo Silver, Away!*

316

I crossed back over the river by Dean Path and Bells Brae, to Queensferry Street and left at Hope, where I tossed the black plastic box I'd brought him in into a public barrel, then happened into Charlotte Square where a little crowd was gathering for the Edinburgh Book Festival—a tent city of the literati. The greensward was filling with bookish-looking sorts—women wearing eyeglasses and fashionable scarves, men with straw hats and briefcases, and around the edges of the green, large tents turned into performance spaces, as if a traveling circus had arrived. The life of fiction—I said to myself—the life of poetry. But I was neither artist nor aficionado. I was a tourist, passing through, my promise to old Hughie kept, suddenly glad for the ticket I kept in my pocket and the home, such as it was, and the life, such as it was, I would be returning to. I left the square, walking up Rose Street, smiling at diners in the outdoor eateries, tossing coins in the hats of the buskers and jugglers and street magicians, making my way without agenda. At the end I turned right and stopped at the Scott Monument before walking down Princes Street through the throngs of revelers and shoppers and souvenir stalls and into St. John the Evangelist at the corner of Lothian. It was a spot Hughie had marked on his map. According to the banner over the entrance to the church, a "Festival of Peace and Silence" was going on inside and I walked in and through that vaulted space among the contemplatives spread among the pews, apparently feasting on peace and silence, until I heard a low din of voices coming from a small room behind the sanctuary. It was the meeting Hughie had directed me to. I went in, put the pound note in the basket, sat down, listened in, and said my piece. An hour later, emerging from that great kirk's interior to the sound of pipers and drummers from the castle above, and the midafternoon's late-season light washing over the swarm of glad-faced humanity, the ancient city in its August festivities, I felt, inexplicably, alive and well. I actually felt it. There was this emergent pang of longing for voices I knew. I wanted to tell them I was better now and coming home and hoped they would still be there when I returned. I looked for a phone to call home on.

I owed it to Hughie, I suppose, to go the distance with him. He'd gone some distances with me since I'd met him thirty years before when I was laid up in the hospital. Fractured hip and pelvis, broken leg and ankle, a couple of compressed vertebrae—I'd fallen from a third-story fire escape. I was hungover and doped up, in casts and

317

traction, and lucky by all accounts to be alive after a party in my rented rooms near the university. It was an old apartment house where I'd been out on the fire escape, a rickety old wooden structure, acting the dark and moody artist, part Dylan Thomas, part Bob Dylan, with my bottle of J. W. Dant Kentucky sour mash, the first clear autumn evening after two weeks of rain.

And it was Eileen Doyle I was trying to impress and Eileen's chest I was hoping to get ahold of, and the J. W. Dant I could, of course, blame it on, on the better-than-even chance that Eileen demurred. That was my plan. After naming a couple of the constellations and saying something memorable, maybe quoting Theodore Roethke or Emily Dickinson, and taking a swig from the bottle of bourbon, I'd begin my advances on lovely Eileen.

She was beautiful and I wanted her to be impressed by the up-and-coming man of letters I was fashioning myself to be. I had a few chords on a guitar and could sing some Leonard Cohen tunes as backup. I had the whiskey to boot. I knew some poems.

And it was J. Doggett Whitacker from West Virginia, our English professor, the son of a bitch, who came out through the window, out onto the fire escape, and began turning Eileen's sweet attentions away from me with his syrupy talk about the lost sister of the Pleiades, then the moon and its phases and the tides, and time.

So I stood up and cleared my throat and, leaning back on the rail to say something unforgettably manful, though I can't for the life of me remember now, I must've leaned too heavily, or the rail was badly constructed, or maybe it was all those recent rains, the rotting wood gone soggy and all; whatever it was, the rail gave way and before I knew it I could feel myself falling backward through mid-air, falling into the oblivion of God only knows what peril, falling, falling.

I'm flat on my back and looking up into it all, the vast basilica of the heavens. I'm seeing stars. And then I can feel myself rolling over, knees and elbows, then arms outstretched, assuming the all-fours, and I can't, for the life of me, get my breath. I can see myself, sort of out of body, as if occupying a balcony seat to this whole daft theater.

"Who is the president of the United States?" Whitacker is shouting at me. "Who wrote 'The Love Song of J. Alfred Prufrock'? Do you know where you are? What day is it? Can you say your name?"

To assure him and the gathering retinue that, though damaged in some yet-to-be-determined ways, my intellect and sensibilities remained intact, I began reciting "Who's Who," word for word, a piece

I'd memorized for just such an occasion—not The Fall, as I later came to call it, but for the likes of Eileen Doyle with eyes such as hers and her perfect skin and her fine round breasts and clear autumn evenings under the stars and the hopes we all have of intimacy.

It was, by all accounts, a stirring recital, perfectly paced and delivered, in the fashionably beleaguered diction of the artist I imagined myself, at the time, to be:

A shilling life will give you all the facts:

I could see the fright in their eyes giving way to wonder as I commenced the recitation, then amazement, that here I was in this epic pose, having taken a dive, albeit inadvertently, that would have killed ninety-nine out of every hundred ordinary men, and yet here I was reciting a sonnet to allay their worries, a man of parts and substance to the end.

Of how he fought, fished, hunted, worked all night

I worked my way through the poem's litany of rhymed particulars, pausing for the stanza's break between lines eight and nine, sighing slightly, turning my gaze ever so meaningfully, looking deeply into Eileen's eyes as she hovered above me, I eased the poem's little dagger home—how the great man who was possibly the possessive *who* of the title, was nonetheless still smitten by the memory of some lovely homebody who did "little jobs about the house," whistled, gardened, and, for reasons still unrevealed by the text,

answered some

Of his long marvelous letters, but kept none.

In the slow motion I always remember this in, tears are welling in Eileen's eyes, those rhymes still sounding in her tiny ivory ears, her bosom is heaving, and she is holding my hand between her breasts and wiping my face with her other hand and Doggett Whitacker is looking utterly vanquished, while the constellations are turning above them all, in the bright firmament of heaven. But in the real-life version, thirty years ago, I no more had Auden's memorable iambs out than I began to puke—all of that god-awful bourbon and, I believe, the remnants of a pepperoni pizza—projectile vomiting, I think they call it, *Gone with the Wind* turned *Exorcist*—and the last thing I remember before blacking out was the look of horror or disgust in Eileen's eyes. I did not know her well enough to know.

And isn't that always the rub? Between the facts of the matter and the way we keep trying to wrestle them into compliance with our remembrance of them? Hardly one for "little jobs around the house," Eileen went to work with the State Department, managed several of the country's more difficult embassies, and resigned to head up an NGO doing relief work in the Congo. Doggett Whitacker moved west, became chair of the English Department at a small college, and wrote a novel that became a movie that was nominated for an Oscar. Their "long marvelous letters" and my own lost in the mail as they always are.

As for me, I never became a rock star or poet, never had "all my honors on" or authored much of anything. My father never beat me. I never ran away. He drove his Lincoln into a bridge abutment one winter night on the way home, and spent two years paralyzed below the waist before he died, grateful there'd been no other cars involved.

"Christ," he'd always say, "they'd've sued us for a fortune."

I stayed home, did not become the doctor he wanted or the lawyer he wanted or the writer or rock star I always imagined myself. I married the Methodist minister's daughter and we went into business doing lawn maintenance and snow removal. Early-morning work for the most part, it left my afternoons and evenings free. Through my father-in-law, who served on the township board, I got contracts to keep the grass mowed, the leaves cleaned up, and the roads clear of snow in the three township cemeteries. When the excavator who did their grave openings died, I bought his backhoe and took over. It was easy work and paid well enough and once folks started cremating more, I put a retort in and then another in the back of the pole barn where I stored my equipment. I hired some kids to do the heavy work—the backhoe and mower part of the business. When I couldn't find kids anymore, I hired Mexicans. I stayed around the office and took care of the cremations. The area morticians would send them over, in wooden caskets or cardboard boxes. I'd pull them from the hearse onto the pushcart with the rollers, check out the paperwork to be sure everything was in order, all the permissions granted, boxes checked—no pacemakers or other explosives—open the retort door and shove them in. A couple hours later, I'd sweep it all out, run the bones through the grinder, pick out any hardware from the caskets, and box up the ashes and label them. Twice a week I'd drive around to the area funeral homes dropping off the boxes or the urns, if they had sent an urn. No one asked about my work. Everyone wanted to be cremated; they just weren't that curious about the fire. It was perfect work for me. Simple, solitary, fixed fees and costs. I could read or tinker with the equipment. The crews would come back from their various duties—burials or mowings, setting headstones. I paid them every other week. By midafternoon I was ready for a drink. I kept a bottle of good scotch in the desk drawer.

It was Hughie MacSwiggan the insurance company sent to see me thirty years ago in the hospital, after The Fall, to offer a settlement of five thousand dollars, in trade for a promise not to sue.

"Of course, the company assumes no fault or negligence. It's only to assist in your recovery. There's hardly any cause of action here—what with the drink that had been taken." Hughie looked like Gregory Peck in *To Kill a Mockingbird*—handsome like that, but flashier, with French cuffs and a bow tie and tassel loafers.

"The doctor said it was a *good* thing I was drinking," I replied. "I didn't stiffen up and break my neck."

I'm not sure if I'd heard that or was making it up.

Hughie smiled, put down his briefcase, removed his hat, pulled a chair to my bedside, and sat near enough to me that he could speak in the voice of a confessor or confidante.

"Listen, kid, do what you like about the money. I'm only the messenger. Here's the thing. It's a crapshoot. You can take the offer, we'll have a check in a week, you'll sign a release, and that's the end of that. Or you can hire an attorney to sue for . . . pick a number . . . and the attorneys can all rattle swords at each other for the next three or four years and after your steadfast refusal not to settle for a penny less than . . . pick a number . . . the court will award you . . . pick a number . . . and your man will get half of it and two-thirds of whatever is left will go for 'costs'—depositions and inquisitions, research and transcripts and such, and after all the dust clears you'll get five thousand, if the guy you've hired is worth his salt. He and our attorney will meet at the golf course to toast your perseverance. Of course, it could go the other way. You could end up with nothing, what with the party and the underage drinking and the designer drugs. The judge might say you're lucky to be alive and let it go at that. Do what you want. It's not my money either way."

I could see why the company would send someone like Hughie. He was what my father would have called a closer—someone who made perfect sense. But then he got even closer still and began to speak in such a quiet, calming tone, I had to watch his mouth to see him shape the words to get them.

321

"But listen, kid, if you really believe that load of shit about how lucky you were to be drinking, how it probably saved your life, if you have really convinced yourself that being drunk when you do a back-flip off of some slum landlord's third story is all to the *good*, you've got more problems than any amount of money will solve. And they'll likely get worse before they get better. So if it dawns on you, after you've spent the next six months in a cast, sleeping on your belly, out of school, out of work, if it ever occurs to you that you might have a problem with drink, well, that's a problem I know some things about. And maybe I can help."

He stood up, buttoned his jacket, straightened his arms so that the monogrammed French cuffs showed just below the sleeves of his jacket. He took a business card from his suit coat pocket, a pen from his shirt pocket, and began writing something on the back.

"The number on the front's for talking money. You can call during regular business hours. The number on the back's my home phone. Call anytime to talk about," he paused to put the pen back in his shirt pocket, "to talk about life. One's no good without the other. Call before you take another drink. Call before you take another dive. Next time you might not bounce."

I never called the number on the back. I took the easy money, spent it on nothing memorable, went on with my twenties and thirties unencumbered by any lasting damage from the fall. Life just seemed to happen to me—the marriage, the twins, the business. I joined the Rotary Club and the Masons. I was president of the Chamber of Commerce. I served on the hospital board and played golf. We went to church. Every year we went camping. We bought a boat and motor home. We had a dog and then another.

I never saw Hughie again except in passing, until twenty years later when I turned up, court ordered, to my first AA meeting after a DUI. The cop who popped me didn't know who I was. I was driving home from a card game at the lodge. It was 2 a.m. and the streets were quiet and he pulled me over for driving without my headlights on. Hell, in the old days Chief Averill would have been playing cards with us and would have called some cars to escort us home safely. He'd hit us up later for a donation to the Police Athletic League. But this kid with his flashlight and steroid physique asks to see my driver's license, asks how much I've had to drink, asks me to step out of my car, asks me to walk along the road, then takes my keys and takes me in. I've never been so pissed off in my life.

My attorney, a fellow Rotarian, was able to keep me out of jail by mentioning my standing in the community and my promise to get help with what the judge, a brother Mason, called my "drinking problem." I was sentenced to "ninety in ninety," meaning an Alcoholics Anonymous meeting every day for ninety days. There were weekly urine tests—the indignity of it—and my driving was restricted to AA meetings and work. Of course I wouldn't go to one of the local meetings, at St. Michael's or the Presbyterians—no need to get the chattering classes going around town. Instead, I went over to a hospital in the next township where they had a couple meetings every day, at midmorning and after dinner.

And there was Hughie, looking distinguished in his midsixties now, handsome as ever but more relaxed—more flannel than French cuffs, more at ease, looking like my father might have looked if he'd missed that bridge abutment years ago. When it came his turn Hughie said his name and that he was "a grateful recovering alcoholic," and then gave anyone who'd listen—some of the inpatients there were too far gone—a brief narrative of his life and times.

How he never drank before he went to war. How he returned from the South Pacific skinny, malarial, and alcoholic, "trained by the US Marine Corps for everything but living life on life's terms. I could survive the jungle, the Japs, and World War II, just not marriage, peacetime, and parenthood." He married the first woman he'd had sex with, not counting the ones he'd paid for in Melbourne and China. He bought a bungalow in the suburbs and went to work selling insurance. After a son and a daughter and more trouble with drink, his first wife left him to "cut her losses." He married again, fathered again, got fired from the agency, and divorced again. There followed a decade of brief incarcerations for bar fights and drunk driving, a bankruptcy filing, and, after a remarkable comeback financially, what he called a moment of clarity when it occurred to him that everything he'd touched "had turned to shit."

"It was the brand-new Cadillac I drove into a telephone pole on Northwestern Highway that made me see the light. I'd been dry for a couple weeks, things were going good, I just stopped into a joint on the way home for a beer. However many hours later it was when I crashed the car, I walked away from it. I got out, like I'd just had a tire gone flat, not head-on into a goddamn telephone pole. I just got out and was walking down the street looking for a telephone booth to call the dealer and tell him to bring me another, like the whole world was my bartender, 'I'll have another,' when the thing blew up—this huge fireball!—that's the light I saw. My 1968 red leather interior, V-8 400-some horsepower exploding lightbulb—that was my moment of clarity."

He joined AA mostly because he couldn't afford a therapist. After the big agency fired him, he opened his own little insurance office and married Annette after she'd kept his fledgling business afloat for several years. They never had any children, but she kept him solvent and upright, made him take her out to dinner and dancing and mended his relations with his own daughters and son, who'd grown distant in his drinking years. They had grown, in spite of his absence or because of it, into adults he loved and admired and had children of their own who thought of Hughie as a kindly "Papa." For reasons he wasn't entirely certain of he had put together "quite a few twenty-four hours of sobriety" and was grateful for the fact that he "wouldn't be drinking today."

"I believe what they told me," Hughie concluded. "We alkies only have three options. Get well, go crazy, or die. If I'm not getting better, I'm getting worse. That's why I keep coming back. I don't take the first drink." He held up the thumb of his right hand for punctuation, then the index finger. "And I go to meetings. Everything else seems to fall into place."

People were nodding and smiling and wiping their eyes and fidgeting in their seats and looking at their watches and Hughie was wrapping up.

"Keep it simple," he said and thrust his thumb up in front of him again with purpose. "Don't take a drink." Then, lifting his index finger beside it, said, "Go to meetings." There was general applause and that was the end.

I did my ninety meetings, kept all my appointments with the probation department, passed my piss tests, and managed to keep from taking a drink for most of the next two years, keeping in contact with Hughie, who'd become my sponsor—someone to call when things got crazy and I wanted to drink.

I might've stayed on the wagon all the way except for the pain in my ass. It would start in my lower back, work its way down my right buttock, down the right leg, and into the ankle, where the whole damn thing would throb away. I couldn't sit comfortably, I couldn't stand for very long, I couldn't walk around the block. It was a low-grade, ever-present, occasionally flaring pain that ran up my leg into the middle of my gluteus damn maximus and down again.

I self-diagnosed as residual damage done me years ago by The Fall or maybe aggravated by lifting too much. It woke me one night with a start, out of a sound sleep, like those sudden dreams of rapid descent, the pain in my ankle flaring badly, and I came downstairs and poured myself one short one, from the bottle I kept for visitors—just to take the edge off the pain of it and to get myself back to sleep. My wife woke me up the next morning in the wingback chair, the bottle empty, the weather channel on the TV, the pain in my hindquarter still killing me. I tried the chiropractor and massage. I even tried acupuncture to no avail. I did the stretching and the hanging from the doorjamb and the ice packs and the heating pads and all the rest. But nothing would soothe it like a stiff drink and some drugs.

After a couple years of on-again-off-again binge drinking and drying out and popping OxyContin for the chronic pain, I found myself fairly dulled to everything. I managed on a kind of automatic pilot, coming and going between the house and office, joylessly, painlessly, biding time, waiting for whatever was going to happen next. The twins were away at college. My wife, it seemed, had developed her own life into which I could come or go as I pleased, like something modular but optional. We stopped eating together. Sex was lackluster, hit or miss. She'd have plans most evenings—something at church or with one of her civic groups. The daily routines lost their meaning to me, becoming a slow procession of dull details. I felt no pain, my own or anyone's. It freed me up to come and go as I pleased. I spent lots of time at the lodge and country club, long boozy lunches with the Chamber of Commerce crowd. I wrote it off to business promotion. I never would have called this happiness, or sadness. The range of my emotions had narrowed. The best I could manage was an absence of pain. I didn't want to chance tampering with that.

For a while, Hughie tried to get me to quit. He'd call me and offer to come get me and take me to a meeting. I'd give him one or another excuse. After a while he quit calling too. Every so often he'd send a card that read, "How go the wars, kid?" or "Had enough?" and always included a number to call, "day or night, 24/7, whenever you're ready." After a while he quit sending cards.

And I stayed at the office more. The area was growing. Farms turning into golf courses and subdivisions, we had a respectable traffic jam through town in the morning, the Chamber of Commerce membership was booming, funeral homes doing land office business, people dropping like flies. I was running the retorts day and night. First it was just the Episcopalians and Unitarians who cremated their

325

dead. Over time even the Catholics did it. What had been the exception was becoming the rule. I sold the landscape equipment to one of the Mexicans, who took over the grave digging and cemetery maintenance. It was all I could do to keep up with the cremations. Along one wall of the pole barn bodies in caskets and cardboard boxes were lining up, waiting their turn in one of the chambers. I walled off one end of the pole barn and put in a shower and toilet and bed. Nobody seemed to miss me at home. First it was only a couple nights a week. After a while the exception became the rule and I only went home for emergencies. Otherwise I more or less lived at the crematory. I'd spend the days reading novels or newspapers, running the retorts, and sorting the paperwork. I'd try not to drink before four or five, after I'd been into town for a meal. I slept in fits and starts. I kept the retorts running. Some nights between the drink that it took to be free of pain and the drink that it took to be entirely numb, when the color of the whiskey in the glass and the tinkling of the ice cubes in the glass still meant something to me, I'd stand out in the pole barn between the retorts and the waiting boxes full of patient corpses and read them poems from a book I bought at the library sale called *The New Modern American & British Poetry.* I'd paid a quarter for it.

I'm nobody! Who are you?
Are you nobody, too?
Then there's a pair of us—don't tell!
They'd banish us, you know.

The particulars of Emily Dickinson's life, detailed by the anthologist, were a comfort to me. How she wrote in private, in secrecy, and a book of hers was never published in her lifetime but after death she became famous. "Keeping herself strictly to herself, she became a mystery, a legend even in her own lifetime."

I'd read them Frost and Rudyard Kipling and memorized that little "Envoy" by Ernest Dowson:

They are not long, the weeping and the laughter,
  Love and desire and hate;
I think they have no portion in us after
  We pass the gate.

They are not long, the days of wine and roses:
  Out of a misty dream
Our path emerges for a while, then closes
  Within a dream.

One night Hughie called. I woke with a start, the book hitting the floor with a flop and him standing in front of me like an apparition. He was thinner, paler, but handsome still, his tweed coat bagging on his shoulders, his flannel shirt buttoned at the collar.

"Your wife said I'd find you here."

"Yes, yes, busy . . . round the clock. . . ."

"How do you sleep with those furnaces going?"

He was shouting a little to be heard.

"I must be used to it. Can't hear a thing."

I wondered how long I'd been out for, what time it was. I was thirsty but with Hughie there I couldn't drink. I offered to make some coffee. He was looking around.

"So here's where we all go up in smoke."

"Yeah, ashes to ashes, dust to dust."

I was trying to sound in better fettle than I was.

"I've told Annette to just cremate me."

He was looking through the open door, out across the pole barn to where the retorts were running.

"Well, don't be in a hurry, Hughie, we don't give any discounts till you make the hundred."

"I am in a hurry, kid. That's why I'm here."

The particulars of Hughie's cancer were unremarkable. He said them without drama or the precision of detail that people with diseases often are given to, and finished with the best guess his doctors had given him.

"Six weeks? Six months? It's hard to know. But I've told Annette to just cremate me."

The operative word in his directive was "just." He just didn't want to trouble them further. He just wanted it all to be over—the second-guessing, the treatments they kept proffering, but never a cure. He just wanted it all behind him.

"You know, I should have died in the Russell Islands. God knows some better men than me died there."

I told him I'd take care of everything, rest assured, he needn't worry. I was not comfortable with all of this. I was very thirsty. I wanted him to leave. I preferred the anonymous dead in their boxes lined up on the wall of the pole barn waiting their turn to the living, breathing, by all accounts dying man I knew some things about, standing before me. I wanted him out of there and to be left alone.

"Easy for you to say—'don't worry'—I'll be the one with my nose

327

pressed up against whatever is out there, or isn't. Don't bullshit a bullshitter, kid."

He sat down in the folding chair I kept by the small table that was the only other furniture in the room.

I asked him about his time in the service. Anything to change the subject.

"Never mind the Marines," he said, "no taps or flags or bugle, no eulogists or limousines, none of that. I'm not paying for a party I can't be at. I just want to be burned up before I start to smell bad, and one more thing."

He pulled his chair closer, leaned in with his elbows on his knees, his hands hanging open with uplifted palms, and fixed me with his slightly jaundiced eyes.

"I want you to scatter my ashes for me. Will you promise me that, kid? You've got to take care of that part yourself. I don't want Annette and the kids . . . Promise me."

I told him I thought his family might appreciate someplace to go and pay their respects on the holidays and birthdays and anniversaries out there in the future after he died. I suggested one of the local cemeteries where three boxes of ashes could be put in a single grave.

"That's just it, kid. I don't want them anchored to me or someplace where I'm buried. They can just keep me in their hearts. That's why I want to be burned and scattered. I want to travel light. Like I'm always saying, kid, 'Let go, let God.'"

I could see he wasn't budging on this. No grave or niches in Hughie's future. No together forever cut in stone.

"And where do you want the ashes scattered?" I asked as if we were talking about something other than him, as if "the ashes" might be easier, figuring maybe some hole on the golf course or in the river or lake, or possibly in the woods out behind his house. It seemed he hadn't considered this part. He was looking off into the middle distance, his eyes narrowing, deep in his contemplations, a wince or a grin—I couldn't be sure—beginning to form on his face.

"Scotland," he said quite matter-of-factly. "Yes, Scotland, that's just the place."

"Have you family there?"

"None that I know of."

I asked when he was last there and he told me he had never been. He'd always wanted to go, since way back in his drinking days when he used to be known as "Friggin MacSwiggan" in the bars. But after getting sober he would never chance it, what with all of those lovely single malts and local whiskeys.

"And Annette doesn't fly," and business was either too good or too bad to take the time away and go. But now that he thought of it, now that he'd be dead before long, he'd really like to go and wasn't I just the man to take him.

"Scotland, kid, that's just the place—take me to Scotland and toss me to the wind. What's that they say? 'I'm worth it'? Well I *am* worth it, after all. So promise me you'll take me there. Or else I'll haunt you, promise."

"But I've never been out of the country," I protested. Except for a cremationists' convention once, in Albuquerque, I'd never even been on a plane.

"All the more reason. Live a little, kid, get out of your comfort zone and see the world. Promise me." He was suddenly serious. "Promise me you'll get me there."

Hughie pulled out an envelope full of hundred-dollar bills wrapped in thousand-dollar packets and quickly counted out five of them. Of course, I objected and of course, he insisted.

"That should cover things. I'll pay the freight, kid. After that you're on your own."

He said nothing about how I'd gone missing from AA. He never asked about my drinking or the prescription drugs. So when he gathered himself up to go, I told him I hoped it would all go well for him, that he wouldn't be in any pain, and that I really wanted to thank him for all his care and kindness over the years and that maybe someday I'd get sober yet.

"It takes what it takes, kid. We all have our bottom. Who's to know? For years I thought it meant giving something up. It wasn't until later I saw it was a gift, sobriety, something I could give myself. All I had to do was ask for a little help from my friends."

I nodded and smiled.

"I'm an alkie who's not dying of alcoholism. That's miracle enough for me, kid. The rest is gravy."

I nodded some more and shook his hand.

"Do you think if they told me when they showed me this cancer, 'So, Hughie, just don't eat cabbage and go to these meetings and this cancer, this squamous-cell metastasized carcinoma, will never kill you'—do you think I'd have any trouble with quitting cabbage or doing the meetings? Not on your life, kid. Well, not on mine."

When Hughie died, Annette kept him at home, put on some Tommy Dorsey and Glenn Miller music and called some of the AA crowd and they announced it at the local meetings and all that evening and the next they kept Hughie there while folks came by to pay their respects and tell Annette and the kids exactly how much Hughie had meant to them. An AA friend who worked for a funeral home fixed him up a little, closed his eyes and mouth, filed the paperwork, and brought a box.

The next morning, his daughters and son lifted his body into the box, into the hearse, and they and Annette all followed behind while the handful of friends and neighbors sang the "Marines' Hymn" while the little procession drove Hughie down the driveway and out of sight. I went ahead to meet them at my place. I had the retort fired up, preheated, and at the ready. I rolled Hughie onto a hydraulic lift, put the little numbered metal coin on the box to keep track of Hughie after the burning, and pushed the box into the retort, closed the door, and pressed the red button that filled the chamber with fire that burned his body and the box. Annette wiped her eyes, thanked me for everything, and handed me an envelope. When I insisted that Hughie had paid for everything she said that I was not to open it until I was on the plane on the way to Scotland. "I'm just following instructions," she told me, then hugged me, then went away.

After everything had cooled, I ground his larger bone structures into a finer substance and dumped all of it into a plastic bag inside a plastic box with a label that bore his name and dates and the logo of the crematory. This greatly reduced version of Hughie was kept on the table in my room till I could arrange for a passport and get my ticket sorted and pack my bags and say my goodbyes and get through the long list of procrastinations that had kept me from going anywhere before. Days went to weeks, which went to months. For the first few nights he was there on my table, I'd pour myself a tall one, cobble some elegiac blather together, hoist the tumbler saying, "Here's to ya, Hughie!" recite some poems, and get a little tipsy with him. But more and more I began to feel stupid, talking to a box of ashes, especially one that had managed, in his own time, to keep sober. I drank less, then little, then none at all. "You've ruined it for me," I whispered to the ashes one night when the whiskey wouldn't do it. And one night after that, I opened the box, undid the twist tie to the plastic bag, and poured the last bit of a near-empty bottle of pricey scotch over Hughie and said, "Have one on me, pal." The poems I kept reading to the box sounded suddenly new to me. I slept well after that. I bought a ticket to Scotland the following day.

I taught one of the Mexicans to run the retort. He said he'd take care of things while I was gone.

When the X-ray at the airport showed "some dense packaging" in my carry-on, I told the security guard it was Hughie MacSwiggan's cremated remains, and asked if she'd like to inspect them further. She looked a little panicked, shook her head, and let me pass. Somewhere over the Atlantic I opened the envelope Annette had given me. Inside was a list of AA meetings in Edinburgh—dozens of them, every day all over town, written out in Hughie's scribble. There was a detailed street map with the locations marked in red ink. And a note from Hughie in the same red ink that read, "Have one on me, kid," paper clipped to a Bank of Scotland one-pound note.

I did not declare Hughie at customs in Heathrow and kept to my own counsel on the train ride north and said nothing checking in at the Channings Hotel. I considered the gardens off Princes Street or maybe some corner of the castle grounds, but the festivalgoers made those impossible—the swarm of them everywhere, everywhere. I toyed with the notion of leaving him in a public house near Waverley Station on the theory that heaven for Hughie might mean that he could drink again. Maybe a fellow pilgrim would find him there and put him to some providential use. But it was the view from Dean Bridge, the deep valley, the "dene" that names the place, the river working its way below under the generous overhang of trees, the scale of it all, and the privacy. I worked my way down into Belgrave Crescent, where I found an open unlocked gate to the private gardens there. But it was a little too perfect, a little too rose gardeny and manicured and I was drawn by the sound of falling water. So I went out and around past the Dean Parish Church and the graveyard there. I made my way down to the water by the footpath and, working back in the direction of the bridge, I found a small waterfall, apparently the site of an old mill, and poured Hughie's ashes out—some into the curling top waters and the rest into the circling pool below. I knelt to the duty of it and watched till every bit of him was gone.

The Hanging Jetty
Michael Upchurch

THE FOOD AND WINE HAD been superb, the service impeccable, the setting otherworldly. They'd had a window table looking out onto the strait, and across the water were hills that belonged to another island. Beyond it rose mountains that were part of another country, while scrolling out onto the bay was a curving jetty, shaping vagaries of tides, its long arm creating seeming shelter.

Their waiter, returning, smiled as he handed them their bill, which was reasonable considering the meal. While her husband searched his wallet for his credit card, she pointed toward the view and asked, "Can you walk out there?"

"Oh, sure," the waiter said. "The beach is public."

"I mean on the jetty."

"People do."

Her husband handed his card to the young man, who accepted it with a flourish. When he returned with the receipt to sign, her husband penned his signature with an even more extragavant flourish. All three laughed, and the wife said, "You live in such a beautiful place—it must be hard to tear yourself away from it."

His laugh finessed itself into a tight little smile: "It is."

Her husband, a little behind the beat, chimed in, "I imagine so."

Then they savored their last few minutes at this perfect table by this perfect window with this perfect view on offer.

They were a couple in late middle age, a pair who had achieved a plateau of sorts. True, they were no longer young, but the things that had once been young about them and made them attractive to each other were still in play, slightly burnished and enriched now. They knew what they had in each other: ideal companionship. They could admire younger couples they saw, especially in a setting like this, and wonder if they enjoyed the same contentment. And they could indulge in these speculations—with a sidelong glance, a half-erotic curiosity—while sending only the mildest ripples of jealousy through their own deep trust in each other. If they'd earned any wisdom over the years, it was in knowing that all things end badly, that it's in the midst of life that all real worth is to be found, and that the time they had already spent together was the truest home they had made for each other. Something lit and nourished them from within, a sort of enduring flame they'd conjured together with their choice of each other. Serenity played over their features. The next stage, they knew, would be health worries: the inevitable caprice of the body's fate. But all their essential questions had been answered, at least to the degree that anyone wants any answers.

Standing and gathering their things, they thanked the waiter, whose smile remained guarded.

"I think we're going out there!" she said, nodding toward the jetty. The roll in her husband's walk took its cue from her merry tone of voice. The restaurant's glass doors closed behind them and the bright evening's light on the windows' glare made their fellow diners into shadows.

The breeze outside was stiff. On the windward side of the jetty small waves smacked against the rock wall while on the leeward side the water surface was both spiraled and smooth, as though the wind didn't affect it but pulling currents did. Children on the beach lugged a small rowboat onto shore, and a ferry in the distance moved so slowly it was hard at first to tell if it was pushing forward or slipping backward. A foghorn sounded, even though no fog could be seen.

Before taking their walk they fetched their windbreakers from the car. It still wasn't summer, no matter how late the light lingered, and the air was brisk up here on the bluff.

Clad in colorful nylon, they followed a path down to the shore and found their way to the jetty. When they stood where it made landfall, it seemed to rise before them. The gift of its curve made the water it swept across seem rounded like an eyeball. And when they looked along the structure's curvilinear spine, they had a surprise.

They had expected it to be cobblestoned on top—paved in some sort of rock that could withstand the brutal force of surf and winds. Instead, it was crowned with a boardwalk built from cedar planks, anchored into concrete by a series of rivets and bolts. This wooden boardwalk was both durable and springy. But the biggest surprise was that it was *painted*, not just in weather-resistant gray or brown, but in a mural . . . a map that, as you walked along it, became an atlas of the world, with all the countries in different colors. And the colors kept changing. China, for instance, started out red but grew a more sickly magenta farther out. And Brazil, which started out a forest green, turned to industrial lime by the time they reached the center of it.

As she and her husband stepped forward, they also stepped upward, borders unspooling at their feet, crude images of the often crude fates of nations. The pictures unfolding were fascinating—and then, as the jetty rose higher and higher, a little frightening. Things grew especially worrisome when she saw how the boards detached themselves from the rivets that secured them. When she looked down through the cracks between these floating planks, she saw unruly water move below and noticed an aching in her hips, some muscle that didn't feel "right" to her—as though, without knowing it, she had strained or injured herself on this long yet gradual walk uphill. And her husband, when she looked at him, had developed a hunched posture from addressing the rigors of this jetty. He had also—but how was this possible?—gone entirely white haired from the pleasing salt-and-pepper shades she had studied over dinner.

He began to stumble. She reached for him and he grabbed her arm with an inconsistent strength. It was an old man's grasp. She had felt it many times when working as a teenager in a nursing home, where, within a day or two, she had come to realize that the fingers were the final thing to go, that their power to grip was the last thing to capitulate.

"Let's head back," she said, and pulled him with her—down toward where China was a healthy red again and farther back to where the former Soviet Union wasn't a dozen separate countries, each with its own distinctive hue, but a single imposing monolith stretching from the Baltic to the Pacific. The mural never stopped moving beneath their feet. Smaller countries appeared and disappeared, only to reemerge again in slightly different shapes and sizes. Poland and Kurdistan—was there even such a country as "Kurdistan"?—seemed to be having an especially difficult time of it. And while this stretch of the jetty did feel a little more solid below them, she began to wonder if they were retreating in the right direction.

The view was still magnificent, even from this far down, and the island landscape and passages of water looked much as they had from the restaurant. But the restaurant itself had grown impossibly dim—a landmark more in theory than in fact. And her husband looked much younger, his hair a long and lustrous black. The jetty, where it retreated, retreated in several directions. And the seashore town where the restaurant held its vantage point was no more distinguishable than the restaurant itself. Instead, there was some meadowland, some salt marsh, and the low and crumbling bluff, now pathless, they had strolled down to get here.

Beneath her feet were the changing shapes of North America. Her own country was vanishing state by state, purchase by purchase, conquest by conquest, until it had dwindled to the original thirteen colonies. Over on the right, Great Britain had gotten out its broom and was sweeping its pale pink systems of education and notions of civic order into India, into Africa—while on a galleon, out in the broad sea road, she could see before her a man with a face not quite her husband's face but with some family link to it, standing on the bridge and giving orders in Spanish, while his crew, onshore below him, did dubious things to the Indians, men and women and children alike.

"No," she said with urgency, "we need to move forward again," and pulled on his arm once more, as she cinched her windbreaker tighter around her.

They had first met when they were thirty—or rather when she was twenty-nine and he was thirty-three. But she thought of it as thirty, as though "thirty" were less a number than a threshold, before which you had no idea what you were doing and after which you saw the road ahead of you. Before "thirty" there was a lot a person could be forgiven; after "thirty" you really ought to know better. And the curious thing now was that, as she moved forward, she could see "thirty" ahead of her.

She pulled her husband toward it until the first gray hairs on his head appeared. Then her curiosity got the better of her. What had he been like in the years before she'd met him? How had he acted when he was younger?

She took a step backward. The global mural beneath her feet seemed to tense as she steered toward the decade she was after. She overreached, hit Batista Cuba, and found herself leading an infant by the hand—with herself just a seed enjoying the oddest addled access to the universe. Panicking, she got him back up into his teens and, with another step, into college, where the jetty, with a youthful swagger, depicted a fraternity prank, a hazing ritual he had sometimes alluded to but never spelled out for her. Now its details surfaced in animal acts, with liquids involved and arrangements of flesh she would scarcely have thought possible. In her own corner, in the bedroom she'd once shared with her sister, she saw only cloying dreams, fluffy surfaces that masked a crude desire to find a man she could control and manipulate, a masculine doll she could lure toward her and spin around . . . until she realized with shame this was no human way to be.

The truth was, they'd both had their weaknesses and flaws, greeds and impulses, thirsts and appetites that had served as foundations for their characters—the characters they strove to be in their best moments or had dinned into them by their parents. Everyone was like this. Everyone passed through phases like these. The single dependable thing was the jetty. But how far could you follow it?

She took a tentative step. She saw the reassuring gray in his hair once more. She took another step, and saw his hair grow sparse in places. Each step felt small yet covered a considerable distance. And the jetty itself hung in fragments here and there: high steps or planks that led miles above the water. There were cracks in these; there were splinters. They loomed over an abyss and offered only an occasional steady toehold, a sort of a crow's nest from which to observe things.

Russia was smaller than she'd ever seen it, and Europe was all one color. As for the Middle East, large parts of it just didn't seem to be there anymore.

She tried looking for her own country, but the jetty, after several shudderings, failed to go in that direction. Then she noticed she was failing too; she had never been so spectral or so thin. She was having trouble holding her head up. And now *her* fingers were the fingers that gripped, gripped fiercely, while her husband's had faded.

Back, back she went again, holding someone or something by the hand—she scarcely knew what. She looked shoreward, trying to see her way there. But the restaurant was dark and its parking lot elusive. The jetty was a mountain, the jetty was a sphere, the jetty was a raft at sea growing smaller by the moment. The jetty rose and rose, in all directions . . . except where it drooped, inadequately suspended. And her husband, his speech badly impaired, was a sort of wraith, trying to say something about the waiter—something unsavory. She could see that in order to steer him, she would have to use some alchemical blend of subtlety and brutality.

Up and down they went along the jetty's various branches, drifting through its labyrinths and perspectives, weaving between predictions and conclusions, trying to find a way off it—the way you do when all other paths have been eliminated.

They kept at it all evening and on into the night, pressing forward even as they withdrew, proceeding and retreating, advancing and receding, trying both to avoid and alight on the moment when the world had last made sense to them and they had last made sense to each other.

The Adjudicator
Brian Evenson

WE HAVE BEEN A LONG time putting our community back into some
semblance of body and shape, and longer still sifting the living from
the dead. There are so many who seem as alive as you and me (if I
may be so bold as to number you, with myself, among the living) but
who already are all but dead. Much has been done that would not be
done in better times, and I too in desperation have committed what
I ought not, and indeed may well do so again.

I have become too accustomed to the signs and tokens of death. I
meet them both in the faces of the living and in the remnants I have
encountered in my daily round: the blackened arm my plow turned
up and which I just as quickly turned back under again; the bloody
marks smeared deep into the grain of the wood of my door and which
I have not the fortitude to scrub away; the man who lies dying in the
ditch between my farm and my neighbor's, and who, long dying,
somehow still is not altogether dead.

Shall I start at the beginning? No, the end. Here am I, waiting for this
same beditched man to either die or lurch to his feet and return to
claw again at my door. I have no crops, my entire harvest having
been pilfered or razed because of all I have witnessed and done and
refused to do. If I am to make it alive to the next harvest, I must carefully pace the consumption of my few remaining stores. I must catch
and eat what maggots and voles and vermin I can, glean and forage a
little, beg mercy of my neighbors if any are still wont to deliver
mercy to the likes of me. And then, if I am lucky, I shall sit here and
starve for months, but perhaps not enough to die.

No, let's have the beginning after all: The end is too much with
me, its breath already warm and damp on the nape of my neck.

At first there are wars and rumors of wars, then comes a light so
bright that it shines through flesh and bone. Then a conflagration,

the landscape peeled off and away, and nearly everyone dies. Those who do not die directly find themselves prone to suddenly erupting into pustules and bleeding from every pore and then falling dead. Most of the remainder are prone to a slow madness, their brains softened so as to slosh within their skulls. All but dead, these set about killing the few who remain alive.

The few who survive unscathed are those in shelters underground or swaddled deep within a strong house. Or simply those who, like me, seem not to have been afflicted for reasons no one can explain. Everything slides into nothingness and collapse, and for several years we all live like animals or worse, and then slowly we find our footing again. Soon some of us, maybe a few dozen, have banded together in this new order despite the disorder still raging in all quarters. We appoint a leader, a man named Rasmus. We begin to grow our scraggled crops. We form a pact to defend one another unto death.

At times I was approached by those who, having heard that I had been left unscathed in the midst of conflagration, believed I might provide some dark help to them. Others were more wary, keeping their distance as if from one cursed. Most, however, felt neither one thing nor the other, but saw me merely as a member of their community, a comrade at arms.

This, then, the fluid state of the world when, of a sudden, everything changed for me in the form of a delegation of men approaching my house. From a distance, I watched them come. The severed arm, having surged up under the sharp prow of the plow, was lying there, its palm open in appeal. Uncertain how they would respond to it, I quickly worked to have it buried again before they arrived.

I watched them come. One of them hallooed me when he saw me watching, and I waved back, then simply stood watching them come. I had grown somberly philosophical by this time and am not distant enough from the conflagration ever to feel at ease. I still in fact carried a hatchet with me everywhere I went, and even slept with it beside me on the pillow. And it was upon this hatchet that Rasmus's eyes first alighted once the delegation had approached close enough to form a half circle about me, and upon the way my hand rested steady on its haft.

"No need for that," he said. "Today will not be the day you hack me to bits."

This remark, perhaps lighthearted enough, based no doubt on the rumors of my past and meaning nothing, or at least little, drew my thoughts to the arm buried beneath my feet. I was glad indeed that I had again inhumed it.

"Gentlemen," I said, "to what do I owe this pleasure?" and I opened my pouch to them and offered them of my tobacco.

For a moment we were all of us engaged in stuffing and lighting our pipes, and then sucking them slowly down to ash; Rasmus kept one finger raised to hold my question in abeyance. When he had finished, he knocked the pipe out against the heel of his boot and turned fully toward me.

"We have an assignment for you," he said.

"The hell you have," I said.

Or at least wanted to say.

I do not know how to tell a story, a real one, or at least tell it well. Reading back over these pages, I see I have done nothing to give a sense of how it felt to have these determined men looming over me, their eyes strangely steady. Nor of Rasmus, with his wispy beard and red-pocked face. Why did we choose him as a leader? Because he was little good for anything else?

So, a large man, ruddy, looming over me, stabbing the air between us with a thick finger, nail yellow and cracking. Minions to either side of him.

What I said was not *The hell you have* but "And it takes six of you to tell me?" Perhaps not, in retrospect, the wisest utterance, and certainly not taken exceptionally well. Not, to be blunt, in the proper community spirit. But once I was started down this path, I had difficulty arresting my career.

He tightened his lips and drew himself up a little, stiff now.

"What," he asked, "was your profession?"

"I've always been a farmer," I said. "As you yourself know."

"No," he said. "Before the conflagration, I mean."

"You know very well what I was before the conflagration," I said.

"I want to hear you say it," he said.

But I would not say it. Instead, I filled my pipe again as they regarded me. Then lit and smoked it. And he, for whatever reason, did not push his point.

"There are rumors about you," he claimed. "Are they true?"

"For the purposes of this conversation," I said, not knowing what

339

he was talking about, which rumors, "you should assume they are all true."

"Paper," he said, and one of the others came forward, held out a folded sheet of paper. I stared at it a long time, finally took it.

"We have an understanding then," said Rasmus, and before I could answer started off. Soon he and his company were lost to me.

After they had gone, I dug the arm up again and examined it, trying to determine how long it had been rotting and if I had been the one to lop it free. In the end I found myself no closer to an answer than I had been at the beginning. Finally I could think to do nothing but plow it back under again.

The matter of my former profession amounts to this: I had no former profession. I was dissolute, poisonous to myself in all ways. At a certain moment, I reached the point where I would have done anything at all to have what I wanted, and indeed I often did. Many of the particulars have faded or vanished from my memory or been pushed deeper down until they can no longer be felt. There was one person, someone I was, in my own way, deeply in love with, whom I betrayed. Someone else, of a different gender, whose self I stripped away nerve by nerve.

When the conflagration came, it was nearly sweet relief for me. And, to be honest, what I did to survive, largely with the hatchet I still carry, is little worse, and perhaps better, than what I did beforehand.

But for Rasmus my profession before the conflagration was a jack-of-all-trades, someone with little enough regard to take on any business, no matter how raucous or how bloody.

How much easier, I think now, *had I just raised my hatchet then and there with Rasmus and his crew and started laying into them. And then simply sowed their bits wide about my field and plowed them in deep.*

There are other things I should tell and perhaps still others forgotten that I shall never work my way back to. There are the rumors he had mentioned, asking if they were true. I cannot say one way or other what he thought they were. Some, as I have said, believe me charmed because of my aboveground survival, others believe me cursed. I am, I probably should have said before, completely devoid of hair—the only long-term change I suffered from the conflagration—and as such look to some homuncular, although not fully formed. I also heal, I have found, much faster than most, and it is, fortunately, somewhat difficult to inflict permanent damage upon me. It could be this that Rasmus was referring to, which has become a rumor that I cannot die: a rumor that may well be disproved this winter. Or perhaps it was something else, something involving the past I have just elucidated above. Or something touching on my deadly skill with the hatchet with which I live affectionately, as if it were a spouse. Who can say? Certainly not I.

The folded piece of paper, once unfolded and spread flat, read as follows:

> *In two days' time a man will approach your door. You will invite him in and greet him. You will share with him of your tobacco. You will converse with him. And then, when he stands to leave, you will lay into him with your hatchet until he is dead. This is the wish of the community and, as a man of the community and one who has often proven himself capable, we call upon you.*

There was, as one would expect, no signature. The words themselves were simple and blocky, anonymous. I screwed the note into a twist and then lit one end of it, using it to ignite my pipe, discarding it in the fire, watching it become its own incandescent ghost and then flinder and flake away into nothingness.

How much shall I tell you about myself? Do I have anything to fear from you? How much can I tell you before I lose hope of maintaining, by whatever tenuous grasp, your sympathy? Or have I already gone too far?

I have no strong moral objection to murder pure and simple, nor for that matter to anything else. Why this is so, I cannot say. And yet I derive no pleasure from it, have no taste for it. I was as content, and perhaps more content, being a simple farmer as I had ever been in my dissolute early life. I felt as if most of my old self had been torn slowly free of the rest of me, and I was not eager to have it pressed back against me again.

True, I had, on the occasions when our community had been afflicted by swarms of the dead or dying, done my part and done it well. After a particular effort, standing blood spattered over the remains of one of the afflicted who had refused to stop moving, I had sometimes seen the fear in the eyes of those who had observed my deeds. But I did not like Rasmus's quick slide from my dispatching the dead to assuming I would do the same without reluctance to the living. Not, again, that I had any reservations against the act of murder, only that I did not care to be taken for granted. And I knew from my past that, asked once, I would be asked again and again.

Still, there are sacrifices to be made when one has the privilege of living in a community. I could see no way around making this particular one, even if I was not, technically speaking, the one being sacrificed.

I spent the rest of the day at work on my house, replacing the shingling of the room where the wood had grown gaunt and had been bleached by wind and sun. The next day I was back to the fields, with plowing and planting to finish and the ditch to be diverted until the near field was a soppy patch that glimmered in the sunset. A pipe at evening as always, and early the next morning a walk two farms away for some more tobacco, trading for it a few handfuls of dried corn from the dwindling stores of the previous year's harvest. Then a careful survey of the property, the dark loamy earth of the still damp fields.

He came late in the day, just before sunset. Had I not known he was coming I might well have been reluctant to swing wide the door, or at least would have opened it with hatchet raised and cocked back for the swing. He was a large man in broad-brimmed hat and long coat, wearing what once would have been called driving gloves.

"I have been sent to you," he said. "They claimed perhaps you could help me."

And so I ushered him in. I gestured to a chair near the fire. I placed

my tobacco pipe and pouch within easy reach. I invited him to remove his gloves, his coat, his hat.

To this point there had been a certain inexorability to the pro-
ceedings, each moment a tiny and inevitable step toward the time
when I would, without either fear or rage, raise my hatchet and make
an end of the fellow.

And yet, when he was freed of hat and coat and gloves and I saw
the bare flesh of his hands, his arms, his face, I suddenly found everything grown complex. What I had seen as a simple death-bound progression now became a sequence of events whose ending I could not
foresee, one in which, from instant to instant, I could not begin to
divine what would happen next.

What was it that threw me into such uncertainty? Did I, as in the
dead art of a dead past, glimpse in the lines and the contours of his
visage the face of a long-lost brother? A long-lost lover? No, nothing
as simple or as clever as that. Rather, it was the fact that his hands
and arms, his face and skull, were completely depilated. Like me, he
had lost all his hair. Had he been a brother or a lover it would not
have been enough to confuse me. But this, somehow, was.

He came in, he sat. His hat and coat I hung from a hook beside my
door. His gloves he paired and smoothed and laid gently over his
knee. His name was Halber, he claimed.

"And who was it sent you?" I asked, though I knew the answer.

Your leader, he claimed. Who had said that I would adjudicate for
him.

"Adjudicate?" I said.

Yes, he claimed, since that was my role in the community or so he
had been told by Rasmus.

I nodded for him to go on.

The story he unraveled was one of the utmost wrongheadedness.
He had once, so he claimed, owned all this property, but when the
conflagration had come he had traveled quickly and hurriedly to try
to throw his body in the way of his parents' death. He had of course
misthrown himself; they had died despite him, his mother going
mad so that in the end he had had to be the one to kill her, and his
father simply having his skin slough off until the bone was showing.
Upon which the man thought to return, but the world being as it

was, he had spent many months just keeping alive, and only now had he managed.

What he wanted, he claimed, was not to reclaim his land. He understood well enough the degree to which everything had transformed. All he wanted was to be given a small plot of land and be allowed to farm it, so he could be back in a place that he knew, and to be accepted into the community. He had said this to Rasmus and his council, and they had deliberated for three days as he awaited their decision. At last they had sent him to me, the adjudicator.

Adjudicator, I thought. *Well, that's one name for it.*

I thought too, with sudden insight, *Normally they would kill him themselves, and perhaps have done so with others in times past. But because, like me, he is hairless, they have sent him here. They are frightened.*

And this made me think too of what they must think of me, and why they had chosen to admit me into the community. And I could not but think it was out of fear or because I was already there, and perhaps it was only because there were those among them who believed I was charmed or cursed and could not die. And perhaps soon, once I had done away with Halber and proven that a man like me could be killed, they would see no reason not to do away with me as well.

"Please tell them," I said, "that I have thought carefully and have adjudicated in your favor. You shall join us."

He stood and awkwardly embraced me, an act I suffered only with great reluctance. And then, gathering his things, he left, leaving me to ponder why I had done what I had done, and what would be its dark consequence.

I was not to wonder long. Late that night I heard shouts and, as I roused myself, a banging had begun at my door. "It's Halber!" a man was screaming, his screams enough to curdle the blood. "It's Halb! Let me in!"

And indeed I almost did. I might well have had I not heard the other voices and sounds that followed, the grunts and indifferent dull sounds of metal slipping into flesh, and heard the pounding suddenly stop. I climbed onto the bed and looked down through the high window. In the pale moonlight I saw him, dying and staring, being dragged away by the legs. Had it been only a pack of the dead and the dying I would have perhaps opened the door and commenced to lay about me with my hatchet, as I had done in the past when the dead came for the living. But as it was, seeing that the faces were those of the living, Rasmus's face among them, I hesitated just long enough to feel that it was too late.

And perhaps it is there that the story should have ended. Perhaps, had I said nothing, done nothing, kept to my house, then my reputation, the myths surrounding me, would have been enough for Rasmus and his council to decide to let me be. Perhaps they would have grudgingly levied a fine, remembered my usefulness in other ways, and life would have gone much as usual, if anything can be described as usual in these days. But we all of us made mistakes that made this impossible.

The mistake I made was in not staying to my house for a few days, deciding instead to tend to my crops, to go about with the business that needed to be attended to on my farm. This, under most circumstances, would not be considered a dire mistake. Or even, to be frank, in most conditions, a mistake at all.

Their mistakes were more severe. Tired of dragging the body, they abandoned it in a ditch halfway between my farm and that of my neighbor. And instead of tearing the head free of the corpse and incinerating it, they left the hairless Halber lacerated but more or less intact.

With every disaster, I have come to believe for my own personal reasons, comes a compensation, a certain balancing of the accounts—not spread evenly about but clumped here and there, of benefit to very few. I heal, as I said, very quickly—or at least I do now: Before the conflagration I did not. There are rumors I cannot die; not having died, these are rumors I can neither confirm nor deny, nor am I curious enough to uncover the truth that I feel compelled to slit my own throat. But from what I've seen of what is happening to Halber, I fear this might well be true, and hardly in the way one would hope.

So, we have reached the day after Halber had been hauled away, my door clawed and scratched on the outside, the bloody marks of his dying smeared there and on the threshold. I stare at the door a moment, checking to see my hatchet is with me. Outside, there are always things to attend to, things to do to keep the farm going. I do them, wondering all the while when the little poultry and livestock remaining in the area will start to breed again, if ever, and if I will ever be able to afford my own chicken. I irrigate my fields again, just enough, then sit on a stone near the field's border and smoke.

That is when I begin to hear it, a slow and distant whistle, a soft wind. At first I think nothing of it. But when it persists I become afflicted with the disease of curiosity.

I stand, trying to ascertain where it is coming from. I follow it in one direction, then another. It slowly becomes louder, just a little louder, just a little louder, a moan now.

It is some time still before I make myself go all the way out to the road and follow it a little way down and find him there, Halber, bloody in the ditch, grievously wounded—by all rights he should be dead.

What did I do? One look was enough to tell me he should be dead. I have dealt with the living turned dead enough to be leery, but he struck me as something different, as a new thing.

He was in any case too hurt to be moved. I went back to the house, brought back a blanket and some water. I wrapped him in the former and dribbled the latter into his mouth. He was delirious and hardly conscious. He would, it seemed to me, soon be dead.

And so I stayed there beside him, waiting for him to die.

Only he did not die. His body seemed unable to let go but also unable to heal itself, and so he struggled there between life and death. I thought for a moment to kill him, but what if he did heal himself? I wondered. Wasn't he like me? Wouldn't he eventually heal himself?

In the end I left him and went home to sleep.

That night I dreamt of him, lying there in his ditch, slowly dying but never dead, breathing in his shallow way but breathing despite everything, never stopping. And then, his breathing no less shallow, he managed over the course of long painful moments to make it to his feet and shuffle forward, like the walking dead. I watched him get slowly up, coming very slowly. Later, much later in my head, I heard a knocking and a dim articulate cry and knew him, suddenly and with, for once, a certain measure of terror, to be knocking on my door.

When I came back to the ditch the next morning I found my blanket was gone, stolen. Some creature had eaten most of one of his hands and the finer portion of his face. But he was still, somehow, alive. And so I slit his throat and watched the blood gurgle out, and then went back to get on with my work.

This seemed to me sufficient, and I must confess that I did not think about him through the course of my day. There were fences to be attended to, wood to be chopped, brush to be cleared. A corner of the field had become too soggy and I found myself cutting a makeshift drainage channel, thinking its course up as I went. By the end of the day I was mud spattered, my bones and muscles aching.

And still, as the sun set, I found my thoughts returning to Halber. I could not stop myself from going to see him.

There are strange things that happen that I cannot explain, and this was one of them. He was as I had left him, but still alive. His throat, I saw, had filmed over, the veins not reconnecting exactly but blood moving there, pulsing back and forth within the film in a kind of delicate bag of blood and nascent tissue, puslike. I watched it beat red then beat pale, in the gap where his throat had been. At that sight I nearly severed his head from his shoulders, but I was too terrified of what would happen, inside of me, if I removed his head and somehow, despite this, he still refused to die.

So instead I went home and sharpened my hatchet.

What can I say about the night that followed, when I chose to become the one who would judge who lived and who died? I have no apologies for what I did, nor any justification either. I did it simply because I could think of nothing else to do. I am neither proud of my actions nor regretful.

I sharpened the hatchet until it had a fine and impossible edge and then in the dark I set out. Perhaps if I had met some of the dying and the afflicted, some of those made vicious and deranged by the conflagration, I would have been satisfied. But the only one I met in my path was Halber, and I gave the fellow a wide berth.

What need is there to pursue in detail what followed next? I did unto Rasmus as might be expected. A single blow of the hatchet and

I was through his door. I caught him on the way out of bed as he moved down the hall and went after his gun, the hatchet cutting through his back and ribs and puncturing one lung so that it hissed. He went down in a heap, groaning and breathing out a mist of blood, and I severed first one forearm then the other, and as his eyes rolled back lopped off his head. His wife arose screaming from the bed and rushed to the window and tried to hurl herself through. I struck her on the back of the skull with the cronge of the handle, meaning only to silence her screams, but it was clear from the way she fell and the puddle of blood that soon spread from her head that perhaps I had struck too hard. Then I approached Rasmus again and very delicately, with the sharpest part of the blade, peeled off his face.

The other five who had come with him to see me suffered the same fate, though I killed them more swiftly, with a single blow, and did not disjoint or decorticate them as I did their leader. There is no need to say more than that, I suppose. In the end I was sodden with blood and gore, and made my way back to my farmhouse, past the still-dying Halber, and slept the sleep of the truly dead.

I awoke to the smell of burning, saw when I burst open the door that they had set my fences afire. My fields too had been trampled apart, then the ditch redirected and trenches dug to wash away the topsoil. Had my house not been stone, they would have burnt that too. I stared at the flames a moment and then, not knowing what else to do, went back to bed.

It was a week before I could bring myself to leave the house. Finally I stripped off my gory clothing, the blood now gone black, and burned it in the fireplace. Then I took water from the irrigation canal and washed in it and dressed myself in my town clothes and set off for my neighbor's farm.

I do not know what I expected. At the very least I expected, I suppose, for Halber to be dead. But he was still alive, still feebly dying in the ditch. I chose not to get close to him.

My neighbor was at his farm, his crops just starting to come in. When he saw me approaching he rushed inside, came out with his rifle.

"Not another step," he said.

I stopped. "Do you think your gun can stop me?" I asked him.

"I don't know," he said, "but if you come any closer we shall find out."

"I have no grudge against you," I said. "I only want those who destroyed my crops."

"Then you want me," he said. "You want all of us, the community."

"But why?"

"Can you possibly ask?"

And I suppose in good conscience I could not, though I thought my neighbor had at least a right to know why I had done what I had done. So I sat on the ground and kept my hand far away from the hatchet and, rifle trained on me, recounted to him, just as I have recounted to you, all that had occurred.

When I was finished he shook his head. "We have all been through much," he said, "and you have made us go through more. None of us are perfect men but you are less perfect than most."

Then he gestured with his gun. "Come with me," he said.

He led me back to the road and toward my farm, to the place in the ditch where the dying man was to be found.

"Is this the man you meant?" he asked.

"Yes," I said. "Halber."

"But you can see for yourself that he has been long dead," he said. "And that when he was alive he was not hairless but in fact replete with hair. Please," he said, "go away do not come back."

But I could not see it. Indeed to me he still appeared as hairless as a baby and, though dying, still alive. I wondered to myself what my neighbor was trying to do to me. Had he not had his gun trained on me I would have turned on him and laid into him with my hatchet. Instead, I simply turned away from him and returned to my house.

Where I have been ever since. I do not know if what is wrong is wrong with me or wrong with the world. Perhaps there is a little of both. I find it difficult to face the man dying in the ditch, and it is clear I and my neighbors no longer live in altogether the same world.

It seems strange to think that after all this, after my years of dissolution and then the hard years after the conflagration, I might die here alone, might slowly starve to death. Assuming it is true that I can in fact die.

I will make do as long as I can and then when my straits are indeed dire I shall leave my house and beg mercy from my neighbors. Perhaps they will show mercy, even if only out of fear, or perhaps they will kill me. Either way it cannot be but a relief.

As for now, though, I shall sit here and write and very slowly starve, waiting part in anticipation and part in fear for the moment when the dying man who so greatly resembles me shall drag himself to his feet and leave his ditch and come again to knock at my door.

This time I shall be ready for him. This time I shall know what to do.

The Pressure Points
Michael Logan

SHE SAID SOMETHING WAS different in her left breast, a thickening. We felt it together. Three doctors, including a surgeon, said it was innocuous fibroid. A mammogram came back normal. She had dense breast tissue and a family history of breast cancer. A mammogram is not a good prognosticator for abnormalities in dense breast tissue.

Six months later, thickening became painful. Take it out, we both said. The surgeon said, "OK, but let's do a repeat mammogram to see what I'm working with." The mammogram showed "a change."—Translation: visible large enough. You are too late if you already knew what the machine now confirms. (Did Pink Floyd already sing this?) A month later, surgeon's office called to change our meeting time to the last scheduled appointment of the day—the encore. We knew then the biopsy was positive for breast cancer but we went and paid our respects. We listened to him tell us there is hope and no hope and he was only a surgeon. Pathology: Grade III aggressive cancer, ER/PR negative, "prognosis: poor." We previewed oncologists.

Fast forward three years: OxyContin and *Do Not Resuscitate* plastic band around the ankle. Cause of death: metastasized breast cancer to the liver. I was part of the death machine. Death conversion kit: mental sexual immodesty, insane jealousy of lovers and family units and pale food. The smell of grocery store sickens. The amount of death poured into brick box to form a deli counter, seafood display, wrapped meats and poultry, cheeses and canned body parts overwhelms. I never smelled previously.

Weeks not hungry punctuated by specific cravings for olives, chocolate, pistachio nuts, and pills—waiting for the death pregnancy test to register positive. Teen year erotic wet dreams discharged between clenched night teeth into amputation nightmares. Biology needed another host to continue. We had no children. The whole family should be dead. I am willing to go back several generations. I understand vampire stories now.

I meet her in a psychologist's waiting room in the dream, down on a knee, begging her back. "You're the reason I'm here," she said. The

351

waiting changes into a death camp and she is tight enough in caress to be a body part. Sensuality is amplified by no future or an inadvertent future because memorialized. Death mocks etiology. Beauty cannot be forged in death. Sex is our most desperate offering, sculpture its apotheosis. Kill Michelangelo.

Humans created music and religion when death didn't respond to lamentation, grief strophes, or logic. Silence echoed, described as "something bigger than us," so humans created art as sacrificial offering and waited. We learned, finally, only death feeds death. American superstition as hero was born—feed death as much cadaver as possible and hope it is satiated without us. Death's lack of an IG tract is ambitionless while we argue what constitutes genocide. Death is the Big Bang, expanding atomically through entropy. All flesh must end, not in the order we want. Beauty expands inexorably until only the minutest available to the woefully lacking human eye pretends a substantive form none of us want—dust into dark matter and the end of the universe. Humans measure time; obviously we have the wrong expectations.

You make decisions already decided elsewhere, study medical terminology a step behind mutations. The Web drowns you: cold clinical details and biological statistics, breathy late-night catechisms and chat rooms, miraculous personal stories and dramatic alternative medicine resuscitations from devouring cancers. Many gurus, only one body to pursue them in; I ride her—we all do, our familial hopes, fears, and superstitions on a corporal beauty and genetic bundle equipped to handle only so much chemistry and hope. I rape her with my eyes for signs of jaundice, cathexis, and remission. Cancer is a blank canvas, spreading white endlessly. You get a paint tool kit, one chance at a masterpiece. My learning curve is steep. I pass on to her my haphazard readings and inexact ruminations on medical science, except instances when she put her finger dipped in red wine to my lips and said, "Don't tell me."

My Cancer Wife (in her own words). Cancer patients used to always freak me out. Bald heads were one thing, but those with no eyebrows or eyelashes really got me. They had an alien otherworldliness about them. I'd try not to stare, but inevitably my gaze would be drawn back. Once in Paris, I watched a couple check out of a hotel. The wife, drawn and tired with a scarf on her head, sat in a chair while her husband handled the luggage. I created a life for them. She was dying of cancer, and this was their trip of a lifetime. I pitied her as I did other cancer patients, but in truth they scared the hell out of me. "Oh my God, what if that was me?" I could work myself to the point of hysteria, obsessing about every ache and pain. So now when those pity stares are directed at me, I understand where the person is coming from. Still, that doesn't make them any easier to take.

The odds are against us. I want a graph of her best day's blood work tattooed to my body: bilirubin, hematocrit, and white blood cell counts arcing across flesh close to the normal range. We feel good when the blood work tells us we feel good. Certain chemotherapies make skin baby soft. I'm obsessed with her pregnant. She asked me if I regretted not having children. I lied, "No." I want a reproduction of her. I'm no artist; I can't sing. Numb bodies, the innocent, are perfect for tattooing because they approximate ice sculptures—no veins. I'm in favor of tattoo visual cued infants, parents pumping foreign languages and Mozart into them. Satiate them with the dark sciences. Get the message in early: Become ice: striations, dark spots, back glare, and opaque fissure mini X-rays Daddy can read. Bottled water isn't going to save you.

My Cancer Wife. Following treatment my hair grew back, and my life with my beloved husband resumed. We traveled to Barcelona and throughout Italy. I returned to work. I had a sold-out solo show of my pottery. Life was good. Then my cancer returned and metastasized to my liver. I was now literally in the fight of my life. Once again I was put on chemo and lost all my hair, including my eyebrows and eyelashes, but this time it was different. As a Stage 4 patient, I would likely be on some form of chemo for the rest of my life. I needed to come to terms with my appearance and how I was going to interact with the world. I couldn't hide in the house forever. The first time around I wouldn't wear a wig. They work for most, but I felt like a clown. I might as well be wearing a football helmet. This time was no different, so I made peace with scarves. But now, I'm a poster child for cancer. Not surprisingly, I'm also the recipient of those pity stares I used to give and have come to dread.

Not just pity stares—"there it is"—death prowling among us. Most would prefer to keep their distance. I have never hated people as much in my life. My end is going to be bitterly alone.

353

Michael Logan

Cancer is War.
Think Positive.
A Proprietary Supplement Blend That Shrinks Tumors.
We want to attack it aggressively.
Oncology miracles happen every day.
Tumor Killer Complex of Medicines and Herbs.
As nerve pain in extremities is a side effect of Doxil intravenous treatment, we recommend ice packs placed on the hands and feet during infusion.
Oncology nurses do it to mutations.
My other head has hair.
Are you asking me to go commando?
Chemo kicks it to the curb.
Insurance won't cover that particular treatment.
I wish I'd seen you before standard chemotherapy did that to you.
Some have been healed with just the laying on of hands.
Every body has a prize inside.

She has small, fragile veins. During a one-week hospital stay (should have been only two days, but there was fever, a possible staph infection, dehydration, and blood pressure sinkholes they pumped three IVs into at once and discussed a blood transfusion) to change out the belly tube drain for internal metal stents within liver bile ducts, they draw blood twice a day until it becomes painful. Several of the phlebotomists can't find a vein, missing, painfully moving the needle around under skin, hoping to get lucky. Her arms are black and blue. We explain to a resident oncologist the blood draws are becoming too painful. We can place a draw port in her neck if needed, he said. She has an Audrey Hepburn, slimly graceful neck. We negotiate the blood draws down to one, at night, after pain medication. We go back to black and blue, try to maintain some dignity above the chest. I realized we would be covered with blankets from then on.

"There is no pain like cancer pain," the hospice nurse told me as we looked upon her body. No extracapillary extension—that phrase gave me hope for a few pathology reading days. At that moment I stopped med school, my mind won't: living rewind in mind fuck time—she could have been saved caught early enough at her first self-diagnosis. I pull out her X-rays late at night and stare at the mirror. I didn't go to the Web, the med-school texts. I had my shirt off,

354

tanning at our income bracket. Mirror gaze graffiti: the man who didn't speed-dial a specialist. I had no W2s, she had a corporate salary, and we vacationed in Italy. We voted left and made money right. You don't hear the bullet. Failure to pursue the obvious (family history of breast cancer) at the inception of creative cellular mutation: should have called a breast surgeon eight months earlier and demanded a biopsy—the hero makes action. I was scared to touch the fragile security we'd erected—a large income neither of us had expected in our lives—but most of all afraid of our good luck. Someone else's story is always someone else's story. We got to the killing floor all those low-down bluesmen sang. She hated most blues. I stood at pit edge, threw our world in, and walked away. Internalized orders against humanity are the easiest to follow.

"We continue living because that's what we do," straight out of the AA handbook, as said by the boyfriend of a friend who should have known better in choice. Individual violence is ridiculous unless utilized at the precise moment of opportunity. Another art form I pose with but don't master. Violence as power is collective implacable pogrom, unjust summary justice, anonymous bloodletting, weak and mentally disabled behind and before the gun. Not easy to kill fifteen thousand Jews by firing squad in one day. Could I have aided and escaped one, a solitary liquid tear formed human, out of the corpse pit's eye? You want to believe the myth of your own bravery, grace under pressure. I now know the answer. Death ridicules the heart as metaphor.

When I thought we were going to save her, my proudest imaginary moments were sitting in the back of a crowded gathering of despised humans, listening to her explain breast cancer etiology, strategies for cancer survival—because cancer survives, and if lucky, you survive with it. When she was dying, I gave over to death the hero's parade. I now enjoy reading about a good genocide. Death is insipid excuse: I couldn't have saved them anyway.

She shivered in late spring night, head in a knit winter hat, wrapped in layers of comforters—fever and chills lapping primitive seizure. I held her and rubbed hard to generate warmth, dead quickly on the surface of blue skin. We renegotiated promises. From the land of the brave she chattered, "I don't know how much more of this I can take, honey." Trained by oncologists to get in twenty-four hours of living no matter cost, convenience, or task, I responded: "Do it for me."

The surgeon showed me the X-ray where the liver tumor scrambled the biliary tree. His pager flashed, he looked at me. "If there's anything you two haven't done but wanted to, I wouldn't wait."

Torture or feckless healthy lover, every spasm told me, "You know nothing." Shivering incessantly, her temperature hits 104. I page our oncologist. "Tumor fever," he said, though I can hear he's somewhat surprised by this event, a small "huh" in the back of his throat, mind off-hours recalling statistical treatment doses and dates, calculated without a chart. I'm impressed. If I was lying on that couch, less so— the divide between the living and dead is never clearer. One promise can't be broken: No matter how sick, she demands no hospital de- livery. This baby will be born at home.

Memory teaches us to remember a person's corporal strong points and beauty marks. Death knows the pressure points, how to dissolve beauty memory. Death knows your body more than ever you will because it *is* your body. You will spend most of your time with death— life is a short ventriloquist act. We spend most of our time not speak- ing of the state we'll inhabit mutely forever.

One night she turned to me with tears in eyes and said, "You could live a long time."

We have a thick notebook of test results I keep—numbers and parabolas painfully straining against flatline.

Treatment Cocktail: Adriamycin/Cytoxan and Taxol. Oncologist satisfied recovery from low white blood cell count complete; she was released from isolation ward of hospital seven days prior. He suggests we lower the dose incrementally, insisting it will have no effect on outcome. "I want the full dose again," she said.

Severe pain is either an accident or unreasonable animal survival. Instinct sucks on pain, because pain is a pulse, until it shuts down every body process trying to keep the pain intact. Oxycontin makes you constipated. It shuts down the GI track. No longer hungry, you wander in your head. Organ shutdown produces brain hallucina- tions. Life after death belief is in this alternative world. Life after death: extremely brief and ecstatic. Brain death may have sedative effect.

Technology began outside the body. It is working its way inward with the potential to revive organs, capillaries, tissue, and possibly reawaken extreme trauma contained in shriveled viscera, stifled interior synaptic ghosts refired at exhumed, reenergized speed. Brain death replayed in car-crash mode. Organizing nightmares is a full workday. It is possible to telecommute.

Death is a social situation with a chain of command. Almost everybody follows orders because they hope to walk away.

For two years she fights off the suggestion of taking an antidepressant. The day she gives in at the oncologist's office surprises me. She is riding a blacked-out train and there is no relief except the death camp. For the first time her gaze between me and the oncologist doesn't say, "Fix me," it says, "Don't let it hurt." Tears are in all our eyes. We have the combined power of lab rats. Pray she gets the overdose of cocaine. We're medicating backward: Even in acute depression she is too strong mentally and too weak physically. We can't say the terrible things we know: It is going to be painful, and a weak, death-impregnated body is going to make it worse.

My new concept for the rock 'n' roll lifestyle—energy bars for peak trauma performance—downers, uppers, SSRIs, cocaine, sugar blended to survive and thrive pre- and posttrauma. The trauma must be timed to coincide to the karmic state synonymous with chemical peak expression. Sobriety is anxiety. Timing is the motherfucker of reality. I sneak out to the funeral home, while she visits with her sister, to guarantee her last wishes are met—cremation, no wake or funeral. The absorbent, empathetically dignified host told me his father died of cancer. After a while, he said, they've been poked and prodded too often and don't want to be touched anymore.

Posttrauma reactive symptoms is your brain explaining death to you.

I miss the Greeks and their orations. Aeschylus: much deader than I, wise, and with my wife. I'm jealous. She'll make him laugh.

I've been taking her Oxycontin at 3 a.m. I know my timing's off. Death won't accept grief. Even when the body is dying, pleasure receptors accept morphine and continue to dampen nerve signals into a mildly euphoric undertow beneath pain.

Let me be explicit: Pain always wins.

More and more morphine is required and the gross load eventually shuts down respiration. Death is the pleasure-centered brain desperate for nerves to return the looped signal and nerves forgetting how, and then forgetting the brain. Brain sucks oxygen like a drunk and lungs hang limp.

The late-war Nam infantry guys figured out self-medication ratio/dose timing to combat stress. Better a nasty OD dream than combat nightmare, the latter hallucinating elsewhere waiting for you to arrive. Death is harmony, merely accepts you. It's a carbon conversion kit.

Sloan-Kettering is a premier cancer treatment facility. The bureaucracy and laboratories behind the facade of normalcy are labyrinthian. An outsized spa whose package includes empathetic pain, the motto should be: You feel great! Except you have breast cancer! The SK oncologist consults with a SK team and concludes they wouldn't be doing anything different than the oncologist group in our small Connecticut town. Treatment equivalence is Pyrrhic victory. She feels like vomiting on the three-hour ride home until the drugs kick in and she sleeps. I think about crashing the car and killing us both. Based on current ratio of helpfulness, I can't guarantee mutual destruction against severe injury. Death business is a killing business and killing isn't so easy, it works in fits and jerks, balance is mentally unavailable. Don't expect to think clearly.

An interventional radiologist explained to me sizing specs for gastrointestinal French tubes. He tells me we'll have to get used to certain things: tubes out of body, fluids and viscera sweat flowing freely in translucence; death recirculating—sorta like air-conditioning.

My hands sterilized, I change and clean the drain, relieving dammed-up fluids from tumor-compressed bile ducts. What is the moment when viscous filament becomes organ poison? Is there a change in color to the flowing tube? Our garbage bags should be marked "biohazard." Death can be functional disintegration and we're organizing, working in the factory, preparing product. She winces at one of my movements, I jerk, and pain is expressed between us, in her body and in my head. I imagine smearing myself with the bile-pus-blood fluid. My visage answer preempting the public domain song—"How's your wife doing?" That's my overly imagined, dramatic, lower brain stem response. The short reality answer—We're doing death at different speeds.

Nauseous fever, again with chills: called oncologist, drove insanely to pharmacy. Pharmacist had mercy on me and passed prescription between the "Sorry We're Closed" grates. I dread post 9 p.m.—anything can happen, drugs are locked out. This time, unexpectedly, the capsules rain capillary manna—usually they don't, or it works but the side effect is worse and another avenue of pain opens. She's sleeping. I want to make love to her I'm so happy to see her face drained of pain lines. I will kiss your shit, God, if you make me a subaltern of pain-free life extensions and sleep. Make me the pill and let me into her nerves and viscera, I'll suck poison. Give me the goods, God, and I'll keep her prisoner forever.

That's macho drug talk: Bet your ass I've become a pusher.

In view of marriage vows, shouldn't we enjoin this together? It should be commonly assumed by the community: "Oh, don't worry, they're a little tipsy, but they're both on a hybrid of Xeloda, Oxy-Contin, Zometa, Abraxane, and Doxil." A little unsteady on our feet at the grocery store, but if we didn't have breast cancer we'd be feeling great!

Cancer symphony, opera, rap-rock album—not dedicated to your mom, but my adorably youthful wife—is anybody out there who isn't in the machine?

I can't sing. One night she is sinking into sleep and asks me to tell her a story. I've learned how to inspect an abdominal opening, which I've just done. Her request stuns me into a mental blank. For all my dreams of gut glory, absorption of her pain, resurrection, and nausea colors, I'm white, extending white limitlessly. My pain has been killed and I am dull. The only story I know is hers. I fall asleep before her, which is always bad luck, pretending I could still die first.

When exactly does revolt become mutation?

We're all freaks—science fiction with fixed data-machine read points of contact to the cellular, closer to genetic bar codes as medicine culturally evolves. The technically skilled often misread. I wanted to offer the radiologist a bribe.

It is not, I have discovered, easy to rid the body of the body. The physical death leftovers don't interest me; I wish the corpse could walk itself to the crematorium, not because it's unattractive, but because death has possession of the ancient story and no mouth. Each death is a summation of an evolutionary strand up to that point. If you're keeping score at home, evolution's a death-dealing biological business. After World War II, the percentage of people requesting cremation rose dramatically.

My wife started a breast cancer research foundation. It is approaching the one-million-dollar–fund-raising mark. Led Zeppelin laughs—it's not enough money for a tour or reparations. They will live forever because they continually draft underage boys.

After the struggle, my body is left, but it is dying rat. I hear falling noises and echoes. Minimal desire to see people and panic attacks: The walls closed in, I floated above myself, watching the vise tighten—sweat exuded animal smell. I made it upstairs into a fist full of her leftover pills, knotted nerves loosened as internal chemistry streamed into and out of neuroepinephrine, dopamine, and serotonin receptors. I transferred her from physical to chemical sensation. Now I understand the seduction of science. Can chemical transaction register touch?

Dying in our bed, she said, "I'm standing over there, against the wall, and I can see myself dead."

I could not resurrect coherence inside my head. It was a balloon on the ceiling. Next day phone calls ensue:

Diagnosis #1: *The shrink speedball: antidepressants, antianxiety meds, and intensive talking treatment.*

Diagnosis #2: *#1 and you need to get out of the house.*

Diagnosis #3: *I hadn't had a blurring session since the killing.*

Diagnosis #4: *Set fire to all your houses.*

The trauma literature boils down to this—after the first, there will always be another. Your body is slave shape memory. The first position ever learned and enforced is fetal. Death shrinks you into your shell. I cannot let go of the body. I wash her, change her clothes, pull my shirt over her head, and dress her. I dawdle, walk in circles, sketch thigh freckles that look like a distant galaxy, babble incessantly as if it were CPR. Cut off a bracelet I want. Rigor mortis is quicker than I expected. Death's silent summation is almost immediate—cold, inert, rigid. There is no way out of this but body bag. As with a newborn, I'm afraid if I fool around too much with this I love, but don't quite recognize as mine, I will hurt her again. Yearning to imagine I have embarrassed her to life so the roseate glow will recharge cheeks—the solitary formality of my ritual is screaming inside my head—Don't snap off a limb. My wife had low blood pressure, was always cold. All I can do to death is light a fire with her in it.

I am at the pharmacy under my name. The facial discrimination of the counterperson, who knows my story in pharmaceuticals rather than conversation, has morphed onto the other side of her face. Empathetic and nonverbal, the pills rattle inside the generic packaging during handoff. She is trying to tell me not to take these alone.

Unequipped to save her, I collapsed, script prewritten in every historical grief manual. "Who doesn't like pills?" David Johansen, lead singer of the New York Dolls, once asked us in concert. What are the pills working on—death or reenactment? Human bodies can simulate death on drugs; brain feedback loops shut down; the feeding tube is pulled out and you are painlessly thick in the throat. One swallow of saliva is a whole meal.

It took two months to get the renowned surgeon scheduled to perform the mastectomy after diagnosis—no difference to outcome. We yielded body parts in the hope of appeasement. During one round of chemotherapy, she said she didn't feel awful enough—it can't be working. I said it was.

My Cancer Wife. I was diagnosed with breast cancer in May 2003. I stayed in the house during my course of chemo. Part of being housebound was fear of infection, but in truth I was hiding. I didn't want to appear vulnerable, looking like an alien. I didn't want to be pitied or stared at. One day my mother-in-law popped in unexpectedly and saw me bald; I cried and cried. She could have cared less what I looked like, but for me it was devastating. It was as if the gig was up; I'd been exposed; the truth was out; I had cancer and had crossed over to the world of "otherness."

She died before they got her hooked up to an intravenous morphine pump. I have a receipt for the order. When I called to cancel the morphine order they sounded surprised. Did I hear right? Husband denied spouse a painless easing from this world, as if I'd chosen the death time as personal pain gauge instead of communal easing off the accelerator. We attempt to align the death process with the grief process in seamless transition, working with the technicians we require. Death is now a tour production. Perhaps they were right. I screamed into the phone—She died in my arms in our bed—peacefully. There was an empty space phone pause before the other voice monochromatically resumed business. I dialed her work voice mail and left messages from the next morning until the company removed it from the phone network.

I wanted to soundtrack into her. Cancer beat me. Say your wife is an iPod, because you can't sing, and constantly vibrates to the music you incessantly introduce into her environment—she's no narc or buffoon, dismissing the ludicrousness of a large percent of your endeavor—but assume reverb: She will fuck me from beyond the grave. It feels good to feel Marvin Gaye. His own dad shot him.

Death sex is alabaster sculptured bodies, veins only open where they bleed into genitalia—the longing for her body tells me I'm living over against her inertness, I'm lukewarm not hot-blooded and bloodied, provoking guilt as tears against the dam holding shut her death, a museum adding space every day—spare me yours, I have lived too long should one more occur today—I want my death to disintegrate into my wife. Death doesn't let you choose: There is no GPS location for death merging. That is why marriage is important in the land of the living.

My Cancer Wife. I do understand that these comments and stares are often generated from true compassion, and other times it's fear. But these individuals will never know how deeply their actions hurt me. The pain of being stared at, pitied, or treated as an invalid is far more painful than any chemo treatment, or how I felt the first time I stared at that bald woman in the mirror. What I want to scream to all who will listen is that I'm still the person I always was, I'm OK, really. Cancer is part of my life, but it is NOT my life. Yes, I wish I didn't have cancer. Yes, I sometimes cry in the shower. Yes, I worry about how much time I have. But in truth, even with cancer, my life is happy. I lead a richer, more fulfilled life than most people I know. I'm active. I walk and swim regularly. I recently walked sixty miles to raise money for breast cancer research. I travel. I have a great job that pays me well and a lovely home. I am a successful artist. I have a circle of friends that could keep the Titanic afloat.

Fluids leaking, it is 2 a.m., I call the doctor. The tube draining her biliary tract, constricted by the metastasized breast CA tumor lodged there, is leaking out her abdomen. He doesn't know why; the day's procedure went well. He is perplexed, his voice mezzo-soprano, questioning his experience, muttering to himself a procedure rerun. I've been changing gauze pads every forty-five minutes to soak up the bile fluid and blood. I would settle for relieving the pain or choking the motherfucker. Last question: Should I make an appointment in the morning at a larger, tertiary hospital farther away, but within emergency driving distance, to halt-solve the leakage? No, no, he states, "I'll schedule her first thing. We can take care of it." Stupid enough, I've taken care of it. Fell asleep draining; no dreams. Awoken by crying, my hands stained awkward yellow. They are the first thing she sees as I grasp bed edge, raised up off the floor.

Later that day in recovery, she is not well but the procedure "went well" again. She's emaciated, shrunk into herself. I see it; she says it. "My spirit is broken, honey." The surgeon who originally diagnosed us notices her. I'm trying to convince nursing staff her blood pressure is always low. I need her home, anything could happen, and a hospital is not a good place for anything can happen. The surgeon greets and moves bedside, holds her hand. Words are passed. His trained eyes move from interior to exterior, arriving out of tubes and sutures, assessing. I watch him shuffle off, a gentle, unassuming man, greatly talented, who practices medicine in impoverished countries during vacations. He slumps at the doctor's desk. My wife can't see him. He hangs his face inside his two open hands. When the wings open, it is a different face.

I now carry a small bottle of antibacterial hand wash with me everywhere. It's become obsessive-compulsive behavior, incidental contact with a potential dirty surface and I'm cleaning-scrubbing off my hands, in public, in private. I'll never get stain free and I'll never get to operate.

I told her, knowing there could be no answer, "I'm coming soon, honey." At what point would death say I'm a liar? Pain will pull you into the death you can't imagine. When is it time to say, "That's not how I envisioned it—is that the right hand?" Death won't respond; it will shut me up.

My Cancer Wife. So the next time you see a cancer patient, don't rush to pity. Look deeper. There is a good chance she doesn't want your pity and plans on beating the disease. And even if her prognosis is poor, she may still actually have a life to be envied.

Don't drink the water. Wash your hands. Study ice and mass killing. Sing. Do it for me.

To Take Place
Joe Wenderoth

YOU MUST DIE. You can do a great many things before you die, but the thing you absolutely must do is die, and this fact—this inevitability—has an impact on everything else. Let's say you decide to take a walk. This is a decision to take a walk *while you still can.* Death tempers relativity in this way. Death says to you: *Your life, in the moment of its completion, will have an absolute shape, and that shape will be the result of what it contained, the final shape of your myriad ongoing decisions.*

*

Poems are not like taking a walk. Poems are not a before-you-die activity. Poems are *pretending to have died.* You pretend to have died and hope that your pretending produces a strong sense of *who* has died, a strong sense of the shape of the life that might have been yours. Poems are a demonstration of whatever it is that is able to pretend—again and again—to have died. Poems are the most serious and the most ridiculous business in the world.

*

There's a big difference between pretending to die and pretending *to have died.* In the former, a character is still being played (however woundedly); in the latter, the sudden absence of that character becomes, in everyone lucky enough to behold it, the stage itself.

*

All goes onward and outward . . . and nothing collapses,
And to die is different from what any one supposed,
    and luckier.

364

Has any one supposed it lucky to be born?
I hasten to inform him or her it is just as lucky to die,
    and I know it.

—Walt Whitman

*

Whitman is not being absurdly optimistic—or at any rate not in the way people so often seem to think; he is invoking our ignorance of the experience of dying. You can't know what dying will actually feel like; you can't know what your last sense of yourself (the imagined whole) will be like; you can't even know *if* there will be a last sense of yourself. And the more you consider it, the more absurd it seems to think that *any* one last version of yourself could be *the finally appropriate one.*

*

When I pretend to have died, I do not do so in preparation for actually dying. The most that can be said about the relationship of my pretending(s) to have died and my actually dying . . . is that the inevitability of the latter is one of the causes of the former. Knowing *that* I will die is what enables me to make that mental leap—the poetic leap—wherein I have died and am able to figure the hypothetical whole of a life, the countenance of my very person. Whitman, in "Song of Myself," removes the *in preparation* part from the equation. In doing so, he finds a new way to invest himself in pretending to have died; suddenly, pretending to have died is to be understood in terms of what it might produce—and in those terms only. Pretending to have died is not, for Whitman, a dreadful inhabiting of the inevitability of annihilation; quite to the contrary, it is the birthing of a whole (however momentary) person, a countenance somehow worthy of the imaginary realm.

*

Whitman's optimism is based on the clear distinction he makes between pretending to have died and actually dying. His suspicion seems to be that we *live* (i.e., pretend to have died) absolutely poetically,

365

but we die absolutely unpoetically. We die, then, without any of the anxiety that usually comes along with our need of a sufficiently imagined whole. This is not to say that Whitman believes we inevitably live in anxiety; no, to the contrary, he says that you have the opportunity to afford your living with a sense of ease and freedom . . . *if* you come to understand the difference between living (pretending to have died) and dying. That is, if you come to understand that you cannot actually die in a wrong way, then death can no longer be conceived of as something fearful—it can no longer be imagined as a kind of final verdict on one's personhood. There will be verdicts, to be sure, but Whitman wants us to believe that they will be many (and profoundly communal too, as we need one another to get a sense of them), and they will be *poetic* in essence; they will be the business of living, not the business of dying. Dying is something else, and produces no verdicts.

*

Dying does not take place. Place exists only in the imagination, and dying occurs elsewhere, in reality. Perhaps not even *there*—who could say? The relevant question is always concerned with what can—or even with what does—take place. Pretending to have died *does* take place. Why do you pretend to have died?

*

It would be a mistake to think that, because you have no experience of death, you are not able to pretend to have died. You have no experience with becoming a cat, but you can certainly pretend to have become a cat. You have seen the cat—the cat has come up close to you. You have seen death—death has come up close to you. The closer it gets, the more foreign it shows itself to be.

*

The luminous matter of galaxies is gravitationally bound to a more massive, sprawling halo of dark matter.

*

To take place is to take place *again*. This is something one learns, despite one's initial dreams of oneself. Dying, when it actually occurs, is occurring for the first time—this is why it does not take place. There is a difference between what occurs (what is *given* place) and what *takes* place. The personhood of the person takes place (or at any rate, it is *possible* for the personhood of the person to take place); that which is outside of the personhood of the person merely occurs. The person has a very strange relationship to that which occurs.

*

When I hear someone talking about the Big Bang, I am sometimes interested. When I am told that someone—someone I in some way know of—has died, I am almost always interested, but the interest is of a different sort. My interest in the Big Bang is poetic, whereas my interest in someone's having died is both poetic and more-than-poetic. If the someone who has died is close to me—beloved—then the balance between the poetic and the more-than-poetic is skewed; the more-than-poetic dominates, and the effect of this domination is to indict poetic interest, or at least to make it confess its basic obscenity.

*

In a chapter on death, Andy Warhol wrote only: "I don't believe in it, because you're not around to know that it's happened. I can't say anything about it because I'm not prepared for it."

*

Consider the difference between knowing *that* someone has died and knowing *how* someone has died. The former is what matters most—it is what ensures the deadness of the dead person. Someone close to us has died, and when we are told of the death (and when we know that we are not being lied to), our first question is almost always: *How?* We ask this question because disbelief, as Warhol pointed out, is very much a part of the foundation of our experience of death. *No . . . how? . . . it can't be. . . .* But the asking of how has another function. Knowledge of the how might be useful to us; with that knowledge, we might construct a final sense of that person.

*

To know how someone died is to be able to turn him into a poem. To not know *how* someone died is, ultimately, to not know *if* someone has died; it is to live with the suggestion that the song is merely endless.

*

The missing mass of the universe led to the theory of dark matter. This dark matter, in order to be consistent with an early-universe annihilation rate (proper relic abundances), should have a small but measurable interaction with ordinary matter.

*

By way of narrative, the personhood of the person is made manifest as an incidental (and intentional) arc. To consider, on the other hand, simply *that death is,* is to invest the personhood of the person differently; it is to invest it in the sensational progress of a disease. The disease progresses not outwardly—not incidentally and not intentionally—but in an inward way, upon an altogether different terrain. To allow for and to carefully register the progress of this disease could be construed as *useful,* but doing so inevitably raises questions about the nature of usefulness. For instance, am I making use of where I am, or is where I am making use of me, or are both true at once? That's just the beginning of the questions.

*

You might find solace in your disease. It invests you in something more immediately your own. It suggests you—surprisingly enough—as a less deniable (i.e., more volatile) ground, upon which the beloved (the shadow-play core of the incidental/intentional arc) is resuscitated and restored to promiscuity.

*

To have died is always someone else's act—it is never mine. *My* death is always (always!) in the future, and it may be that it is something I do not have the ability to experience. So there are really two kinds of death: the death of an other, and the death of myself. The death of an other is something I might take possession of, in a sense, in that I might be in proximity to it and know *that* it has occurred. At the same time, the death of an other is conspicuously inaccessible to me—it is an experience I quite decisively have not had. My death, on the other hand, is something I will never have the opportunity to take possession of or be in proximity to. I will not attend my own funeral. My death differs most significantly from the death of an other in that it can never be a part of my past; it is not something I will ever have the chance to figure, to pull into the on-going business of world formation and world inhabiting. Death is simply the ceasing of the on-site savoring of one revision arc.

*

Is the inaccessibility of an other's death different from the inaccessibility of my own death? Yes and no.

—Yes, in that the barriers differ. I am excluded from the other's death by the difference in our bodies; I am excluded from my own death by time. The inverse is also true: I am included in the other's death by way of time, and I am included in my own death by way of body.

—No, in that it would not be possible for me to conceive of my own death, let alone its being inaccessible to me, without the other's death and that death's being in some sense inaccessible to me. The inaccessibility of the death of the other, then, must be instrumental in the formation of the inaccessibility of my own death.

*

Pretending to have died is profoundly social. It is an attempt to overcome death's inaccessibility. It is an attempt to enter into the other just as it is an attempt to enter into oneself.

*

Pretending to have died is profoundly antisocial. It is to identify oneself as the god-power capable of demonstrating the death of oneself, and it is to presume that this demonstration is the beginning of a never-to-be-occupied history.

Joe Wenderoth

*

Scientists have been trying to observe proton decay, but have not succeeded as of yet. The challenge consists of finding a place to do the testing; that is, the challenge is to find a place in which a proton might be sufficiently shielded from cosmogenic events. Most testing has been done deep underground, beneath miles of rock. It's interesting to think that observing the most fundamental decay of the universe cannot be accomplished because said universe contains no site from which this kind of observation of itself is possible.

*

To bear witness to someone's pretending to have died is the same as being someone who is pretending to have died. That is, it is social; it implies that you and I are *next of kin*.

To bear witness to someone's pretending to have died is antisocial in that it suggests a welcoming of the presence of a god (presence, in this case, being coextensive with speech) who brings everything to an end.

*

That god is my tool, I tell myself, if only to express how unlikely it is for you to have known me.

Triage Along the Nile
Edward Hoagland

HE COULD POINT AT Katire and Torit, Obb and Farajok, Magwe and
Palotaka, Karpeto and Kerripi, settlements like pimples in the heaving ocean of vitality, tracklessly green and stretching twenty-eight
hundred miles to Liberia and Sierra Leone—sufficient to sap the
bravado of any bush pilot except the likes of Mickey, who was beating a rhythm on his knee with his fist or eating hummus from a can
with a forefinger, and drinking thermos coffee. It didn't seem a particularly funereal or hairy flight to him because he often flew into
rebel-held enclaves in Congo, Somalia, or Sudan without any pro-
tective clearance or diplomats aboard for a guarantee. The Allied
Democratic Forces, fighting Uganda from Zaire; or a rump Nuer fac-
tion fighting the Dinkas from the swampy village of Lafon, north of
Torit; or the Equatorial Defense Force, of Mandaris, Baris, and others
the Dinkas had persecuted; or the homicidal lunatics of the Lord's
Resistance Army, who cut people's lips off in the name of the Christian God: All might be operating somewhere underneath us, not to
mention the SPLA's militias, or their Arab enemies. That's why Leo
and the nuns, during the two-week walk from Opari to Chukudum,
if the car broke down or had become dangerous to use, would need
the protection of people who loved him from his years of pastoral
care. Just one jughead with a Kalashnikov could splat them as anony-
mously as some small band of Somali *shifta* searching below a ridge-
line for gold or ivory, and themselves fair game for anybody.

Mickey hadn't known these Norwegians because they came to
Africa on three-month stints and left. "But Ruthie's a good old bag,"
he said. "One time I had hepatitis and she could tell by looking at
my eyes and told me to lie down and get treated. Otherwise I'd have
kept right on flying and collapsed someplace you wouldn't ever want
to be."

He pointed to the collection of hills surrounding her church at Loa,
when we reached the river, and down to the Catholics' chapel and
mission, twenty miles north of Ruth's. We could also see Juba—my
first glimpse—a scattered locality including an airport with tower

and runways expanded for the military, and a dock on the Nile where a defunct ferryboat was moored, two or three blocks of cement stores, a paved street with several squat brick administrative buildings, some bungalows or villas for the honchos in charge, barracks for the soldiers, a down-at-heels one-story stucco hospital, and an awful sprawl of slum neighborhoods of thatch in disrepair and mud, oily with stagnant sewage, hodgepodged by the three-year siege and housing a couple of hundred thousand wretched souls who hadn't managed to tiptoe through the rings of scrubby minefields both sides had laid irregularly around the city one night or another and get safely out. It was ugly. There were vultures on unburied bodies, both goats and humans, in this huge circle, and jackals that glanced up at us with flesh hanging from their mouths. And people who made it through encountered famously rough treatment from a Dinka cadre suspicious of why they had remained in Juba for so long in the first place.

Besides the ring of mines—where two goats that hadn't finished dying, apparently panicked by the birds, were staggering, trying to stand—the city's spraddled slums had been partly appropriated for military use, and mortar-blasted by the SPLA. Other mortar shells had strayed into the pathetically jammed-together hovels where women, children, and the elderly had been trying to survive the siege, fed by the Lutherans' weekly flights into Juba from Kenya, balancing the Catholics' feeding of "our" side. In Nairobi, the aid facilitators joked mordantly about how they might have been unintentionally prolonging the war—Lutherans feeding Muslims, Catholics the animists—which was not what they wanted, regardless of the egging on they might be getting from the diplomats. To look down for the first time at the squalor and privation our side's siege was inflicting upon tens of thousands of trapped civilians was breathtaking—"enemy territory," and there *was* the Antonov that bombed us, and two MiGs, on the airfield waiting for us to do our business and the truce to end. But when Mickey chuckled and reminded me of how I'd demonized those hired Slavs, "you with your CIA guys," I had to admit I might be flying against the Dinkas myself if I was living inside the siege lines.

We saw muzzle flashes, burning huts, and a blackish tank askew on a roadway as we banked. Inside that broken circle of machine-gun sniping and mortar explosions nobody was moving as in a normal provincial city, just scurrying for bare essentials, even though the breakout had loosened the guerrillas' grip on the perimeter. My sorrow spread so far beyond the three Norwegians who had died for their idealism that I wished I was back in the Berkshires teaching American schoolkids about our own Civil War, instead of watching this one. From the air, you could spot the positions that were crumbling and who, hunkered there, was doomed. The disintegrating siege line reminded me of burning my bridges in Alexandria, after watching my company's ships being destroyed in the Umm Qasr Harbor on CNN during the Gulf War, and how I'd emptied their Egyptian bank account of as much as I would ordinarily be authorized to and stuffed the cash into my girlfriend's body stocking before we flew to Heathrow. On the flight itself, joking with Amy about the corporate "coffers," I'd realized I had committed an irreversibly stupid mistake. She later changed her name by marrying someone else, and wasn't a signatory anyhow, bless her, so I was more a target. And here I was, slanting steeply toward the Norwegians' hand-mown, stone-picked airstrip, a dozen miles south of Juba, wishing I wasn't, especially when Mickey muttered, *"Holy shit."*

The MiGs had vaulted into the sky behind us, but instead of plugging us were bulleting away toward one of the other government towns under siege: Wau or Kapoeta, Torit or Malakal. Our location being known, every other battleground in Equatoria was open to them. We could see the Maryknolls' stubby steeple up the curly, gorge-gouged Nile, which boasted a slick stretch near where the Norwegians had built their infirmary, and where the Irish girl and several others were waving frantically. Mickey's gray hair shone silver in the sunlight, to match his wicked grin at how bumpily we were going to hit the runway, the crescendo of a trip for him. But the blitzed hospital building wiped us clean of our preoccupations.

The bodies, black and white, were mangled, discolored, concussively dispersed, and not yet in bags, as we had anticipated. The surgeon still registered his amazement, but his wife, the nurse, in her green scrub suit, looked agonized, with ghastly shards of glass and stone and wood embedded in her, punctures that had bled plentifully. The second Norwegian man, the anesthetist, appeared to have lived a while, crawling aimlessly, hemorrhaging from his gashes. Four or five times as many Africans had died, patients and helpers strewn as if after an eruption. The wounded had been lying for all these hours untended in the jumble of the crushed building, with any means of helping them also smashed and crushed. The Irish girl was not a nurse, had no bandaging or morphine, and felt constrained not to move the corpses until they had been photographed. So, except for a few starvelings who had been scavenging for survival items like dented containers, stained tarpaulins and gurneys, fly-covered scraps of bloody cloth, it was unmitigated horror.

She had assembled a pitiful pile of belongings to go with them. But in the meantime, the injured Africans were begging for water, pain-killer, a tourniquet, a situation to recline in without stones poking their backs. We unloaded the coffins. The coroner and diplomat indeed took pictures. We then washed, adjusted or painstakingly tended to, and wrapped the three eloquent white bodies, speaking volumes in the din of war, though not so poignantly as the living who pleaded for care. They and the unburied dead had no relatives or buddies around to minister to them. Nobody was digging either graves or fox-holes, and it became unutterably sad when a bloodstained English speaker upbraided us, then wilted to the ground.

"We kept our hopes up because we thought a doctor would come," he said. That is, a replacement on the plane, not merely a burial party. Mickey and I were loading Al's trunkful of frontline medications into the back of the jeep, along with the hundred kilos of cornmeal he had sent. Moira, the Irish girl, had given me the key, kissed her Dinka officer goodbye, and vanished onto the plane to keep the coffins company. He radioed permission for me to cross the Nile to Ruth's side on a certain secret ferry the SPLA maintained now that the bridges had been bombed out, then jogged off to rejoin his unit. The aerial still sported a Norwegian flag, to which I added a square of white sheeting, and I topped up the gas tank from my jerrycan, in case that got grabbed at the first roadblock. The hospital's fuel drums had exploded in the raid. Only masculine pride kept me from sneaking right back onto the plane.

The moaning of the dying asking for family, for shelter, for water had been a counterpoint to our hasty undertaking arrangements—the folding of amputated arms, closing jellied eyes, capping the doc-tor's half-scalped skull. The temporary coffins, one-size-fits-all, seemed uncomforting. No respectful proprieties were possible when we were all in such a hurry, and yet the Zanzibari suggested in passing that it was a much more compact scene than a militia massacre, where the dead and dismembered have run in all directions to escape the ma-chetes: "So you take it in only gradually and forget it more slowly when you are home."

I was surprised. I was digging out a vial of morphine, intending to leave now with the plane in order not to be swarmed by rubber-neckers who needed something to eat, if left alone here. But I wanted to give some relief.

"It was not human." He pointed upward at the air. "That you can forget: but not what the machetes do."

One person was herself a nurse and instructed me as to how much to shoot her with. A Dinka, her humor was intact, thanking me when she saw she wasn't going to be evacuated. "Tell Ruthie I had a hysterectomy"—pointing at her gory wound. She had managed to crawl into the brush for some shade. Ambulatory patients with shrapnel in them thronged around as I administered a couple of other lethal doses to those worse off; and Mickey yelled.

Under my driver's seat I'd felt a few days' worth of Norwegian army rations and a first-aid kit. Mickey started his engine and yelled again, so I walked over, noticing Moira in the copilot's seat and really no room for me, though I'd half hoped he was telling me there was. Instead, he surprised me by throwing out his emergency fanny pack, which contained a compass, duct tape, water purifier, Cipro, hard-tack, kippered herring, and the like.

"God luv ya, man! See you in Juba if they catch you—or Khartoum! Al will pay me back." He laughed, being used to dropping daredevils off in goosebump situations, and pointed me toward the jeep, so we could leave at the same time. Gripping the yoke, he taxied to the leeward end of the strip. "The doctor, the doctor!" people were shouting, as they recognized for sure that they were being abandoned with no assistance, no food, unless the Arabs brought them some. White man style, I scrammed, slipping my motor into gear to reach the spindly road just as he mounted over the trees and could no longer radio the SPLA to rescue me from the crowd. And now, when Juba's control tower confirmed his departure, the offensive would no doubt resume in earnest.

Once clear of the disaster zone, I drove slowly, with my pennants fluttering from the aerial and the good-guy logo on the door, hoping not to tempt any hair-trigger bozos at either side. Roadblocks might be my least risk, compared to ordnance hidden at free-fire angles to kill an APC or tank and infantry advancing south, that you'd never see till you were safely past. And the road was fitfully mobbed with civilians burdened by bundles on their heads and tired, undernourished, disoriented children frightened by the crump and thump of shelling behind us—which, although they parted for me without cat-calls, sometimes startled them right back into the middle of the lane I had. I drove with one foot on the clutch, the other on the brake, wasting precious gas, as I suppose you must when bugging out of a civil war.

I wasn't forcibly stopped. Nobody set a baby down in front of my wheels or banged on my fender with a club. But lame, wraithlike people cried out to me in Bari, Arabic, Dinka, or English for a lift, with that edge of hysteria when norms are breaking down. They had self-hacked canes and blistered sores and a mango or a wad of cassava in hand and were bent into the shape of question marks. But the huts along the way had not been torched, the trees not stripped of their leaves for soup, and kids who weren't clinging to their mothers, piggyback, might hop for fun with a stick like a vaulting pole. The casualties lay behind, where the noise was, and the grief of leaving them. People were in survival mode, dazed, yet trekking by the thousands through the rolling, tawny, still luxuriant landscape in the direction of Uganda. If they were footsore now, they'd be reeling soon.

I'd kept excusing myself for not picking any riders up because I was going to turn off, and finally a wooden crosspiece on a post did finger me left to the ferry landing at a fat stretch of the Nile where islets could conceal the rope and an acacia forest the pulleys on either bank. The Dinka soldier who was preventing civilians from boarding nodded at the sight of me, and the Bari ferryman chocked my wheels on the raft, as he and his son began to pull us toward the opposite side. The currents, greeny brown, revolved like supple cylinders or parallel crocodiles, though I noticed an actual crocodile swimming crosswise to them, like us. The man said he worked mostly at night when the MiGs didn't fly, and this had been his grandfather's livelihood, paid for at first by the English and the Italian White Father missionaries.

"No oil here. Why this war?" he asked. The oil was beyond Juba and Malakal downriver; he hadn't been that far north. When I tapped his biceps, he showed me trotlines he had strung from an island into the river that kept his family well supplied with protein. When I asked what he would do when the Arabs arrived, he waggled his thumb at a pirogue hidden next to the slip he was pulling toward.

"They don't swim. I know them! Not watermen. No camels here." He pointed at a mountain torrent joining the river beyond where we were. "Scared," he said, as if shivering; then showed me a black-and-white fish eagle soaring to dive on the fish bewildered by the water's change in flow, and gave me a piece of white crocodile tail meat to chew.

A Dinka guard helped him, me, and his son to push the jeep up the landing to the dirt road on this east bank, where an equivalent crowd, inflamed by rumors that the guerrillas were no longer able to hold their positions surrounding Juba, was fleeing south. Mostly Dinkas, not from these local river tribes, they weren't afraid to step right up and harangue the Dinka soldiery: *If you have already lost your cattle herds and homelands, do you want to lose your children and old people as well?* They couldn't melt into the forest on ancient footpaths and shelter with relatives who might never have made either army aware they existed. Though it was their fight, not mine, being on Ruth's side of the river, I could fill my empty seats with a handful of the thousands of souls who needed a ride. Fearfully raucous, shedding the discipline the SPLA had imposed on its refugee camps, the retreat was not yet a free-for-all, and neither deferential nor hostile to my NGO logo. I wanted to find Bol, but the name is a common one and nobody responded to my inquiries except with puzzlement.

I let a broken-legged old man with a spear lie on top of the grain sacks and medical gear on the understanding, conveyed by sign language, that he would defend them if necessary. Next to me in front, I allowed an exhausted, bulgingly pregnant woman to sit, whose stained toga indicated that her sac had burst. It was a crazy notion, but could you have turned her down? She had no one else; Ruth might help. And children climbed in and out, over the back bumper, because I drove with stymied intensity, seldom above five or ten miles an hour in the crush. Crones and geezers were attempting to evacuate and women of all ages with or without toddlers in tow— long-legged savannah folk but limping from the downed timber hereabouts, with shins barked, knees knobbed from weeks on a meal or less per day. Some figures leaned or lay a few yards off the line of march, awaiting their fate or for the pain to let up, or their marrow to release more calories. If they were already dead, nobody knew.

I met no vehicles. The guerrillas had thrown their stake-sided trucks and pickups into carrying troops, not acting as ambulances, and mounted machine guns in the latter. So I was afraid that a cruising MiG might spot me, only a minute's flying time south of the fighting, and assume I must be a commander. I didn't want to go slower than I could help, yet couldn't drive fast. Whole families were walking in front of me, whose ears were hearing echoes of the crackle of battle, not attuned to a minor motor nudging their heels. Gamins and gravid ladies strode like marathoners, carrying whichever members of the newest generation had endured. All turned in vague alarm at the snout of my jeep, expecting a hollering commandant. SPLA politics were so lethal, relief mixed with chagrin that a last NGO was leaving, in their expressions.

I thought of Herbert and Craig, who always cleared out before the shit hit the fan. Herbert, after his three passports spilled out of his bag in my presence, had opened up a little, not to speak of his intelligence work but saying he had "a cocoon" at home (wherever that was) where his wife raised dogs, and he had a "den" with all of Bach and Mozart at his fingertips and the finest technology to render it "soothing," he said.

Passing a man stumbling in gait, his hip bones, almost fleshless, wagging as laboriously as a sick fish's tail, needing both food and first aid, I realized I would have picked him up at any other time. Too many blackbirds were sailing in the sky, as if congregating off the mountainsides to head toward the civilian conclaves down where Ruth's clinic was. Her fence had been knocked down. Her compound was filling, Makundi, her Kamba assistant, had told Al, sounding uncommonly worried on the radio, with a babble of squatters as background noise behind him, not because they imagined she still had rations to feed them, but the Arabs might not bomb her church for fear of "angering America." When the exodus reached them, a panic would block our route.

I was still wondering whether Ruth's baby jackal had gone into one of Makundi's stews; whether Bol was at the front, or I might meet him again; when suddenly on a hunch I spun the car to the right into the tall grass, a dip in the ground, practically flipping it, simultaneously with my ears registering the bass banshee hurricane scream of a jet cannoning the road where we'd just been. I lost my backseat passengers, wrenched my shoulder, bloodied my nose, and the lady beside me began to miscarry and therefore shriek. I was gasping in simpleton's shock, spitting nettles and spiderwebs out of my mouth, till the pain in my shoulder, almost out of its socket, became nothing compared to hers. The baby must have been crushed: would have to be extracted; I dragged her out of the jeep.

The tangly turf of the jungle, such as it was, had cushioned the falls of the old spearman and two or three small orphans who had been riding with him. He reassembled his dignity, his three good limbs, scrambled to the road, and began badgering passersby to help. The trouble, of course, was that things were worse. I had never assisted in a birth, aborted or not, but wiggled the inert fetus out of the canal—the mother's hands like trapped birds beside mine—along with a horrendous flow of blood. Easing her into a peaceably woozy position in which to lose consciousness with the child beside her was the saddest moment so far, but a wider devastation had been inflicted on the stream of pedestrians next to the shell craters and strafing pattern scribbled on the road. They were now in louder agony and nobody could minister to them either. In the chaos and congestion we did enlist enough bystanders to right the car, and I found another 10 cc vial of morphine, good for ten quick shots, and some absorbent compresses.

A stillbirth in the midst of a famine, a bombing, an auto accident, and triaging. I tied tourniquets onto stumps that, alone, were not going to save anybody's life, but the anguish of the surviving family was diminished. We bounced on, another very pregnant woman in the passenger seat, and the broken-legged man, with a retaped splint, lying on the bags and trunks, yelling imprecations in Dinka when necessary at new arrivals, unmaimed, who surged around, walking south but begging for a ride. She was a Kakwa, with relatives in Atiak, she said in storekeeper English, watching the MiG perform more important errands on the horizon than coming back for us, its afterburners banging as it climbed away from any Stinger that might be fired in retaliation. I believe in premonitions, or a sixth sense that saves your life, but the plane had probably not been supersonic so close to the ground on its strafing run at us: So I might have heard it, as an assist to my hunch. She had seen our escape but lost a sister in the attack, and thus was betting on me, split between hope and grief. *He* had a voice like a herder, sharp and loud, rattling his spear, but she could negotiate better for us through a crowd, using Juba's Arabic argot or Kakwa, which is close to Bari. She was also softhearted, so we soon had kids perching on both front fenders and the spare tire bolted to the rear, which disarmed the walking wounded who otherwise might have yelled at us. Another woman, stick armed yet pouch bellied, tall yet bent, with pain creasing her face, and too timid to look at me, swung herself aboard in the backseat area at the invitation of my friend with the spear—he explained the reason in Dinka, and she yammered to him in her distress like, perhaps, a fellow villager.

People stepped around the more outlandish dead, depersonalized by ghoulish wounds or grotesque postures, when a sort of all-fours, slaughterhouse animalization had occurred during the throes. But if I couldn't drive around, I needed to drag them, with the kids' help, out of the road. Or I might stop anyway, visualizing how the tank treads would chew them up if they were left where they must have collapsed. Sensible individuals would have availed themselves of the

379

woods to die, but who's so sensible, or not afraid of hyenas, at that tipping point? Better the company of the living before the vultures land. We hauled them underneath the nearest tree: and people in convulsions, not finished with the process yet—braying in misery at the departure point. There is no dignity to dying of dysentery along the roadside among the myriad feet of a retreat. The tanks would suspect an ambush and grind right over them.

Waifs and walking wounded I steered around, becoming acclimated. The spearman growled half sympathetically at how I trembled: our close call catching up with me. New crowds swallowed us, oldsters wagging their bones like a carp's tail, laboring south on the shoulders of the road. The adrenaline still had me panting. I ached. My wrists and fists remembered how hard they'd wrenched us off into the ditch. A granny holding hands with four children blocked our way, but I didn't honk, or even regret leaving Nairobi. I was in the flow, Uganda incongruously the safest haven. Incidents were blurring together because people held their youngsters up for me to see— whether to take them or inoculate them, feed them—and I didn't stop, except finally in the case of one woman who appeared to be dying. Afflicted as though by a stroke by some shrapnel she seemed to have in her, only half of her face worked to express her urgency. She was besmeared and encrusted, with another woman, who was shattered likewise. I'd spread my hands to indicate my inability to take them anywhere that would have mattered, even if I'd had the space, and pointed at a shady tree where they might sit. My motor stalled in the milling crowd. Then the jeep felt jostled, but before I could get irritated, the detonations of an Antonov carpeting a refugee camp followed. More panic and congestion would ensue.

What good would it do? I signaled. They were supporting each other at my driver's-side window. Bandages, penicillin, if I stopped and rooted them out and wasn't swamped by other petitioners, would be of no real use now. What the mother with aphasia or semiparalysis wanted, however, was to pass, with the help of her friend, a boy of kindergarten age, catatonic with fright, from their slippery arms into my lap. Whatever might happen to him was better than watching her die. The mortuary immobility of her face told me that, and he didn't begin to grab for my ears and eyeglasses until I'd driven away. The kid on the rear fender yelled at him in Dinka to quit that.

I needed a sling to ease my shoulder's ache, but would see a person losing blood at a catastrophic rate. Even though I didn't stop, the vehicles behind me would be less merciful. It might be a charnel house

380

by then—tomorrow. My spearman's bad leg looked wizened, badly set, lucky perhaps that it didn't smell of gangrene, and his spear mostly functioned as a cane. But he groaned at the anxious scenarios we squeezed through, the dramas of families split by who could continue to walk and who could not, believing, I think, that needier people ought to have his space in the car and he should be facing the Arabs with his spear: Take one with him. I hadn't stopped for him to catch the chance to slide out, but at the Maryknolls' former post, now teeming with refugees, I felt duty bound to check in, as if Father Leo's voice were prompting me. A few parishioners and a Tanzanian X-ray technician left behind, whose machine had broken long ago, were preserving order inside each building's shell, and my presence bolstered them, especially when I said that the NGOs were all coming back, regardless of who won the war. Surviving the next month or so would be the trick. Those whose starvation had progressed to the monkey-cheeked, eye-socket stage had been provided with a dimly illuminated concrete room to lie in; malarial patients, another. The latrines had flooded.

My car was claustrophobically surrounded, and I was surprised the Tanzanian stranded, but, raising his eyebrows, he indicated the thronging children, the veneer of civility still masking desperate circumstances. How could he desert? Leo and the nuns were "precious, God's instruments." It was crucial they not be killed by mistake, like the Scandinavians. I hugged him and gave him one of the fifty-kilo bags of maize I'd brought (Leo's brogue prompting again), which was immediately set boiling in the fifty-five-gallon steel drum they cooked mush in. My spearman lay down on guard in the weeds, and we lost our collection of urchins to the prospect of a palmful of cornmeal apiece.

I took the opportunity to skedaddle, but my remaining passengers, the heavily pregnant Kakwa and the other woman, were so dismayed I gave them energy bars from a Meals Ready to Eat and snacked on one myself. Around a couple of bends we met more waifs in the road, who mounted the fenders and the spare tire fastened upright in back. I picked up a third ailing woman, to fill the backseat—the eye is hardwired for triage, I think—and peeled a tangerine for the child in my lap. Unfortunately he was wetting it from more than one orifice, but I had resisted the awful impulse to leave him at the Catholics' place, to be smothered in terror. A railroad train could not have collected all of the women and children in need of rescue. The listlessness of true famine was spreading, people eking out their final calories by as little exertion as possible, and I had no radio to start the aid groups in Gulu moving north to receive them.

We slowed to a crawl again when a soldier with a Kalashnikov, although nodding in recognition at my logo, squeezed off a warning shot and peered at my passport, then asked for a candy bar. Imagining the furor in the European press about the Norwegians' deaths, I wondered what the rumor mill in Nairobi's NGO community was doing with Ruthie's holdout status. Selfless, or neurotic and pigheaded? She and our piffling organization, Protestants Against Famine, were minor players on the overall scene, but this disaster would train a spotlight on her. She was probably going to apologize for endangering me, but would she even be considered employable out on the edge again? Combined with what was already some gossip about her labyrinth and witches' globe and spirit stick (maybe the truckdrivers had snitched), would this seem a stunt signifying unreliability? People knew of her sudden return to Ohio a year or two before, but not that she'd come back to Africa precipitously because she'd felt suicidal there. Burning out was OK; anybody might do that. The code involved how you handled it.

"I don't believe in tragic sacrifices," I muttered to myself, as if rehearsing my first comments to Ruth. My shoulder hurt as I eased the tires over the bumps, praying none was going to go flat, and blaming her was easy. On the other hand, I'd begun to anticipate seeing Bol. Now, in the anarchy of the rebels' defeat, I might be able to rescue him, help him fulfill his dream of reaching the cities of the West. The river in its purring gorge was lit by curvaceous intensities of tawny light, the hills like combers over it, overenthusiastically endowed with flora. But in my lap the little kindergartner who had been thrust upon me, and was clinging to my sore ribs and interfering with my driving, had also vomited up the pieces of an energy bar he had eaten and further dehydrated himself by releasing more of his diarrhea onto my pants, as though to remind me that this was an ambulance I was driving, and I was probably about to dump the patients out in Ruth's churchyard to await the tanks. The pregnant woman next to me, in tribal dress, with necklaces, amulets, earrings, a hairband, but bone thin, offered the scrawny boy the bits he'd thrown up in her tweezer fingers. When he shook his head, she popped them in her mouth. Gracious, was I kidding myself that I could save her and him, as well as the carload of people I had undertaken to pick up?

"God luv ya!" Mickey had called from the cockpit, when he'd

tossed me his crash rations and kit with flashlight and so on. And I was thinking how accidental it was, whom you "saved." Makundi instead of this famished Kakwa, or *her* instead of another of the women in their seventh or eighth month I had noticed struggling along, but passed? A stooped fellow clutching a few cassava roots by the roadside (and relieved I wasn't stopping to steal them) indicated by gesturing that Bol might still be around, when I said the name. I thought of my legendary Clancy ancestor, who as a child had starved with his family through the Great Potato Famine in Ireland a hundred fifty years ago. And when they sent him out to search the fields one last time, after nobody else had strength enough to go, he walked back, like this man, with three in his hands and knowledge of an undiscovered pocket, to save their lives. A sumptuous sunset had begun, as large as the sky. Would we get away by dawn? I didn't dare leave Ruth's till daylight or we might face mob rule.

"God bless you!" She grinned wearily, when I drove through the ruined gate. The courtyard was like ten Gypsy encampments piled together, with hunger the theme. Her hair had whitened, so she looked sixty instead of fifty, and even Makundi, who had been skinny before, was thinner still.

"You find us in reduced circumstances," she added self-mockingly, while grimacing at the arrival of yet more weakened women, swelling toward deliveries that were sure to be wretched and sad: also the small boy curled fetally, with his snot bubbling into my lap. Two Dinka clan chieftains' wives, Nyadoul and Nyajal, one in a red toga, the other in blue—"They are heroes," Ruth said—took charge of my last fifty kilos of cornmeal, though it would need to multiply like Christ's five loaves and two fishes in order to nourish the multitude who gathered around the steel fuel drum to smell the aroma as sticks were lit.

"This way they're dying by inches," she said, and, turning, asked me, since I had remained almost silent, "Should I apologize?" In fact, according to Al, she had, over the radio. Yet on the scene I was uncertain. Maybe you really ought to stay as long as you could, if only as a witness.

I cleared my throat. "I don't know." Because that sounded a bit stupid, I added, "Truthfully."

Ruth was sleepwalking by now, compared to when I'd left, but still cherishing young Leo, who continued to hug her right hip in addled confusion, and therefore was none too pleased by my introducing an obviously sickly, faintly weeping new waif right into the household, so to speak, who might be fatally contagious. I wasn't either—he'd been handed to me as a stranger by a stranger a couple of hours ago and had been dribbling on me from both ends ever since. But his mother's anguished expression from the side of her face that still worked was potent, imperative, as Ruth, without asking, could see. Not touching him, she examined him sympathetically.

"No measles," she said. "They have measles in Kajo Kaji. Can you picture what will happen if those two armies come tearing through here and all get the measles and everybody on their feet keeps running?"

The drone of the Antonov, never grounded as early in the evening as the MiGs, moved us indoors to "the priory," as she called her quarters jokingly, to collapse into chairs for a pot of tea. Not that the roof made it safer than the dinky ditch she'd had dug for a bomb shelter—and which stunk now of feces—but you could ignore more. She was in a diminished mood. There was no protocol. She wolfed down a Meals Ready to Eat from my stash, chewing pieces little Leo could swallow to finger into his mouth. I gave my boy soup. The generator had run out of fuel, so we used a candle. The radio's battery was dwindling. The baby jackal had gone into one of Makundi's stews.

"It's so random it's bedlam," she said. "You have to believe in heaven, and I don't know if I do."

We did reach Felix, nearby in Uganda, who ran the closest NGO station and could relay news to Al the next morning that I'd arrived at Ruth's. His radio was on because he was attempting to reach the German embassy in Kampala, in case they could pressure an army commander to organize a convoy of food north along his road from Gulu. A mine probably planted by a rump group of rebels called the Allied Democratic Forces had blown up under a routine delivery, killing the truck driver, and set off a drivers' boycott. Knowing an avalanche of refugees was tumbling his way, he sounded frantic to get resupplied. "I can feed a hundred at most for one day," he said. Ruthie groaned. We were watching a line of our own souls, supervised by Nyadoul and Nyajal, each receive a handful of mush to last them indefinitely. These rebels weren't crazies like the Lord's Resistance Army, but a collection of leftover military folk who had served previous dictators, so their mines weren't meant to disable aid groups, but Museveni's army. The Lord's Resistance Army's evil genius wished to punish the whole world for its sins.

I wanted Ruth to massage my sick shoulder, but she was too tired to ask. She showed me a knapsack she'd packed for tomorrow's vamoose. Makundi, meanwhile, was guarding the jeep. She also pawed through the meds that remained in the chest for what to distribute to patients she recognized before we left—irritated now that Al hadn't remembered to put in powdered milk and eggs for Leo.

"But he's never met Leo. And we had about ten minutes," I pointed out, though afraid then of being blamed myself.

The complaint was shelved when the Antonov pooped a crapload of explosives onto a temporary settlement down the road a bit, where it might impact the exodus the most. The route must be choked with the injured, the panicky, throttling the possibilities of either resupply for the front or an orderly guerrilla retreat. Flames flashed up like blood briefly, and I pictured the airplane's crew, Soviets cashiered at the end of the Cold War without ever having had the chance to bomb American targets; this could be their apotheosis. We continued doling out germicides, rehydrating salts, malaria pills, so nothing would be left to fall into less deserving hands, a random, surreptitious process nonetheless, because everyone needed stuff. The chairs, beds, blinds, bins would disappear as soon as we were gone, and after I emptied the rest of my jerrycan into the gas tank, I rinsed it obsessively to carry our water, since the jugs had been stolen already. The other jeep's tires, up on blocks, which I'd hoped to cannibalize for the Norwegians' vehicle, had been cut up for rubber sandals.

Makundi wore a pair—and so did Bol, when he showed up, looking skeletal. I hugged him, gave him an energy bar. No, no firing squads; nothing for him to fear if, like us, he made a dash for it. The big, bright rising moon tempted us—if it might not tempt the Antonov into trying another bombing run—instead of the alternative, succumbing to a nap. But, coughing badly, swallowing an aspirin, he advised us not to.

"At night people have less conscience, you know? No witness. In daylight they know you did good, so they wouldn't hurt you."

He didn't want to discuss what had befallen his various schoolboys, except that the Unaccompanied Minors program had been scrapped by the SPLA even before the offensive. No food for those not drafted, and so the twelve-year-olds-and-under scattered, chasing bush squirrels and grasshoppers. He grabbed at the air, as you'd do to catch the latter and crunch them in your mouth. I fell asleep on my cot while we caught up, but Ruth, being worried that his cough was tubercular, did not act welcoming, and Makundi, no fan of the

Sudanese, had always been cool toward Bol. He liked to say that the Brits had given the Sudan its independence on a silver platter well before Kenya's and without anything like the fight Kenya's Mau Mau had had to wage. So here they were, fighting each other instead—Arabs versus Dinkas; Nuer and Zande against the Dinkas. Bol would scowl defensively. "Do you think we've made no plans?" But Makundi in their arguments had just evoked the chaos everywhere within a hundred miles by waving circles in the air.

This wasn't in contention now. And Ruth was preoccupied with preserving the poor toddler, Leo, still marked with the monkey eye sockets and cheeks from the starvation he had endured before Father Leo had happened to scoop him up. Like Bol's, her attention had narrowed, but still had a child to focus upon, whom she wanted to situate at Ohio State, her father's alma mater, someday, and in the premed progression that he had wanted for her, instead of nursing school, until her mother's suicide in the swimming pool had derailed both of their lives. She had no soap left to scrub with after touching her patients, which bothered her visibly when Leo was standing by wanting to be touched too. No food to give them either—the cornmeal I had brought vanished even before the end of the line reached the cooking barrel—but a gargantuan scale of privation within a stone's throw of the church itself. People may have congregated in the churchyard in hopes it would be spared in order not to anger the Christian powers, but flickering on the hillsides all around were campfires anchoring individual families against the atavism of the sky.

The Task of Memory
Sarah Manguso

WE VOTED THAT ONE person born per week per nation would receive a monument in the earth. The rest would be incinerated. First there was a committee, which grew corrupt immediately, then a lottery, which grew corrupt immediately. Then there was chaos. The rich used their own land or bought more. Then there was a new lottery, determined by machine. But the programmers were corruptible. For a long time there was dissent, then the people built a new machine that wrote the program that determined who got buried. The only rule was that none of the builders could be chosen, and none were chosen, and it was a very long time ago and so we say God built it and we obey it and it has been like that for many years now but we don't know how many.

In every week in every nation one infant born was selected for burial in the earth, with a six-inch-square memory object. Plenty of dissenters buried their dead anyway, and they were plowed up during the building of the new structures and were incinerated. Despite the problems with the new plan, far fewer took up space in the earth, and it was good.

In the time that passed, the earth filled with us. We changed a week to a month. From one person born per week to one person born per year per nation. Then to one person born per year per everywhere. Sometimes many were buried in the same year. Some years no one was. Probabilities were calculated and perverted immediately by willful or accidental misapplication of the words and figures.

Finally almost none could be buried. The insane offered themselves to the fire to make room for the reasonable. The reasonable tried to stay alive, waiting for a time when the people would die a little faster, so they could die and stay in the shapes of themselves longer, maybe even under a memory object marked with words and figures. Most of the remaining land was made of us but we didn't know it because there was nothing to remember us by.

We drew and wrote and sang of those who had lived just before us, and in time our words and our songs grew very hard to understand,

and in the pestilences and the wars and the vowel shifts and the quakes and the cold times, year by year we forgot the arrangement, and now when we bury our dead we notice the space being taken, and we worry, and we wonder when the earth will fill with us, and whether we should come to a decision to prevent it from happening.

A Room on the Eighth Floor
Peter Mountford

I AWOKE TO A SINGLE reedy voice calling out an incomprehensible refrain, some nasally phrase he'd repeat all morning. I had requested an eighth-floor room hoping to avoid this. I opened my eyes. The day's first light glowed pale blue at the edge of the curtains. Another voice—this one burpy, froggish—joined in; his phrase was shorter. What could they be selling at that hour? I had no idea. A third voice entered, and they were a chorus, singing some garbled tune, a puzzle of phrases, all intoned with that distinctive blend of eagerness and sloppiness used by street vendors across the world. Ten minutes later, car horns added a blunt and percussive layer. A police officer brought a whistle to the intersection, hoping to encourage order, but all he added was another note. Still, the sound didn't find its center until the buses and micros joined in, shoving their way down the city's narrow roads, their engines growling. And with morning light warming at the edge of a heavy curtain, I knew that the din had reached its peak, a dull howl that would last sixteen hours. It'd fill a whole day and carry on halfway through the night. This was the music of metropolises across Latin America—a symphony forever tuning up before its concert. It was a menacing, tuneless song, pure dissonance.

I got up and showered, careful not to let any water into my mouth; typhoid fever, amoebas, hepatitis, and dozens of varieties of parasites swam in those pipes. Tap water smelled different down here. Brackish, and a little chalky. The water was so hard it swept the soap off my skin before I could lather up. After shaving, I went back to my room with the tiny towel wrapped around my waist, slid open the curtains, inhaled the air, which smelled of rotting kelp, and looked out at the dirty blond light burning on the hazy south Pacific.

This was my second of two days in Lima. I was alone. I have gone down to South America often in the last ten years and I have always gone alone. After Lima, I would spend a couple of days in Cusco and Machu Picchu and then continue down to La Paz for a few weeks. I had brought a digital camera, three yellow legal pads, a fistful of pens.

I called the concierge to ask if he could recommend a city tour. He seemed flummoxed by the request. *A tour of Lima?* Apparently, no one had asked for a tour before. Why would they? He put me on hold. I stared out at the dreary sea. I listened to the mob below. A truck's backfire echoed through the city like distant artillery.

A few minutes later, the concierge returned, pleased to tell me there was a tour after all. In his heavily accented English, he said it departed at two.

Huaca Huallamarca, a pre-Incan mud-brick pyramid, had been blanched beige by 1,800 years of constant exposure. The pyramid was surrounded by what could best be described as a concrete fence. It looked like an inverted quarry. A heap of dirt in a dusty field.

Our guide stood at the front of the bus with a battered microphone in his hand and explained that the site had been used for religious ceremonies, namely the sacrifice of animals and humans, including babies. A century before the conquistadores landed, Incans started limiting their sacrifices to animals and virgins. "They were very civilized," he said, but this attempt at humor provoked no response from us. The guide was stocky, his skin oily. He had a truncated forehead, broad mouth. His resting expression looked pained. He was totally devoid of humor, barely managing to roll out the "jokes" built into his routine.

The tour was in English. We were maybe eight, and all of us were white. Four were young backpackers—Australians from the sound of their accents, hungover from the smell of their breath. The neighborhood surrounding the pyramid was typically bleak for Latin America. The buildings were boxy, with huge rectangular windows. They looked vaguely Soviet. The streets were clogged with pedestrians and decrepit buses and cars. Near our bus, a griller of meats stood by his shabby stove, burning homemade charcoal that emitted noxious effluvia, motor oil, and sour beef. I looked upward, to the tops of the buildings where thick concrete posts sprouted. Rebar poles stretched from the posts like bones from which all flesh had been sheared. The rebar represented hope. It meant another level could be added, if money ever permitted.

Looking at the city from inside the bus, I felt as though I'd been roused from a narcotic torpor. The guide continued talking about the deaths that were once doled out on that pyramid, but I wasn't listening anymore. I directed the overhead air-conditioning vent at my face. I had a fresh pad open on my lap, but wrote nothing down. I had my camera too. I took no pictures.

Our guide finished his speech and the bus grumbled back to life.

The first time I went to South America, I never wanted to leave. It was ten years ago. I almost tore up my return ticket. It sounds trite, probably was, but I felt more alive down there, away from what seemed like the oppressive strictures of the "First World." It's easy to overlook those strictures when you live here, and yet—compared to the rest of the world, and compared to the rest of human history— we live in an incredibly well-ordered, prosperous, and secure society. In most of Latin America, a car will pause at a red light, and if no one seems to be coming, the driver will proceed through. That's it. If a policeman happens to be there, he won't bother issuing a ticket. It's not a big deal, of course, until you see how it's part of a whole out- look on life, a blasé attitude toward the rule of law, toward the notion of safety itself. That lack of order appealed to me, because I felt as if it would enable me to dodge the demands of a sensible adult- hood, which were bearing down on me. I was twenty-one, and didn't feel especially implicated by the poverty around me: It seemed like an abstraction, something completely hypothetical, just like my own mortality did.

I enjoyed that freedom for a while. But eventually something about me changed, and I had to leave. Though I still return regularly, I enjoy nothing about these trips. While down there, I feel a bottom- less loneliness. People stare at me because I'm tall and white. Because I'm tall and white, I've been robbed or mugged at least a dozen times. I'm constantly on edge. I get insomnia. I am beset with nightmares of a postapocalyptic world in which everyone I know is dead. I'm the only one left and I won't last long. I have to step over piles of emaciated and withered cadavers on my way to forage cans of food from the desolate supermarket near my house in Seattle. Dust covers everything. There is no electricity, no running water, and I'm utter- ly alone.

Still, whenever I tell friends that I'm going to go down to Latin America, they express envy that I'm heading off to such an "exotic" place, and I have trouble explaining why I'm dreading the trip.

Once, on the northern coast of Ecuador during an outbreak of cholera, I met a doctor who told me that they used Gatorade to hy- drate patients at the main hospital in Esmeraldas, a city of a hundred thousand, because they didn't have enough IVs or saline drips. (The best treatment is one or more simultaneous saline drips and a barrage of antibiotics.) "It seems like you're ejecting it all in a constant stream of vomit and diarrhea," he explained, "but if you keep pushing the sports drinks whenever you're conscious, you really do have a decent chance of survival." This, as if he were describing the best route to a restaurant. We were in Atacamas, a dilapidated "resort" town half an hour south of Esmeraldas, and it occurred to me that if I were to get seriously ill or injured—even if all I needed was a shot of penicillin—I would probably die.

Wearing sunglasses and carrying bottles of water, we debarked at a museum in downtown Lima. We'd been instructed not to give anything to the children who crowded around the bus, begging, so we hurried along as they swarmed, tugging on our fingers and mumbling.

Inside, we stared at gold headdresses mounted behind thin sheets of glass. We stared at gold breastplates, gold ax blades. The room was small, overlit, awkwardly arranged. The display seemed meager to me. Our guide told us there had been so much gold in the Incan empire that the Inca did not consider it especially valuable and were happy to give it to the Spanish. The previous night I had read that La Paz, my final destination, would never have existed were it not for the gold in its Choqueyapu River. By the time the Spanish had drained every nugget from the river, the surrounding city was big enough to sustain itself without the gold. Now, the river—slick with toxic waste and sewage—runs underground, where the stench won't bother anyone.

The guide led us to a smaller room in the basement, where we stared at Francisco Pizarro's eviscerated and mummified corpse. The thorax and abdominal cavity had been stuffed with cotton balls. The remaining flesh looked like old kippers. Our guide said nothing. He just looked at the body for a minute, then led the way out of the room.

Upstairs, we bought bottled water from a kiosk and stepped outside. Diesel exhaust singed my nostrils. The air was damp but not hot: The Pacific Ocean kept it cool.

The weather in Lima never changes. It's cool at night and humid always. It never rains. When I was there, it hadn't rained at all in ten years. It averages a fraction of an inch of precipitation per year, mostly in the form of a gauzy predawn mist. It's hostile to life. There are few native plants or animals. It's so arid the streets have no gutters, no drains. Roofs are flat and not water resistant. Were it actually to rain, the city would be in chaos: Ceilings would collapse, streets would fill with water, and disease-carrying mosquitoes would flourish. Like any arid city, Lima is highly combustible. On the last day of 2001, a vendor in Lima's fireworks bazaar attempted to demonstrate one of his wares for a customer and the place ignited in a multicolored inferno. Within an hour 276 people were dead, and the whole market had been reduced to ash. People had been incinerated in their automobiles as they sat in gridlock on the street out front.

Back in our bus, the tour continued. Our guide pointed at buildings and described them. This is Moorish architecture, he said, and that is baroque. The guide projected a pride I was not prepared to believe. The city was dun colored, a vast smudge. The guide pointed out the American ambassador's house, gleaming white, and said it was bigger than the Peruvian presidential palace. We chuckled politely. Beyond the high black fence, I could see cameras tucked in under the eaves. Men with M-16s and Oakley sunglasses patrolled the verdant lawn.

Our final stop was a sixteenth-century cathedral and adjacent Franciscan monastery. Out front, a dry fountain occupied the center of a pigeon-filled square. More pigeons were embedded in the cathedral's brickwork, and vultures lumbered clumsily around the spires.

Inside the monastery, a red-and-white tile path surrounded a small courtyard. Each of the pillars had a painting of a monk on it: The monks were being crucified on the blue pillars, beheaded on the yellow. A series of rudimentary paintings on the walls showed a sickly-looking Saint Francis ministering to the Indians. Saint Francis always held a human skull in one hand and the Bible in the other. The guide told us that Francis was never painted with a skull in his hand in Europe; it was a uniquely Latin American feature. The skull, he said, was the symbol of poverty. The most scrupulous order of monks with their vow of poverty, Franciscans were also the most ruthless missionaries in the New World. They slaughtered all natives who resisted conversion. To this day, indigenous populations are smaller in areas of Latin America where the Franciscans had a major presence.

We entered a hall at the far side of the courtyard. This was the library. Two dozen statues had been carved at regular intervals along the mahogany shelves. These were the monks who died on missions to tame "savages." Each was depicted in a way that indicated how he had died: The beheaded held their heads at their chests, the ill were emaciated, one monk had three arrows through his torso, and another had been dismembered. Our guide's voice echoed off the domed ceiling. I saw he was scanning the group, trying to figure out how many of us were listening. I would like to say that I was the only one listening, but in truth I wasn't listening either.

I could already smell the catacombs. Over centuries, the stench of carrion had mellowed into something musty and earthy. Down the thin stone staircase the odor grew stronger, sharper, and the air cooled. Our guide led us through a series of chambers where Incan corpses had been disposed of with an efficiency that would have impressed the commanders at Buchenwald. The monks who were charged with this task toiled at it daily for centuries. They built a row of twelve narrow wells, each thirty feet deep. A souring cadaver would be dumped into one and covered with a layer of lime and charcoal dust. The next body would be dropped on top, covered in lime and charcoal. And so on. Once a well could hold no more bodies, the monks would move to the next well.

After a year, the monks could return to a full well and exhume its contents. Upstairs, in the courtyard, under the relentless sunlight, they would sort through the mud and bones. The mud and the smaller bones were cast into the sea, but they kept the sturdiest bones in a series of pits throughout the catacombs. There were a series of separate pits for femurs, for skulls, and for pelvises. The largest pit, at least twenty-five feet wide, contained a painstakingly arranged pile of femurs and skulls. All told, our guide said, the monks had stored the remains of around seventy thousand people. As I looked at these bones, I knew I was staring at the detritus of a history erased, the husk of a civilization wholly eradicated. And yet I felt nothing. I hadn't felt anything all day but a familiar listlessness, an itchy impatience to get back up north, back inside the bubble. Still, here I was, in Lima, and I had brought three pads of paper, a fistful of pens. I had brought a digital camera. I had come down intending to extract my pound of flesh—my notes.

Notes, then:

The skulls are dusty, grayish. Holes in the smooth crowns of some give evidence of a musket ball or a saber blade. No forensic exam needed—the cause of death can be identified from across the room. Musty. Low ceilings.

That's all I wrote in Lima.

Still, I remember more. I remember that once we made our way back upstairs to the library, the air that had seemed so stale before smelled fresh. And the guide—a little brusque now—told us that the bus would pick us up in ten minutes.

We shuffled out into the blinding square, where a barefoot and toothless old woman begged, groaning, her knotted gray hair askew. She smelled of livestock. She looked like an exile from a previous century. I could see the structure of her skull under her skin. Her gums had receded so badly that I could see where her long, narrow teeth entered her jawbone. She muttered, *"Ayúdame"* ("Help me"), like some miserable mantra. *"Ayúdame, ayúdame . . ."*

I turned away and encountered two boys—eyes yellowed with hepatitis—trying to sell me tiny boxes of gum. As I marched across the square, they walked backward, muttering at me softly. It sounded like they were speaking in tongues, and I thought of the garbled voices I'd listened to that morning. I thought about that first man: his forlorn, reedy voice, begging *someone* to buy what he had to sell, although no one else was even awake. There, in that square, with every step, the children seemed to multiply around me; they were coming from behind too, pawing at my waist. I gripped my wallet and sped up, pleading, *"Déjame en paz, déjame, por favor . . . déjame . . . por . . . favor. . . ."*

As quickly as they had materialized, the children dispersed. I turned and watched them swarm around another member of our group, their grubby hands darting around his waist. Clusters of pigeons waddled around too, scavenging, all of them.

I looked around the square: I needed another bottle of water, but there was no one selling. On the square beside the cathedral, some military police loitered around their armored vehicle, atop which sat a mounted fifty-caliber machine gun for crowd control. There hadn't been a coup since Fujimori was kicked out in 2000, and I suppose they wanted to make sure there wouldn't be another.

Most history is written in disappearing ink, the vanished story of how chaos was put down and the ensuing calm sustained. The erasure is necessary for the comfort of future generations. It's why they put those skulls underground, safely out of view. It was to ensure my own comfort that I had avoided taking any pictures in Lima. It was why I had requested a room on the eighth floor of my hotel. It is why people from the United States don't usually go to places like Lima or Bolivia for pleasure: The brutal part of their history is under way, and it's disturbing to see that. More to the point, it's disturbing to discover our own part in it, that we—by merely being citizens of the United States—have a prominent role in this bloody process.

The fact is that my experience—and the experience of any gringo down there, no matter how long he stays, no matter how fluently he speaks the language—is of a neocolonialist visiting the colonies. To suggest otherwise is naive. The blood has dried up and blown away. The maggots have sprouted wings and vanished. But still it is *that* place: the site of our ghastly plunder.

I was standing in the square in front of that monastery, finally free of those children, when I took out my camera. I snapped a picture of the soldiers and their vehicle. I turned back and took another of the cathedral, with one of those children running into the pigeon-littered frame. Finally, I turned and took a picture of our guide, sitting down at the monastery's entrance. Those were the only three pictures I took in Lima. The following day, I took dozens of pictures in Machu Picchu. Up there, in the damp highlands, the Incans built their monuments from stone; they never used mud bricks, their monuments would have melted at the first heavy rain.

There are memories we want to keep and memories we want to lose. It may be foolish to think we have any say over what memories will remain, but for better or worse, that is how we cope with the magnitude of history: We crop it down into acceptable frames. Although I know this well, I also know that won't be the last time I try to edit my own memory. It won't be the last time I go to South America looking for something, only to avert my eyes once I locate it.

Back in our bus, the air-conditioning hissed as we rode along a cliff over the sea. The tour was done, so the guide and the driver spoke to each other quietly in Spanish. Otherwise, the bus was silent. Black raptors groomed themselves on the street lamps. It was dusk and the sun was melting into a ribbon of gray at the horizon. The Pacific Ocean was fetid and streaked with silt. It belched up clouds of sewage. A bank of pink foam undulated beyond the waves. There were eight million people in the city, but not a single person on those five miles of tropical beach.

At my hotel that night, I ordered a Monte Cristo sandwich from room service and ate it in bed, watching the same sitcoms I would watch in Seattle. After a while, I didn't even notice the subtitles anymore. Fading a little, I turned off the television, turned off the lights. I rolled onto my side, closed my eyes, and lay there, motionless, listening to the cacophony around me.

Some Old Words Were Spoken
C. D. Wright

beside the hole, a photograph was
taken in which everyone is seen
touching everyone else. In the light
unmoving I lie, fixed on a stationary
sky of birds flying upside down
over a hill gone deep in its coloring.
Amid weird collisions of feeling
and gladioli, first and foremost, I want
to thank my dearest adversary for
putting a fire up under my words, for
releasing my husband when a stunned
fish emerged from an aqueous pit,
spit on his hands, and threw his old
house out the window. Thanks to those
who exposed the hairy, buff eggs
of my anxieties, their pupae of little
hypocrisies. Bravo, I say to the one
who pulled the shivering rug from
my bones, he who knelt over my face
drenched in self-inflicted tears, tendered
his pen and left me spinning the poetry
of white hair in advance of its years,
left me mouthing the sticky clusters
of regret, talking to a god in whom none
believe, then took me over the edge
of enchantment, my thanks. To the child
who refused to abdicate his ecstasy,
encore. Between hammer and nail gun,
an ear is caressed by the sweet quibbling
Spanish of roofers through a scrim
of firs. Otherwise no one here but me
to break the frame, gnashing quietly.
For dying this way is a snap: no menus,

no wine lists, no taxis, no tickets,
no bulging duffel riding a conveyor belt
in the wrong capital; no one waiting
at the gate with a hand-lettered
sign. No, in fact, destination in mind.
Just an unseasonable chill. For dying
this way is nothing. Is like losing
a sock. A photograph is being set up
by my friend, the wedding photographer,
in which everyone is touching
everyone else and then everyone drifts off
into separate cars trailing swirls of dust.

(An unidentified observer reports that the caravan drove from Ultima
Thule to Paraclifta, where they found nothing but a string of catfish heads
hung on a wire and some doves flying around an abandoned gymnasium.)

Three Poems in Search of Small Gods
Jim Harrison

HARD TIMES

The other boot doesn't drop from heaven.
I've made this path and nobody else
leading crookedly up through the pasture
where I'll never reach the top of Antelope Butte.
It is here that my mind begins to learn
my heart's language on this endless
wobbly path, veering south and north
informed by my all too vivid dreams
which are a compass without a needle.
Today the gods speak in drunk talk
pulling at a heart too old for this walk,
a cold windy day kneeling at the mouth
of the snake den where they killed 800 rattlers.
Moving higher my thumping chest recites the names
of a dozen friends who have died in recent years,
names now incomprehensible as the mountains
across the river far behind me.
I'll always be walking up toward Antelope Butte.
Perhaps when we die our names are taken
from us by a divine magnet, and are free
to flutter here and there within the bodies
of birds. I'll be a simple crow
who can reach the top of Antelope Butte.

LARSON'S HOLSTEIN BULL

Death waits inside us for a door to open.
Death is patient as a dead cat.
Death is a doorknob made of flesh.
Death is that angelic farm girl
gored by the bull on her way home
from school, crossing the pasture
for a shortcut. In the seventh grade
she couldn't read or write. She wasn't a virgin.
She was "simpleminded," we all said.
It was May, a time of lilacs and shooting stars.
She's lived in my memory for sixty years.
Death steals everything except our stories.

EASTER 2008

Death is liquid, the scientists are saying. We'll enter the habitat
of water after giving up the control we've never had. There will
be music as when we used to hear a far-off motorboat while
swimming underwater. Some of the information is confusing,
though water makes music simply being itself. Since we won't
have ears and mouths it will be a relief to give up language, to
sense a bird flying overhead without saying *bird* and not to have
to hear our strenuous blood pumping this way and that. You
don't need ears to hear the planets in transit, or the dead who
have long since decided there is nothing more to say but *glory*
in their being simply part of the universe held in the arena of a
thrall called home. When Christ rose from the water he wondered
at seeing the gods he had left far behind when he finished his
forty days in the wilderness.

Andalucía

H. G. Carrillo

LABOR DAY. AND ODD, he thinks, it is again a September that rounds the clever hopes of a low, dishonest decade toward expiration.

Waves of anger; waves of fear, an angry young woman sings at the top of her lungs as he pushes the button on the dashboard and the radio runs a circuit from pop station to pop station. It was only recently, when he was doing an article on her for *Rolling Stone* as part of its yearlong fortieth anniversary celebration, that he discovered she did so without knowing its source.

Oughtn't I what? she had asked, and he told her who Auden was, indicated the allusion the song makes, and she said it was *Just something I remember hearing from somewheres. I'm all ironical like that,* batting the long false eyelashes she told him were genuine mink.

Liquid mascara had run and dried from her left eye to the middle of her cheek, and despite the NO SMOKING sign directly above him, she had lit cigarette against cigarette, patted her wildly exaggerated black waterfall of a beehive whenever she wanted to add importance to what she was saying, and she told him she was bringing it back—*Like Ella, with a hint of Etta and some of the Nancys—Wilson, Sinatra, Simone—thrown in*—old school.

She had told him she was hella fierce, dividing the words with a rush of smoke into four syllables he had needed to hit PLAY and REWIND several times to decipher. But in the end, her publicist had insisted he remove them anyway, saying it was implied.

Fury is its own invention these days, a friend had recently written in another magazine, to which they all said, Right-on, only to ask each if anyone still said Right-on anymore.

The left turn signal is flashing, and, as if moving on its own, the car obeys. Minutes before, he had heard the pronouncement, the last sad little clicks of the breathing machine. And it seemed as if ten years of excuses that had come hard had gone quickly. He had written an article in which the mention of an O-ring reiterated a national horror, though within a few short weeks, an O-ring had been the

402

punch line of jokes on more than one late-night talk show, and now he doubted if he could find a handful of readers who remembered the event that started it at all. And—like *Define sex; I have sinned,* he had recently written, as with *It depends on what the meaning of the word "is" is*—the reference is receding into something everyone knows comes from somewhere, but has no idea where.

The difference was, they now said, they were living in a country at war. They often said it or would punctuate it with what sounded to them like great pronouncements of what they called the State of Things. Yet the shift from saying the Gulf War to the Second Gulf War had been so seamless it was as if what could be confused as a veer from course in a yachting expedition had become something handy as they all began saying to each other, Same war different decade, as if it hadn't been said before.

A friend had written a piece in the *Post,* which had subsequently been syndicated nationwide, on the cookie in the shape of the Twin Towers that was being sold at Ground Zero. *Like the breast cancer cookie,* she had mentioned, though another friend was quick to point out that equating the two was the same as comparing apples to monkey feces.

And although they all scorned her—Soft politics, they said. No backbone. So afraid of dealing with the real issues, they muttered—when they all talked to each other on the phone, eventually each of them found some way to be forgiving of her.

We've all done things for money, they all told her, at one time or another, though, clearly, none of them believed that he or she had.

They would all be headed toward their forties, or would be well into their forties, they were saying just the decade previous. And had said they would be making the decisions that would run the country, run the world, without their knowing they had begun a slide into a time when democracy had become theory.

They wrote articles, and knew people who wrote articles, and knew many of the people in the articles they read. And each had, at one time or another, taken a stab—thinking himself clever, thinking herself profound—at trying to expose what dictators do, and the rubbish they talked to an apathetic grave without knowing it. Yet without so much as a ripple in a puddle that seemed to have the implacable depth of oceans.

We bumbled it, we fumbled it, we let it slip from our hands, a friend had written in what during their childhoods had been thought a venerated New York magazine, but rather than admit they might be fucking up their chances, they allowed their subscriptions to lapse, and claimed embarrassment by the football reference.

And, Oh my God I was so embarrassed for him. We were so embarrassed for him, they said to each other, Embarrassed, they said of many, but hardly ever of themselves.

Someone who had done all the right things only to find out they were all wrong often told them that she felt very much like another one of their friends who had moved from Oxy to smack to rehab, to whatever it was they were calling that thing that came after EST.

None of them talked to either of them anymore, yet somehow they all knew one of them had landed a plum production job at CNN—had met Christiane Amanpour, did a convincing impression of her saying, Coming to you live from Turkey—and the other had a teenaged son who lost an arm in a meth lab explosion—the right one, someone would remind them all whenever the story came up at parties they all still held in their homes as they had when they all had lived in apartments ten years before—but no one knew what had happened to which.

They had all started the decade talking about how everything that was reliable was only relatable through narrative, but somewhere along the way seemed less and less inclined to tell any of their stories let alone those of others.

Later all the friends who had attended a book party, at another more intimate party, had claimed they were unable to finish reading what they had earlier proclaimed a *celebration.* And it was then and there, a little drunker than he usually allowed, for the first time he found himself saying he wasn't sure if anyone ever read anything anymore and believing it.

The green light in front of the windshield has gone weird with unfamiliarity, strange as if he had been picked up and turned around, left still looking forward for the direction in which he had been headed. An hour and twenty-seven minutes had passed since the time of death had been called and he had felt a hand on his shoulder and a voice, and another voice, and yet another. I'm so sorry, they had all said in one way or another.

If the clock on the dash is right—he has never known, it has never been his job to set it—their friends would now be at a barbecue in a friend's yard lined with fig trees in Arlington, where, counting backward from drinks in hand, they would be trying to appear as though they weren't calculating the risks of bridges and darkness driving back to the city.

Hairpin turns, slick pavement, in the winter black ice, were brand-new fears that they had begun trying on, finding themselves writing about things like drinking water, school testing, and people who believed in God in the same way they had taken on bombs and covert action, implicating everything from the lack of school funding to the abundance of pesticides in cattle feed. *Though God,* a friend had written, *may be our last repository of hope,* yet in the opposing editorial that shared the right side of the page, the friend's wife had written, *Love the prayer, but do not hesitate to damn the supplicant when necessary.*

Along with coffee or decaf, warm figs with clotted cream, there would be talk of cholesterol accompanied with a certain nostalgia for a time when it wasn't part of their collective vocabularies of fret, when they ate what they wanted and slept with people they had no need to keep track of.

The low orange and purple sun; how shadows were becoming visibly shorter of late, faster than the previous summer and the one before that; and the cost of heating in the coming winter. They would be talking about anything except what was directly in front of them.

Even an odd silence between them warranted discussion. Let go, they could spin into the darkness of unfinished projects, blank pages and empty computer screens, and the ways in which uncompleted plans simply indicate poor preparation. And what did that mean? they would ask each other until it was clear—their hosts will have wilted; in a corner, under an umbrellaed table, a half-eaten bowl of hummus will have become watery and clouded with mosquitoes—it was past time to go. Like failed boys, waiting for never-ending summers, they count minutes, and before the last have run out, one of them will ask had anyone heard anything or did anyone know what was going on.

Recently he had written that he had never dreamt, *never dreams that it is the smell of hospitals—a combination of rubbing alcohol, disinfectant, and whatever it is that they use to mask the redolent cheddaring that occurs when the enthusiasm of one hope passes through the widening rings of sorrow of another—that one longs for.* It was to be a series of articles to be published in a magazine. Brave, most of their friends said last week when the first of them appeared. Over the phone, with tears in her voice, a friend said how impressed she was when she read it the first time, the second time, and the third by his lack of sentimentality.

Work all day—teach; tend to a family; other people's gardens, a bar; sign multimillion-dollar deals that conjoin previously warring companies—though now the ends of your days no longer end with shared meals in front of the television or a conversation about the day's paper. There are no more movies at which to rendezvous, lists of dinner invitations to be sent, or arguments to be had. There are specialists to check in with, nurses' consults about the maintenance of things like plans for extubation and peripheral IV lines, and plastic containers of Jell-O.

And as she continued to read his words back to him—*You forget the vacations you've taken together, what it will cost to put a new roof on the garage, the time you had bad raw-milk cheese in Lucerne and the tiny bathroom you share, because now the walk, the evening stroll, you most look forward to is down the hall and past the nurses' station to a room with wetly thumbed magazines*—he heard them all, all of their friends.

He was brave, their friends told them, They—the two of them—were doing the right thing. They'd do the same, their friends said. Yet in print they said, *It's not like it was in the eighties . . . not the same worries we had back then.* A friend had described it as *the new diabetes, manageable through any myriad of drug cocktails out there.*

They all cared, they all wished, they all approved. They all called—How are things? When do you think? You know I've got your back? they asked—though over the past five months, he saw less and less of them.

Waiting outside the room for what would be the fourteenth and final bronchoscopy, he had flipped through his notebook to find the week previous he had dedicated a page to the words *recede, receding,* and *receded.* Knowing it was an image of erosion, something to do with *water, peeling paint,* and *nails bitten raw to the cuticles* that would never crystallize into whatever it was that was lodged somewhere in the back of his head, and that their friends—who on their answering machine offered help and prayer—no longer came to the hospital.

Headed home, he finds he has gotten lost in the rotaries, driven around the Capitol Building twice, passed the Pentagon without thinking about much more than the fact that there had been a time when they had hoped, they had promised, they had come to terms with the ways in which they believed their parents had gotten it wrong—Yeah, got it wrong, they said, and they had said it often—though with everyone outside the city, he surmises that there were just as many if not more people living on the streets, more tourists, though now they came and went as if the city were an amusement-park ride, and they were waiting for T-shirts proclaiming their survival of the experience.

The District was either at parks, at summer homes, or in backyards, around barbeque pits. The distracted, the homeless, singular figures—people living under the brush in Rock Creek Park and the men waiting for handouts at the church in the shadows of the Watergate—people they had always said, always thought, always wrote, that they would be the voices for are the only ones who seem to be walking about in the late afternoon.

The streets are quiet but alive with activity. Motion not available to him as if it is happening in a language that he recognizes but does not understand.

And stopped by a traffic light as he reaches Dupont Circle he is nearly thrown by the agitated start of his own body as a dark black man in a spangled purple dress and pink shiny lipstick leans in the window, the back of his head nearly lying on the steering wheel as he sings, He was a deep-sea diver with a stroke that could not go wrong. He sings, Deep, deep, deep-sea diver, baby . . . hard and strong.

And it startles and runs though him so quickly—sends him instantly into the kind of sick he can taste—that the blare of horns and the cackling laughter is behind him before he realizes he has run the light, closely missed a line of parked cars at the corner of Connecticut Avenue, and stopped traffic in all four directions.

Rafa, he hears himself saying his own name. Rafa—Rafa, Rafa, Rafa, Rafa—because nothing will have changed in their house, except for that. Next to his computer he will find an empty yogurt container with a sticky spoon still in it, the bed is unmade, there is a pile of socks and underwear near the hamper. He says Rafa as he opens the front door.

Rafa, he says and with a sweep of his forearm takes the line of switches that turn on the front porch lamp, all the lights in the foyer, living room, and front hallway.

He hears Jesús, the muscular gray stripe they have fed regularly but never claimed, yowl and scratch the front door. His bowl by the back door is empty, but Rafa ignores his cries and turns on the light above the end of the hallway that causes the bleed of canvas above the table where they had always put their keys to shine and pulsate.

Years ago, a woman neither of them knew then, but both later befriended and eventually brought into their circle of friends, had

407

written that the signature in Hugo's paintings was always a mystery, *the moment that one thinks that the work is unsigned his signature rises as if organic into the foreground.* And it is a bloodied serpent, ragged, a hangman's noose of letter spelling out the letter H and Hugo's surname that reaches toward him.

Red paintings. It had been red paintings. Hugo had been giving a lecture on red paintings when they first met. Red paintings and how he would be trying the rest of his life to make one.

Red on red on red does not equal red, he had offered the crowd, and the audience in front of him had chuckled, applauded, celebrated as if they knew him, as if they had always known him. They had Uh-huhed, said, Isn't that the truth. He's always been a pragmatist, they had said as if they were competing to appear to each other as though they knew him better, longer, more intimately, more importantly.

Titian, Picasso, Bacon, Bacon, Bacon, Bacon, Van Gogh's *Red Chestnuts in the Public Park at Arles.*

He had only gone to the lecture on assignment, knew little about Hugo or his work before, and found he had become more interested in the click of the slide projector than the images blown up on the enormous screen, found himself settled in the deep furrows Hugo's voice dug into the darkened room rather than what he was saying.

Yet, just last week, Rafa had listened to the tapes that he made that day again—Hugo saying that even though the focus of the painting, its intention, what the artist set out to do, is red, it's never the feature, really the feature. . . . It is the glade that surrounds it, the woman encased in the dress, the chestnuts, the moss and teal overstuffed living room through which the burning dog runs that allows us to see it—though even after all of these years, Rafa understands, finally understands, but has no idea what to do with the interviews.

After the talk, when they had gone for coffee—Vas tocar una café-cito conmigo, he had singled out Rafa, who in turn heard the mutters of disappointment issued by the others who lingered afterward—Hugo smoothed back the heavy black forelock the way that he had at the podium, but at the time Rafa thought that it was just for him, just so that he could see Hugo's face, his dark deep-set eyes and the strong line of his once broken nose, while he listened as Hugo talked about studying under Ray Yoshida and Mel Bochner and Ed Paschke and Jim Nutt and how lineage was what people looked at first, and about meeting Louise Bourgeois for the first time, about a daughter from a teenaged romance while he was still in La Habana that necessitated a marriage that ended unhappily, about study in Barcelona and working as a barback, a busboy, and a boy whore before coming to the US and living in a crawl space for three months in Miami, about grapes from the Loire region versus anything that comes from Napa Valley, the Brahms C minor String Quartet, the best place to get fresh figs, Mark Grace and Alan Trammell, and light that can only be seen, only be fathomed, light that only seems real in Andalucía.

And long before they even talked about calling it an evening— before they parted ways in the wet streets and he found himself thinking of ways that he could accidentally brush his bare arm against Hugo's—though it had never occurred to him before, Rafa knew that he would one day see all that blinding white sunlight that Hugo said went straight through the top of your head, would pierce your brain scatty and open in radiant beams out of your eyes, your mouth, your ass.

We should do this again sometime soon, Hugo had said at the end of the night. It's been fun.

Though—there were no visible signs; *Robustly handsome, energetic, and dynamic* were the words used to describe him in the next day's *Times*—what Rafa had heard was, Vaminos, chico, Run with me, Come with me, Sit by me, Be with me, Be mine, Reclámeme, and when it comes time, kill me, mi amor.

And without being told, Rafa knew.

He had written about it in the *Sun Times* and *The New Republic.* He still had the files. He was often a source they called whenever any of his friends were writing articles that began something like *If Reagan . . . If the first Bush;* repeating in print—*Silence=Death*— things from the T-shirts they wore until they eventually no longer fit and had been turned into household rags.

Before Hugo, they wrote about the numbers of funerals they attended, placed hope in AZT. *Now, in recent years, like thinning hair and biannual cancer screenings, they had become accustomed to going into friends' bathrooms or kitchens, and no longer sucked back the next breath as they were confronted by the rows and rows of white plastic bottles. . . . Retrovirals they were familiar with, knew the names of, were no longer the end of something,* Rafa had recently written, *seemed to so many answers rather than questions.* And another summer had begun to run out of itself.

Had anyone asked when they first met, Rafa would have said he knew what he was taking on. He knew how to protect himself, how to remain healthy, uninfected. He had read enough to know what questions to ask doctors and what signs to look out for, how to predict when a change in Hugo's color would mean a cold was coming on, or something more serious, like the five months early on when Hugo was wasting.

He learned to cook Cuban the way both their mothers had, and he had a friend he played softball with, a newspaper writer, who had married a woman who was an important painter. And over the years he watched and mimed some of the man's gestures. The way he stepped out of the way when the press wanted to talk to his wife, when photographers and gallery owners wanted a part of her; the man took care of the children most of the time, kept house, answered the phone, fended off eager students who showed up at their door, so she could work.

Very early on Rafa had told himself, I can do this. And he learned to build stretchers, gesso canvasses, he found the best caterers that happily delivered at a moment's notice. He turned a blind eye to at least three indiscretions that he could think of, and kept his own secret and few. He knew where to buy wine by the case, had interviewed a diplomat who for years sent them boxes of Partagás on their birthdays, Christmas, and the day they claimed as their anniversary, and he found a way to have several bottles of a brandy that could only be gotten in Granada.

He fought when they had needed to fight, and lied when the truth would have been unnecessarily hurtful. He had written about how and when to acquire a gun, ones that shot bullets that exploded like a deadly sparkler on contact, and consulted with a forensics physician about the precise angle at which one could place a barrel into one's mouth and be certain to take left and right hemispheres as well as the back of one's head. On a warm summer's afternoon, he and Hugo had driven out into the country in Virginia, and walked to a favorite secluded spot. Earlier that year, he had written in support of a man—*whose wife's insides were mapped black with cancer*—and how in an interview the man had told him that somehow the greatest act of lovemaking between the two of them was the look they gave each other right before he had left her in the room with enough morphine to stop an elephant in midcharge.

For years, he had lived with a presence larger than his, a life force that had seemed stronger and more important than his own. When asked, How?—by friends, by family, by onlookers in celebration, in envy, in fear—How had they survived the good and the bad? Rafa simply said from the beginning he had told himself that he knew what the rules were, knew what he was up against, knew what he was supposed to do.

But the truth was that he hadn't, couldn't, and didn't.

Even though the house is still warm from having been shut up all day, outside there is chill enough in the air for a thin membrane of fog to have begun a slow creep against the ground.

Jesús yowls and bats a paw at a dining-room window. A rhythmic slap, slap, slapping as demanding as a heartbeat, and Rafa falls forward into the darkened room and his palms leave two wet streaks in light blue paint around the row of rheostats along the dining-room wall, setting the wall pockets and chandelier ablaze.

Stifling, itchy warm, wet everywhere, he finds it hard, almost impossible, to pull air in. A button flies and clatters against the wood floor in circles of echo as in one motion, he pulls the loosened tie, dress- and undershirt over his head. Without unlacing them, he steps from his shoes and without bending—heel against toe—he pulls his feet free from his socks.

The flagstone is cool and dark and smooth and uneven under his feet as he rounds the butcher-block island. The overhead light charges the copper pots and they reflect and gleam with spears of orange so sharp—they slice, they bite—they are nearly shrieks.

And it is as he pushes his head under a spigot of cold water that he thinks to plug the stopper. And as it fills around him, a puddle that moves into a stream, a river, a flood, an ocean to his face, he opens his eyes until his contacts dislodge and fall away, leaving him nearly blind as he thinks about everyone he will have to call.

Hugo's mother in Miami, gallery owners, the museum where he was to have given a talk next month.

Just last week Hugo had gotten an e-mail from a friend, asking where the hell was he; didn't he know that there were those less fortunate, they needed his voice, his funds, his presence. He was planning a trip to South Africa, was in the process of starting a coalition of artists. *Get off your lazy ass and do something, hombre,* the friend had written.

After sixteen years there was little Rafa had no idea how to do. Put any of Hugo's suits in front of him and he would know which shirt, which tie, if it was a capped- rather than a square-toed shoe that went with it. It was always orange over apple unless there were bananas. Salad over dessert. Very short sentences; Courier New, ten point; all in lowercase; Rafa signed with a small "h."

There had been what would be comparable to fan letters: art-school

411

students, housewives, collectors, a graduate student in Cologne who wondered about the significance of one of Hugo's landscapes—*Andalucía #237*—in the Pardo, a painting in London, the current retrospective in New York, a purchase—an early work, mostly blues and greens—the sea rather than the land—that was part of an estate and needed verification of its provenance.

And though at first he had typed `drink the water` to the friend headed to save South Africa, he had deleted it and started again because all he could hear was the sound of his own voice in it.

Rafa smiles as the sink fills his ears, wetting the back of his head.

It is cool on the back of his neck, and it is only when he can feel it spilling over the sides of the sink, running down the front of his trousers and puddling at his feet that he is unable to hold his breath any longer.

Like rain, it runs off his forehead to his neck, along his back and past his belt. Cool between his buttocks. Circling his thighs.

It's being in the center of things, Hugo had said as they stood on top of the Mulhacén in the Sierra Nevada—*the almonds, the olives, the grapes, walnuts, cherries; legacies left by the Tartessians, Visigoths, and Moors; the flat-roofed houses left by the Alpujarras*—during the visit the year after their first meeting. It was as if Rafa could see a storm moving toward them and Hugo was merely part of the landscape.

Landscape within the landscape, he had paid no attention to the fluttering at the edges of the canvas he had secured to the ground with stones—Rafa had recently found in one of the notebooks he carried that May through August—*the painter's hair stood on end as if attached to the flashes of lightning that jagged the sky in yellow and orange ziggurats.*

And from those notebooks he had written—*Cuban-born painter Hugo Cartagena*—in an article for *Art in America* when they returned—*erupts as if a force from the center of each canvas in declaration of all the elements around him. His shoes, trousers, arms, naked torso, and hair covered with paint, he is his own extension of matter and light as he thinks it.*

Next to the article was a photograph of *Andalucía #120*, a torment of red, blue, and purple, the clouds, the lighting, the brush that clung to rock in spite of the wind, held on where there seemed nothing to hold onto. Because, Rafa recalls, it seemed at the time they were invincible, they were off, they were unstoppable.

You're right to move to the District, friends had said, it will be good for you, you for it, they said. They'd be closer to the action, Closer to the Cause, the Cure: Things that mattered. Hugo would paint, Rafa would write, they'd tell it. Tell it to them good, their friends had said. Tell it, Tell it, Tell it to the mountains, a friend who was now seven years sober, weaved when they first found Rafa and Hugo, first closed on their house when they and their friends called buying in Adams Morgan innovative rather than a wise investment or shrewd move. Tell it! Tell it! Tell it! the friend had yelled, until his voice was indistinguishable from the police sirens screeching up P Street.

It is like the taste of rain that floods Rafa's mouth. Warm and bitter, along the edges of his tongue, so much like a threat, swallowing arm-length gulps that press against and expand the lining of his stomach nearly to splitting, and throw him back against the kitchen table.

Fighting to catch his breath, he closes his eyes tighter. The sink continues to roar, and he wraps his arms around himself and rocks on his heels and feels water splashing against his ankles.

Neck back so far, his Adam's apple strains, he opens his eyes to the fog from outside, rolling like clouds above him, the ceiling near the exhaust hood above the range threatens rain. His mouth is full of the grit of red clay the way that it can only be found in the centers of blue-black grapes or in the sediment in the bottles of home-made wine.

They will; They were; They would be, they had all written at some time or another. And though there were those who had once typed them with impunity, the thought cowed and braved them at the same time now, but did little else as they often found themselves connecting it with the approach of that which at one time seemed so distant it was impossible.

They all knew that in time they would have to begin testing out, if only in idle conversation—*They will; They were; They would have been*—if only to see how they would one day feel, crossing their tongues, teeth, and lips. But like so many things that they had stuck Post-its to, they never got around to trying them out.

Instead they went to Andalucía the same way that they had since he had started going with Hugo; when Hugo's annual trip, two months each summer, had begun part of each of his summers since, and eventually their friends' winters, their springs. As if it were a collective resting place, they vacationed, they got away, they told other friends, chance acquaintances. It became a place where they sought renewal, their friends took those they needed to see surreptitiously as well as those that they needed to see most immediately.

And it seemed at what they had long predicted would be their moment of true clarity, the day they would own the world—Rule the land, they had said—it seemed to Rafa that after a while they all wrote *Andalucía*.

¡Bienvenidos al Andalucía! the article in the Travel Section of the *Times* read that a friend had called to say how hard she had worked to keep the title in Spanish. There had been an article dedicated to Egyptian and griffon vultures; their friend had traveled to the Sierra Monera for the black vultures that could be found there, while his wife produced a pretty little monograph that she wanted Hugo to illustrate on a varietal of wild irises, growing in the lumpy fields, along roadsides.

The summer before the last election year, the Guadalquivir ran in a series of sections in a glossy New York magazine; at the ceremony for the award the piece had won, its author was praised for his attention to detail, and the rich portrayal of the history of the political life that has existed along the river since the 1400s was mentioned by the presenter so many times that anyone new coming to the group joined in and referred to the author as Rich Portrayal without understanding the joke, which had become a little sad recently when the author began dating a beautiful young woman in her twenties who didn't read very much, thought Rich's last name was Portrayal and had no idea why his friends laughed at her confusion.

The Taliban had officially stopped receiving open invitations to the White House when they were celebrating the book a friend had assembled from the postcards that they had sent each other from Seville, Granada; there were nearly a hundred images of Córdoba. A coffee-table book with French flaps, a success that led to a job at Condé Nast, and a house in Connecticut that they all visited from time to time.

They wrote about the almonds, La Mezquita, and the effect the Euro had had on their ability to travel. In turns, there were eloquent pages of longing for the days of cheaper travel, a time when flamenco was much less commercialized, a bitterness about what it takes to get wickerwork, silver, glass, leatherwork through customs these days.

They wrote on the anniversaries of both *Carmen* and *Quixote* as bombs exploded in Azerbaijan, and though they knew enough to write op-ed pieces berating newscasters and political officials for *among a list of many areas of the world in which the United*

States was acutely aware, Azerbaijan was among those that they were unable to pronounce properly, yet without considering, once again, that they lived in a country without language or alphabet for that which did not directly affect them. And why those who claimed to know more than the others now chose criticism and called it activism.

The world around them was slipping into itself, off of itself, onto itself while they wrote *Andalucía*.

The house vibrates around Rafa. An acrid whir of the air above him being sliced to bits as a helicopter rattles a single pane of glass in the panel of windows that overlook the garden. Red poppies, sweet william, phlox. From the beginning of summer, there are thirteen different varieties of roses that bleed a border around the garage that they had long ago converted into Hugo's studio. Zinnias in crimson, burgundy, colorado, rojo de sangre that will hold on to their color until the first good frost. Japanese red grass, Saint Paulina, gerberas. Rubrums he has to imagine, remember where they had planted them in the dark.

Unlike the police choppers, he had been among the first to have written, *or the copters headed toward Howard or GW's hospitals, they throw no light. Light would only mean an opportunity for pictures, for a news crew to get pictures. Were they to have the stealth of a puma or a disease it would be easier to imagine the neighborhoods passed over unaware, but it is an active "not listening" they work through as they make dinner, sing children to sleep, put their feet up, and turn on the news.*

And despite the drag at the hems of his pants from the water around his ankles, he follows the noise above out into the yard. He can feel it as it moves closer, and he stands in the path, the diagonal they have worn through the yard over the last couple of years, as they make their way to Virginia.

The wounded, a friend had written after him, *from Iraq are stabilized in Germany and airlifted to Virginia where they wait on the tarmac until dark.* And it is knowledge like a rush of gooseflesh to his ankles, his toes in the grass, that speeds from Rafa as the helicopter passes over him. *Broken bodies, bandaged yet still bleeding, torn apart, pass over them at dinnertime, before bedtime, as though dreams, the stuff of phantoms, because the press has never gotten a picture of them as they head toward Walter Reed.*

He lets the sound vibrate through him, wants it to rip him apart, because dancing sweaty in discos they had wished to make deals with God, get him to swap our places, and keep running up that hill. Though they now wrote about how the sound of the helicopters had become as ambient as street arguments and the cries of fire trucks. He lets it burn, bite into him as it moves into the distance over the Safeway, though a friend had written a piece about how they disturbed her dog so she had employed the skills of an animal psychologist. And they all laughed at the ways in which her attempt at irony had failed, cursed the young, damned what they called the establishment, and mixed more drinks.

Jesús hisses either at Rafa or something he sees that Rafa cannot in the dark.

With the lights on in the studio a line of stacked, failed, or unsold *Andalucías* glitter. There is the smell of linseed oil and what he would find in Hugo's armpits, and on the back of his neck after he had been working long hours, a smell that he looked for in the T-shirts, socks, and underpants that he had brought back from the hospital the past couple of months that he would launder and take back with him the next day.

On a canvas that stretches over twenty feet across the far wall an abstraction of the penitentes of La Semana Santa remains unfinished. Rafa is able to make out the peaks of hoods in the background, the precursor to Klansmen's robes; a green eye exposed through the hole cut in the sheet dominates the left side of the canvas, and la cruz de guía in the background on the left, but Rafa thinks you would have had to have been there, seen it happen to understand what the painting had been meant to do. Nuestro Padre Jesús el Cautivo, Cristo del Gran Poder, Cristo de Pason, Virgen del Rocio, Virgen del Esperanza, Virgen de Victória, they pray.

This career-long fascination with a single place? a pretty Spanish reporter had asked Hugo just the year before, though she refused to believe him when he told her that he was lazy; he knew the language, the food, the weather, and the people agreed with him. *Ever modest,* she wrote, before she gave it new valence, turned it into something that it wasn't—*iconographic, inspired*—something he, who had been there when most of them were made, was uncertain could be found on any of the canvases.

If it should happen, their friends had called in response to an article around the same time that Rafa had published in a magazine declaring a definite when. A set of instructions, in which he had illustrated the kinds of arrangements that needed to be made with one's lawyers that would exonerate one's partners, family, and

416

friends from culpability; the kinds of music that should be playing in the room; the meal the night before; the light—*Yes, it could be candlelight, or it could be the most dizzying light imaginable, light that shocks open the senses, that is reminiscent of everything that has never left you the same*—that was to be in the room; the kinds of pills that doctors might be prescribing for the day-to-day that could be horded and stockpiled. There were many choices of asphyxiations, some simple as a gasoline-soaked rag and a Hefty bag, and the brave dinner the surviving partner was to have at a nearby restaurant: *Lájugar trout grilled with Trevélez cured ham; spicy arroz with quail and rabbit; Moruna; goat cheese cured in ashes with manzanilla for desert.*

If, two friends wrote, not directly implicating Rafa, but clearly in response to him, in two separate carefully constructed articles, which talked of hope and the possibility of cure at the same time avoiding the void of evidence to confirm their findings. *If,* they wrote the same way that a friend of theirs who had died in what each had written off as *that first wave—the realization,* one had called it; *that first shock,* the other wrote—*If,* they used to say, it were a fifth we'd all be drunk. They wrote as though it would never come the same way that Rafa had believed at that moment, the moment that they had all talked about—the moment of true feeling, the moment Rafa looked at him and said, now—he would not go gently.

None of them had imagined that moment would pass as though it had never happened and that days would go by, and stretch, and linger into months. None of them could have predicted that they would watch seasons change, find other things to do, and go on with jobs and dinner parties and the dust that collects under beds and bookcases with the sound of breathing so shallow, so scratchy it was reminiscent of the sound of a twig brushing against a windowpane, and not be the one to defy convention, break the law, push forward, and flick the switch off. Or that he would be here now in his bare feet—Rafa, his whispers, Rafa, Rafa, Rafa—with the water in the kitchen still running.

NOTES ON CONTRIBUTORS

JOHN ASHBERY's most recent collection, *Notes from the Air: Selected Later Poems* (Ecco/HarperCollins), won the 2008 Griffin International Poetry Prize. The first volume of his collected poems will be published this fall by Library of America. An exhibition of his collages from 1948 to 2008 was held at Tibor de Nagy Gallery in New York this fall.

MARY JO BANG is the author of five collections of poems, including *The Eye Like a Strange Balloon* (Grove Press). Her most recent, *Elegy* (Graywolf Press), won the National Book Critics Circle Award. She teaches at Washington University in St. Louis.

DORIS BETTS is the author of nine books of fiction, most recently *The Sharp Teeth of Love* (Knopf).

JAY CANTOR's latest book is the novel *Great Neck* (Knopf and Vintage Books).

H. G. CARRILLO is the author of the novel *Loosing My Espanish* (Pantheon/Anchor). His short stories have appeared in *Kenyon Review, The Iowa Review, Glimmer Train, Ninth Letter, Slice,* and other journals and publications. He is assistant professor in the Department of English at George Washington University in Washington, DC, where he is currently at work on a novel.

ROBERT CLARK is the author of four novels and four books of nonfiction, most recently *Dark Water: Flood and Redemption in the City of Masterpieces* (Doubleday).

JOHN D'AGATA teaches creative writing at the University of Iowa.

SUSAN DAITCH is the author of two novels, *L. C.* (Harcourt Brace) and *The Colorist* (Vintage), and a collection of short fiction, *Storytown* (Dalkey Archive Press).

NICHOLAS DELBANCO's most recent books are a collection of essays, *Anywhere out of the World* (Columbia University Press), and a novel, *The Count of Concord* (Dalkey Archive). He is the Robert Frost Distinguished University Professor of English at the University of Michigan.

MARK DOTY's newest book is *Fire to Fire: New and Selected Poems* (HarperCollins). A short handbook for writers, *The Art of Description,* is forthcoming from Graywolf.

GEOFF DYER's most recent book, *The Ongoing Moment* (Vintage), won a 2006 Infinity Award from the International Center for Photography. His new novel, *Jeff in Venice, Death in Varanasi,* is forthcoming in the spring from Pantheon.

BRIAN EVENSON is the author of seven books of fiction, most recently *The Open Curtain* (Coffee House Press), which was a finalist for an Edgar Award. A novel, *Last Days*, and a new collection of stories, *Fugue State*, are forthcoming in 2009. He directs Brown University's Literary Arts Program.

MARY GORDON's latest book is *Circling My Mother* (Pantheon). She teaches at Barnard College and has been named New York State Writer for 2008–10.

DAVID GUTERSON is the author of four novels, *The Other*, *Our Lady of the Forest* (both Knopf), *East of the Mountains*, and *Snow Falling on Cedars* (both Harcourt). He lives in Washington State.

JESSICA HAGEDORN is the author of *Dogeaters*, *The Gangster of Love*, and *Dream Jungle* (all Penguin). She is at work on a new novel, which is forthcoming from Viking.

JIM HARRISON is the author of thirty books of poetry, fiction, and nonfiction. His new novel, *The English Major*, is forthcoming this fall from Grove, and a book of poems, *In Search of Small Gods*, will be published in the spring by Copper Canyon Press. He is a member of the American Academy of Arts and Letters.

BRENDA HILLMAN is the author of seven collections of poetry, the most recent of which are *Cascadia* and *Pieces of Air in the Epic* (both Wesleyan). She is the Olivia C. Filippi Professor of Poetry at Saint Mary's College of California.

EDWARD HOAGLAND's twentieth book, *Early in the Season*, is forthcoming this fall. "Triage Along the Nile" is an excerpt from a novel in progress about Africa.

DAVID HUDDLE is the author of the novels *The Story of a Million Years* and *La Tour Dreams of the Wolf Girl* (Houghton Mifflin/Mariner). His most recent book is his sixth poetry collection, *Glory River* (LSU Press).

DAVID IVES is the author of the one-act comedies *All in the Timing* and *Time Flies*.

SHELLEY JACKSON is the author of *Half Life* (HarperCollins), *The Melancholy of Anatomy* (Anchor Books), and hypertexts including *Patchwork Girl* (Eastgate Systems). She is also the author of children's books including *The Old Woman and the Wave* (DK Ink) and *Sophia, the Alchemist's Dog* (Atheneum).

PETER KETTLE calls his style of painting fictional realism, and exhibits regularly at Llewellyn Alexander gallery in London, in addition to his numerous commissions. His Web site is www.peterkettle.co.uk.

ANN LAUTERBACH's eighth collection of poems, *Or to Begin Again*, will be published by Penguin in April 2009. She is Schwab Professor of Languages and Literature at Bard College and visiting Core Critic in Painting and Sculpture at the Yale School of Art.

MICHAEL LOGAN is a writer of creative nonfiction presently at work on "Asylum," an investigation of the mental health of the *Einsatzgruppen* paramilitary units in World War II.

THOMAS LYNCH's poems, essays, and stories have appeared in *The New York Times, Granta, The Atlantic,* and *The Times* of London. He lives in Michigan and West Clare, Ireland.

SARAH MANGUSO is the author of four books, most recently the memoir *The Two Kinds of Decay* (Farrar, Straus and Giroux). A 2008 Rome Prize fellow, she teaches at the Pratt Institute.

TED MATHYS is the author of *Forge* and the forthcoming *The Spoils* (both Coffee House).

KYOKO MORI has published two nonfiction books, *The Drum of Water: A Memoir* and *Polite Lies: On Being a Woman Caught Between Cultures* (both Henry Holt). She has also published three novels, *Shizuko's Daughter* and *One Bird* (both Holt), and *Stone Field, True Arrow* (Metropolitan). She teaches in the MFA program at George Mason University.

PETER MOUNTFORD is currently finishing his first novel, *The Pillage.*

JOYCE CAROL OATES is the author, most recently, of the novel *My Sister, My Love: The Intimate Story of Skyler Rampike* and the story collection *Wild Nights!* (both Ecco Press). The story in this issue will appear in her story collection *Dear Husband,* forthcoming next spring from Ecco/HarperCollins.

LANCE OLSEN is the author of many books of and about innovative fiction, including, most recently, the novels *Nietzsche's Kisses* (FC2) and *Anxious Pleasures* (Shoemaker & Hoard). He teaches at the University of Utah.

JAYNE ANNE PHILLIPS's "Leavitt's Dream" is an excerpt from *Lark and Termite,* a novel forthcoming from Knopf in January 2009.

MELISSA PRITCHARD is the author of a biography and six books of fiction, most recently *Disappearing Ingenue* and *Late Bloomer* (both Doubleday/Anchor). She teaches creative writing at Arizona State University.

In addition to numerous stories and essays, TOM ROBBINS is the author of eight novels, including *Even Cowgirls Get the Blues, Jitterbug Perfume, Half Asleep in Frog Pajamas,* and *Villa Incognito* (all Bantam).

LUCIUS SENECA (c. 4 BC–AD 65) was the leading Stoic philosopher in first-century Rome.

BOB SHACOCHIS's sixth book, *The Woman Who Lost Her Soul,* is forthcoming next year from Grove/Atlantic.

CHRISTOPHER SORRENTINO is the author, most recently, of *American Tempura* (Nothing Moments). His novel *Trance* (Picador) was a finalist for the National Book Award.

TERESE SVOBODA's books include *Tin God* (University of Nebraska), *Trailer Girl and Other Stories,* and *A Drink Called Paradise* (both Counterpoint). "My Brother's Dust" is an excerpt from a work in progress, *Dog on Fire.*

MELANIE RAE THON's most recent books are *Sweet Hearts* (Washington Square Press) and *First, Body* (Owl Books/Henry Holt). Her work has appeared in *The O. Henry Prize Stories,* the Pushcart Prize anthology, and *Best American Short Stories.*

SALLIE TISDALE is the author of several books, including *Stepping Westward* (Henry Holt), *Talk Dirty to Me* (Doubleday), and, most recently, *Women of the Way: Discovering 2,500 Years of Buddhist Wisdom* (Harper). She is a lay teacher at Dharma Rain Zen Center in Portland, Oregon.

MICHAEL UPCHURCH is a novelist whose books include *Air, The Flame Forest* (both Available Press/Ballantine), and *Passive Intruder* (Norton).

ELIOT WEINBERGER's books include *An Elemental Thing* and *What Happened Here: Bush Chronicles* (both New Directions).

JOE WENDEROTH's books of poetry include *Disfortune* and *It Is If I Speak* (both Wesleyan), and, most recently, *No Real Light,* published by Wave Books. Wave Books is also the publisher of his novel, *Letters to Wendy's,* and *The Holy Spirit of Life: Essays Written for John Ashcroft's Secret Self.*

C. D. WRIGHT's most recent title is *Rising, Falling, Hovering* (Copper Canyon).

Open Letter. Fall Books.
www.openletterbooks.org

Marguerite Duras
Rubem Fonseca
Ričardas Gavelis
Jan Kjærstad
Bragi Ólafsson
Dubravka Ugresic
subscribe.

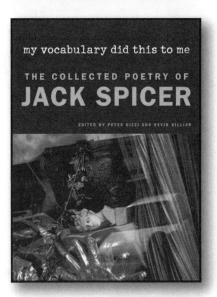

master of fine arts in writing

Poetry & Fiction

NOON

A LITERARY ANNUAL

1324 LEXINGTON AVENUE   PMB 298   NEW YORK   NEW YORK   10128

EDITION PRICE $12 DOMESTIC $17 FOREIGN

siglio

uncommon books at the intersections
and interstices of art & literature

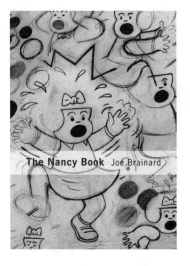

The Nancy Book by Joe Brainard

AVAILABLE NOW

From 1963 to 1978 Joe Brainard created more than 100 works of art that appropriated the classic comic strip character Nancy and sent her into an astonishing variety of spaces, all electrified by the incongruity of her presence. Brainard's Nancy traverses high art and low, the poetic and pornographic, the surreal and the absurd, reveling in as well as transcending her two-dimensionality. With 78 full page illustrations, an original essay by Ann Lauterbach, and collaborations with Bill Berkson, Ted Berrigan, Robert Creeley, Frank Lima, Frank O'Hara, Ron Padgett, and James Schuyler.

THE NANCY BOOK LIMITED EDITION is slipcased with a beautiful, hand-pulled, numbered lithograph of "Untitled (Nancy with Gun)," housed in a foil-stamped portfolio. More info about the book and limited edition as well as a library of essays about Joe Brainard, reviews of *The Nancy Book*, and other resources at **www.sigliopress.com**.

Several Gravities by Keith Waldrop

SPRING 2009

For nearly four decades, Keith Waldrop has been creating a lyrical and provocative body of visual work that mirrors his extraordinary oeuvre of poetry, fiction, and translation. His collages are dense with arcane, romantic drama and rich with textual and visual play. Edited by Robert Seydel, a substantial selection of these radiant collages will be published in a full color, hardcover edition with an essay by Waldrop that speaks to the relationship between his visual and poetic practices. The concurrent limited edition will include an original collage and can be reserved by contacting Siglio.

Sign up at **www.sigliopress.com** to receive a 15% discount coupon (mention Conjunctions!).
All Siglio website orders also receive special edition ephemera available nowhere else.

Move a couch, save the world?

"A lot of people are looking for magic in the world today, but only Benjamin Parzybok thought to check the sofa, which is, I think, the place it's most likely to be found. *Couch* is a slacker epic: a gentle, funny book that ambles merrily from Coupland to Tolkien, and gives couch-surfing (among other things) a whole new meaning." —Paul La Farge

Couch: a novel
Benjamin Parzybok

9781931520546
pb · $16

The King's Last Song
Geoff Ryman

"Ryman's knack for depicting characters; his ability to tell multiple, interrelated stories; and his knowledge of Cambodian history create a rich narrative that looks at Cambodia's "killing fields"both recent and ancientand Buddhist belief with its desire for transcendence."
—*Library Journal*

★ "An unforgettably vivid portrait of Cambodian culture."
—*Booklist* (**starred review**)

9781931520560
pb · $16

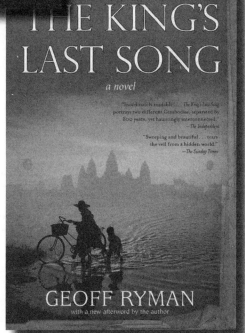

small beer press

DICHTEN =, No. 10: Sixteen New (to America) Poets

A magazine issue of German-language poets mostly in their 30s and 40s: Ann Cotton, Franz Josef Czernin, Michael Donhauser, Ute Eisinger, Daniel Falb, Hendrik Jackson, Marget Kreidl, Bert Papenfuss, Steffen Popp, Monika Rinck, Farhad Showghi, Hans Thill, Raphael Urweider, Anja Utler, Ron Winkler, and Uljana Wolf. Translated from the German by Andrew Duncan, Tony Frazer, Nicholas Grindell, Christian Hawkey, and Rosmarie Waldrop.

Poetry, 144 pages, offset, smyth-sewn, ISBN13: 978-1-886224-92-6, original pbk. $14

Isabelle Baladine Howald: *SECRET OF BREATH*

[Série d'Ecriture, No.21; translated from the French by Eléna Rivera]

A suite for two voices — voice of one living, voice of one dying — in a race against death and toward death. Caught in a narrative frame and a landscape marked by war, snow, cold, speed, and separation, the voices, even while facing death, embody the approach of love. The secret of breath is as much a kiss as a last sigh.

Poetry, 64 pages, offset, smyth-sewn, ISBN13: 978-1-886224-91-9, original pbk. $14

Recent Prizewinners:

Catherine Imbriglio, *PARTS OF THE MASS*:
Norma Farber Prize for Best First Book of Poetry, 2008

Ulf Stolterfoht, *LINGOS I-IX*, tr. Rosmarie Waldrop:
PEN Award For Poetry In Translation, 2008

Dallas Wiebe
1930-2008

"If you read this book, your life, not to mention your conversations, may become more interesting."—Charles Alexander, *Rain Taxi*

"Wiebe has always written with classical simplicity and power. His stories are smart, tough, elegant, and unsettlingly original: each holds your heart and mind in an unrelenting if compassionate grip."—Harry Mathews

"one of our best writers of innovative fictions"
—Doug Bolling, *American Book Review*

"Though it's more improbable than a dead Irish author writing a great American novel, there is a Dallas Wiebe who lives in Cincinnati and possesses a Flann[O'Brian]ish sense of the absurd... If you expect conventional mystery tales, you will be disappointed... Wiebe quickly leaves the mystery genre to plunge deeper into Mystery."—Mark Swartz, *Village Voice*

"enjoy the humor...of this carnevalesque world."
—Susan Smith Nash, *Review of Contemporary Fiction*

Going to the Mountain Stories, 192 pp., ISBN 978-0-930901-49-3, pbk. $14
Skyblue's Essays Fiction, 160 pp., ISBN 978-1-886224-02-5, pbk. $14
The Vox Populi Street Stories 312 pp., ISBN 978-1-886224-64-3, pbk. $15

Orders: Small Press Distribution: 1-800/869-7553, www.spdbooks.org. In Europe: www.hpress.no
www.burningdeck.com

BARDMFA

Since 1981 our summer-based MFA degree program has offered a non-traditional approach to the creative arts. Our emphasis on individual conferencing with faculty, school-wide interdisciplinary group conversation/critique, and a flexible schedule combine to both challenge the student and allow space for artistic growth.

Our Writing discipline emphasizes awareness of a variety of verbal, aural, and textual structures, and students develop an individual process of composition as well as a critical understanding of their field. Forms such as innovative poetry, short fiction, sound, and mixed-media writing are particularly well-suited to the structure and nature of the Bard MFA program.

Writing faculty include:

Anselm Berrigan, co-chair	David Levi Strauss
Linh Dinh	Tracie Morris
Robert Fitterman	Leslie Scalapino
Paul La Farge	Fiona Templeton
Ann Lauterbach, co-chair	

Call or email us to schedule a campus visit, or check *www.bard.edu/mfa* for a list of upcoming information sessions.

Milton Avery Graduate School of the Arts
Bard College
Annandale-on-Hudson, NY 12504

845-758-7481 • mfa@bard.edu • www.bard.edu/mfa